The Supplement of Reading

BY THE SAME AUTHOR:

Dark Interpreter: The Discourse of Romanticism

The Supplement of Reading

FIGURES OF UNDERSTANDING IN ROMANTIC THEORY AND PRACTICE

Tilottama Rajan

Cornell University Press

ITHACA AND LONDON

First published 1990 by Cornell University Press.

International Standard Book Number 0-8014-2045-8 (cloth)
International Standard Book Number 0-8014-9749-3 (paper)
Library of Congress Catalog Card Number 90-55122
Printed in the United States of America
Librarians: Library of Congress cataloging information appears on the last page of the book.

♾ The paper in this book meets the minimum requirements of the American National Standard for Permanence of Paper for Printed Library Materials Z39.48-1984.

Contents

C. *Deconstruction at the Scene of Its Reading*

Acknowledgments

Chapter 1, "The Supplement of Reading," appeared in a slightly different form in *New Literary History* 17 (1985–86): 573–94. Chapter 6, "Wollstonecraft and Godwin: Reading the Secrets of the Political Novel," appeared in *Studies in Romanticism* 27 (1988): 22–51. Chapter 11, "Deconstruction or Reconstruction: Reading Shelley's *Prometheus Unbound*," also appeared in a slightly different form in *SiR* 23 (1984): 317–38. Parts of Chapter 2, in an earlier form, are appearing under the title "Representation and Self-Representation: The Canonical Hermeneutics of Hegel and Kierkegaard," in *Parabasis V*, ed. Michel Bareau (Edmonton: Alta Press, 1990).

This book was begun with the aid of a leave fellowship from the Social Sciences and Humanities Research Council of Canada during 1984–85, partially supplemented by Queen's University. It was completed with the help of a fellowship from the Guggenheim Foundation during 1988 and the generous support of the Graduate School at the University of Wisconsin–Madison. Travel grants from the American Council of Learned Societies as well as from the graduate schools of Queen's University and the University of Wisconsin enabled me to do the necessary work in manuscript collections. None of this would have been possible without the generous professional support of several colleagues, whose own work has likewise been a continuing source of stimulation to me: Geoffrey Hartman, Jerome McGann, Hillis Miller, Robert Essick, Stuart Curran, Leopold Damrosch, Frederick Garber, Milton Wilson, and Ross Woodman. I am also grateful to the following libraries for allowing me to look at manuscript material by Blake and Shelley: the Bodleian Library, the Prints and Drawings Collection of the British Museum, the

Huntington Library, the Library of Congress, the Pierpoint Morgan Library, the Yale Centre for British Art, and the Beinecke Library. My thanks are due to Kathy Dauck and Barb Bosold, who have wrestled valiantly with the Infernal Machine and its attempts to transform this book into experimental fiction.

David Clark and Ross Woodman have read virtually all of this book at some stage of its composition, and I am particularly grateful for their careful and always sympathetic criticism. Without the many conversations I have had with David Clark, my thinking on Blake would not have got to where it is, and I owe him a debt that cannot be adequately registered in a footnote. The chapter on the conversation poems likewise germinated, appropriately enough, in conversations with Ross Woodman. But I must also thank him in ways that cannot easily be articulated, for his special sensitivity to the connection between academic and emotional support, and for his understanding of how one's life is part of one's ideas. To my parents, who have supported me in ways that go beyond the academic and who have thus made it easier for me to work productively, I also owe a profound debt. Finally my most unusual debt is to four very special squirrels: to Tangerina, Chloe, and most of all to Twinkle and her daughter Periwinkle. They have helped me to relearn the language of romanticism, which had once seemed to me an object of critique only, and to understand the deeply hermeneutic nature of the relationship to the other. For they have wanted to communicate despite the absence of a spoken language, and if I have sought the illusory immediacy of speech, their choice of gesture and mime has told me that they know understanding to be by signs only. Sharing some of their life with me, they have not shared their death. But they have allowed their death to be signified, by a child or by a sister, so that the silence and solitude of their absence would not be vacancy.

TILOTTAMA RAJAN

Madison, Wisconsin

Frequently Cited Texts and Abbreviations

A	G. W. F. Hegel. *Hegel's Aesthetics: Lectures on Fine Art.* Trans. T. M. Knox. 2 vols. Oxford: Clarendon, 1975.
AW	F. W. J. Schelling. *The Ages of the World.* Trans. F. de Wolfe Bolman. New York: Columbia University Press, 1946.
BL	Samuel Taylor Coleridge. *Biographia Literaria.* Ed. J. Shawcross. 2 vols. London: Oxford University Press, 1907.
CI	Søren Kierkegaard. *The Concept of Irony.* Trans. Lee M. Capel. 1965; rpt. Bloomington: Indiana University Press, 1971.
CUP	Søren Kierkegaard. *Concluding Unscientific Postscript.* Trans. David Swenson and Walter Lowrie. Princeton, N.J.: Princeton University Press, 1941.
CW	William Godwin. *Caleb Williams or Things as They Are.* Ed. David McCracken. New York: Norton, 1977.
E	William Blake. *The Complete Poetry and Prose of William Blake.* Ed. David V. Erdman, with commentary by Harold Bloom. Rev. ed. Berkeley: University of California Press, 1982. (In citations in the text the abbreviation 'E' is followed first by the page number; the numbers following the semicolon indicate the plates and lines. Page numbers only are used to cite very brief texts.)
GL	Friedrich Schleiermacher. *A Critical Essay on the Gospel of Saint Luke.* Trans. Connop Thirlwall. London: John Taylor, 1825.
H	Friedrich Schleiermacher. *Hermeneutics: The Handwritten Manuscripts.* Ed. Heinz Kimmerle. Trans. James Duke and Jack Forstman. Missoula, Mont.: Scholars' Press, 1977.
HK	Friedrich Schleiermacher. *Hermeneutik und Kritik mit besonderen Beziehung auf das Neue Testament.* Ed. Friedrich Lücke (1838). In *Sämmtliche Werke,* Erste Abtheilung, zweiter Band. Berlin: G. Reimer, 1864.

IDP	Friedrich Schleiermacher. *Schleiermacher's Introductions to the Dialogues of Plato.* Trans. William Dobson. Cambridge: J. J. Deighton, 1836.
LB	William Wordsworth and Samuel Taylor Coleridge. *Lyrical Ballads: The Text of the 1798 Edition with the Additional 1800 Poems and the Prefaces.* Ed. R. L. Brett and A. R. Jones. London: Methuen, 1968.
LJ	Friedrich Schleiermacher. *The Life of Jesus.* Ed. Jack Verheyden. Trans. S. Maclean Gilmour. Philadelphia: Fortress Press, 1975.
MWW	Mary Wollstonecraft. *Mary and The Wrongs of Woman.* Ed. James Kinsley and Gary Kelly. Oxford: Oxford University Press, 1980.
O	Friedrich Schleiermacher. "The Hermeneutics: The Outline of the 1819 Lectures." Trans. Jan Wocjik and Roland Haas. *New Literary History* 10 (1978): 1–16.
P	William Wordsworth. *The Prelude 1799, 1805, 1850.* Ed. Jonathan Wordsworth, M. H. Abrams, and Stephen Gill. New York: Norton, 1979 (quotations from 1850 version).
PM	G. W. F. Hegel. *The Phenomenology of Mind.* Trans. J. B. Baillie. Revised ed., 1931. Rpt. New York: Harper and Row, 1967.
PV	Søren Kierkegaard. *The Point of View for My Work as an Author.* Trans. Walter Lowrie. New York: Harper and Row, 1962.
SPP	Percy Bysshe Shelley. *Shelley's Poetry and Prose.* Ed. Donald H. Reiman and Sharon B. Powers. New York: Norton, 1977.
St.L.	William Godwin. *Travels of St. Leon.* London: Henry Colburn and Richard Bentley, 1831.
STC	Samuel Taylor Coleridge. *The Complete Poetical Works of Samuel Taylor Coleridge.* Ed. E. H. Coleridge. 2 vols. Oxford: Clarendon, 1912.

The Supplement of Reading

Introduction

The impetus for this book lies in a sense of dissatisfaction with my own previous work on the problem of representation, of making present, in romantic literature.[1] Deconstruction, even when it takes a psychological or phenomenological form and does not abolish the desire for reference by reducing consciousness to a mere ghost in the machine of language, has remained a postformalist mode, at least on this continent.[2] While it does not attribute a self-identical meaning to the text, the dissemination of meaning is something that happens 'inside' the text and not also between the text and history or the text and its readers. Any move to include the 'outside' of the text is unlikely to transcend deconstruction, for history and the text's readers are themselves involved in textual processes. Or put differently, outside and inside are not so much opposite as diacritical terms. But dissemination implies both scattering and communication, and to consider the latter is to reinscribe the

[1]Tilottama Rajan, *Dark Interpreter: The Discourse of Romanticism* (Ithaca, N.Y.: Cornell University Press, 1980).

[2]I am assuming here that 'deconstruction' is a broader term than 'poststructuralism,' which is only its most recent manifestation. Characteristic of all varieties of deconstruction are the dismantling of binary oppositions and the finding of subtexts within texts. But deconstruction, as pioneered by Schopenhauer and Nietzsche, historically predates the structuralist emphasis on the purely linguistic nature of the subject. It is thus possible to conceive of a deconstruction that is postorganicist rather than poststructuralist and that does not make consciousness into a mere effect of language. My own previous work is deconstructive in this way, as is the early work of Paul de Man. For a more detailed discussion of this subject see my articles "Displacing Post-Structuralism: Criticism of the Romantics after Paul de Man," *Studies in Romanticism* 24 (1985): 451–74, and "The Future of Deconstruction in Romantic Studies," *Nineteenth-Century Contexts* 11, no. 2 (1987): 131–47.

affective and referential aspects of literature. To consider the outside of the text is correspondingly to see how texts produce meanings, but in the sense of 'producing' something as in a play, or 'producing' something that participates in an economy and therefore a system of representation.

In focusing on the role of the reader in romantic theory and practice, I suggest that the assumptions of the period often preclude consideration of a text purely in terms of its internal relations. But an inquiry into the outside can take several forms, and this study is concerned with the 'outside of the text,' rather than with the material documentation of what is outside the text. More specifically, it explores the recourse to the 'supplement of reading' as a way of reconstructing a written *text* unable to achieve identity with itself into the ideal totality of the *work*.[3] The pressures of derealization in romantic texts often coexist with a strongly affirmative conception that invites the reader to bridge the gap between conception and execution, and to supply a unity not present in the text. As if to insure our cooperation, the romantic text often makes the appropriate reader a part of its rhetoric, as in Coleridge's conversation poems, which address themselves to a kindred spirit who must suspend the disbelief into which the poems themselves wander. The deferral of achieved meaning from the text to its reading finds a critical parallel in the rise of hermeneutics: broadly speaking, the theory of interpretation, but in this context the increasingly 'psychological' rather than exegetical form it takes as meaning is located in a creative consciousness behind the text. Superficially, hermeneutics may resemble the rhetorical criticism of Samuel Johnson or Horace in its focus on the reader. But Johnson conceives of the reader as recipient rather than supplement: it is the text that must persuade the reader, and not the reader who must complete the text. At the same time, the supplement of reading is also a highly problematic concept. As in the case of a supplement to an encyclopedia, the need for it points to a gap in the written text even as it fills it. Moreover, in transforming the reader from recipient to supplement, the author renounces his authority over the reader. Actual readers do not necessarily follow the roles prescribed for them within texts or by culturally limited critical conventions. Texts exist within the circuit of communication, and their 'intentions' are often displaced by an awareness of such readers, which puts authors themselves in the position of interpreters rather than prophets.

Though there has been no systematic study of the subject, attention to

[3]I borrow this distinction from Roland Barthes, "From Work to Text," in *Image, Music, Text*, trans. Stephen Heath (New York: Hill and Wang, 1977), pp. 155–64. The distinction is of course critical rather than real.

the role of the reader in romantic aesthetics is by no means new. Kathleen Wheeler cites Jean Paul's notion that the author provides an outline which the reader is to fill in creatively.[4] Similarly, David Welberry writes, "Romantic hermeneutics is a model of understanding as the re-cognition of the sponsoring spiritual source of a work."[5] Over the years there have been discussions of individual texts that focus on their rhetoric or their construction of an implied reader. Many of these earlier studies assume a work that can be reconstructed from the text and are reluctant to explore how problematic a recuperative hermeneutic can be in the texts themselves.[6] More recently, Jerome McGann has drawn attention to the need to situate hermeneutics itself, and others have begun to explore the interpretive fluidity created by the interchanging of writer and reader.[7] The early studies, however, remain valuable in articulating paradigms that enter romantic texts on the level of desire (even granted that desire is itself a representation rather than a moment of consciousness prior to language). Or to put it differently, the models developed in traditional hermeneutics simply recognize explicitly the strategies of supplementation often assumed by modern scholarship. Thus Northrop Frye reads Blake in terms of a canonical hermeneutic that reinterprets the early poems according to the later 'system.' And editorial projects like "Shelley and his Circle" draw on a romantic linkage between philology and organicism to contextualize texts in their author's literary life. Building dialogically on both the studies stimulated by contemporary theory and those that precede it, this book looks at how the activity of reading is

[4]Kathleen Wheeler, ed., *German Aesthetic and Literary Criticism: The Romantic Ironists and Goethe* (Cambridge: Cambridge University Press, 1984), pp. 11–15.

[5]"E. T. A. Hoffmann and Romantic Hermeneutics: An Interpretation of Hoffmann's 'Don Juan,'" *Studies in Romanticism* 19 (1980): 455.

[6]Examples include Michael G. Cooke, "The Mode of Argument in Wordsworth's Poetry," *Acts of Inclusion: Studies Bearing on an Elementary Theory of Romanticism* (New Haven, Conn.: Yale University Press, 1979), pp. 185–215; Jerome McGann, "The Aim of Blake's Prophecies and the Uses of Blake Criticism," in Stuart Curran and Joseph Wittreich, eds., *Blake's Sublime Allegory: Essays on the "Four Zoas," "Milton," "Jerusalem"* (Madison: University of Wisconsin Press, 1973), pp. 3–21; Leslie Tannenbaum, *Biblical Tradition in Blake's Prophecies: The Great Code of Art* (Princeton, N.J.: Princeton University Press, 1982); E. S. Shaffer, *'Kubla Khan' and The Fall of Jerusalem: The Mythological School in Biblical Criticism and Secular Literature, 1770–1880* (Cambridge: Cambridge University Press, 1975); Morris Eaves, *William Blake's Theory of Art* (Princeton, N.J.: Princeton University Press, 1982). A highly complex version of this approach, one that reconstructs a traditional hermeneutic across the theoretical abyss introduced by the sublime, is Vincent de Luca's "A Wall of Words: The Sublime as Text," in Nelson Hilton and Thomas Vogler, eds., *Unnam'd Forms: Blake and Textuality* (Berkeley: University of California Press, 1986), pp. 218–41.

[7]"The Ancient Mariner: The Meaning of Meanings," *The Beauty of Inflections: Literary Investigations in Historical Method and Theory* (Oxford: Clarendon, 1985), pp. 135–72. See also Jean-Pierre Mileur, *Vision and Revision: Coleridge's Art of Immanence* (Berkeley: University of California Press, 1982); Donald Ault, "Re-Visioning *The Four Zoas*," in Hilton and Vogler, eds., *Unnam'd Forms*, pp. 105–40; William Galperin, *Revision and Authority in Wordsworth: The Interpretation of a Career* (Philadelphia: University of Pennsylvania Press, 1989).

narrated in a wide range of romantic texts and how the role of the reader is projected and complicated by romantic theory itself.

Making the reader a constituent of the text, as H. R. Jauss's studies of medieval literature suggest, is not unique to romantic literature.[8] What may be unique is the manner in which this move is theorized into a crisis in signification by developments in romantic hermeneutics that both reflect and influence the organization of texts. The result is an increasingly metafictional literature that makes theory a subject of reflection within the text itself. This book therefore falls into two parts. The first part reconstructs romantic concepts of reading from German theories about the relationship among expression, communication, and understanding. The decision to focus on English romantic texts but to develop a historically grounded framework for their analysis from German theory of the period is probably no longer something that needs to be defended. Because English criticism remains empirical while German literary theory forms part of an encyclopedic philosophic project, we can expect the latter to develop explicitly theories of interpretation that are less systematically present in the criticism of the English romantics. I use the term 'traditional hermeneutics' to indicate an initial romantic position on reading: one committed to F. A. Wolf's definition of hermeneutics as the art of grasping the "thoughts of another person . . . just as he has grasped them himself."[9] But this definition by no means sums up perceptions about reading. Hence, the second part of this study concentrates on romantic writers at the point where they begin to reflect upon traditional hermeneutics in scenes of reading that often textualize their own theoretical assumptions. The fact that the literature questions as well as enacts a traditional hermeneutic means that some of the theoretical writings examined in the first part are read against the grain, so as to uncover those aporias in them that result in their emerging as problematic in romantic practice. But these writings, too, are self-interrogating, and in the course of the period the hermeneutic theory of reading rewrites itself as a 'heuristic' theory that displaces but does not entirely dismantle the former. It is important to recognize that this development takes place within hermeneutics itself. Poststructuralism has accustomed us to an ahistorical and prescriptive use of terms like 'hermeneutics,' 'phenomenology,' and 'philology,' which associates them with a naive metaphysics of presence. But the meaning of these terms is not fixed, and if they are used historically to describe a series of writers who em-

[8]"Theses on the Transition from the Aesthetics of Literary Works to a Theory of Aesthetic Experience," in Mario J. Valdes and Owen J. Miller, eds., *Interpretation of Narrative* (Toronto: University of Toronto Press, 1978), pp. 145–47.

[9]Quoted by Tzvetan Todorov, *Symbolism and Interpretation*, trans. Catherine Porter (Ithaca, N.Y.: Cornell University Press, 1982), pp. 146–47.

ploy them rather than to describe a normative position, they emerge as far more complex, indeed, self-revising.

They also revise our own critical map. In looking at romantic texts in the light of a nineteenth-century aesthetics re-visioned in contemporary terms, this study attempts a kind of new literary history. New literary history is not simply the reinscription of a history-of-ideas criticism as 'theory,' according to a genetic logic that makes the former an embryonic version of the latter. It is also a reinscription of theory in the history of ideas that configured theory differently. The first chapter discusses the problems presented by the supplement of reading. It distinguishes in the abstract two varieties of recuperative reading: a positive hermeneutic that synthesizes the text by arranging and expanding elements actually given in it, and a negative hermeneutic in which the act of reading supplies something absent from and in contradiction to the textual surface. These attempts to ground meaning through interpretation are increasingly self-undermining and lead to a heuristic theory of the text as a stimulus for the production of meanings that cannot entirely be fixed. Subsequent chapters trace the directions taken by theories of reading in the romantic period itself. The second chapter begins with Friedrich Schleiermacher, whose notion that a "grammatical" reading of the *text* needs to be complemented by a "psychological" reading that grasps the wholeness of the *work* provides a model for the positive hermeneutic earlier described. Hegel extends this tradition so as to expand a purely literary hermeneutics into an ontological hermeneutics but also renders it deeply problematic by making interpretation projective and teleological rather than reconstructive. In the work of Jean Paul and the later Schelling we find models for a negative hermeneutic that increasingly identifies meaning with what is *not* said, deferring it to the imaginary. Finally, in Kierkegaard's *Concept of Irony* a hermeneutics of absence is staged, so as to bring out both the insistence of the desire for meaning that motivates it, and the tenuousness of the meaning so constructed. In moving from Schleiermacher to Kierkegaard, I try to bring out the paradox of romantic hermeneutics, as a movement that simultaneously initiates and masks the deconstruction of representation and ultimately unweaves its own recuperative strategies. I also see an emergent awareness of this paradox on the part of the theorists.

The third chapter therefore examines the reconception of hermeneutics as it emerges from the later work of Schleiermacher and from Kierkegaard's *Point of View for My Work as an Author*, where the relationship between reading and authority is a constant concern. One of the more puzzling aspects of this study may well be the way Schleiermacher surfaces as protagonist of two narratives about hermeneutics: a traditional and a revisionary narrative. That is because it is extremely difficult to identify him with a single position without distorting his work. Positions that have now become hypostatized as schools intertwine in the more fluid context of romanticism, with its emphasis on (critical) texts as unfinished processes, on textuality as intertextuality. Because this earlier theoretical terrain is, to adapt Shelley, like the "chaos of a cyclic poem," it can be mapped in more than one way. For a long time our perception of Schleiermacher has been mediated by Wilhelm Dilthey, and he has been associated with what Hans-Georg Gadamer brands a false romanticism of immediacy.[10] This Schleiermacher is treated in the second chapter and is as much a historically true figure as any other 'Schleiermacher,' because the text of a certain strain in romantic hermeneutics writes itself around him. The simultaneously deconstructive and phenomenological Schleiermacher discussed in the third chapter is similarly a 'historical figure,' in the double sense that he is not an imaginary construction but is at the same time a 'figure,' produced through the intertextual inscription of contemporary theory in an earlier critical discourse.

The inclusion in this section of philosophers like Hegel and Schelling, who are concerned with understanding but not strictly with literary hermeneutics, may seem more unorthodox to the critic than to the philosopher. It has, nevertheless, a historical sanction from Dilthey who, in his biography of Schleiermacher, relates the latter's theory of reading to post-Kantian idealism and even to Goethe's work in botany and anatomy. Describing how Goethe explains metamorphosis and difference in organisms as part of a uniform structure, Dilthey sees the organic hypothesis as yielding principles for the interpretation of parts that do not initially appear to fit into a whole.[11] Following Dilthey, who sees a parallel between the reading of nature and the reading of texts, I extrapolate from Hegel and Schelling principles that can apply to the reading of texts as well as the interpretation of Being. Thus Hegel's *Phenomenology of Mind* attempts something like the anagogic level of exegesis in the medieval theory: namely, a reading of history that will recomprehend individual events in the light of the entire history of mind. From it we can extrapolate a 'canonical' hermeneutics, which rereads the individual text in relation both to the author's oeuvre and to a world-historical poem that is still unfolding.

Writers like Blake, Wordsworth, or Coleridge, who either created or planned a magnum opus, used the canon as a figure of reading in their texts. But such figures always prove self-complicating, and the second part of this book is concerned with what happens to them when they are

[10]*Truth and Method* (New York: Seabury Press, 1975), pp. 164–69.

[11]"The Schleiermacher Biography," *Dilthey: Selected Writings*, ed. H. P. Rickman (Cambridge: Cambridge University Press, 1976), pp. 61–62. See pp. 46–67 in general.

inscribed in literary texts and opened up to the intertextual processes of reading. These chapters therefore do not follow the 'narrative' of the first part by tracing an evolution from texts that encode a positive hermeneutic, through ones whose strategies of recuperation are more dubious, to texts that abandon interpretive closure. To approach the texts purely in terms of the traditional models would now be redundant, in that it would restate in a rhetorical rather than thematic vocabulary existing interpretations tacitly informed by hermeneutic paradigms. But it is also one of my contentions that texts become problematic at the point where they raise the question of their own reading. Those texts that ask to be read on a hermeneutic as well as a mimetic level inevitably function at a reflexive level as well, inscribing rather than exemplifying the traditional models. We can make a schematic distinction between 'hermeneutic' texts uneasily committed to their recuperative strategies and texts that incorporate these strategies in more self-critical ways. But all the texts considered in the second part are effectively or intentionally open to some degree of heuristic reading. Or to put it differently, a study of romantic theory may locate the models in an approximately historical sequence. But it is more difficult to fit authors or even texts into a genetic narrative that allows the traditional models an untroubled, if temporary, identity as stages in an individual or historical evolution.

Accordingly, these chapters explore the presence of the traditional models in various texts but treat them as already under erasure. Chapter 4 discusses how the psychological subtext of Coleridge's conversation poems displaces their attempt to model a decorum of reading drawn from positive hermeneutics. These poems are 'hermeneutic' texts still committed to what they render problematic. Less reluctantly reflexive, *Prometheus Unbound* (the subject of Chapter 11) articulates a positive hermeneutic in the dialogue between Asia and Panthea, questions it in the dialogue with Demogorgon, and tenuously reinscribes it through its use of the performative mode of drama. Chapter 6 looks at how the fragmentary status of Wollstonecraft's *Wrongs of Woman* both encourages and limits the text's plea to be read through a hermeneutics of reversal. It then considers how Godwin, in his revision of *Caleb Williams*, reflects upon this hermeneutic, which the first version had invoked as a supplement to its unhappy ending. The chapters on Blake again include texts such as *Urizen* and *Europe* that can be read in terms of a negative hermeneutic but consider how such readings are displaced by the intertextual aesthetic of the early work. Moreover, the models do not constitute a series of positions that authors go through in a certain order. Blake returns in his later work to a theoretically 'earlier' hermeneutic. His development is an exception to any claim about a historical movement from 'hermeneutic' to 'heuristic' texts. But his simultaneous reprinting of early poems that are what Barthes describes as 'writerly' texts[12] also problematizes any cultural authority he reclaims by returning to more traditional figures of understanding.

The second part, then, is not concerned with 'pure' forms of the traditional models. If they occur anywhere in English romanticism, it may be in theoretical writings by the authors considered. Accordingly, the sixth chapter discusses an essay in which Godwin elaborates a divinatory hermeneutics, and Chapter 5, on Wordsworth, begins with the "Preface" to *Lyrical Ballads*, which expands poetics into hermeneutics so as to make language part of a project of cross-cultural understanding. But classifying something as 'theory' rather than 'text' is itself a critical choice, and the blurring of the line between the two parts of this study through the inclusion of theory in the sections on texts is meant to qualify any metadiscursive authority the various models may have acquired in the first part. Thus, Chapter 4 approaches Coleridge's theory of reading not through his biblical writings but through the *Biographia* considered as a narrative, which generates asymmetries between authority and its reading that are paralleled in the conversation poems. More unusually, the chapters on Blake use texts as sources of theory and treat *Milton* and *The Marriage* as contrasting theories of reading. The textualizing of theory is the particular concern of Chapter 10, which looks at Shelley's *Defence* as composed by different theoretical 'voices,' at the relationship of supplementation and displacement between these voices, and at the intertextual relationship between the essay and its subsequent readers.

As these comments indicate, whereas chapters in the first part are stages in an argument, those in the second part consider an array of *intersecting* problems. Thus, the tripartite subdivision of this section is itself a heuristic schema and picks out issues by no means confined to the chapters in which they are given titular attention. These issues include ones that lie dormant in the hermeneutic tradition, such as the relationship among reading, history, and culture. The concept of divinatory reading projects the text into history so as to make reading the means to its future empowerment. But there is little sense of history as a site of rereading, though it seems implicit in the idea that texts are still in process. The chapter on the political novel therefore explores the incorporation of hermeneutics into a revolutionary aesthetic whose romanticism itself becomes subject to reflection. As important are issues of cultural difference bracketed by a tradition that believes in a common human nature, yet raised by the very format of Dilthey's essay on hermeneutics, as a critical *history* in which romantic hermeneutics is situated

[12]Roland Barthes, *S/Z*, trans. Richard Miller (New York: Hill and Wang, 1974), pp. 3–4.

as a specifically post-Kantian form of interpretation. The chapters on Wordsworth and Coleridge thus take up the dialogizing of hermeneutics that occurs in texts where the romantic ideology is culturally situated. Built around his differences from the Wordsworth circle, Coleridge's conversation poems model reading as a transcendence of difference, but raise the issue of what Gadamer calls "prejudice" as a way of historicizing authority. By using the heteroglossic form of the collection, the *Lyrical Ballads* more explicitly question their attempt to make literature part of a social hermeneutic. The section on Blake, necessarily extensive because its subject is the Blake canon, deals with the politics of 'canonization' and with the early Blake's development of a counterhermeneutic sensitive to the imperialism of canonical reading. These chapters all recognize the challenge posed to the conservatism of hermeneutics by the text's insertion into shifting cultural contexts. But they also see reading itself as generating an intertextuality that produces this insertion. They therefore mediate between hermeneutics and various forms of cultural critique. The final chapter, by contrast, tries to mediate between hermeneutics and deconstruction. Focusing on what has become an exemplary text for the deconstruction of reading, it suggests that *The Triumph of Life* cannot be reduced to a manuscript that proves unreadable, just as the possibility of reading cannot be judged according to the still formalist criterion of whether we can arrive at an interpretation. Rather, the work, like the procession that includes not just Life but her participants, is constituted by the ongoing intertextual transactions between manuscripts, reading texts, and readers.

The recognition of the pivotal role played by the reader has several consequences. As recently as 1977 Tzvetan Todorov suggested that the romantic period is marked by the demise of rhetoric (in the old sense of persuasion) and the rise of aesthetics: of a Kantian notion of art as disinterested and self-contained. He cites Karl Philipp Moritz on the 'intransitivity' of art: "The nature of the beautiful object consists in the fact that . . . [it] explains itself—describes itself through itself—. . . . No sooner would a beautiful work of art require, beyond that index finger, a special explanation, than it would become by that very token imperfect."[13] In stressing the importance that the romantics attached to reading, this study questions the formalist view that they saw the work of art as ontologically complete and that they sought to insulate it from acting

[13]Tzvetan Todorov, *Theories of the Symbol*, trans. Catherine Porter (Ithaca, N.Y.: Cornell University Press, 1982), pp. 111–12, 159–60. The view that the romantics paid no attention to the reader is an influential one. See also M. H. Abrams, *The Mirror and the Lamp: Romantic Theory and the Critical Tradition* (1953; rpt. New York: Oxford University Press, 1971), pp. 22–26; Jane Tompkins, "The Reader in History," in Tompkins, ed., *Reader-Response Criticism: From Formalism to Post-Structuralism* (Baltimore: The Johns Hopkins University Press, 1980), p. 214.

upon or being affected by extra-aesthetic discourses. But in using the figure of the reader to de-autonomize the work, it also differs in certain ways from the questioning of textual identity carried out by a certain form of deconstruction. My differences from what we can call rhetorical poststructuralism[14]—as well as my debt to it—will, I hope, emerge in the way I treat those 'scenes' of reading and writing that have come to preoccupy much recent discussion of the romantics under the seminal influence of Paul de Man. For de Man such scenes disrupt representation by drawing attention to language rather than to what it signifies: their effect is thus to imprison the text in a hall of mirrors. By a 'scene,' however, I do not mean (as de Man often does) a figural moment in which the text draws attention to its tropological structure, but an extended *narration* of the process of communication or expression. We must ask why romantic texts (unlike the lyrics of Baudelaire or Mallarmé) so often go beyond the inclusion of figural moments to represent the problem of representation in a scene. Scenes are more complex than figural moments, both in what they express and in their effect on a reader. A scene arises from a surplus of meaning that cannot be reduced to a conceptual statement. We narrate fundamental problems because our attempt to state them logically does not fully explain them. Moreover, narratives are situational and provisional: a particular episode occurs in a context of events that allows us to imagine that the story might be different in altered circumstances. Finally, though scenes are expansions of figural moments in that they unmask the textuality of whatever happens in literature, they simultaneously have the opposite effect: because a scene is a narrative with characters and events, it also represents textuality as something that happens in the world.

To give but one example, Coleridge's opening description of the jasmin and myrtle in "The Eolian Harp" as "meet emblems" of innocence and love (*sic*, l. 5) discloses as a trope the poet's attempt to argue for the consubstantiality of mind and nature. To some extent, the scene of reading at the end of the poem, where Sara unmasks Coleridge's pantheistic pretenses, is an elaboration of this figural moment. But it is also much more than a simple reduction of 'truth' to rhetoric. The scene brings into play the kind of reading described by hermeneuticists from J. A. Ernesti to Schleiermacher, who consider the text in its biographical and psychological context. But far from grounding the meaning of the text, philology, as Nietzsche observes, is "ephexis" or "undecisiveness" in

[14]I use this term not to describe the work of Foucault, Barthes, or Kristeva, but to designate the work of the later de Man and his followers, which concentrates almost exclusively on figures and tropes.

interpretation.[15] Knowing Coleridge's domestic situation and knowing that in 1795 he was just beginning his literary career, readers may ascribe his renunciation of his pantheistic vision to insecurity, and through a hermeneutics of reversal they may reconstruct the benediction of this vision absent from the text but present in other, parallel, conversation poems. At the other extreme, they may see the poet's evocation of these contexts as self-serving and feel that 'Coleridge' is using 'Sara' as a scapegoat for the inherent figurality of his vision. Alternatively, because these readings are not really separate and autonomous, readers may recognize that Coleridge's vision is merely metaphoric and yet not feel that Sara's response is the right one. The point is that the substitution of characters and circumstances for tropes encourages the reader to elaborate the scene in a variety of different ways. Moreover, as we interweave various elaborations of the concluding scene, it ceases to be just a figural moment: we live through these alternative scenarios even while deconstructing them, and living through them is different from seeing through them.

We might better state the difference between the figural moment and the scene by saying that the latter asks to be approached as 'discourse' rather than 'language.' As Paul Ricoeur observes in his version of the distinction between *langue* and *parole*, discourse occurs and is read in time, and cannot be detached from a relationship to speaker, audience, and situation. As important, it therefore carries the intention of reference: "the signs of language refer only to other signs in the interior of the same system so that language no more has a world than it has a time and a subject, whereas discourse . . . refers to a world."[16] Micro-units of a text are much easier to read in purely linguistic terms than are episodes, scenes, or entire narratives. To treat a scene of reading as simply a figural moment is thus to evade the claims that the form makes on us. One of the aims of this study is to show how 'reading' the text is a partly figurative process, something about which scenes are staged and fictions constructed. But an equally important purpose is to show that romantic texts resist being read as language and ask to be treated as discourse. By including characterized readers and staging scenes of reading, they create a relationship with speaker, audience, and situation, and ask us to consider not simply the structure of signs but also the life of signs in literary communities and in psychic life.

[15]Friedrich Nietzsche, *The Anti-Christ*, in *Twilight of the Idols and The Anti-Christ*, trans. R. J. Hollingdale (London: Penguin Books, 1968), p. 169.

[16]Paul Ricoeur, *Hermeneutics and the Human Sciences*, ed. and trans. John B. Thompson (New York: Cambridge University Press, 1981), p. 133.

PART I

CHAPTER ONE

The Supplement of Reading

The Disappearance of Actualization

It is now a commonplace that the period once associated with an organicist aesthetic that naturalizes the sign produced a large number of texts that are intentional in structure, "able to posit regardless of presence but, . . . unable to give a foundation to what [they posit] except as an intent of consciousness."[1] This study takes as its starting point what I shall call the disappearance of narrative, dramatic, or conceptual 'actualization,' a phenomenon that results in the absence from romantic writing of embodied or achieved meaning as opposed to discarnate meaning. The problem is most obvious in the many texts that are fragments, where the written 'text' does not coincide with the hypothetical totality of the 'work.' In Coleridge's *Christabel,* for instance, the work is not limited to Christabel's captivation and ontological deconstruction by Geraldine. It may include a happy ending, in which the difference of Christabel from herself is annulled, as she and Sir Leoline are reconciled and Geraldine is either vanquished or saved. But this ending, sketched by Coleridge in comments to friends, is never incorporated into the text, which concludes with Christabel's being rejected by her father, and which intimates the ending only negatively, as a desire for something that might correct the present unjust state of affairs. Similarly, in Keats's *Hyperion* Apollo's deification is intimated at the end but is undermined by the perfunctoriness of the description and the abrupt termination of

[1]Paul de Man, "The Intentional Structure of the Romantic Image," *The Rhetoric of Romanticism* (New York: Columbia University Press, 1984), p. 6.

the text in a series of asterisks. For Apollo undergoes no psychological development until he somewhat unconvincingly ingests the lessons of several millennia of history in five lines, as though to make us aware that his deification is not something that happens in divine history, but is a linguistic event, subject to doubt and dismantling. To bring the poem to its 'conclusion' we must leave the text, which derealizes itself, for the unheard melodies of a work 'intended' by the author.

But the disappearance of actualization is not just a feature of fragments. Blake's major prophecies present a completed action culminating in the reintegration of the divided psyche. Yet the characters are often flat and abstract, notations for characters rather than fully developed personalities. Moreover, the action, though predictable, does not unfold logically, but proceeds discontinuously through a series of imaginative leaps. As Ronald Grimes suggests, the characters "do not develop biographically." At the level of the plot "connective devices are muted. The spaces between events seem to be blank, as if inviting the reader to fill them in by himself."[2] As 'visionary forms dramatic,' to use Blake's own phrase, the prophecies require the participation of the reader if vision is to be dramatized, made concrete. Leslie Tannenbaum has discussed with reference to biblical hermeneutics this notion of the reader's actualizing the text in a "prophetic or apocalyptic theater, which . . . through the communication of [the] prophecy, is relocated in the mind of the reader."[3] Much the same can be said of *Prometheus Unbound*, which is technically complete but does not follow the semiotics of Aristotelian drama, in which the play is the imitation of a probable action and not of an intention. Although in this case the arrival of the Promethean age is described in the text, it remains allegorical: a sequence of visionary abstractions spoken by dramatis personae who are voices and not persons. That a mythopoeic text cannot be realistic is obvious. But verisimilitude can be psychological or metaphysical as well as photographic, and this kind of verisimilitude is achieved only if we as readers stage the play in the theater of our own experience.

The disappearance of actualization is not just a feature of fictional texts. We find it also in expository prose, where continuous argument normally serves the function of plot and narrative syntax. Coleridge's *Biographia Literaria*, for instance, is made up of disjunctive and unsynthesized parts. Its centerpiece is a redemptive theory of imagination

[2]"Time and Space in Blake's Major Prophecies," in Stuart Curran and Joseph Wittreich, eds., *Blake's Sublime Allegory: Essays on the "Four Zoas," "Milton," "Jerusalem"* (Madison: University of Wisconsin Press, 1973), p. 64.

[3]*Biblical Tradition in Blake's Prophecies* (Princeton, N.J.: Princeton University Press, 1982), p. 48.

as a reconciliation of opposites that reduplicates the primal act of creation. But the link between Coleridge's aesthetics and the ten scholia from Schelling that precede it and provide its metaphysical grounding is not made in the text. Moreover, though Coleridge promises a hundred-page treatise on the imagination, the very extensiveness of which would give the theory philosophical credibility, what he provides are two elliptical paragraphs that must be fleshed out by the sympathetic reader. Characteristic of all these texts is an erosion of the reportorial, psychological, or even conceptual realism that comes from creating transitions between parts. The text becomes like the script for a film or the score for a piece of music rather than the film or music itself. It would be all too easy to conclude that much romantic literature is technically incompetent, especially since at first sight it lacks the self-consciousness about technique that might lead us to defend it as experimental. But in fact we are dealing with a series of far-reaching shifts in concepts of the location and nature of meaning, the relationship of reader to text, and finally the status of discourse itself.

Corresponding to this shift in literature itself is a shift in romantic aesthetics, from a concern with the text as a finished product that contains its own meaning to a concern with the creative and receptive processes as loci of meaning. An aesthetics of pictorialism is replaced by one based on feeling as a way of achieving 'immediacy,' making meaning present. Wallace Jackson traces through the eighteenth century the decline of the idea that literature should approximate to painting in order to summon up its subject before our eyes, and its replacement by a Burkean aesthetics of the sublime that makes us feel the experience instead of painting it for us.[4] Presence comes to be located not in depiction but in an effect, something that happens in the consciousness of the reader, and correspondingly definiteness ceases to be a criterion for rhetorical success. This undoing of the model that underwrites the idea of art as a making visible[5] has far-reaching implications. But for the moment it is enough to note that it aims to preserve, not to deconstruct, an aesthetics of presence. As important as the fading of pictorialism is the diminishing emphasis on genre, as a means by which the text encodes and institutionalizes what it says. Here, too, the desire is not to question, but to relocate at the level of organic form, the presence of a unitary meaning. The decline of generic criticism is matched on the

[4]*Immediacy: The Development of a Critical Concept from Addison to Coleridge* (Amsterdam: Rodopi, 1973), pp. 27–69.

[5]For a discussion of the relationship of pictorial and visual metaphors to a metaphysics of presence, see Allen Thiher, *Words in Reflection: Modern Language Theory and Post-Modern Fiction* (Chicago: University of Chicago Press, 1984), pp. 1–5.

intratextual level by a diminished emphasis on the structural grammar of the text emphasized by neoclassicism.[6] In chastising Milton for those breaches of decorum that make *Paradise Lost* and "Lycidas" fail as acts of representation, Samuel Johnson assumes that stylistic and structural integrity are versions of logical proof, and that a text marked by aesthetic dissonances is unpersuasive. But though a first-generation romantic like Coleridge continues to give some emphasis to matters of construction, such as the relationship of part to whole, he already designates as *secondary* imagination the capacity for formal shaping that is specifically the possession of the poet, and describes as primary imagination the originating creative perception that precedes and gives value to aesthetic structuring. We see in Coleridge the beginnings of a shift from a formalist aesthetics of craft to a phenomenological aesthetics of genius, though he stops short of rejecting structural actualization as unimportant. In this he resembles Schleiermacher, for whom psychological interpretation is primary, though grammatical interpretation is also necessary. But from here it is only a short step to a second-generation romantic like Shelley, who at times introduces a dualism between inspiration and composition that can shift the locus of meaning away altogether from the written text. Though the work behind the text is assumed to be a totality, the written text is no longer required to be an autonomous formal unit. The text may become the trace, the re-presentation, of a signified that precedes it in the creative process. Or it may become an intent of consciousness, the catalyst for a signified to be produced in the reading process. More commonly it becomes both, in a hermeneutics that sees the reading process as a corrective that recovers the separation of signifier from signified that occurs in writing.

Of interest here is the movement away from narrative realism described by Hans Frei in biblical interpretation as it develops from the seventeenth to the nineteenth century. What Frei traces, in delineating a shift from a system that codifies the rules governing the interpretation of subject matter to a hermeneutics of understanding that locates meaning in the interpretive act, is not a change in representation itself, but rather a change in the conventions of reading the Bible. But assumptions in biblical hermeneutics about the presence and location of meaning exerted a profound influence on the construction as well as the

[6]Eric Rothstein points out that alongside the Aristotelian aesthetics of unity there developed in the eighteenth century an aesthetics of the "non-finito": "Ideal Presence and the 'Non-Finito' in Eighteenth-Century Aesthetics," *Eighteenth-Century Studies* 9 (Spring 1976): 307–32. Sometimes the role of the reader seems largely prestructured by the text, but sometimes the non-finito is conceived as more genuinely open-ended. The romantic emphasis on the role of the reader obviously has its roots in this development, but it goes much further, particularly in the working out of a 'negative' hermeneutics.

reading of secular scriptures in the romantic period. Frei describes how an increasing focus on the synoptic gospels, which are disconnected and aggregational in form, erodes the reading of biblical narrative in general as novelistic or history-like. More and more it is felt that the "cohesion of depiction with subject matter on the one hand, and of subject matter with its accessibility to present understanding on the other, requires something more than the narrative account itself."[7] Hence the 'essential meaning' is deferred from the text itself to the *cogito* of the author, to a macrocosmic version of this *cogito* known as the Spirit of the Age, or to the text's 'applicative' reading.

Crucial to this development is Schleiermacher, at least as the nineteenth century culminating in Dilthey saw him. Schleiermacher's notion of a reading that takes place on two levels begins the erosion of a belief in the self-sufficiency of the text. Though the text can be studied "grammatically"—in terms of its structural and linguistic parts—it must also be studied "psychologically," through "a projection into the inner creative process," if we are to grasp the wholeness of the work.[8] More importantly, Schleiermacher anticipates the Derridean sense of writing as something that threatens the identity of meaning, though he does not share in the deconstruction of a dualism that privileges *parole* over *écriture*. Psychological reading restores to a text made up of 'isolated signs' the presence that comes from making contact with the voice behind those signs. The point is that the growing emphasis of hermeneutics on the reader as coproducer of the text is initially a response to an anxiety about the self-sufficiency of the linguistic system and its subset, the textual system. This is not to say that Schleiermacher denies the presence of meaning in the text. For in the 1819 Compendium, at least, he avoids any disjunction between work and text by seeing the psychological and grammatical readings as complementary. Yet he stands on the edge of a radical shift from a concept of literature as mimesis to one of literature as a re-presentation that defers the presence of a unitary meaning. From here it is but a short step to a hermeneutics that sees this 'meaning' as present only in the writer's intention, which becomes a separable mental entity from the process of working out thoughts in language.

It would be wrong to say that this step is taken in *The Defence of Poetry*. For if Shelley intensifies a movement away from the text to consciousness, in the end he also reimplicates conception in expression by turning reading into a heuristic rather than hermeneutic activity. But he does seem intermittently to be mounting a hermeneutic defense of logocentr-

[7]Hans Frei, *The Eclipse of Biblical Narrative: A Study in Eighteenth and Nineteenth Century Hermeneutics* (New Haven, Conn.: Yale University Press, 1974), p. 189.

[8]Wilhelm Dilthey, "The Rise of Hermeneutics," trans. Fredric Jameson, *New Literary History* 3 (1971–72): 243–44.

ism in the wake of a growing uneasiness about the stability of the sign, and it is this strand in his aesthetics, as representative of a romantic trend, that will concern us for the moment. Early in his argument Shelley proclaims a view of language as a free-standing system similar to that conceived by Saussure, in which words bear a direct relationship to thoughts, or in which the acoustic image evokes the concept signified by it. Acoustic images or "sounds" (to use Shelley's word) "have relation both between each other and towards that which they represent" (*SPP*, p. 484), and it is the former, the syntagmatic and paradigmatic relations among signifiers, that guarantee the coherence of the signified and its uptake by the reader. But Shelley also questions this belief that the relationship between conception and expression is unproblematic, describing the mind as a fading coal and lamenting the fracturing of the sign that occurs between inspiration and composition. Given this disjunction between signifier and signified endemic to writing, a self-present meaning can no longer be located in the text but must be sought in the conception that exists before it is formulated in a language that makes it different from itself. The view of the communicative process here voiced by Shelley goes far beyond Schleiermacher's: it short-circuits grammatical reading of the text by seeking a fusion with the author on a subliminal or transverbal level. Correspondingly, it also eliminates the need for structural actualization:

> a word, a trait in the representation of a scene or a passion, will touch the enchanted chord, and reanimate, in those who have ever experienced these emotions, the sleeping, the cold, the buried image of the past. (*SPP*, p. 505)

> A single sentence may be considered as a whole though it may be found in the midst of a series of unassimilated portions. (*SPP*, pp. 485–86)

Moreover, Shelley can go far beyond the concept of reading as an actualization of the text to a concept of reading as reversal, which will be discussed later. His own readings of Dante and Milton are hermeneutic but not exegetical. Instead of explicating what is in the text, he locates the meaning of the work in an intention radically at odds with the published text, and thus inaccessible except to a purely psychological reading.

We can only touch on developments in language theory that might have led to the emphasis on the reader and to the declining importance of the grammatical level in hermeneutics itself. The radical shift after the Renaissance from an Adamic theory of language as divinely ordained to a theory of the sign as arbitrary does not unsettle signification. Instead, the earlier theory is displaced into rationalist projects for a universal language developed by thinkers like Leibniz and John Wilkins. Of the two factors that contribute to the stability of the sign, one is an 'atomistic' conception of language.[9] The possibility that language might displace ideas does not occur because the relationship between the signifier and the signified is considered only in terms of single words, and not in terms of propositions or groups of words. The myth of referential stability is also maintained by the nature of the atoms involved. These consist of categorematic terms, nouns and adjectives that refer to substances and qualities, and not of syncategorematic terms such as particles whose function is to connect words with words. Through the emphasis on what come to be called 'matter-words' (nouns and verbs), as opposed to 'form words' (particles and pronouns) "which express our perceptions as modified by numerous relations of Space and Time,"[10] the illusion is created that language is positive, that it always names or posits something.

But Enlightenment semantics is also the scene of a more unsettling shift from the sign to the proposition as the minimal unit of discourse. This shift inaugurates an awareness that relationships between words may be complicating factors, and that ideas themselves are not simple entities but associative compounds. Stephen Land traces from a different perspective the erosion of the positivist and atomist theories of language. Thus Locke emphasizes matter-words but also concedes that there are words that name not substance but the absence of it.[11] As significant is Horne Tooke, who begins *The Diversions of Purley* by arguing that we cannot deal with the formation of ideas without first dealing with language, and that a consideration of primarily linguistic terms like particles must therefore precede a discussion of ideational terms like verbs and nouns. His bizarre etymologies, which short-circuit this radical thesis by resolving particles into nouns and verbs so as to make them "the Name of a Thing,"[12] betray a deep anxiety about the slipperiness of these words that refer only to other words, and that therefore make language a system of relational rather than positive terms. The ideational consequences of such a theory of language are suggested by Hugh Blair, who draws on associationist psychology to point out that no object

[9]See Hans Aarsleff, *The Study of Language in England, 1780–1860* (Minneapolis: University of Minnesota Press, 1983), p. 124; Stephen Land, *From Signs to Propositions: The Concept of Form in Eighteenth-Century Semantic Theory* (London: Longmans, 1974), pp. v, 2–22; Ferdinand de Saussure, *Course in General Linguistics*, ed. Charles Bally and Albert Sechehaye, trans. Wade Baskin (New York: McGraw-Hill, 1966), p. 113 and "Translator's Introduction," p. xvi.

[10]F. W. Farrar, *Language and Languages* (Edinburgh: Ballantyne Press, 1877), p. 107.

[11]Land, *From Signs to Propositions*, pp. 184–85. Such words also include negative nouns like 'silence,' which represent the absence of something.

[12]Horne Tooke, *The Diversions of Purley* (London: Thomas Tegg, 1840), pp. 15–25, 631.

"presents itself to our view *isolé* . . . but always occurs as somehow related to other objects; going before them, or following them . . . ; resembling them or opposed to them."[13]

There is evidence that in the nineteenth century concepts of language move in an increasingly diacritical direction. Thus F. W. Farrar, who draws on a wide range of European sources, argues that words "cannot express an intrinsic meaning. . . . They are nothing more . . . than organizations of relations."[14] According to Land, the shift from signs to propositions and the related displacement of interest from nouns to connectives results in a protostructuralist theory of language in which its relational nature determines rather than disseminates meaning. But often, as we will see in the case of Shelley and Blake, it is in these terms that connect words with each other or stand in place of other words that a precise referent seems to vanish. Once a fixed meaning can no longer be located in individual word-atoms considered as signs of things or as reproducing the logical status of referents, the question arises of how we grasp what is not quite in the words but between or behind them. It is here that semantics rejoins the recuperative project of hermeneutics. Tooke uses the grammatical term 'subaudition' to explain how we construct a meaning not present in the particular word or phrase. Subaudition accounts for abbreviation in grammatical constructions and describes a process by which the listener restores something not explicitly voiced so as to clarify the construction or the etymology.[15] Much later Michel Bréal in his *Semantics* focuses on the problem of 'polysemia' and returns to the concept of subaudition to posit an "interior syntax" that allows the listener to fill in "what is missing" and to clarify "the uncertainties of language."[16]

Subaudition is the grammatical equivalent of psychological reading at the level of larger interpretive units. But it is also apparent that both are

[13]*Lectures on Rhetoric and Belles Lettres*, 3 vols. (London: Strahan and Cadell, 1785), I, 354.

[14]*An Essay on the Origin of Language* (London: John Murray, 1860), p. 39. See also *Language and Languages*, pp. 251–54. See also Rousseau's distinction between colors, which have an "independent" meaning, and sounds, which have meaning only in relation to each other: *Essai sur l'origine des langues*, ed. Charles Porset (Bordeaux: G. Ducros, 1968), p. 173.

[15]Aarsleff, *The Study of Language*, p. 64.

[16]Aarsleff, *From Locke to Saussure: Essays on the Study of Language and Intellectual History* (Minneapolis: University of Minnesota Press, 1982), pp. 320, 387–88; Michel Bréal, *Semantics: Studies in the Science of Meaning*, trans. Mrs. Henry Cust (1900; rpt. New York: Dover, 1974), pp. 139–41, 106. Aarsleff compares Bréal's notion of going behind the word to the thought and the similar attempt by Cartesian linguistics to go beyond the surface grammar to the deep structure (*From Locke to Saussure*, p. 388). But the differences between Bréal's semantics and the tradition that extends from the Port-Royal philosophical grammar to Chomskian linguistics are equally instructive. On this tradition see Noam Chomsky, *Cartesian Linguistics: A Chapter in the History of Rationalist Thought* (New York: Harper and Row, 1966), pp. 29, 31–33, 35, 44. In the latter the changes that occur when deep structure is converted to surface structure are syntactic rather than semantic: surface structure is a

highly problematical concepts. The rise of hermeneutics is the beginning of a massive but still unacknowledged change in romantic concepts of discourse. For one cannot shift the location of meaning to the reading process without also changing the very status of meaning as a fixed essence that does not vary between readers. David Simpson points to a tendency in romantic aesthetics toward the "disestablishment of the text as an authority and the stressing of its function as a heuristic stimulus."[17] But the fact that hermeneutics inaugurates the disestablishment of authoritative meaning was not recognized by its practitioners. Indeed, they turned to hermeneutics because of its apparent logocentrism: its origins in biblical interpretation, which also committed it to preserve the authority of various secular scriptures. Yet the contradictions in the hermeneutic concepts of author and reader will eventually lead to the dismantling of its fervent logocentrism. While denying the authority of the text and its classic or historically invariable status, romantic hermeneuticists often conceive of the author as a grounding center. Equally problematical is the role assigned to the reader. For hermeneutics grants the reader as producer of the text a large degree of autonomy from the letter of the text, while initially requiring a fidelity to its spirit that takes away the very liberty conferred on the reader.

Varieties of Hermeneutic Reading

The degree to which the construction of romantic texts displaces their 'meaning' from the mimetic to the hermeneutic level will obviously vary. At the simplest level there are poems in which the parts of the whole are present in the text but unsynthesized. Blake's *Marriage of Heaven and Hell*, for instance, consists of disparate sections of parable and proposition that must be dynamically connected by its readers if such a marriage is to be accomplished in our consciousness. The concluding "Song of Liberty" provides, as the rest of the text does not, a narrative sequence for this process. But it consists of twenty numbered sentences that indicate the stages of an action without actually embodying it. Harold Bloom speculates that each sentence was meant to be a caption for an engrav-

reordering of deep structure but is not more ambiguous than the former (cf. Chomsky, p. 49). By contrast, for Bréal grammar has become ambiguous and inadequate: "it is an undoubted fact that language designates things in an incomplete and inaccurate manner" (Bréal, *Semantics*, p. 171).

[17] *Irony and Authority in Romantic Poetry* (Totowa, N.J.: Rowman and Littlefield, 1979), p. 25. Simpson conflates hermeneutic and heuristic concepts of the text-reader relationship. This conflation exists in nineteenth-century hermeneutic theory, but I see romantic writers as gradually discovering the distinctness of the two.

ing.[18] As the text stands, however, the links between them are omitted, as are the plates that might concretize them and bring them to life, so that the responsibility for making the shorthand of the text into an imitation of an action rests with the reader.

The disappearance of actualization may occur at a structural level through the omission of links in the narrative syntax of the text. But this process of derealization may also occur at the level of smaller semantic units. Donald Davie has suggested that the language of Wordsworth's *Prelude*, which hovers between the concrete and the abstract, is made up of words that signify rather than embody their meaning: 'fiduciary' symbols that, like coins as values of monetary exchange, possess their value as a result of a social contract. Wordsworth's words, he argues, "will carry the reader only so long as he does not loiter . . . [they] have meaning so long as we trust them."[19] What is at issue here is a loosening of the strict denotative bond between sound and sense that exists in similarly philosophic works like Pope's *Essay on Man*. In Wordsworth the acoustic image, as Davie sees it, becomes a stimulus to us to produce through sympathetic understanding a signified that we half create and half perceive. Here, as in *The Marriage*, the elements of a completed meaning are present in the text, but the reader must participate in the process of actualizing them, sometimes by reading through or around certain aporias in the text that might otherwise deconstruct it.

A more complex case is Blake's *Songs*, where it is not simply the animation but also the organization of the parts into a whole that is left unaccomplished. In the *Songs* the exact sequence of the poems is not specified. It is clear enough that we are meant to do more than simply proceed from *Innocence* to *Experience*, but where we set a terminus to the endlessly complex process of intertextualizing poems and states of mind is less clear. Blake himself, in ending different editions of the *Songs* with different poems, seems to have produced the *telos* of the textual process in more than one way. A traditionally hermeneutic reading, however, would reconstruct 'Blake's' intention from such larger contexts as the author's oeuvre and the spirit of the age, combining the poems dialectically so as to generate from the contraries of innocence and experience a progression in the reader's consciousness toward the state of organized innocence.

The texts so far discussed are all special cases in that they are not simply dependent on the reader to interpret them but also to supply something that they do not contain. There is no poem in the *Songs* that

[18]*Blake's Apocalypse: A Study in Poetic Argument* (1963; rpt. Ithaca, N.Y.: Cornell University Press, 1970), p. 96.

[19]*Articulate Energy* (London: Routledge and Kegan Paul, 1955), pp. 106–7.

actually consolidates the state of organized innocence, for the Lyca poems celebrate it as fantasy and therefore as an abstraction from reality. But in all the cases considered the components of a completed meaning are present in the text. It is simply that the meaning is not produced in the text but by the reader and is therefore accessible only through psychological reading, or through applicative reading, in which meaning is validated through our application of the text to our own lives. Much the same is true of the expository prose so far considered. What happens in *Biographia Literaria* is not that the goal of Coleridge's argument is unclear. Rather, he leaves his argument rhetorically unactualized and concludes with a merely embryonic definition of the imagination, lest the insertion of self into language, the process of elaboration and demonstration, turn out to be a process of dismantling. The onus is then on the imaginative reader to restore the unity of the work. But a different case arises when the terminus of the work is quite literally absent from the text and the reader must reconstruct not something that is partially present but something that is not there at all.

An initial example of such a work is *Christabel*, where the projected ending not only does not follow from the events that lead up to it, but also does not follow the rest of the text. There is a cryptic conclusion to part II that may, if we interpret it allegorically, tell us that the wrath of Christabel's father is the reverse side of love, and that his apparent rejection of her is the other side of a coin that the imaginative reader can turn over to reveal the happy ending. This conclusion stands in place of the happy ending Coleridge sketches elsewhere, and re-presents it as a deferred presence. But it is tacked on in such a way that it can be no more than a sign, a token of faith. Moreover, it does not function in the same way as the ending of Keats's *Hyperion*, where the text at least points to the work; rather, it stands in place of comments about a happy ending that Coleridge made to friends and is a supplement to an absent signifier that can be restored only if the actual ending of the narrative is disregarded or reversed. It is a signifier that stands in place of a further signifier and not even of a signified.

If the first group of texts calls for a synthesising hermeneutics, this second group requires a much more radical hermeneutics of reversal, in which the positive essence of the work must be grasped across the barrier of the text's negativity, and in which the reading process does not simply complete the creative process but compensates for the deconstructive momentum of the latter. The model for a hermeneutics of reversal can be found in the later work of Schelling, and more problematically, in Kierkegaard's *The Concept of Irony*, both of which are discussed in the next chapter. What is interesting for our purposes is that Schelling employs literary terms such as 'irony' to interpret the text of Being, which allows us to reverse his procedure and to see his ontology as a hermeneutic. Arguing that every element contains the seed of its opposite, he sees the created world as characterized by envelopment and irony. In other words, its apparent meaning envelops a deeper and quite opposite meaning; its signs must be read ironically, as expressing a demonic or inverted world in which God, through his "art of dissimulation or irony displays the reverse of that which he genuinely wills" (*AW*, p. 77). A poem like *Christabel* has already introduced the negative stage of the rhetoric of envelopment in showing how the apparently 'good' Christabel bears the psychic trace of the 'bad' Geraldine. Within a hermeneutics of reversal, the reader is asked to bring to light the contrary envelopment of good within evil by believing that the good Christabel is still present within the defeated Christabel, and that God, for reasons unknown, is temporarily displaying the reverse of what he genuinely wills.

One may well ask how the reader is to reconstruct the hidden meaning of a work if that 'meaning' is not even partially present in the text. One answer is that it is present, but so carefully concealed as to be evident only to the discerning reader. A second answer is that it is made explicit somewhere else in the canon. The same process of inference from whole to part which allows us to read through the aporias in an individual work must be seen as operating between the authorial canon as a whole and the parts of that canon composed by individual texts. In other words, we are asked to break the hermeneutic circle at the level of the oeuvre, projecting into the individual text a set of meanings that it does not have in isolation, and perhaps even reversing the reading that emerges when the text is made its own context. Schelling's phenomenology allows for the placing of irony as a moment in the unfolding of the cultural unconscious. It allows for the presence of the positive within the negative, if we imaginatively complete the process by which the seed becomes the plant. Similarly, the hermeneutic notion of a canon, whether completed, as in the case of Blake, or hypothetical, as in the case of Coleridge, permits a reversal of the textual reading by allowing us insight into a later stage in the phenomenology of the author's spirit.

Canonical reading is not the only strategy for interpretation implicit in romantic theory and practice. Because in Shelley's phrase "a word," or a "trait" is sufficient to reanimate a narrative archetype (*SPP*, p. 505), the reader may complete a text by referring it to a completed parallel in literature or myth. Such a strategy informs Keats's *Endymion*, where the repeated evocation of the "old tale" that the modern redaction is not quite able to imitate serves as a figure of reading that inscribes the narrator's desire for a certain kind of ending. A similar strategy informs *Hyperion*, where a parallel between the first three books of *Paradise Lost* and the three books of Keats's poem supplies a movement from light to darkness not clearly present in the text itself. A variant of this strategy is behind Blake's statement that the Bible is "the great code of art," a statement that calls for typological reading of authorial canons. Yet another strategy for psychological reading that informs the rhetorical construction of romantic texts involves supplementing what is in the text with other transcripts of the author's 'intentions' (notebooks, letters, lectures), with sympathetic awareness of the author's life and the goals to which it is oriented, or with knowledge of what was thought in the author's circle. The process of understanding texts by bringing them to life is a feature of the hermeneutics that subsumes philological scholarship in the nineteenth century. But more important, it is part of the rhetoric of romantic texts, which often place themselves in "life" by referring to actual people and to the time, place, and circumstances of composition, so as to invite the reader to identify with the writer.

An example of how canonical reading can be used to facilitate a hermeneutics of reversal is *The (First) Book of Urizen* by Blake, or more properly, the critical treatment it has received.[20] On the face of it the poem presents the phenomenology of spirit, both individual and cosmic, as a series of degenerative cycles and thus seems to decenter the Blakean journey toward Jerusalem. But critics are often able to give the poem a positive meaning as an antithetical moment in the dialectic of Blake's canon. Crucial to a negative hermeneutics that 'saves' the positive meaning of the text would be an analysis of the rhetoric of parody and satire as presenting inverted worlds whose very grotesqueness motivates the reader to reverse them. But equally important would be a redemptive analogy between the corpus of Blake's texts and the biblical canon, which similarly contains infernal moments. The readings sketched here are of course considerably more complex than the other 'hermeneutic' readings offered earlier and involve the reader in a kind of somersault rather than a simple reconstruction or completion. The psychological reading here does not so much anchor itself in the grammatical reading as it effects a canceling and sublation of the latter. The canonical reading of *Urizen* is certainly not impossible. But as will become apparent when the poem is discussed in greater detail, like all traditionally hermeneutic readings, it is problematical. One difficulty is that Urizen is by no means a purely parodic figure, an Ubu Roi, but is often dispiritingly sublime. The Urizenic order can at times seem inevitable, and we cannot always persuade ourselves that it is inverse as well as perverse. Moreover, the lapidary structure of the poem, which consists of discrete chapters subdivided into disjunct verses between which the reader must construct

[20]Cf. Tannenbaum, *Biblical Tradition in Blake's Prophecies*, pp. 201–24.

causal and chronological bridges, makes the text radically ambiguous. The metaphysical narrative that we construct if we see the entry of self-consciousness into the world as error rather than self-discovery is already a discourse in a text that has no story. If readers center the poem's significance in the manner suggested, it is because they know (or think they know) from other works that in Blake's mythology Urizen is a villain and not an antihero. But readers who recognize the repressive critical function of concepts such as author, canon, and system used to homogenize the text may well choose not to follow the hermeneutic reading suggested. Indeed, Blake himself may thematize the inconclusiveness of the hermeneutic reading through Fuzon, who represents the energy that breaks out of the Urizenic prisonhouse in which readers who read logically, literally, and therefore pessimistically are trapped.

Hermeneutic and Heuristic Reading

It should be clear by now that any attempt to explain the disappearance of actualization by a hermeneutics that locates meaning outside the written text is fraught with problems. The absence of a self-identical meaning results partly from a feeling that language is not product but process, or to quote Wilhelm von Humboldt, "Language is not a work (*ergon*) but an activity (*energeia*)." Both Humboldt and Schleiermacher argue that because written language is an "incomplete, mummified depository," the reader must be dynamically involved in the generation of meaning if literature is to become a psychological as well as a semiological event.[21] But the absence of actualized meaning also results from a disjunction between signifier and signified in the text of the social and human psyche, a feeling that the meaning of events in the world is not given, and thus that literary discourse can no longer codify meaning but can only be a heuristic stimulus to its production. In its initial stages romantic hermeneutics both initiates and masks this crucial change in the status of discourse. Because it sees literature as a productivity rather than a product, it inevitably sees literary meaning as implicated in larger processes such as communication and history. But at the same time traditional romantic hermeneutics neutralizes this recognition by making reading a process but positing as the goal of this process a product, a fixed center behind the text called the 'work.'

The argument for the importance of traditional hermeneutics to an understanding of romanticism is not based on any assumption that it

[21]Wilhelm von Humboldt, *Humanist without Portfolio*, trans. Marianne Cowan (Detroit: Wayne State University Press, 1963), p. 280.

WORD ↔ THING

Figure 1.

provides a key to the texts, but rather on its presence at the site of certain formative tensions in romantic views of discourse. The disappearance of actualization can very well lead to our viewing the text as the locus for a deconstruction of meaning. For in its displacement of meaning from language to consciousness, hermeneutics recognizes that the relationship between signifier and signified is problematical. But by seeing this relationship as something that has psychological and interpersonal as well as semiological dimensions, it also attempts to forestall the poststructuralist fracturing of the sign. The crucial historical role of hermeneutics as conserver of a continued though problematical logocentric impulse in romanticism will be apparent if we consider the different possible views of the linguistic sign. Theories of language that posit an innate resemblance between words and things, such as the seventeenth-century ontotheological theories of language as something given by God to Adam, allow for a direct correspondence between word and thing that we can express through the dyad in Figure 1. But the moment language is conceived of as a conventional system in which signification involves a relationship between acoustic image and concept rather than word and thing, the correspondence becomes more problematical. Structuralist theories of language continue to see the linguistic system as a freestanding whole in which the correspondence between signifier and signified can be expressed in terms of the dyad in Figure 2. This arbitrary correspondence in the individual semantic atom is subtended diacritically by systematic syntagmatic and paradigmatic relations between elements of the system. In considering the problem of meaning in both traditional hermeneutics and poststructuralism, however, it is useful to think in terms of the tetrad in Figure 3. For many nineteenth-century hermeneuticists, writing disrupts the bond between signifier and signified that exists before expression. The reader, however, is able to mediate between language and actuality, and to restore this link. We do so by penetrating into the consciousness of a centering subject, the author, and thus guaranteeing the sign as intention though not as reference. The hermeneutic circuit is then completed as in Figure 4 through a reading that is application as well as divination: the reader transforms intention into reference, and reunites the signifier and signified by an

ACOUSTIC IMAGE ↔ CONCEPT

Figure 2.

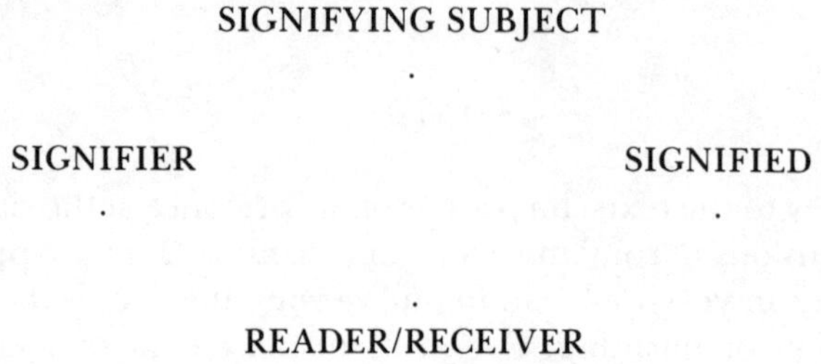

SIGNIFYING SUBJECT

SIGNIFIER SIGNIFIED

READER/RECEIVER

Figure 3.

act of emotional commitment. In poststructuralism, by contrast, the links between all elements of the tetrad are disrupted, and thus it becomes impossible to restore the bond between signifier and signified. It is precisely this radical fracturing of the work as sign that traditional hermeneutics recontains by introducing the subject (reader and author) into the impersonal network of language and making signification a matter of communication between persons as well as of correspondence between words and referents.

Yet such readings are undermined by the fact that they compensate for the supplementarity of writing by substituting for it what can fairly be called the supplement of reading: writing, which stood in place of an absent signified, is now replaced by reading, which stands in place of writing. Hence the relevance of traditional hermeneutics to romantic texts can only be a corrective one: it reminds us that literature is the interaction of text and reader, and not simply the interplay of text and subtext. But this interaction, as was apparent in the case of "The Eolian Harp," is much more complicated than a hermeneutic reading will allow. If we attempt such readings, it is because the currency and influence of a traditional hermeneutic in the romantic period means that they are of-

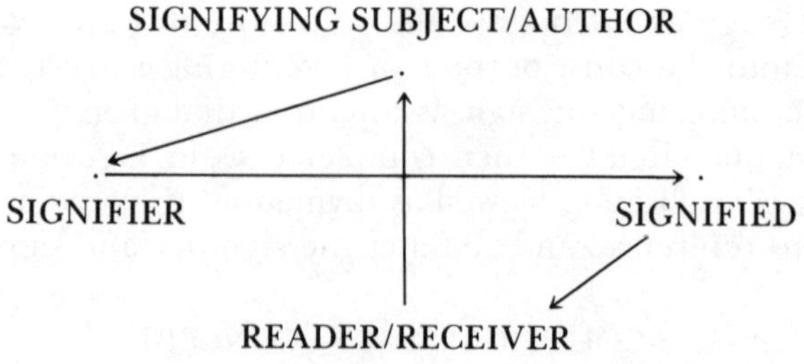

SIGNIFYING SUBJECT/AUTHOR

SIGNIFIER SIGNIFIED

READER/RECEIVER

Figure 4.

ten suggested in the text or in the canon. As Roland Barthes indicates, however, the author enters the text as a "guest . . . inscribed . . . like one of his own characters, figured in the carpet."[22] Similarly, the hermeneutic recovery of authorial 'intention' must also be seen as a guest in the text, possessed of no more authority than other possible readings. And indeed, the hermeneutic tradition itself develops toward such a recognition, as the notions of intention and authority work themselves out in the texts of Kierkegaard and of Schleiermacher himself.

The rise of hermeneutics speaks for a romantic belief that texts, even if they are intentional in structure, are productively engaged with something outside the prisonhouse of language. But while the disappearance of actualization does not make the text into the site for an erasure of meaning, it also does not allow for a reinstallation of the verbal icon in the inner temple of the work. Implicitly or explicitly, romantic texts function as heuristic stimuli for the production of meanings that are historically and personally variable. For texts that project an ideal reader or inscribe within themselves a model of the reading that will make them complete jeopardize their own closure by making the sympathetic reading a figure within the text. Thus, increasingly there are also texts that seem designed as what Barthes calls 'writerly' texts, in which the reader becomes in some sense a writer of the text.[23] The distinction between the two kinds of texts is easier to maintain in theory than in practice. Often the second kind will suggest its own authorized reading, but as a construction of desire that nevertheless does constrain the free play of reading. Not surprisingly, the overlap between hermeneutic and heuristic texts is more likely to occur in texts that do not simply imply a model of reading through genre and mode, or include figures of reading, but in those that thematize the problem of reading more extensively in a scene of reading or through numerous (and significantly different) scenes of reading.

Coleridge's conversation poems provide an instance of the poem that is designed as traditionally hermeneutic. At the other extreme, some of Blake's early texts exemplify what Umberto Eco calls "works in movement": a designation more specific than the larger category of the "open work." Works in movement do not simply elicit the "*theoretical, mental* collaboration" of the reader in interpreting "a product which has already been organised in its structural entirety": they consist of "unplanned or physically incomplete structural units," which call on the reader to do all or part of the organizing.[24] Characteristic of Blake's early texts is their

[22] *Image, Music, Text*, trans. Stephen Heath (New York: Hill and Wang, 1977), p. 161.
[23] *S/Z*, trans. Richard Miller (New York: Hill and Wang, 1974), pp. 3–4.
[24] *The Role of the Reader: Explorations in the Semiotics of Texts* (Bloomington: Indiana Uni-

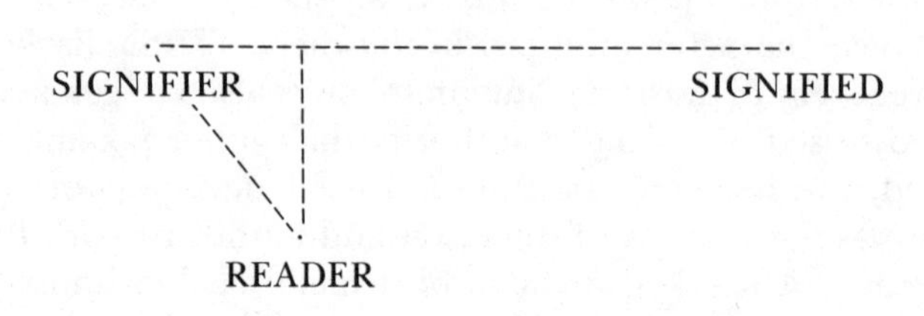

Figure 5.

paratactic organization in terms of disjunct units that must be synthesized by the reader, or in terms of fractured prosodic and thematic planes that make the text, in Kristeva's words, "an *intersection of textual surfaces* rather than a *point* (a fixed meaning)," "a dialogue among several writings."[25] Leopold Damrosch has summed up this tendency in describing the Blakean text as kaleidoscopic, composed of "transferrable parts," and thus resistant to a holistic analysis deriving from notions of organic form.[26] The result is that these early texts do not 'contain' their meaning. They are decentered texts, but with consequences that are productive and generative. Traditionally, Blake criticism (not without encouragement from Blake himself) has taken the early works and read them in the light of the later system. This reading of the canon, however, is a fiction developed within the canon itself. For Blake's habit of intertextualizing poems (as in the addition of the *Songs of Experience* to the *Songs of Innocence*) and of reprocessing his own material by returning to the same nexus of events and characters in successive prophecies means that he himself constantly unseals the work he has written and makes it into a text. Blake's texts represent a kind of text we have not so far discussed, which functions without the protection of a theory of meaning that guarantees the individual reader's production of meaning will also be a reproduction of something encoded by the author. As Figure 5 indicates, the heuristic text renounces the power to codify meaning associated with the authority of the author, but it also retains the power to refer to and affect reality, with the result that text and reader mutually make and remake each other.

---

versity Press, 1984), p. 56. I obviously do not agree with Eco's view that open works (and the aesthetics that legitimizes them) do not exist before the late nineteenth century (p. 53).

[25]Julia Kristeva, *Desire in Language*, trans. Leon Roudiez (New York: Columbia University Press, 1980), p. 65.

[26]*Symbol and Truth in Blake's Myth* (Princeton, N.J.: Princeton University Press, 1980), pp. 349–50.

A heuristic concept of discourse shares with a hermeneutic one the assumption that literature has an affective power, but it also renounces the closure of the sign to which the latter remains committed. Reading can no longer be conceived as the reconstruction of an original meaning but must be seen as the production of a new meaning. Consequently, the signifying complex constructed by the reader out of the text—the discourse of reception—cannot be related back to a transcendental signified in the author's psyche, and remains an intent of consciousness. What we have hitherto called the 'work' is of course of the same order as this complex constructed out of the text, so that the heuristic concept of discourse collapses the distinction between work and text. Reading does indeed engender signification: in the act of reading signifier and signified are fused through a third element—involvement, or what Ricoeur calls "appropriation" (*Aneignung*).[27] But this fusion does not occur through a reading that reconstructs the meaning of the text and thus institutionalizes itself by making the work into a signified and then into a book. Early romantic hermeneutics assumes three key elements that we shall call 'text,' 'work,' and 'book.' Using the text (which is understood through grammatical reading) as a pre-text, the reader through divination generates the work. The text may stand in relation to the work as a positive transparency (as is the case in a reconstructive hermeneutics), or as a negative transparency, a displacement (as is the case in antithetical hermeneutics). But the point is that the usefulness of the text ceases as soon as the work has been constructed from it. The work, however, is still no more than an intent of consciousness, until the reader has confirmed it as reference by relating the signifying system of the work to a transcendental signified in the reader's psyche. At this point, through a series of readings leading from the grammatical through the psychological to the applicative, we have moved from the text, through the work, to the book. The book is something public: it can be placed in libraries and prescribed in courses. Although the work exists only in the consciousness of the author, the book is something that cannot be created without the existence of the reader, hence the pivotal place of the reader in hermeneutics.

The explicitly heuristic text, as we shall see, is not reducible to a single formula. One way of describing it is to say that it presents reading as performative rather than constative: although it does not legitimize reading as the repetition of an anterior meaning, it assumes that the very performance of reading will authorize the meaning so constructed. The term 'performative' suggests a mode of understanding that temporarily

[27]Paul Ricoeur, *Hermeneutics and the Human Sciences*, ed. and trans. John B. Thompson (New York: Cambridge University Press, 1981), pp. 182–93.

brackets the self-reflexive: in other words, such reading, in which the heart becomes its own oracle, constructs a unified if hypothetical meaning out of a disjunctive text through a will-to-power. Thus we may expect to find in the spectrum of texts to be considered a certain number of 'performative' texts, Blake's *Marriage* and Shelley's *Prometheus Unbound* being examples. Unlike 'hermeneutic' texts, these texts are highly self-conscious and present themselves as linguistic entities. They assume that they exist only as they are performed and may go so far as to inscribe a particularly desirable performance, but only as a fiction. Paul de Man has questioned the legitimacy of the performative as a category in asking whether "the language of truth (*episteme*)" can convincingly "be replaced by a language of persuasion (*doxa*)" as a means of restoring to literature the power to give a foundation to what it posits. Rhetoric, he suggests, "considered as persuasion . . . is performative but when considered as a system of tropes, it deconstructs its own performance."[28] But the performative text makes us aware that the problem can also be seen the other way round. Considered as a system of tropes, it suggests, rhetoric may be self-consuming, but considered as persuasion it can still be performative.

Nevertheless, there is a sense in which performative reading is no more than a historicized version of hermeneutic reading, similar to the latter in deferring the responsibility for constituting a unified meaning from the text to the reader, but different in that it locates its authority in a culturally variable reading community rather than in an origin. While conceding that a text can be performed in different ways, it segregates these performances from each other, so as to make each reading internally consistent and thus persuasive. But it is not really clear that each reading can really remain untroubled by others, in a joyous pluralism of complementary performances or in a competing economy of cultural free enterprise. Thus we can also expect to find among heuristic texts a certain number that thematize reading as a simultaneous construction and unraveling of meaning, so as to recognize that it may be implicated in the same pressures as writing. As extended scenes of reading, poems like Shelley's *Triumph of Life* explore how reading complicates and disseminates as well as performs meaning. Such a view of reading may sound very similar to the one taken by de Man. But as we shall see, the heuristic text still allows us to take a phenomenological view of speech acts as having the form (if not the content) of an understanding, of a movement behind appearances to their ground. Put very simply, there is a difference between reading a poem as writing, and reading it as ad-

[28]*Allegories of Reading: Figural Language in Rousseau, Nietzsche, Rilke, and Proust* (New Haven, Conn.: Yale University Press, 1979), pp. 130–31.

dressed to a reader. The latter brings into play the desire to understand, or what Ricoeur calls "appropriation." As my constant blurring of the line between heuristic reading and heuristic texts suggests, this difference is not simply an interpretive convention but is grounded in the texts themselves. Ricoeur's distinction between language and discourse is once again useful. The heuristic text requires to be read as discourse, as something addressed by an author to a reader within a temporal framework. The increasing focus on the reader, then, is at the center of an important shift in romantic concepts of the status of literature: of reading and writing and the stability of the meaning they convey. Clearly, there are problems in the attempt—whether hermeneutic or heuristic—to recover the authority of the sign through the supplement of reading. But we cannot dismiss as a futile postponement of semiotic nihilism the sense that the problem of the text's difference from itself must be reconceived in terms of the reader. Writing is already thought of as an alienated medium that exists in the gap between signifier and signified. But reading in the romantic period is still to some extent conceived as an action, hence a medium in which the fracturing of the sign can be momentarily overcome, through a desire that creates understandings even if it does not uncover truths.

CHAPTER TWO

The Hermeneutic Tradition from Schleiermacher to Kierkegaard

So far we have considered the general forms taken by the commerce between author, reader, and text, but not the figures who make romantic hermeneutics different from its precursors. The history of hermeneutics from Schleiermacher to Dilthey is the history of an expansion of the field of study to include not only biblical and secular texts but all human phenomena—from texts to gestures and actions—that use sensory signs to convey an inner spiritual reality.[1] This expansion has consequences for modern semiotics that will not be pursued here, for the romantic period initiates an awareness of empirical 'realities' as textual phenomena. But it is the increasing sense that signs may not adequately convey interiority that will be the concern of this chapter. To begin with, this inadequacy is the product of a temporal distance between author and reader that we can overcome through a process of historical reconstruction or re-experiencing (*Nacherleben*).[2] More and more, however, the inner meaning of a text is deferred to the future and becomes something to be projected rather than recovered by the reader. This chapter traces the movement from a positive hermeneutics that deepens or completes the text to a negative hermeneutics that resists it. It follows this movement through the work of Schleiermacher and others to that of Hegel, which stands ambiguously on the borderline between the two varieties of hermeneutics, and finally to the work of

[1]Wilhelm Dilthey, "The Understanding of Other Persons and Their Expressions of Life," *Descriptive Psychology and Historical Understanding*, trans. R. M. Zaner and K. L. Heiges (The Hague: Martinus Nijhoff, 1977), pp. 123–24.

[2]The term is Dilthey's but it can apply equally well to Schleiermacher (ibid., p. 132).

Schelling and (more self-critically) Kierkegaard.[3] In the process it also discloses the increasingly problematical status of the supplement of reading. For the growing estrangement of the 'true' meaning from what appears in the written text or the language of events comes perilously close to deconstructing the transcendental signified. If this meaning cannot be represented, we must ask, is there any guarantee that it exists? Kierkegaard's *Concept of Irony*, as a form of what he later calls "doubly reflected communication" (*PV*, p. 156), simultaneously manifests and reflects on its own desire for authoritative meaning. It therefore marks a fitting close to one chapter in the history of hermeneutics and an appropriate transition to another. This further chapter, which is simultaneous with rather than subsequent to the first, explores the continued importance of reading as a way of renewing writing. But it replaces the work as origin with the work as originating productivity, and thus radically reconceives what is involved in the supplement of reading.

Positive Hermeneutics: Schleiermacher and His Circle

The separation of form from meaning seems to begin with Schleiermacher's sense of the need for a 'psychological' as well as 'grammatical' or literal reading of texts. This need is first articulated only in the 1819 Compendium[4] and distinguishes him from his predecessor J. A. Ernesti,

[3]I do not consider the hermeneutics of Dilthey in detail because chronologically as well as intellectually he falls outside the range of this study. Dilthey marks the return of hermeneutics to a positivist concern with textual expressions as interpreted through a structural hermeneutics. This chapter traces an increasingly metaphysical tendency in romantic hermeneutics. The next chapter outlines an emphasis on the linguisticality of understanding, which is, however, phenomenological rather than structuralist.

[4]The development and textual history of Schleiermacher's hermeneutics are complicated. For a long time the only available edition of the *Hermeneutics* was that of his student Friedrich Lücke, based on the manuscript now referred to as the Compendium of 1819, supplemented by lecture notes taken in 1828–29 and 1832–33. In 1959 Heinz Kimmerle brought out an edition of the various handwritten manuscripts of the hermeneutics, beginning with the aphorisms of 1805 and including the first draft of 1809–1810, the Compendium (the only substantial manuscript), the 1829 "Academy Addresses," and the less complete material written between 1826 and 1833 (cited in text and notes by the abbreviation *H*). The effect of Kimmerle's edition is to make us aware of shifts and tensions in Schleiermacher's thinking, which are not necessarily confined to those outlined by Kimmerle himself. Kimmerle argues that the early Schleiermacher is much more committed to the identity of thought and language than the later Schleiermacher, who tends toward a psychologism that posits thought as something ideal and separable from its verbal expression. The 1819 Compendium is a transitional work that begins this move, but in which the linguistic emphasis is still evident in the decision to retain the label of 'technical' interpretation for the detailed account of the second level of reading, instead of the term 'psychological' interpretation introduced for the first time in the general introduction. Thus it is not until the "Academy Addresses" of 1829 that "the second part of the theory of understanding developed in a way that corresponds to the introduction of 1819" (*H*, p. 39). Behind

who makes other forms of reading mere aids to grammatical interpretation. Briefly, grammatical study is concerned with the meanings of and interconnections between individual words (*H*, p. 147), but not with form or structure in an aesthetic sense. Psychological reading, on the other hand, understands the text from within and thus breaks the hermeneutic circle. It seeks an "identification with the author" (O, p. 10) through a return to the point of origin of a text (*Anfangspunkt*), a point that simultaneously reveals the *arche* and *telos* of the discourse (*HK*, p. 154), by way of a circular understanding that comprehends the unity of the work through its parts and understands the significance of each part

---

Kimmerle's project is a desire to defend Schleiermacher against the criticism of Gadamer, by making available his early theories on hermeneutics. The view that Schleiermacher neglected language, as Kimmerle points out, comes from Dilthey's account of him in "The Rise of Hermeneutics" (*New Literary History* 3 [1971–72]), and Dilthey in turn relied on Lücke's edition, which draws only on Schleiermacher's later work.

My own treatment of Schleiermacher follows two divergent lines, one of them revisionary, but in a different way from Kimmerle's treatment. In the present chapter, I discuss the Schleiermacher popularized by Dilthey and criticized in our own time by Gadamer and Kimmerle himself, who favors the early Schleiermacher. There is obvious evidence in the later hermeneutics for a psychologistic reading of Schleiermacher. However, I argue in the next chapter that the later Schleiermacher is actually much more complex than either Dilthey or Kimmerle allow, and that he uses the 'psychological' in a much more explicitly problematic way than either Hegel or Schelling. If the early Schleiermacher is something of a structuralist in his use of grammatical and linguistic models to illuminate 'technical' interpretation and in his assumption that the technical and the grammatical are related like *parole* and *langue*, the later Schleiermacher is romantic in his concern with the psychological but incipiently deconstructive in his treatment of 'psychology.' Moreover, he remains committed to the interconnection between thought and language, but the 'linguisticality of understanding' now implies a language that is different from itself—hence my reference to the 'interconnection' rather than the 'identity' of thought and language.

For obvious reasons I have used the Lücke version of the hermeneutics as well as the Compendium. As Kimmerle admits, his own edition does not make Lücke's superfluous, because the latter draws on lecture notes by Schleiermacher's students (*H*, p. 230), which are considerably fuller than Schleiermacher's notes of 1832–33 published by Kimmerle, yet are in no way inconsistent with these notes. My discussion in these chapters therefore draws on the following texts: (*A*) The translation by Jan Wocjik and Roland Haas of "The Hermeneutics: The Outline of the 1819 Lectures", *New Literary History* 10 (1978): 1–16. I have preferred this abbreviated translation (cited in text and notes as O) to the English translation of the Kimmerle edition (*H*) because it seems more faithful at certain points. Where the Wojcik translation is incomplete, I have also drawn on the "Compendium of 1819" (MS 3) as printed in the English translation of the Kimmerle edition. This consists of an introduction, a first part on 'grammatical' interpretation, and a brief second part on 'technical' interpretation. (*B*) The "Draft for the Presentation of the Second Part" (MS 3′, 1826–27) and "The Separate Exposition of the Second Part" (MS 4, 1826–27), both in *H*. (*C*) "The Two Academy Addresses of 1829" (MS 5) in *H*. (*D*) "The Marginal Notes of 1832–33" reprinted in *H*, and the Lücke edition (cited in text and notes as *HK*). The latter is valuable not only because it provides a fuller account of 'psychological interpretation' than is available from the marginal notes, but also because it indicates that in his final lectures Schleiermacher devoted an autonomous (and apparently lengthy) section to psychological as distinct from technical interpretation.

in the light of the whole. A third level of reading often discussed in biblical and legal hermeneutics, the applicative,[5] is also tacitly present in Schleiermacher's theory. For psychological reading also requires readers to engage in a more conservative version of what Paul Ricoeur calls *Aneignung*, making the text our own, in order to grasp it as part of our lives and not just as a historical document.[6] Because the concept of application locates the significance of the text partly in its effect on the reader (*Wirkung*), it raises a problem implicit in psychological reading as well: namely, that meaning is not something contained in the text, but also something that remains suspended until it is confirmed through understanding and enactment.

Whether the need to go beyond grammatical reading of the text in order to actualize it denies the presence in it of incarnate meaning is a question that has troubled interpreters of Schleiermacher. Two antecedent traditions in hermeneutics—the theological and philological—are worth mentioning, because they indicate that multileveled reading does not have to result in the severance of the inner from the outer. Already in Francke's *Praelectiones* and Rambach's *Institutions* we find distinctions between the grammatical, literal or real, and the spiritual senses of a text. The similar vocabulary suggests that Schleiermacher's hermeneutics may have begun as a secularized version of medieval exegesis, replacing the anagogic by the psychological level, and translating the moral or tropological level as applicative reading. The fourfold method, too, raises problems of the separation of meaning from depiction, which Christian theorists argue around. Summing up the tradition, Erich Auerbach distinguishes allegory, which empties out the sensory level by making it a mere sign, from figural writing and interpretation, which permit both "poles—the figure and its fulfilment—to retain the characteristics of concrete historical reality."[7] Psychological reading may well have been conceived on the model of figural interpretation, as informing the grammatical rather than replacing it. Similarly, philologists before Schleiermacher had introduced the notion of multilayered reading without moving in a phenomenological direction. Spinoza, for instance, distinguishes grammatical, structural, and historical reading, which focus respectively on the meaning of words, the coherence of the text,

[5]David Hoy, *The Critical Circle: Literature, History, and Philosophical Hermeneutics* (Berkeley: University of California Press, 1982), p. 53.

[6]*Hermeneutics and the Human Sciences*, ed. and trans. John B. Thompson (New York: Cambridge University Press, 1982), pp. 182–93.

[7]*Mimesis: The Representation of Reality in Western Literature* (Princeton, N.J.: Princeton University Press, 1953), pp. 195–96. On the difference between allegory and typology see also Leonhard Goppelt, *Typos: The Typological Interpretation of the Old Testament in the New*, trans. Donald H. Madvig (Grand Rapids, Mich.: Eerdmans, 1982), pp. 7, 13.

and the historical context, including knowledge of author and reader.[8] F. A. Wolf posits three complementary methods of reading: the grammatical, the historical, and the philosophic[9] (or at other times the rhetorical).[10] Grammatical interpretation is concerned with the signifier (though regarded as referentially stable), historical interpretation is concerned with the text's contexts, and philosophic interpretation counteracts the centrifugal tendencies of history and biography by returning to what the text says. Schleiermacher was critical of Friedrich Ast, who was much more romantic in the use he made of multilayered reading, envisioning a spiritual (*geistig*) rather than a philosophic reading at the third level. As the term *geistig* with its premonitions of Hegel indicates, such a reading is concerned with the spirit of the work as part of the spirit of the age and the world-view of its author. For the early Schleiermacher such encyclopedic notions take hermeneutics in a metaphysical and idealist direction.[11]

But despite these qualifications, which apply largely to his early work, it is not possible to put Schleiermacher on the conservative side of the great divide between philology and phenomenology. For on a theoretical level he increasingly develops in the direction of Ast. His replacement of Wolf's 'philosophic' reading with psychological reading marks a shift away from pure philology, though in an unorthodox way he always remains a philologist. Moreover, in borrowing from Ast the concept of the hermeneutic circle, Schleiermacher commits himself to precisely the approach he sometimes condemns: to reading the work as a totality and thus to a reliance on intuition foreign to philology. The analogy between psychological and figural reading similarly masks a problem. For it is arguable that figural reading cannot really escape the privileging of a 'deeper' meaning, and that the opposition between figure and allegory is tenuous. Indeed, Auerbach concedes that Christianity may be shadowed by an "antagonism between sensory appearance and meaning" and that the figural may be a compensatory attempt to overcome tensions between the letter and the spirit,[12] recognized by the interpretive tradition of Augustine, Origen, and Philo.[13] In terms of his practical criticism, it is

[8]Benedict de Spinoza, *A Theological Political Treatise and A Political Treatise*, trans. R. H. M. Elwes (New York: Dover, 1951), pp. 101–104. The terms 'grammatical,' 'structural,' and 'historical' are those of Tzvetan Todorov, *Symbolism and Interpretation*, trans. Catherine Porter (Ithaca, N.Y.: Cornell University Press, 1982), pp. 140–42.

[9]Richard Palmer, *Hermeneutics* (Evanston, Ill.: Northwestern University Press, 1969), p. 82.

[10]Todorov, *Symbolism and Interpretation*, p. 154.

[11]Palmer, *Hermeneutics*, p. 85.

[12]*Mimesis*, pp. 49, 75.

[13]Origen, too, has a theory of multilayered reading, consisting of the somatic (grammatical-historical), the psychic (moral), and the pneumatic (allegorical-mystical). But his theory is formulated in terms of an opposition between the body and the spirit which devalues the

not always easy to say where Schleiermacher stands. In his *Life of Jesus* he appears to favor texts that make the spiritual present at the literal level, and only reluctantly devises a hermeneutic for texts that fail to do so. But in his *Introductions to the Dialogues of Plato,* external and inward readings of texts are opposed in terms of a romantic vocabulary that privileges the inner as closer to life and the outer as more mechanical. It may be that as a practical critic Schleiermacher found it difficult to construct a general hermeneutic that would apply to all texts, and that his interest for the future lies precisely in the fact that he is not theoretically monolithic.

For the purposes of this chapter, however, Schleiermacher's position in romantic hermeneutics will be measured not so much in terms of what he first 'intended' as in terms of his influence, and in terms of those shifts in nineteenth-century thought for which he created an opening. It is generally felt that his work consolidated a movement away from the rules of exegesis to the theory of understanding, even if the latter was still bound up for him with what Peter Szondi calls the earlier "material hermeneutics."[14] Arguments for Schleiermacher's conservatism depend on a genetic fallacy that allows the interpretation of his later work to be governed by his earliest statements on hermeneutics. But it seems clear that he moved away from a hermeneutics centered on 'grammar,' even if certain tensions remain in his writing. And since Schleiermacher himself suggests that interpretation must be 'divinatory' as well as 'historical,' it seems appropriate to read him in the light of his own principles. The historical method examines the text as a finished product, whereas the divinatory method grasps it as a moment in a process and considers how a discourse that is produced by a certain line of thought in turn reacts upon those thoughts, so as to require a reader who will understand "better than its creator" the potential within it (O, p. 9). From a divinatory perspective Schleiermacher prepared the ground for a hermeneutics that looks for something more than what is actually given in the text, and in his analysis of Plato and the gospels he focused on a disintegration of coherence at the grammatical or literal level that made this more inward reading necessary. Thus he spoke to a specifically romantic dilemma, in a way that Ernesti and Wolf could not. The structural, stylistic, and ideological problems that he saw in classical and biblical texts were

former. See Peter Szondi, "Introduction to Literary Hermeneutics," *New Literary History* 10 (1978): 24–25. See also Karlfried Froehlich, "'Always to Keep the Literal Sense in Holy Scripture Means to Kill One's Soul': The State of Biblical Hermeneutics at the Beginning of the Fifteenth Century," *Literary Uses of Typology from the Later Middle Ages to the Present,* ed. Earl Miner (Princeton, N.J.: Princeton University Press, 1977), p. 22. On Philo's relation to this tradition see Goppelt, *Typos,* pp. 42–53.

[14]"Introduction to Literary Hermeneutics," p. 19.

also those that existed in romantic texts, and the recourse to interpretation as a way of making the text present to itself was typical of an age that saw self-consciousness as a way to heal itself.

What is less clear is whether psychological reading recovers the identity of the text, and whether in the end romantic theorists see such identity as desirable. The counterplot of romantic hermeneutics and phenomenology, however—their disclosure of how the recourse to reading and speech disseminates meaning—is something that will be considered in the next chapter. Paradoxically, a principal figure in this counterplot is Schleiermacher himself. For the divinatory reading of his work that developments in contemporary theory permit is very different from the one attempted in this chapter: from the reading actually assumed by Dilthey, who considered only the later version of the hermeneutics compiled by Friedrich Lücke and used it to link 'Schleiermacher' to a psychologism Dilthey himself was to leave behind.

'Schleiermacher's' statements on hermeneutics took form between 1805 and 1833, and have been read as moving increasingly toward a psychologism that separates thought from language. The 1819 Compendium, the first extensive outline of the hermeneutics, occupies a transitional position in this development. Already Schleiermacher distinguishes between discourse (*Reden*) and text (*Schrift*) and postulates a "difference" between them caused by the absence of the living voice (O, p. 1). The aim of hermeneutics is to move behind the text to this living discourse (O, p. 10). But it would be wrong to assume that this discourse is something unavailable through language or even writing. For at this stage, though the term 'psychological' occurs, it is used synonymously with 'technical,' which has to do with the author's subjectivity as it finds expression in aesthetic forms. In a sense the technical is an extension of the grammatical,[15] concerned with form rather than syntax, with the unique style that informs an author's connecting of words, but also with those larger organizations of parts into a whole that yield "the unity of the work" or the "theme" (O, pp. 12–13). The technical reading does not seem to create a fissure between the psychological and the grammatical, but rather acts as a bridge between 'discourse' and text. Indeed, the following description of technical reading makes clear the formalist assumptions that counterbalance the phenomenological distinction of discourse from text: "The ultimate goal of the psychological [technical] exposition is nothing other than to perceive the consequences of the beginning; that is to say, to consider the work as it is formed by its parts,

[15]Gadamer also notes, in reference to Schleiermacher's later tripartite division, that the technical is analogous to the grammatical: "The Problem of Language in Schleiermacher's Hermeneutic," in *Schleiermacher as Contemporary*, ed. Robert W. Funk (New York: Herder and Herder, 1970), p. 82.

and to perceive every part in light of the work's overall subject as its motivation; this is also to say that the form is seen to be shaped by the subject matter" (O, p. 13).

On the other hand, it would be equally wrong to argue that Schleiermacher moves decisively against the concept of a meaning that can be intimated by but not embodied in the text. The Compendium also contains an important distinction between the historical and the divinatory or prophetic methods, which is used to intersect the initial division of reading into the grammatical (objective) and the psychological (subjective). Thus Schleiermacher introduces four categories: the objective-historical, the objective-divinatory, the subjective-historical, and the subjective-divinatory. Whereas the historical is concerned with the text as achieved form, the proto-Hegelian concept of the divinatory is concerned with the text as part of an ongoing process that requires an imaginative leap on the part of the reader to discern its direction. Objective-historical reconstruction concerns itself with the text as a product of the existing system of language, including genre as well as grammar, and objective-divinatory reconstruction assesses how "the discourse itself developed the language" (O, p. 9). Subjective-historical reconstruction is similar to what Schleiermacher later defines as 'technical' reading: it considers the text as an objective correlative of the author's mind. But subjective-divinatory reading seems to go beyond the merely technical to consider what has not yet found expression in the text, namely, the process initiated by but not completed in its writing (O, p. 9).

Between 1826 and 1833 Schleiermacher considerably expanded what he had to say about psychological reading, not, as is sometimes supposed, in order to replace the term 'technical' with 'psychological,' but in order to create two autonomous subdivisions within the psychological: the technical, and the psychological proper. These two readings strain in opposite directions, toward and away from attention to what he calls the "text" (*Schrift*), and it is by no means clear that they can be made concentric to each other. Already in the Compendium, Schleiermacher allows that classical and romantic works require different methods of reading (O, pp. 4–5), and so it seems logical that some works might yield more to psychological than to technical reading, and might not be readable as works that have fully actualized their meaning. In the final lectures the long section on psychological reading that follows the briefer account of technical reading repeated from 1819 begins by distinguishing "the indefinite, flowing thought-process" from the "finished thought-complex" (*HK*, pp. 148–49). It is the latter that is the object of a technical analysis concerned with "a definite thought and will to representation" and with "the objective realisation" of this creative resolve in the text (*HK*, p. 154). Technical analysis, in other words, focuses on what

Schleiermacher calls "meditation and composition," the linear shaping of a creative intention into a text. But psychological reading is concerned with the "rise of thought out of the entirety of the life moments of the individual" (*HK*, p. 152), with the intuitions in which thought has its inception, and therefore not simply with the thought expressed but also with underlying and collateral thoughts (*Grundgedanken* and *Nebengedanken*).

As in the 1819 Compendium, where he insists that grammatical and technical reading are complementary, Schleiermacher here emphasizes the interdependence of the technical and the psychological. In order to grasp the discourse as a whole, it is necessary to understand it from its point of inception and thus to read psychologically; but in returning to the conception, we also see it taking form and thus engage in technical reading. That reading involves a back-and-forth movement between understanding the thought process and its formalized expression is undoubtedly true. Yet it does not follow that there is a symmetrical relationship between conception and expression. For there seems to be more behind the text than is articulated in it, and what there is behind it is also more inchoate. To the extent that Schleiermacher is committed to grasping the life moments of the author as a *unity*, the psychological reading has to take a divinatory form by discerning a direction in the indefinite thought process—something that the reader would not have to do if the finished text already fully articulated that direction. In other words, the reader must try to understand "the discourse just as well and even better than its creator" (O, p. 9).

Hans Frei emphasizes that Schleiermacher does not intend to make words "a secondary expression of a putatively more real internality."[16] But he also points to the difficulty Schleiermacher has in maintaining the unity of the psychological and the grammatical—a difficulty that only increases after him. To recognize how far his theoretical work[17] marks a turning point in the history of hermeneutics, it is worth considering two other theorists more strictly philological than he: his precursor J. A. Ernesti, and August Boeckh, who wrote somewhat later. Ernesti's *Institutio Interpretis* (1761) occupies a pivotal and complex position. From a later perspective he seems a fundamentalist, concerned with the literal meaning of texts and committed both to the clarity and unity of such texts. On the other hand, he is also a product of Enlighten-

[16]*The Eclipse of Biblical Narrative: A Study in Eighteenth and Nineteenth Century Hermeneutics* (New Haven, Conn.: Yale University Press, 1974), p. 309.

[17]I use the term 'theoretical work' because I suggest in the next chapter that Schleiermacher's commentaries on Plato and Luke are strongly philological and use philology not to fix meaning but as part of a dialectical process designed to make the reader see through precisely this attempt.

ment rationalism and of its reaction against pietist hermeneutics, which sought to place the meaning of the text outside it, in the coincidence of the interpreter's reading with the voice of the holy spirit. Thus, on the one hand, Ernesti seems conservative in his attitude toward interpretation as the fixing of meaning and argues that the Bible is incapable of contradiction: if "any contradiction should appear to exist, a suitable method of reconciliation is to be investigated."[18] On the other hand, he insists that the unified meaning of the biblical text is not to be sought outside it: "when different reasons for the meaning of a word oppose each other," greater weight ought to be given to "the accurate interpretation of words" than to "the illustration of previously formed opinions."[19] Following the Enlightenment view that there is a direct but customary correspondence between words and things, Ernesti argues that there are three criteria for the interpretation of texts: the meaning of words, the historical context governing their usage, and the author's intention.[20] But none of these criteria lead beyond the grammatical level: as Hans Frei observes, "Ernesti does not think of the author's intention as a privileged realm beyond his words. . . . The words constitute the intention."[21]

In contrast to the later Schleiermacher, Ernesti thus sees the grammatical level as primary. Though he uses what Ast and Wolf call historical reading, the purpose of context (whether biographical or cultural) is to redirect our attention to the individual words rather than to supply what is implied between the lines or explain what the words cannot fully articulate. 'Psychological reading' is not a term that Ernesti uses, and he has little patience with allegorical reading, which is often fanciful in constructing a meaning beyond the literal. To the mystification of allegorizing he opposes the scientific procedures of philological understanding, which deals only with what is there.[22]

It is arguable that Ernesti's privileging of the grammatical is hard to sustain. For one thing, he relies on the atomistic theory of language common at the time, which focuses on single words as positive terms and thus brackets the erosion of referential stability that would arise if meaning were considered at the level of larger units like the proposition or the narrative episode. As a result he does not have to move beyond the grammatical level to recover that self-identical meaning that seems the goal of traditional hermeneutics. It is also arguable that he does not

[18]*Principles of Biblical Interpretation*, trans. Charles H. Terrot, 2 vols. (Edinburgh: Thomas Clark, 1843), I, 38.

[19]Ibid., I, 37; II, 193.

[20]Ibid., I, 28, 63.

[21]*Eclipse of Biblical Narrative*, p. 252.

[22]Ernesti, *Biblical Interpretation*, I, 25; II, 189, 192.

even succeed in locating meaning at the grammatical level. For as soon as one recognizes that words are governed by custom, it is necessary to refer to contexts beyond the words themselves; nor are such contexts always sufficient, as Ernesti himself concedes.[23] But in terms of his aesthetic and hermeneutic norms, the search for a meaning that is not grammatically actualized is illegitimate, an embarrassment when it must occur.

To turn to Boeckh is to recognize the difference made by Schleiermacher's hermeneutics. Boeckh, who studied with Schleiermacher but was also influenced by Wolf, is also dedicatedly philological. But philology for him is not the study of words, but rather "the understanding of what has been produced by the human spirit." It is part of Boeckh's concept of the encyclopedia, which involves a global version of the hermeneutic circle in which particular areas of knowledge are to be understood only in relation to the entirety of human knowledge.[24] Between Ernesti and Boeckh philology itself, once synonymous with a solidity that could not be accused of idealism, has moved from the grammatical level to what Ast called the *geistige* level. Similarly, at first glance Boeckh's various kinds of reading seem designed to minimize the psychological element, and terms like 'divinatory' and 'prophetic' are notably absent from his writing. He distinguishes two forms of objective understanding, the grammatical and the historical as in Wolf, and two forms of subjective understanding, the generic and the individual, the latter being rather like technical interpretation. This fourfold scheme seems designed to exclude anything beyond the words and form of a text. But it is not just that Boeckh is more sensitive than Ernesti to the destabilizing forces within grammar, nor even that he is more inclined to defer the act of understanding to the historical or generic level. He recognizes that the sufficiency of the grammatical level varies markedly in texts and diminishes considerably in some.[25] Moreover, he envisions a situation in which the supplement of reading becomes an internal constituent of texts: a situation in which "the speaker or writer presupposes, consciously or unconsciously, that the people to whom he is addressing himself will not only understand his words grammatically, but will in connection with them think of more than they actually say."[26] In the end, despite his philological bias, he comes very close to Schleiermacher in feeling that the hermeneutic circle is not broken in an objective way, but through the construction of hypotheses about intention that depend

[23]Ibid., I, 178–79.
[24]August Boeckh, *On Interpretation and Criticism*, trans. and ed. John Paul Pritchard (Norman: University of Oklahoma Press, 1968), pp. 31–33.
[25]Ibid., pp. 78, 53. Cf. also Schleiermacher (O, p. 5).
[26]Boeckh, *On Interpretation*, p. 77.

on "intuition" and on a special affinity between reader and author.[27] Most importantly, he recognizes the slipperiness of such interpretations. The attempt to ground interpretation through an appeal to historical facts is itself dependent on an act of interpretation to constitute those 'facts' as facts. The attempt to stabilize a text through "individual" interpretation of an author's lexicon is similarly problematic, because the assumption that "the subjective essence of the speaker mirrors itself in his language" encounters the obstacle of deciphering persona and narrative voice.[28]

As we consider the development of hermeneutics in the nineteenth century, it is clear that it changes from being an exegetical to a phenomenological method. But another development is also worth remarking: namely, the expansion of hermeneutics to the understanding of signs generally. Such a development does not have to lead in a metaphysical direction, but until Dilthey applies hermeneutic principles to the human and social sciences at the turn of the century, the main new trend is in fact the expansion of textual hermeneutics into a hermeneutics of being. This development has two consequences. The increasingly metaphysical orientation of hermeneutics intensifies the commitment to understanding as the finding of a transcendental signified, a ground outside the play of language. We have already seen this tendency in Schleiermacher. But inasmuch as his attitude to metaphysics is ambivalent, his notions of origin and ground will also emerge as more unstable than I have suggested. Second, with the broadening of literary into ontological hermeneutics, the rules of philology become less important, and psychological reading moves closer to what the term implies for a modern audience. This is not to say that the philological tradition disappears (Boeckh being an example to the contrary), but simply that ontological hermeneutics weakens the role played by "evidence" in interpretation, because being cannot very well be approached in terms of anything factual such as the literary or historical context. The notion of historical reading—an autonomous category in Ast and an autonomous mode of both the grammatical and psychological categories in Schleiermacher—largely disappears, leaving psychological reading to develop in a more intuitionist direction. The deemphasis on evidence can only augment the tendency for reading to become the reading of consciousness rather than of texts, and for poets to assume such a reading. As usual, Schleiermacher stands somewhere in the middle of this development, and it may be useful to compare him with another member of the Jena circle, Schelling, in order to see what happens

[27]Ibid., p. 82.
[28]Ibid., pp. 76, 89.

to a hermeneutics of texts when it is rewritten as a hermeneutics of being.

Schleiermacher himself does not strictly adhere to his own restriction of hermeneutics to the study of written documents, since both his life of Jesus and his essay on Socrates deal with figures who are known only through the writings of others. Nevertheless, he himself does not take hermeneutics in an ontological direction. But the introduction to Schelling's *Ages of the World*, concerned as it is with the interpretation of being in its various stages of development, makes use of concepts with clear parallels in traditional hermeneutics to do precisely that. Whether the parallels represent the influence of Schleiermacher is not something that will be explored here, since the *Ages* was written between Schleiermacher's early and later courses of lectures, and since much that is in those lectures is not unique to him. Appended to one of the cornerstones of Schelling's later philosophy, the introduction seems a development of the earlier and more affirmative philosophy of identity—hence, the appropriateness of considering it here and not in conjunction with the later work. By the philosophy of identity we must understand not only the identity of self and other, but also the resulting achievement of identity with oneself. By extension we must also understand by the term the identity of author and interpreter, and the consequent grasping of the identity of the text or of the object being studied. Schelling is not so naive as to believe that this can be achieved (*AW*, p. 88), but it remains a goal which we can and should approximate. He suggests that understanding, as it pertains to the interpretation of being, involves a dialectic between two voices within the interpreter: an inward self connected to the origin of things, and a lower and more self-conscious ego. The higher self is the ground of all truth but is ignorant of what it knows and needs the lower self in order to "make distinguishable, express, interpret" what otherwise remains inchoate (*AW*, p. 85). Through the lower self, then, the higher is able to "view itself, represent and become intelligible to itself" (*AW*, p. 85).

In this manner Schelling takes a principle fundamental to his and Hegel's dialectics—namely, that the subject must become estranged from itself and become an object to itself before it can return to itself—and uses it to explain why vision must go through the detour of signs and their interpretation, why presence must be re-presented in order to become self-present. For our purposes, however, it is enough to note that the higher self is associated with immediate vision, where the lower self proceeds "piece by piece in a fragmentary way, with divisions and gradations" (*AW*, p. 88). The lower mode of understanding, in other words, corresponds to grammatical reading, where the higher parallels the psychological reading necessary to break the hermeneutic circle.

Like Schleiermacher, Schelling claims not to argue for a hermeneutics of the ineffable and believes that the psychological and grammatical approaches are mutually necessary (*AW*, pp. 87–89). Yet the hierarchy of lower and higher indicates where his emphases lie. As significantly, visionary understanding occurs not through the reading of outward signs or historical evidence, but rather through the awakening of an "archetype . . . [that] slumbers in the soul like an obscured and forgotten, even if not completely obliterated, image" (*AW*, p. 85). Part of the function of the lower principle is to raise to the level of consciousness representations that lie in the soul as pure forms without material content (*AW*, p. 84n). On one level, Schelling's account is more satisfactory as a description of how divination occurs than that of Schleiermacher. For the 1819 Compendium offers no explanation of divination, and the later definition of it as the recovery of secondary trains of thought is too linguistic to express that particular term. At the same time Schelling's more precise awareness of divination and of the psychological as the "unconscious" crosses a new threshold in romantic hermeneutics. With this development goes a return to a hermeneutics of faith, though not in the conservative way practiced by pietist hermeneutics.[29] In different ways the theorists to be considered have recourse to a form of imaginative faith to supply what is not empirically given, Hegel by default and the later Schelling by design.[30] With this recourse to faith comes a further separation of consciousness from its textual appearances, at least on the level of desire.

Hegel and the Hermeneutics of History

With Hegel we enter a new stage in the history of hermeneutics, namely, the expansion of a literary hermeneutics into a general hermeneutics concerned with all products of the human spirit. Paradoxically, this expansion has two different but intertwined effects. It makes hermeneutics more metaphysical in its claims, as interpretation claims to get at Truth and not just at the truth of a text. But it also makes metaphysics for the first time the subject of textual analysis. As we shall see,

[29]For a discussion of Rambach see Frei, *Eclipse of Biblical Narrative*, pp. 38–39.

[30]Since Hegel saw himself as continuing the rationalist and positive tradition of the Enlightenment, he would not have recognized that he was asking the reader to supply something that is not present in the history of Spirit. However, the later Schelling's position vis-à-vis Enlightenment theology (and any secularization of it into a spiritual anthropology) is somewhat different, because he applied the pejorative label of 'negative philosophy,' among other things, to developments in post-Renaissance theology such as deism.

the uneasy marriage between metaphysics and a hermeneutics that inevitably implies the linguisticality of understanding comes close to breaking in later enactments of the hermeneutic project like Kierkegaard's *Concept of Irony*. But as we shall also see, the result is not to refute categorically the hermeneutic claim that one can proceed beyond the merely semiological to something deeper.

The assumptions of hermeneutics pervade Hegel's work and are not just found, as one might expect, in his *Aesthetics*. Indeed, *The Phenomenology of Mind* is a hermeneutics of intellectual history, which develops principles that Hegel will later apply to aesthetic genres and techniques. The most important of these principles is that 'false' or failed forms of awareness are versions of truth and must be reread in a historical perspective. Spirit goes through the three stages of being-in-itself (*an sich*), then being-for-itself (*für sich*), and finally being-in-and-for-itself at once. Correspondingly, the Idea is at first undeveloped because it is un–self-conscious, then it becomes fully self-conscious but mental and intentional, and finally it becomes fully elaborated and concretely present in life. The teleological structure of the human project allows us to unfold individual modes of consciousness toward their completion through a divinatory reading. Thus Hegel often seems to approach the analysis of a mode of consciousness deconstructively, by showing it as thwarted by its internal discrepancies. But he also suggests that the perspective of history allows us to read aporias into a logic of contradictions. As in typological reading, of which his method seems a secular variant, the relationship between past and present modes of consciousness provides the logic for leading present modes of awareness in the direction of the future. Thus stoicism (in retrospect) prefigures scepticism in the movement toward absolute freedom. Stoics free themselves from the world as it is but imprison themselves in a single attitude: namely, the rejection of life. Sceptics still fail to participate in life but at least exercise freedom in the domain of thought, by refusing to be tied to any single position (*PM*, pp. 244–45). As scepticism is more complete than stoicism, so we can imagine present forms of awareness such as the unhappy consciousness being progressively freed of their contradictions in the advancing spiral of intellectual history. What should be clear is that Hegel's method of reading fissures within a form of consciousness so as to posit their eventual closure derives from the hermeneutic procedure of understanding the part in relation to the whole. He breaks the hermeneutic circle at the level of history and sublates the grammatical reading of the history of ideas as a process riddled with contradictions into a psychological reading of it as a purposive development. Indeed, the adjective 'psychological' is his as well as Schleiermacher's, because Hegel places his semiology of history in a psychology of history and defines the latter term as the study of spirit determining itself in itself, as a subject for itself.[31]

In the *Aesthetics* Hegel provides a historical typology of modes designed to explain the asymmetries between content and execution found in symbolic and romantic art, in such a way that they, too, seem generative rather than deconstructive. Hegel's approach to art is phenomenological and psychological rather than structural: he defines the forms of art as "the different ways of grasping the Idea as content" or "the different relations of meaning and shape" (*A*, I,75). Ideally, art is "the actualizing and unfolding of the beautiful," "the Ideal in its actualization," the embodiment of ideas in a concrete and therefore persuasive form (*A*, I,299,105). The completed work of art is also the self-actualization of the artist as medium of the world-historical spirit: in it one "produces" oneself in an external medium where one enjoys "in the shape of things only an external realization of himself" (*A*, I,31). Hegel thus distinguishes in art two terms, which he variously calls "theme" and "execution," "meaning and shape," "Idea and presentation," or "inwardness and external manifestation" (*A*, I,96,300,74,301). The perfect work, ontologically speaking, is "the union of meaning with its individual configuration" (*A*, I,101). Psychologically speaking, it is the finding of an adequate outer shape for something inward, so as to bring about "the unity of the artist's subjective activity with his topic and work" (*A*, I,602).

But of the three historically successive modes of art that Hegel analyzes—the symbolic, the classical, and the romantic—only the second achieves this unity of the technical and psychological. Classical art is the "adequate embodiment of the Idea" (*A*, I,77). It is the achievement of an organic form, in which the presence of a form that is indwelling rather than a shape that is superinduced reflects the fact that the Idea has become concrete. But in both symbolic and romantic art meaning is separate from the shape that it tries uneasily to inhabit. Symbolic art, being the product of the earliest phase in the phenomenology of mind, fails to achieve identity with itself because of a deficiency of self-consciousness. Its content remains indeterminate and its forms "rather a *mere search* for portrayal than a capacity for true presentation" (*A*, I,76). Sometimes a symbolic work may be overpatterned, in an attempt to determine externally a content that is still vague (*A*, I,133). In romantic art, on the other hand, the Idea is fully developed, but external forms have become inadequate to embody it. Once again, as a consequence, the art form manifests a discrepancy between inner and outer, a failure to

[31]Hegel, *Encyclopedia of the Philosophical Sciences*, trans. William Wallace (Oxford: Clarendon Press, 1971), pt. 3, sec. 387, p. 25.

objectify meaning. A useful gloss on Hegel's triad of aesthetic modes is Schelling's distinction between schematic, symbolic, and allegoric art in *The Philosophy of Art*. Schematic art uses the general to point to the particular. It has an abstract and formal grasp of the Idea, that has been unable to root this understanding in the concrete world. By contrast, allegoric art uses the particular to point to the general: it conveys a subjectively complete grasp of the Idea, which it is unable to universalize. The middle term alone, symbolic art, is the union of subjective and objective.[32]

Although the *Aesthetics* is not explicitly a theory of reading, Hegel is concerned to emphasize the aspect of understanding: the fact that art is not an autonomous structure but is created "for a public" (*A*, I,263–64). The classical work seems not to require the supplement of interpretation. It "describes itself through itself" and "unfolds itself before our eyes."[33] But for the most part Hegel deals with art forms that lack this clarity. Moreover, he does not just describe the decorums characteristic of a rhetorical criticism that dismisses texts that are not 'classical' and universal. He also engages in the deeper reading of surface failures that characterizes a hermeneutic criticism that tries to grasp even the spirit of imperfect works. For instance, the decorum of epic, in contrast to that of lyric, requires a maximum of detail if clarity is to be achieved. But Hegel is also concerned to understand the historical reasons for techniques in major narrative forms that derealize what is being conveyed. His *Aesthetics* is thus a phenomenology of art not only in the traditional sense of trying to grasp the spirit behind individual forms, but also in the more contemporary sense of considering forms in terms of their effect on the reader. Among the characteristics of romantic art that have the effect of derealizing content is indeterminacy of characterization: the "undisclosedness, . . . absence of outward shape . . . lack of expression and development" that distinguish a character "based in inwardness" (*A*, I,580). Such a character can appear as flat and unconvincing (*A*, I,582), so that the nexus of thematic concerns associated with it lacks solidity. Also characteristic of this kind of art is a disordering of the events that occur in the objective world: "The spirit has withdrawn into itself out of the externality of appearances which now on their side are shaped no matter how, for they are unconnected with the subject since his inner world no longer sees itself in them" (*A*, I,586–87).

The *Aesthetics* provides an anatomy, not of criticism, but of aesthetic

[32]See Tzvetan Todorov, *Theories of the Symbol*, trans. Catherine Porter (Ithaca, N.Y.: Cornell University Press, 1982), pp. 208–12. Schelling does not use the word 'symbolic' in the same way as Hegel, but uses it, like Goethe and Coleridge, to indicate the synthesis, not the separation, of the particular and universal.

[33]Quoted in ibid., pp. 159–60.

response, and these examples give only the faintest impression of its synoptic aims. Part of this aim is to educate a superreader who will know how to read in the absence of conventional structural codes. For instance, Hegel's descriptions of how romantic art disorganizes the empirical surface by fragmenting character, plot, and setting can well apply to Blake's later prophecies, which present an action that is essentially inward, and leave the "material of the external world . . . to go its own way," (*A*, I,594), like an autonomous language whose activities are irrelevant to the true spirit of the narrative. Perhaps more than any other romantic, Blake strains against the limits of the aesthetic, defined as the presenting of "the Idea to immediate perception in a sensuous shape and not in the form of thinking and pure spirituality" (*A*, I,72). The Hegelian method allows us to understand the anti-aesthetic elements in Blake as part of the historical movement of romantic art toward a mode of understanding that it can bring into being only through its own collapse. This method, especially when it is a question of romantic rather than symbolic art, is best described as hermeneutic rather than rhetorical. Occasionally, Hegel will follow the evaluative tendencies of neoclassical criticism and simply judge works of symbolic art as defective, because they fail as acts of persuasion. But the underlying assumption in his presentation of the romantic is that discontinuities between meaning and shape are historically produced, and that the reader committed to grasping the spirit of the work will liberate it from the constraints of formal representation.

Hegel's reading of cultural history leads naturally to a canonical hermeneutics. Texts are read so as to reconceive fissures within them from the higher vantage points of the author's canon, the romantic canon, and finally that project to which Shelley refers as "that great poem, which all poets, like the co-operating thoughts of one great mind, have built up since the beginning of the world" (*SPP*, p. 493). Such a macrohermeneutics is certainly not new in romantic theory, Friedrich Schlegel's concept of a progressive universal poetry being an example.[34] But where earlier theorists often conceive of the canon as a series of self-contained stages, Hegel's dialectical aesthetics sees each phase as intentionally oriented toward something that it is not, namely, a subsequent phase that may be its antithesis. In assuming a deeper reading that in some ways must negate a grammatical reading, Hegel's work finds itself at a threshold between a positive and a negative hermeneutics. That he nevertheless saw his hermeneutics of cultural history as positive, and that he saw history

[34]For an account of Schlegel's hermeneutics see Margaret Higgonet, "Organic Unity and Interpretative Boundaries: Friedrich Schlegel's Theories and Their Application in His Critique of Lessing," *Studies in Romanticism* 19 (1980): 176, 182, 186.

itself as a rational process unfolding from *arche* to *telos*, is clear enough. Indeed, Hegel insists that in symbolic art "the shape and meaning are strange to one another from the start, . . . yet they stand in no negative relation but in a friendly one" (*A*, I,512). But whether the *Aesthetics* consistently enacts a positive hermeneutic is less certain. In speaking of discrepancies between theme and execution, Hegel implies that the positive content of a text is apparent, but that for historical reasons its form is not adequate to its content. The reader's function in the case of a symbolic text is to project the reconciliation of form and content, and in the case of a romantic art form to read through (but not to reverse) the grammar or form to arrive at the real content. But Hegel also suggests that form reflects rather than disguises content, and that "defectiveness of *form* results from defectiveness of *content*" (*A*, I,74). If that is the case, he must envisage a supplementary reading that corrects or resists the content, instead of simply discarding the form to unfold the content.

The problem of how complete the meaning is even at the level of conception surfaces in the specific discussions of symbolic and romantic art in terms of 'indeterminacy.' Many of the symbolic forms that Hegel discusses—allegory, parable, didactic poetry—posit a meaning that they simply fail to make concrete. Didactic poetry provides a content "already cut and dried and developed explicitly as meaning in its therefore prosaic form" alongside an artistic form "tacked on . . . in an entirely external way" (*A*, I,423). Blake's *Marriage*, which uses the parabolic and didactic forms, may be an example of a symbolic text requiring no more than positive animation from the reader. But, on the other hand, Hegel frequently distinguishes symbolic from romantic art in terms of "indeterminacy": meaning and shape remain separate in symbolic art, because the meaning is "not yet conscious of itself."[35] He also describes the "relation of the Idea to the objective world" as "a *negative* one" (*A*, I,77) and thereby suggests that a hermeneutics of the symbolic must negate both content and form to arrive at the Idea. Coleridge's *Christabel* might be an example of a text that is 'correctly' understood only from a vantage point in the future, and only if the indeterminate relationship between Christabel and Geraldine is determined and morally schematized. In the indeterminate text, meaning is not represented in a positive but abstract way; rather, the reader must avoid working through what is in the text and must construct what is not there. Romantic art seems far simpler in that its content is supposedly determinate but purely inward (*A*, I,519), and withdrawn from that immersion in corporeality constituted by artistic form and language. Yet there is something troubling about describing as 'positive' a reading that requires one to burn away the language in

[35]*Encyclopedia*, pt. 3, sec. 561, p. 295.

which the 'meaning' is expressed. Moreover, in Hegel's own terms, the deficient form must express some deficiency in content, and a divinatory reading will once again have to imagine a content that is not there and to repress the aporias in what *is* there.

This discussion can only touch on some of the more general ways in which Hegel takes the hermeneutic project beyond his predecessors. To begin with, he displaces an organic into a historical model of understanding and translates the synchronic identity between subject and object affirmed by Coleridge and the early Schelling into a constantly deferred identity. The interpretation of spirit is now something that has to occur through difference, process, and displacement. Friedrich Ast had developed from the philosophy of the early Schelling a hermeneutics that was temporal but not historical. The identity of the text was grasped through the equivalent of the subject-object fusion: namely, a reading that identified author and reader. This understanding was not immediate, but it occurred through a sequence of more or less contemporaneous acts. But in Hegel's hermeneutics the art form must be understood by placing it in a context that is still unfolding, and we must project ourselves forward to a point in the literary historical process from which we can re-vision a form that could not fully understand itself at the time of its composition. In other words, Hegelian hermeneutics stands more perilously at the threshold between a meaning that is potentially present and one that is still absent.

For Hegel, then, texts are not just historical in the sense that their original spirit is obscured by time, but also in the sense that their meaning is unfolded and even changed by history. Hegel's introduction of the historical dimension into hermeneutics thus renders problematic the notions both of an original meaning and of a definitive reading. Previously, psychological reading had unlocked the meaning of the text by putting us in contact with the author's voice. But for Hegel there is no author in the sense of an origin. The author is merely the medium through which the conflicting voices of a given historical period speak, and the aporetic texts or systems of thought thus produced can be properly read only as they are unfolded toward their resolution in the historical process. The disappearance of the author is inevitably the disappearance of the implied reader as well. Hegelian hermeneutics, even as it tries to determine the direction of reading, actually leaves much more to the constructive powers of the explicit reader than does traditional hermeneutics. To put it differently, Hegel's methods are constantly at odds with his hermeneutic goal of getting at the truth. Try as he will to salvage an essentialist concept of meaning by using metaphors of inner and outer, soul and body, to separate the Idea from its appearances in the discourse of history, Hegel cannot really disentangle a transcendental signified from the process of its signification, which constantly makes and unmakes it. Moreover, his own readings open up interpretive options that his system seeks to foreclose. Even as he assumes a reading that will reconstitute the positive meaning of the art form across its negativity, the readings he provides show how art forms do not cohere. It is not of course to individual readings that one looks for this higher strategy of interpretation, but to their cumulative relationship as a typological series. But the story told in *The Phenomenology of Mind,* the story of how 'spirit' progressively understands itself as it constitutes itself in successive systems of thought, is not always one of diminishing contradictions. It is not clear, for instance, that the unhappy consciousness is closer to identity with itself than scepticism; indeed, it seems to deepen rather than resolve the problems of the latter. The hermeneutic story told by the *Aesthetics* is similarly ambiguous. Hegel seems to present the movement from symbolic to romantic art as a development from shadowy types to truth, in which the reading of discontinuous forms becomes progressively easier because romantic art, which has a definite though purely inward content, guarantees that the indeterminacy of symbolic art was always the potential presence of a fixed meaning. In this story, though the need for a psychological reading at odds with the grammatical one persists throughout the history of the cultural text, the requirement ceases to raise problems about the identity of the text. But the opposition between symbolic and romantic art often seems a tenuous one. It is just as possible that the *Aesthetics* tells a different story: one of repeated unreadability rather than increasing readability. Romantic art is haunted by the same problems as a symbolic art: a collapse of meaning at the obvious level that is not clearly accompanied by the reconstitution of a firm meaning at a deeper level. In classical art, where meaning is completely adequate to shape, the need for interpretation is momentarily eliminated, but in romantic art the disappearance of a referent once again becomes a problem.

Both Hegel's *Phenomenology* and his *Aesthetics* yield a model of canonical interpretation that incorporates methods from typological reading to create a logic and a *logos* binding past, present, and future. Such interpretation aims to be a grand expansion of the 'positive' hermeneutics earlier discussed, which sees itself as developing a meaning that is always embryonically present. But, as we have seen, the introduction of the historical dimension renders problematic the presence of determinate meaning. Yet an awareness of this indeterminacy coexists in Hegel with a powerful desire to interpret and direct it. I have used the term 'negative' hermeneutics to indicate a reading that resists the elements of difference and negativity in the text to posit a meaning that is highly speculative. Schelling, too, saw Hegelian phenomenology as 'negative' in the sense that it failed to deal with positive facts.[36] It is also negative in that it fails to deal with language, with what it has itself articulated in language. Despite the fact that dialectic (as Adorno has pointed out) is committed to the linguisticality of understanding,[37] Hegel's exaltation of the 'romantic' finally signals a rejection of representation. But Schelling's own 'positive' philosophy, to which we shall now turn, is even more negative in finally demanding a leap of faith that bypasses his careful articulation of things as they are. With Schelling, the crisis of a hermeneutics committed to cognitive theism deepens, as does the impossible separation between the 'true' text and the language of events.

Envelopment, Involution, and Irony: Schelling's Hermeneutics of Negativity

So far, the hermeneutic procedures described share an assumption that the grammatical level of the text intimates the psychological level. Yet if the nineteenth-century emphasis on the supplement of reading is radical in a way that its eighteenth-century precursors in an aesthetics of affect were not, it is because the connection between levels is increasingly disturbed, and the referent becomes more and more a projection of interpretive desire. We spoke earlier of a group of texts that require not simply deepening but reversal if their 'true' meaning is to be unfolded. The incorporation in such texts of 'figures of reading' that encourage a reversal of the text's grammatical meaning can be linked to an important shift in the concept of mimesis, from the imitation of what is there to what is in fact absent. This shift, of course, is not a sudden one. It may have its genesis in the earlier idea of an imitation that improves rather than copies, but it also moves beyond this notion in supposing an 'imitation' that must oppose rather than improve the original. Thus for Jean Paul literature is still the imitation or reflection of something that objectively exists, yet what it imitates is not empirical but hidden. Poetry, he argues, "should neither destroy nor repeat but decipher reality." She "represents that highest life which is eternally lacking in all our reality, even in the most beautiful reality of the heart; she paints the future drama on the curtain of eternity. She is no flat mirror of the present, but

[36]See David Punter, *Blake, Hegel and Dialectic* (Amsterdam: Rodopi, 1982), p. 61. I disagree, however, with his comparison of Schelling's critique of Hegel to that of Marx. The 'positive facts' that Schelling sees Hegel as neglecting are not material but metaphysical facts.

[37]Cf. Theodor Adorno's comment: "Hegelian dialectic was a dialectic without language, while the most literal sense of the word 'dialectic' postulates language": *Negative Dialectics*, trans. E. B. Ashton (London: Routledge and Kegan Paul, 1973), p. 163.

the magic mirror of the time which is not yet."[38] Even more significantly, Jean Paul sees poetry as a mimesis that can be at odds with what it ostensibly imitates. The copy may contain "more than the original" or even produce "its opposite," because "a double nature is being imitated: an outer and an inner one."[39]

Jean Paul is concerned with literature and not with its reading. But it is difficult for the text to conflate the real and the ideal in this way without seeming escapist—a dilemma that often bothers Jean Paul, who feels that the "organic synthesis . . . between the old realism and the new idealism" may elude him.[40] Thus in the practice of romantic literature it is often not the text that supplements reality, but the reader who must supplement the text of reality through a reading that deciphers rather than repeats, an interpretive copy that contains more than the original. The hermeneutics of reversal, however, is subtended and legitimated by a shift in the sense of what it is that constitutes poetic imitation. That Jean Paul's notion of aesthetic production would even bear the name of imitation is interesting, as we consider the curious survival of metaphors like the mirror in a period that has supposedly discarded a mimetic in favor of an expressive aesthetics. It suggests the continued importance of the norm of representation, as a source of anxiety about any aesthetic or hermeneutic that is not mimetic, because it defers the presence of meaning from the text to some medium like authorial consciousness or reader response that lacks the tangible materiality of the former.

As already indicated, the metaphysical underpinning for a hermeneutics of reversal can be found in the later work of Schelling. Schelling's philosophy went through several phases. He himself distinguished two: an initial phase encompassing the *Naturphilosophie* and the *System of Transcendental Idealism* (1800), and a later phase that he characterized as his 'positive' philosophy—somewhat puzzlingly, given its proto-existential awareness of contingency and its historical position as a bridge between Hegel and Kierkegaard. From the early 'philosophy of identity,' which seems to resolve the subject-object dialectic that is temporalized and deferred in the later philosophy, Friedrich Ast actually developed a hermeneutics of identity. The famous concept of the hermeneutic circle describes three stages in the reading process that parallel three similar stages in the spiral of the creative process itself: from an uncritical presentiment of the work's unity, we move through a grammatical analysis of its parts that often seems inimical to a grasp of its wholeness, to a critical understanding of its totality informed by a knowledge of its particu-

[38]Jean Paul, *Horn of Oberon: Jean-Paul Richter's School for Aesthetics*, trans. Margaret R. Hale (Detroit: Wayne State University Press, 1973), p. 309.
[39]Ibid., p. 24.
[40]Ibid., p. 306.

larity.[41] It is arguable that Ast ignores those buried complexities in the philosophy that the later Schelling himself could not so easily put aside. The positive philosophy attempts to remedy what Schelling saw as the twofold deficiency of Hegel's and his own earlier philosophy. On the one hand, Schelling, like Kierkegaard, felt that Hegel's phenomenology failed to be positive: Hegelian dialectic was essentially negative, and without its "terminus ad quem" in the utopia of Absolute Spirit, "Hegelian being would remain unfulfilled as what it is, namely, nothing."[42] The positive philosophy, by contrast, would reveal the presence of being within existence rather than simply deferring it. On the other hand, the shortcoming of what Schelling called the negative philosophy was paradoxically that it did not take sufficient account of the negative momentum within existence: of the primacy of lack and nonbeing, and of the irrational ground of things. Idealism, defined as the denial of the primordial negating power, is to be eschewed. Schelling's later work thus involves two important recognitions: that the Hegelian attempt to posit a presence behind the signs of history actually turns out to be negative in that it does not succeed in actualizing anything, and that any future hermeneutic must ground itself in those obstacles to positive activity that Hegel reveals but does not recognize. As such, it initiates both an increased awareness of the crisis of representation in romanticism, and a deepening of that crisis. For Schelling deconstructs hermeneutics as it exists in his time: he recognizes that romantic philosophy has not succeeded in communicating the presence of a positive referent, despite strategies of deferral which allow this referent to be conveyed on other than a grammatical level. And yet he intends to ground his own positive philosophy on a conscious embrace of precisely those things that had turned Hegel's philosophy into a negative hermeneutic.

To speak of Schelling's philosophy as a hermeneutic and to extrapolate from it methods of reading literary texts is not as much of an imaginative leap as it may seem, given his frequent references to God as an artist and his use of literary terms like 'irony' to characterize this artistry.[43] It is not so much that Schelling sees the same productive activity at work in nature and art, as had been the case in the *System of Transcendental Idealism*. Rather, the history of consciousness—whether of metaphysics, of art, or of myth—is a series of signs, a book that calls for

[41]On Ast see Rudolph Makkreel, *Dilthey: Philosopher of the Human Studies* (Princeton, N.J.: Princeton University Press, 1975), p. 268.

[42]Quoted in Karl Lowith, *From Hegel to Nietzsche: The Revolution in Nineteenth-Century Thought* (New York: Doubleday/Anchor, 1967), p. 114. For Kierkegaard's similar criticism of Hegel, see *CUP*, p. 34n.

[43]See *AW*, pp. 71, 77, 168. See also George Seidel, *Activity and Ground: Fichte, Schelling, and Hegel* (New York: Georg Olms, 1976), pp. 123–24.

interpretation, but not in the conventional sense of a *liber naturae* that already contains the meanings to be decoded, because it also calls for reading, for a productive and applicative understanding that will unfold what is only potentially in it. Indeed, Schelling signals the fundamentally hermeneutic nature of his project in *The Ages of the World* by introducing the unfinished account of the ages with the inquiry into the nature of understanding already discussed. But the text itself goes far beyond any hermeneutic outlined in its introduction. Schelling apparently conceived of three ages in the history of consciousness: past, present, and future, and wrote the introduction as an approach to understanding the first of these through "recollection" or retelling. The understanding of the future as what is "divined" rather than what is "known" will necessarily proceed on very different principles (*AW*, p. 83). We might expect from the introduction that the extant text will be a fragment, the first part of a three-part project. In fact, as F. de Wolfe Bolman indicates, it is more or less complete (*AW*, p. 68n.): a collapsed philosophic epic, a recollection of the past as seen from the present in such a way that it points toward the future. The principles outlined for the understanding of the past by itself are thus too limited to represent adequately what Schelling actually does in combining the archeological hermeneutics of recollection with the teleological hermeneutics of divination.

The Ages is an attempt to understand being, to discover its *arche* and *telos* (*AW*, p. 93). But it begins with the premise that what confronts us as we look at the past is the absence of being, the very negation of what the interpreter seeks. Briefly, Schelling argues that the ground of the positive must be sought in negativity and unfolded through a dialectic of reversal. Such reversal is possible because everything contains the seed of its opposite, so that negation contains a hidden root of positivity (*AW*, p. 208): "only an inversion, a turning out of what is hidden and a turning in of what is manifest, is needed in order to transplant and transform, as it were, the one into the other" (*AW*, p. 114). That something is absent does not mean that it does not exist, for nonbeing is the ground of coming-to-be: the "power of negation displaces, we said, the will of love and that of the spirit, yet only from the present. It posits these wills as not *being*, yet in no way therefore as nonbeing, but as future, and, as such, to be sure, also as being (only concealedly)" (*AW*, p. 205).

Much of Schelling's text is concerned with the theological problem of a *deus absconditus*. But his discussion bears on the linguistic problem of whether there is a transcendental signified, because his approach to the disappearance of God is essentially hermeneutic. The *Ages* is about how to read the signs of creation correctly, so as to go beyond their manifest content by substituting a psychological for a grammatical reading. Like Schleiermacher, Schelling uses the term "divination" to describe such a reading, but he also requires us to make an imaginative leap from the grammatical to the psychological in order to see nonbeing as the dialectical ground of being. The concept of absence as a deferred presence explains the absence of "external revelation" (*AW*, pp. 205–6) in literature as the consequence of a temporary problem in the semiotics of history and requires us to unfold the true meaning of a narrative by reversing it. Crucial to Schelling's hermeneutics of nonbeing are the notions of envelopment, involution, and irony. "Envelopment" describes the transitional state in which God appears to have withdrawn from the world, because the positive power has been hidden inside the negative power (*AW*, p. 205). "Involution" similarly describes a state of being turned inside out (*AW*, pp. 205–6). The assumption that a positive meaning is enveloped within a negative one allows Schelling to propose an almost mathematically neat formula: "the negating power is the only manifest aspect of God; the real essence, however, is the hidden aspect. The whole therefore stands as A, which, outwardly, is B" (*AW*, p. 110). The systematic counterreading of textual signs is summed up in the principle of irony, which Schelling uses to describe the text of creation as an inverted world produced under conditions where there is a gap between essence and existence. In this inverted world, God himself "disguises himself and appears to be another, and in consequence of this divine art of dissimulation or irony displays the reverse of that which he genuinely wills."[44] Schelling's description of divine irony applies equally to the ontology of the text, which similarly requires antithetical reading if the work within it is to be unfolded.

Schelling himself links the envelopment of a positive within a negative revelation to the typological reading of the Bible (*AW*, pp. 158–62). But there is a significant difference. Fixing on the shadowy tokens of hope in order to unseal the envelope of a disastrous narrative is partly justified in the case of the Bible by the fact that the New Testament exists. *The Ages*, like the romantic texts and canons of which it is representative, does not contain its own future. It relies, somewhat circularly, on the biblical parallel in order to place the ironic moment within a secular scripture that, if it existed, would justify the placing of irony within it. But the dilemma posed by what the romantics very broadly called irony is not so easily resolved. The increasing concern with this mode can be explained by seeing it as a focus for a cluster of anxieties regarding the disappearance of a referent. For irony at its most basic puts in question the existence of literature as a positive activity, that is, as an activity that posits something. In theory, Schelling provides a model for producing something positive from the ironic text. In practice, given that the re-

[44]Quoted in Bolman's introduction to *AW*, p. 77.

reading of irony requires a supplementary critical act, this model has the effect of a double negation. On the one hand, it allows readers the freedom to imagine something other than things as they are and thus negates empirical reality by making us feel that it must be the sign of something beyond it. On the other hand, any alternate state of affairs envisioned by the reader is negated by the fact that it is not yet real.

The Text of Absence: Kierkegaard's *Concept of Irony*

In *The Concept of Irony* Kierkegaard elaborates in textual terms the hermeneutics of the negative developed by Schelling. But he also explores the problems minimized by the latter's assumption that the process of reversal, once begun, can be arrested, and that the psychological meaning is somehow less figurative than the grammatical meaning. For Kierkegaard's essay does not really provide a method that can be abstracted from the process by which it is developed. Unlike Hegel's work, it does not attempt a metacritical stance, irony being its mode as well as its subject. Rather, it reenacts the strategies of earlier hermeneutics so as to demonstrate their continued hold on the imagination, but also so as to push them to an extreme where they disclose themselves as figures of reading. Written fairly late in the hermeneutic tradition, *The Concept of Irony* both deconstructs that tradition and continues it on the level of desire. Through the figure of Socrates and (implicitly) Jesus, it explores those margins of the hermeneutic enterprise approached by Schleiermacher, where the psychological meaning vanishes, because the person being studied is known only through testimony of disciples. It also brings out more clearly the problems of interpreting the unsaid by placing it—as Hegel and Schelling do—in a larger context so as to defer the positing of meaning to the future.

The Concept of Irony is concerned with a unique problem: the interpretation of meaning where none is posited, or the reading of what one might call the silent text. Where the text as Schelling conceives it says the opposite of what it means, the text that interests Kierkegaard is one that is constantly vanishing. For the central figure in Kierkegaard's discussion is Socrates, who committed nothing to writing or speech and presents himself as an absence: "He was not like a philosopher lecturing upon his views, wherein the very lecture itself constitutes the presence of the Idea" (*CI*, p. 50). Rather, Socrates' method being irony, whatever is said is simultaneously unsaid. With the extension of methods from literary interpretation to the reading of persons, and particularly to someone like Socrates, we have reached the ultimate challenge to the hermeneutic tradition. The possibility that the representation of meaning may be unnecessary for reading to occur has been raised explicitly. At the same time the hermeneutic recuperation of meaning from within its derealization has been pushed to a limit where it comes to seem absurd, in the philosophic sense of that word.

Within the spectrum of tropes used by the romantics to crystalise some relationship between appearance and reality, and hence between the surface and depth of the text, irony stands at the opposite pole from the symbol. Symbol is defined by Solger as "the presence of the Idea itself in existence." Translated from metaphysical into literary terms, it becomes the mode of the fully actualized text, in which the complete unity of inner and outer form makes it unnecessary to search for a hidden meaning:

> in the true symbol the external object has merged itself with the light of the inward essence, and is entirely one with it, so that this inner light is not to be found by itself in a particular part, nor even in the inner core of the thing, but equally over its entire external surface; and one could well say that it is the task of the artist to turn the inwardness of things into their outwardness.[45]

Irony and its cognates, however, provide only "disintegrating external forms" that must be given a deeper interpretation if they are to yield anything meaningful. Humor turns "everything to nothing, including the idea," though it can be seen more profoundly as "the sublime turned upside-down, or a finite applied to the infinite." More positively, wit is a "spark that leaps suddenly over intermediate steps" but that, because of the way it functions, consumes what it suggests. Finally, irony itself may be the negation of a positive truth (as it is in Schelling), or more commonly, the suspension of any truth whatever.[46] On the face of it, what Kierkegaard attempts is a hermeneutics of irony, the philosophic standpoint that Hegel had dismissed because of its "infinite, absolute negativity" (*A*, I,68), and around which cluster romantic anxieties about texts that derealize themselves. This attempt to reconceive in a positive way a mode that threatens to deny altogether the positive power of language is not without precedent. Hegel to the contrary, Friedrich Schlegel sees the decreative power of irony as consistent with the teleological project of a progressive universal poetry and finally connects irony (particularly Socratic irony) with love. Indeed, as Marshall Brown points out, romantic irony is often linked to allegory and hence to the abstract positing of

[45]Karl Solger, *Erwin, or Four Dialogues on Beauty and Art*, in Kathleen Wheeler, ed., *German Aesthetic and Literary Criticism: The Romantic Ironists and Goethe* (Cambridge: Cambridge University Press, 1984), p. 130.

[46]Ibid., p. 128.

meaning. If irony and allegory both disjoin appearances "from the world of significance, with only the secondary difference that allegory points toward the higher meaning and irony does not," ironic destruction and allegoric anticipation are frequently coupled together,[47] so as to yield an idealism that is dialectical and critical rather than dogmatic.

Amidst these attempts at idealization, what is remarkable about Kierkegaard's essay is that he does not elide the deconstructive potential of irony by perceiving it as creative and fertile.[48] Unlike Solger, Kierkegaard is not interested in wit and humor, nor does his concept of irony (like Schlegel's) include these modes in all but name. Within the triad of ironic forms that Solger studies, wit and humor display a certain positive energy that colors his understanding of the third term, irony. But Kierkegaard, in contrast, emphasizes the negativity of irony, seemingly in order to argue that though it is everything Hegel says it is, it is still consistent with the assumption of wholeness in the individual's history. Beginning his account of irony with Socrates, he focuses on the enigmatic nullity of the Socratic personality which, as we strip away the attempts by Plato and Xenophon to give it a positive identity, turns out to be an "empty space," a "nothingness" (*CI*, p. 56). Some of the problems explored by Kierkegaard had already been raised by Schleiermacher in his essay on Socrates: the enigma of a philosopher who is not present in his discourse, the difficulty of trying to know him through the contradictory accounts of Plato and Xenophon, the difficulty of disentangling 'Socrates' from 'Plato,' and indeed the question of whether there *is* a real Socrates.[49] These problems in turn suggest various problems in literary hermeneutics. They include the difficulty of grasping truth when there are different versions of it, and also the question of how to find the true voice of the author behind the figurative voices that represent and displace it in subsequent critical traditions. It is an indication of Kierkegaard's difference from the philological positivism of earlier classical study that he cannot rest with Schleiermacher's view that Socrates created something, namely, the dialectical method. As Kierkegaard attempts to disentangle the Socratic from the Platonic voice in the dia-

[47] *The Shape of German Romanticism* (Ithaca, N.Y.: Cornell University Press, 1979), pp. 99–100.

[48] I refer to Anne Mellor's discussion of romantic irony, which she identifies with Schlegel. Mellor emphasizes the unstable though fertile character of irony, without giving sufficient attention to the continued transcendental element in it: *English Romantic Irony* (Cambridge, Mass. : Harvard University Press, 1980), pp. 3–25. Another recent discussion of nineteenth-century theories of irony is Lillian Furst's *Fictions of Romantic Irony* (Cambridge, Mass.: Harvard University Press, 1984), pp. 23–48.

[49] Schleiermacher, "The Worth of Socrates as a Philosopher," in *The Apology of Socrates, The Crito and Part of the Phaedo, with notes from Stallbaum, Schleiermacher etc.* (London: Taylor Walton and Maberley, 1852), pp. cliv, clii.

logues, Socrates' contribution turns out to be the evacuation of originary meaning, where the attempt to fill this ideological void through systematic philosophy and myth is Plato's addition. There are according to Kierkegaard two kinds of questions, of which only the second is authentically Socratic: "One may ask a question for the purpose of obtaining an answer . . . or . . . to suck out the apparent content with a question and leave only an emptiness remaining" (*CI*, p. 73). Similarly, there are two kinds of dialogue: the "constructive dialogues which are distinguished by an objective and systematic presentation" and which are essentially Platonic, and the ironic dialogues, in which alone the truly Socratic emerges in the form of a refusal to use language to construct meaning (*CI*, p. 90).

This may not sound like promising ground for a phenomenological rather than poststructuralist concept of irony. Indeed, Kierkegaard seems to have deconstructed the hermeneutic project, by following the classic strategies of traditional hermeneutics only to parody them. For he goes from a grammatical reading of the texts in which Socrates is represented (the dialogues), to a more psychological and inward reading of the person himself, only to disclose Socrates' personality as an absence. This is not the end, however. For Kierkegaard then goes on to reverse his deconstruction and to reconstruct the identity of the Socratic 'text' from its apparent nonidentity. The seeming nothingness of Socrates becomes, in turn, a surface that invites further reading, and this deeper psychological reading, of Socrates and of the irony that is his modus vivendi, reveals that absence is the representation of a still unarticulated presence. Kierkegaard then introduces his famous gloss on the Hegelian definition of irony, a gloss that seems to create a transcendental signified from its very disappearance, and to refute Hegel by placing the Socratic moment within the larger context of the history of Spirit: irony "is negativity because it only negates; it is infinite because it negates not this or that phenomenon; and it is absolute because it negates by virtue of a higher which is not" (*CI*, p. 278). Kierkegaard does not believe in a world-historical spirit or in the rational unfolding of history, and would feel that Hegel emphasizes the collective spirit at the expense of the individual. Nevertheless, there is something Hegelian about this suggestion that the present is the ground of the future, and that the signs of the present must be given not just a literal or even a psychological reading, but also a divinatory reading. The conclusion, furthermore, draws on some of the most orthodox strategies of Christian hermeneutics. It seems to elide the problem posed by romantic irony, by seeing it as a false type of Socratic irony, and it further seems to reorient the negativity of the latter, by seeing Socrates as a type of Jesus, who similarly confronts the interpreter with a textual silence that is not an absence.

The parallel between Socrates and Jesus, earlier drawn by Hamann,[50] allows Kierkegaard to make the ironic mode a type—though not an equivalent—of the prophetic mode:

> For the ironic subject the given actuality has completely lost its validity; it has become for him an imperfect form which everywhere constrains. He does not possess the new, however, he only knows the present does not correspond to the Idea. . . . [he] is in one sense prophetic, to be sure, for he constantly points to something future; but what it is he knows not. While he is prophetic in this sense, his position and situation are nevertheless the opposite of the prophetic. (*CI*, p. 278)

Kierkegaard's essay could be seen as providing, through a phenomenology of the ironic spirit, a model that allows for the reading of the apparently unreadable text. The canonical readings of Blake which reinterpret the ironic stance of *Urizen* by making it prefigure the prophetic stance of *Jerusalem* employ such a model, perhaps without any awareness of Kierkegaard. But throughout this discussion I have used the word 'seems' because it is not at all clear whether Kierkegaard is providing or playing with hermeneutic models. For one thing, the strategies of reading he uses repeat those he criticizes in others. For example, his argument that irony can be counterread into something positive depends on a binary opposition between a 'true' Socratic irony, which is the prelude to something positive, and the 'false' romantic irony of Schlegel and Tieck, which continually negates. But Kierkegaard himself undermines this opposition. For instance, his description of Socratic irony as "hovering" uses language reminiscent of Schlegel (*CI*, p. 279). And in his discussion of Socrates and Plato he is unable to see Platonic positivity as the fulfilment of Socratic negativity, dismisses it as a mere supplement, and thus raises the question of why any future positivity should be any less supplementary. In undoing the opposition between Socratic and romantic irony, he thus veers toward the 'romantic' position that defines irony as infinite (but not absolute) negativity. Second, Kierkegaard's negative hermeneutic, which he developed as a way of grappling with complexities ignored by post-Enlightenment thinkers like Schleiermacher and Hegel (at least as the nineteenth century saw them), involves a series of readings rather like Chinese boxes. It radically destabilizes the process of reading by making it potentially endless. It is, to be sure, a dialectical hermeneutics, but that is not to say the dialectic is progressive. For if we move from reading the representation of Socrates in the dialogues to a more inward reading of Socrates as a person, only

[50] J. C. O'Flaherty, *Hamann's Socratic Memorabilia: A Translation and Commentary* (Baltimore: The Johns Hopkins University Press, 1967).

to find that this inward reading of him as phenomenologically absent is again an outer shell that conceals something potentially more positive, who is to say that this new 'inner' meaning is not a further representation that fails to get at the truth? We are not quite prepared for this textual vertigo when we read Kierkegaard's definition of irony as a figure in which the word is in opposition to its true meaning, and the reader simply negates the word to arrive at this meaning (*CI*, p. 265). The trope of irony allows the reader, through a hermeneutics of reversal, to posit what the text does not. The mode of irony, however, is more complicated. In Kierkegaard's own enactment of a negative hermeneutic, which considers irony as a modus vivendi rather than in the more limited form of a trope, the process of supplementing the text through the act of reading seems to turn back on itself, and reading ceases to be a positive activity.

In the end it is difficult to say whether the essay on irony dismantles the hermeneutic project or continues Schelling's endeavor and shows it triumphing over incredible odds. Kierkegaard's essay is the first of the works considered in this chapter to present itself as text and not simply theory, although other works may in practice function this way. Our reading of it will depend on whether we give priority to the theological or aesthetic side of his work, to what he says or to how he says it. Pierre Macherey suggests that one think of a text as "exhibiting" rather than expressing an ideology, as repeating ideology so as to display its gaps and become "the mythology of its own myths."[51] This view of the text as "criticism," as the displacement of ideology, is very different from and more subtle than the work to which Barthes refers as "ideological criticism and semiological dismantling."[52] Semiological dismantling analyzes a text or a tradition of ideas in such a way as to uncover the gaps that expose it as a product of false consciousness. But a critique generated by repetition rather than explicit deconstruction allows mythology to display its gaps by letting it speak and thus also display itself. Kierkegaard exhibits the strategies of traditional hermeneutics in such a way as to defamiliarize them as textual strategies. But emptied out, they become available for repossession by the reader as strategies with which we can play. Perhaps Kierkegaard himself provides the best description of how the simultaneous affirmation and unsettling of an idea functions, when he points out in the *Concluding Unscientific Postscript* that "to write a book and revoke it is something else than not writing it at all" (*CUP*, p. 548). He provides another useful gloss on this procedure of ambiguously

[51]*A Theory of Literary Production*, trans. Geoffrey Wall (London: Routledge and Kegan Paul, 1978), p. 60.

[52]Roland Barthes, *Image, Music, Text*, trans. Stephen Heath (New York: Hill and Wang, 1977), p. 166.

dismantling and reproducing an ideology in his term "dialectical reduplication," which involves a translation of a truth intellectually apprehended into the terms of actual living (*PV*, pp. 16–18, 166). A text can be seen as the dialectical reduplication of a theory, a repetition that simultaneously enacts it and throws it into relief, translates the theoretical into the real and the proper into the figurative.

The dialectical reduplication of a system of ideas is in a sense its deconstruction. Yet Kierkegaard's use of deconstruction differs considerably from what recent theory has accustomed us to, in reinscribing everything that it criticizes. The unique method of *The Concept of Irony* may seem less puzzling if we remember that Derrida distinguishes between two forms of deconstruction. The more common form, used by Nietzsche, involves a decision "to change terrain, in a discontinuous and irruptive fashion, by brutally placing oneself outside, and by affirming an absolute break and difference." But there is also a form of deconstruction that attempts "an exit . . . without changing terrain, by repeating what is implicit in the founding concepts and the original problematic, by using against the edifice the instruments or stones available in the house." Derrida is concerned with the tendency of both modes to reinstate the habits of thinking they attack. A deconstruction based on ironic repetition "risks ceaselessly confirming, consolidating, *relifting*" what it deconstructs, whereas one based on rupture inverts the oppositions it exposes, "thereby inhabiting more naively and more strictly than ever the inside [it] declares [it] has deserted."[53] But Kierkegaard's avoidance of rupture needs to be seen as deliberate and productive rather than dangerous. For the fact that he is no less committed to placing existing categories of thought under erasure than a more ruptural thinker like Nietzsche and yet will not openly break with the hermeneutic tradition is surely one of the most significant things in the rhetoric of that tradition's attempt to read itself. In the next chapter we will explore the ambiguities of the Kierkegaardian deconstruction, as well as the revisionary hermeneutics that emerges from his work and, less vertiginously, from that of Schleiermacher.

[53]Jacques Derrida, *Margins of Philosophy*, trans. Alan Bass (Chicago: University of Chicago Press, 1982), p. 135.

CHAPTER THREE

Kierkegaard and Schleiermacher Revisited: The Revisionary Tradition in Romantic Hermeneutics

So far we have seen hermeneutics as providing a framework in which to view romantic literature, while also placing hermeneutics within the problematic which it frames. Such an approach brings out the interrogation of concepts like meaning and identity present in the subtext of hermeneutics itself. But it does not necessarily dismantle the postulate of a consciousness behind the text which legitimizes psychological reading, as opposed to the grammatical reading Schleiermacher saw as inadequate, and the rhetorical reading that has now replaced exegesis in an era that believes truth to be a mobile army of metaphors. This approach simply suspends the idea that this consciousness can ground the meaning of the text, or that this consciousness can achieve that identity with itself that will end its having to narrate itself to itself. The history of romantic hermeneutics is of a movement complicated by its emergence within a chain of substitutions. When writing fails to represent adequately the thought or speech that precedes it, it is replaced by reading, which is thus open to a similar failure. Moreover, the hermeneutic tradition itself is involved in substitutions that further unravel its project. If Ast and Schleiermacher defer meaning from the text to the author's consciousness, Hegel further defers it to the unfolding of the world-historical canon, and Schelling is unable to find meaning in a canonical reading that expands the text and instead must project one that negates it. This series of deferrals culminates in Kierkegaard's essay on irony, where the hermeneutic myth of a consciousness present to itself behind the screen of its textual appearances lays itself open to deconstruction.

But the history of romantic hermeneutics also shows the impossibility of deconstructing consciousness itself, considered as lack, desire, or will.

For Kierkegaard remains profoundly phenomenological in uncovering behind irony a desire to posit, if not an ability to do so. Indeed, his description of irony is highly phenomenological. Even though it does not contribute to the "content of personality," irony, according to him, can be understood only in relation to personality: "It has the movement of turning back into itself which is characteristic of personality, of seeking back into itself, terminating in itself—except that in this movement irony returns emptyhanded" (*CI*, p. 242n.). Thus, it may be more accurate to speak of what happens between Schleiermacher and Kierkegaard not as the dismantling of hermeneutics, but as a displacement already present in the writings of Schleiermacher himself. Kierkegaard concedes the linguisticality of understanding, which compels anyone trying to penetrate the disguises of irony to return emptyhanded. But *The Concept of Irony* is not simply an earlier version of *Allegories of Reading*. For unlike de Man, Kierkegaard suggests that the failure to transcend the linguistic must itself be understood in psychological, not linguistic terms. Whether we see this coupling of the linguistic and the psychological as spelling the death of 'hermeneutics' will depend on how monolithically we define a term that is itself historical and subject to change. If the aim of 'hermeneutics' is to fix the meaning of a text, Kierkegaard shows the emptiness of the hermeneutic project. But if its central postulate is that reading is psychological rather than purely rhetorical or grammatical, he remains within the hermeneutic tradition. Hermeneutics, as the study of the relations between textuality and reading, was and is committed to the value of the word. *The Concept of Irony* is an early instance of a revised hermeneutics that treats the consciousness of the text and the text of consciousness as twin paradoxes. In it, reading remains an attempt to understand the intellectual personality behind the text, and a process with consequences for the intellectual life of the interpreter. But the special circumstances of reading, in which authorial identity is made available only in textual form, complicate both this identity and the interpreter's attempt to understand himself or herself through the text (and consequently as a text). For the normal situation of texts, as texts of the first degree produced by their authors, tends to suppress their textuality and lets the reader use them as a window to the author's intention. It is precisely to emphasize the special nature of reading that Kierkegaard chooses a text of the second degree, one in which the comforting link with the author has been broken, and instead of a text written by Socrates we have one written by a reader (Plato) to supply the place of an absent text.

But Kierkegaard's exposure of reading as supplementary also dramatizes how involved it is with needs and desires, and thus how powerfully psychological it remains. What he does implicitly in *The Concept of Irony*, namely, to "relift" hermeneutics at a "more certain depth," he will do more explicitly in a later text, *The Point of View for My Work as an Author.* In this retrospective interpretation of his own oeuvre he exhibits one direction taken by the revisionary movement within romantic hermeneutics: toward the reinstatement of a psychologically oriented reading decoupled from the notion of origins. But the continued emphasis on reading is purchased at the cost of conceding that the author has disappeared, and thus that reading cannot be aletheological, because what it reproduces is not something outside the reader but simply the dialogue of desire and scepticism within the reader. The cryptic absences of the author, as it were, generate readers who are never anything but supplementary. Although the *Point of View* differs from *The Concept of Irony* in reintroducing the author (Kierkegaard himself), this author is never more than a reader, a guest in his own text. Romantic hermeneutics is not always content with thus renouncing the figure of the author as source. For the disappearance of Socrates from his text is matched by the many cases in which authors attempt to appear in romantic texts, if only to have their authority challenged, as in *The Prelude*, or to appear as figures in their own texts, as in *The Triumph of Life*. The presence of the author as figure in so many romantic texts suggests that we need to define a second way the relation between reading and textuality can be reconceived: one that will preserve the link between psychological reading and the search for origins, while pluralizing the origins themselves.

Considering certain crucial margins in the work of Schleiermacher, where he becomes concerned with the speech or discourse of the text, allows us to explore a revised model of psychological reading that is thematized in poems like *The Triumph of Life*, and that is also implied in Shelley's *Defence of Poetry*. Unlike interpretation, the focus for Kierkegaard's inquiry into the experience of reading, discourse is not one-sided and projective, but involves an activity of exchange. The focus on the discourse of the text allows for a reconceiving of the reading process somewhat different from Kierkegaard's. Kierkegaard does not really deal with the activity of writing or speaking, but simply with how the reading of what has already been written becomes self-complicating. For Schleiermacher, too, reading remains disseminative. But the emphasis on the discourse of the text involves an interest in texts from the point of view of the author as well as the reader, and thus crucially changes the relation between reading and original meaning(s). Instead of being purely self-referential, the text becomes an intent at meaning that generates in the reader a corresponding intent at understanding. What is understood is not simple, just as what is meant is not self-identical. But just as the disappearance of the author in Kierkegaard results in an eclipse of the text's aletheological dimension, so his 'appearance' (and I use the word deliberately) results in a sense that texts do indeed disseminate truths, lead to temporary understandings. His appearance, in other words, restores to the text what Ricoeur calls its outside as opposed to its inside: its "transcendent aim," which makes it something "which is addressed to someone about something."[1]

Reinscribing Hermeneutics as Reader-Response Theory: Kierkegaard's *Point of View*

A study of how the romantic tradition reconceives hermeneutics can begin with Kierkegaard's *Point of View*, often taken as the key to his 'canon' but just as clearly part of its enigma. This later text repeats from *The Concept of Irony* the deconstruction of a critical metalanguage outside the play of signifiers by promising an interpretation of Kierkegaard's texts, which itself calls for further interpretation. But it also goes beyond *The Concept of Irony*, where a higher perspective from which to refocus the texts's negativity had not yet emerged. *The Concept of Irony*, in other words, remained fundamentally deconstructive, in that it did no more than express the need for psychological reading, but as a desire that still lacked an outside, a will that had not yet achieved representation. *The Point of View* actually figures for us this reading of the canon, based on a hermeneutics of reversal, while according it a merely 'lyrical' status. As such, it brings out the importance of desire in producing psychological reading and simultaneously compromising it. It refuses to dismantle the phenomenological notion of a will accompanying the writing and reading of the text, a *telos* that may not precede and direct the linguistic process but that is still produced along with it. But more important, Kierkegaard's approach to the problem is not monolithic: he is as much concerned with 'readings' as intellectual events that occur regardless of whether they have any ground, as he is with the very activity of 'reading' itself as something that has become suspect. He suggests that there are modes of reading just as there are literary modes. A lyrical reading will be different from a discursive reading: it may not be logically persuasive, and yet it cannot therefore be discarded. We will see Shelley adopting a similar strategy in *Prometheus Unbound*, where the dialogue between Asia and Panthea on dreams provides a lyrical reading of the text that is problematized by being set in the discursive mode of drama. There is a considerable distance between the recognition that reading is figurative and the analysis of its complicity with emotional needs and fears, on the

[1]Paul Ricoeur, *Hermeneutics and the Human Sciences*, ed. and trans. John B. Thompson (New York: Cambridge University Press, 1982), p. 153.

one hand, and the claim that texts are unreadable, on the other. That distance marks the difference between a Kierkegaard and a de Man, between someone who is concerned with how desire produces readings and someone who is concerned to reduce all reading to a figure of desire. The difference is nowhere more apparent than in the rhetorical ramifications of their respective styles. For de Man's is a metalinguistic criticism that analyzes figural moments in literature, whereas Kierkegaard's 'theory' is itself conveyed through scenes of reading, which involve us in their dialectical reduplication and thus compel us to elaborate and live through their figures.

The Point of View begins with a hermeneutic dilemma: how to find the 'real' Kierkegaard, given that 'Kierkegaard' produced fictitious as well as religious texts, pseudonymous as well as authorized texts, and that he thus allowed his canon to be inhabited by a certain 'ambiguity' or 'duplicity.' We are not concerned here with the nature of Kierkegaard's Christianity so much as with his conception of 'truth,' and with how the attempt to ground the meaning of his works is complicated by the existence of different authorial voices, which in this case happen to include the religious. Clearly, the oscillation between voices, one serious and one playful, one that appears directly referential and one that is implicated in metaphoric processes, is part of a problem to be found in other writers like Blake and Godwin, who also combine the polemical and the imaginative. As Kierkegaard points out, the discrepancy between the voices cannot be explained by positing an author who evolved from the aesthetic to the religious, for the canon is simply not arranged as a progress of the soul. The priority of 'truth' over 'falsity' is constantly jeopardized by the intertwining of the aesthetic and the religious (*PV*, pp. 10–12). Precisely when pseudonymous works seem to be replaced by authorized religious works, "as a testimony and as a precaution" comes "the little aesthetic article by a pseudonym, *Inter et Inter*" (*PV*, p. 14). Precisely when "direct communication" (*PV*, p. 40) seems to have taken over, the threat of obliquity is reintroduced.

'Kierkegaard's' response is to argue that his duplicity functions pedagogically, like Socratic dialectic (*PV*, pp. 39, 41), and thus incidentally to complete the placing of Socratic irony as a type of Christian truth merely hinted at in the essay on irony. He argues for a reading of his aesthetic texts in terms of a hermeneutics of reversal, with the difference that what lies beneath the actual text (the religious) is now supplied in other texts by the author. The duplicitous use of the aesthetic and the ironic, with their endless deferral of meaning, is not something done by 'Kierkegaard,' who is himself caught in the dialectic, but by the "Governance," a religious equivalent to Hegel's world-historical spirit, or more realistically speaking, to the Lacanian unconscious. In constructing the aesthetic as a surface to be consumed, the Governance at once accommodates the power of things as they are and allows readers to be surprised by their own error into resisting the text of actuality:

> For there is an immense difference, a dialectical difference, between these two cases: the case of a man who is ignorant and is to have a piece of knowledge imparted to him, so that he is like an empty vessel which is to be filled or a blank sheet of paper upon which something is to be written; and the case of a man who is under an illusion and must first be delivered from that. Likewise there is a difference between writing on a blank sheet of paper and bringing to light by the application of a caustic fluid a text which is hidden under another text. Assuming then that a person is a victim of an illusion, . . . if I do not begin by deceiving him, I must begin with direct communication. But direct communication presupposes that the receiver's ability to receive is undisturbed. But here such is not the case; an illusion stands in the way. That is to say, one must first of all use the caustic fluid. But this caustic means is negativity. (*PV*, p. 40)

The valorization of the religious over the aesthetic is of course undermined by the very terms of Kierkegaard's argument. For a genetic metaphor that makes the religious texts more mature than the aesthetic texts he substitutes a spatial metaphor that makes the religious stratum of his thinking more profound than the aesthetic. But his insistence on how the two voices have been intertwined throughout his career makes it difficult for him to have recourse to metaphors of surface and depth, whether horizontal or vertical, teleological or geological. Derrida has shown how in Husserl's *Ideas* the "geological metaphor" that posits a grounding stratum gets insensibly associated with a "*textual* metaphor" in which "the 'strata' are 'woven'; their intermixing is such that the warp cannot be distinguished from the woof."[2] In Kierkegaard the rejection of a geological, archeological, or teleological model of understanding in favor of a textual model is quite explicit. Hence it is surprising to find him positing, through the Governance, a deep structure of events and using methods he has called into question. Moreover, the idea that Kierkegaard only came to understand the methods of the Governance over a period of time seems a version of the genetic postulate earlier discarded as illusory. In the light of his own argument, we must be suspicious of those reassuring words drawn from a genetic logic that gradually reenter the *Point of View*: references to a "turning-point in my whole activity as an author" and to a "transition to the series of purely religious writings" (*PV*, p. 53). Once again we have the paradox of a text

[2]Jacques Derrida, *Speech and Phenomena and Other Essays on Husserl's Theory of Signs*, trans. David B. Allison (Evanston, Ill.: Northwestern University Press, 1973), pp. 110–12.

performing what it has shown to be impossible, and thus taking away the interpretation that it offers.

Just as important in terms of introducing and unsettling the hierarchy of the religious and aesthetic is the concept of dialectical reduplication. Dialectical reduplication involves a translation from one mode to another: the translation of theory into practice, of religious commitment into the terms of actual life. As the living through of what is abstract, it is part of the existential aspect of Kierkegaard's hermeneutic, in which understanding must occur through application. The idea is introduced to explain why the Governance, instead of communicating its religious intentions directly, reflects them in the distorting mirror of the aesthetic. For the religious position to be truly understood, the process by which one is converted to it must be experienced. But a dialectical reduplication is not a simple translation of theory into practice: understanding is inevitably shifted through its application. Put differently, dialectical reduplication involves an enactment that repeats and defers or differs from what it enacts. Hence, it is by no means clear that the attempt to reduplicate the religious position existentially by making it emerge from the aesthetic will necessarily return us to the religious position. Corresponding to dialectical reduplication as the Governance's method of writing the Kierkegaard canon is the idea of 'repetition' as Kierkegaard's own method of reading it. Elsewhere Kierkegaard distinguishes between repetition-as-recollection and genuine repetition: between repetition backward as the recollection of what has been, and repetition forward as a second chance that allows us to have everything double.[3] Such repetition, although not a reproduction of the same, claims not to involve the nonsynthetic difference of Derridean repetition. 'Kierkegaard's' retrospective reading of his aesthetic texts involves the second kind of repetition: he retraces his past as part of a spiritual therapy in order to make it produce new insights. There is no guarantee, however, that returning to the aesthetic texts to perform a divinatory reading will deliver precisely the new truths within them that 'Kierkegaard' wants disclosed. Similarly, Kierkegaard seems aware of the dangers that lurk in reduplication, and his description of it as "dialectical" indicates a desire to see complication as progressive, differences as returning to an identity instead of proliferating. But the metaphor he uses to argue that duplication and duplicity produce truth is deliberately disturbing:

> as a woman's coyness has a reference to the true lover and yields when he appears, but only then, so, too, dialectical reduplication has a reference to

[3]Søren Kierkegaard, *Fear and Trembling, Repetition*, ed. and trans. Howard V. Hong and Edna Hong (Princeton, N.J.: Princeton University Press, 1983), pp. 131, 149, 220–21, 294.

> true seriousness. To one less serious the explanation cannot be imparted, for the elasticity of the dialectical reduplication is too great for him to grasp: it takes the explanation away from him again and makes it doubtful to him whether it really is the explanation. (*PV*, p. 17)

Especially given Kierkegaard's concession that "the mark of a dialectical reduplication is that the ambiguity is maintained" (*PV*, p. 17), we must wonder whether coyness and play ever do become serious, whether there is a true lover who can bring into play a coyness that is without subterfuge.

Through the dialectical reduplication at the heart of his work, namely, the replaying of theory as fiction, Kierkegaard repeats the strategies of traditional hermeneutics so as to make them self-reflexive. The result is a radical revision of hermeneutics, in which the author is reduced to the status of a reader, and the text becomes a heuristic stimulus: "That I was 'without authority' I have from the first moment asserted clearly and repeated as a stereotyped phrase. I regarded myself preferably as a *reader* of the books" (*PV*, p. 151). As reader he provides us with a 'psychological' interpretation of the canon that cannot ground its meaning, since it does no more than reflect his own need for stability. Such a reading of his own work is a "lyrical satisfaction to me *qua* man" (*PV*, p. 18) and thus has the status not even of an originating desire but rather a desire after the fact. The effect of allowing the text to exist only as it is read is to grant the text a linguistic and historical autonomy from the author's intention. Thus Kierkegaard begins his second chapter with the heading "The Explanation: That the Author is and was a Religious Author." But he goes on to add:

> It might seem that a mere protestation to this effect on the part of the author himself would be more than enough; for surely he knows best what is meant. For my part, however, I have little confidence in protestations with regard to literary productions and am inclined to take an objective view of my own works. If as a third person, in the role of a reader, I cannot substantiate the fact that what I affirm is so, and that it could not but be so, it would not occur to me to wish to win a cause which I regard as lost. (*PV*, p. 15)

'Kierkegaard' might argue that the *Point of View* does indeed substantiate from the perspective of the reader the claim that Kierkegaard is a religious author. But then 'Kierkegaard' is himself a fictional construct. In the end the *Point of View* tells us the truth about the author's work, but this truth is a moving army of metaphors and metonymies, subject to further reading. Of particular interest is his slippery use of the term 'poet,' for paradoxically the status of religious interpretation depends on the status of the 'poetic.' Initially it seems that the term 'poetic' is associated with the purely fictitious, with the weak, the aesthetic voice in Kierkegaard: "There was allowed me again a period for poetical production, but always under the arrest of the religious, which was on the watch" (*PV*, p. 86). But later on there is a curious statement that identifies the religious interpretation of Kierkegaard's life with poetic mythmaking.

> I have nothing further to say, but in conclusion I will let another speak, my poet, who when he comes will assign me a place among those who have suffered for the sake of an idea. . . . The dialectical structure he [Kierkegaard] brought to completion, of which the several parts are whole works, he could not ascribe to any man, least of all would he ascribe it to himself; if he were to ascribe it to any one, it would be to Governance, to whom it was in fact ascribed, day after day and year after year, by the author, who historically died of a mortal disease, but poetically died of longing for eternity. (*PV*, pp. 100, 103)

The religious 'truth' that allows us to ground the reading of Kierkegaard's texts is in some sense 'poetic' and duplicitous.

What do we make of this interweaving of the 'aesthetic' and the 'religious,' initially made to oppose each other as false and true, under the rubric of the 'poetic'? The suggestion is surely that religious truth, and the hermeneutic concept of Governance, are themselves figures contained within the ambiguity they seek to contain. But this does not mean that they are untrue, for if the religious world-view is poetic, by the same token the poetic is religious rather than fictitious, a source of values, though one that is always under the 'arrest' of the aesthetic. This is also the point made by Kierkegaard's regretful distinction between being a religious author and a religious man: "it was not at all my original intention to become a religious author. My intention was to evacuate as hastily as possible the poetical—and then go out to a country parish" (*PV*, p. 86). To write about his religiousness instead of simply being religious allows Kierkegaard to inhabit the discrepancy between the religious and the aesthetic impulses, between the metaphysical and the playful, without excluding either one.

The metatext that begins by offering us the end of a golden string ends, in short, by leading us further into the labyrinth. At one point Kierkegaard uses the curious metaphor of spying to describe his religious reading of his aesthetic self, and suggests that this agent who detects counterfeiters must himself be under the suspicion that he exercises:

> I am like a spy in a higher service, the service of the idea. I have nothing new to proclaim; I am without authority, being myself hidden in deceit; . . . I am

> not a holy man; in short, I am a spy who in his spying, in learning to know all about questionable conduct and illusions and suspicious characters, all the while he is making inspection is himself under the closest inspection. Observe that this is the sort of people the police make use of. They will hardly select for their purposes the sort of people whose life was always highly honest; . . . the police are far from disinclined to have under their thumb a person who by reason of his *vita ante acta* they can compel to put up with everything, to obey. (*PV*, pp. 87–88)

Despite the later disclaimer that the divine police are purer than the civil police, this analogy is a good example of how the poetical mode complicates or dialectically reduplicates religious 'truths' by incorporating them into scenes of reading: scenes with a plot and a cast of characters that can be interpreted in more than one way. We can of course accept 'Kierkegaard's' claim that the analogy applies only to him as spy and not to his employers. But if the reader who pries out the truth is himself concealing something, the motives of his Kafkan employers would seem no less dubious. The gesture of humility by which 'Kierkegaard' confesses his own duplicity so as to absolve the Governance from any blame may be precisely that: a fiction that conceals his desire for a religious certainty that nothing in his life authorizes. We might wonder also about the compulsion that the Governance exercises over 'Kierkegaard.' What emerges from this passage is a theory in which reading is concealment as well as decipherment, an activity that penetrates secrets and reveals truths but at the same time harbors its own secrets.

The potential endlessness of reading is further compounded because the writer is always in the position of reading something already written and is never in the position of actually writing it. He thus speaks from outside rather than inside his own words. Lest this sound too much like the death of the author,[4] however, it is important to note a particularly romantic caveat that Kierkegaard inconspicuously inserts. This caveat seems at odds with the insistence elsewhere that the author is without authority, and that the text has an autonomy that makes original and final intentions irrelevant. Here, by contrast, Kierkegaard seems to criticize the writer who withholds a signature and is subsumed into the text:

> in our age, which reckons as wisdom that which is truly the mystery of unrighteousness, viz. that one need not inquire about the communicator, but only about the communication, the objective only—in our age what is an author? An author is often merely an x, even when his name is signed, something quite impersonal, which addresses itself abstractly, by the aid of

[4]Roland Barthes, *Image, Music, Text,* trans. Stephen Heath (New York: Hill and Wang, 1977), pp. 145–47.

> printing, to thousands and thousands, while remaining itself unseen and unknown. (*PV*, pp 44–45)

The voice here makes an existential demand that the author (in this case Kierkegaard) declare himself as an individual and put himself at risk (*PV*, p. 44). The demand is not so inconsistent with the voiding of authority as it may seem, for this writer does not confer authority on his text: rather he renounces a claim to objectivity and admits that as a "single individual" he is quite insignificant. He enters the circuit of communication, where to assume a position is to lay oneself open to attack, as well as to the "control which in practical life must always be exercised over everyone who wishes to teach others," the accountability that allows the audience to judge whether the writer's personal and intellectual life comports "with his communication" (*PV*, p. 45). In other words, as Kierkegaard commits himself, his life becomes part of his text. This view that authors must declare a reading of their texts, even if that reading is subject to further reading, marks what is particularly romantic about Kierkegaard's idea of the literary transaction, which insists on the presence of the personal element as part of the play of signifiers. Kierkegaard's theory of authorship does not involve a classical theory of impersonality, in which it is the invisibility of the author that lends the text its authority, nor does it involve the theory of egotistical sublimity wrongly associated with romanticism, in which that authority derives from the massive presence of the author. But he also does not argue for the modern 'scriptor,' who is born simultaneously with the text and written by its decentered processes. There is for him a dialectical tension between author and text, in which the text assumes a degree of autonomy, but in which the writer, too, must take a stand (or a series of stands) outside these differences that never seem to progress toward identities. Such, for instance, is the tension in Blake's *Songs* between a series of poems that endlessly displace and rewrite each other, and the voice of the bard, which in some sense clearly does represent 'Blake' himself, but without making Blake present to us.

This demand that the authors declare themselves is explored more fully in the *Concluding Unscientific Postscript*. Against the attempts in philosophical and religious hermeneutics to establish through objective critical procedures a truth that only turns out to be vulnerable to further reading, Kierkegaard insists on the need to grasp truth subjectively (*CUP*, pp. 23–33). But he soon concedes that a subjective truth, though emotionally different from an objective one, is not logically more certain, because it is no more than contingent (*CUP*, pp. 68, 68n). Moreover, it is kept in perpetual motion by Kierkegaard's wariness about the mutual constraint exercised on each other by the institutions of 'author' and 'reader.' Not surprisingly, he is critical of any attempt to tell the reader what to think. He dislikes "direct" or "ordinary communication," a truth without figure that omits "the elusiveness" and "has no secrets" (*CUP*, pp. 76, 73), because he wants to leave the reader free to interpret "something which was not stereotyped for insertion in a systematic formulary, but which the trained dialectical gymnast produces and changes and produces again, the same and yet not the same" (*CUP*, p. 64). What is more unusual is a sophisticated reception aesthetics that leads Kierkegaard to suspect the institutional power of the audience and consequently to deconstruct the sympathetic reader favored by other romantics. A hostile or contemptuous reader, he argues, does not curtail the liberty of the author:

> An admirer on the other hand, is not so easily disposed of. His tender assiduities become so many burdens laid upon the object of his admiration, and before the latter has an inkling of what is taking place, he finds himself groaning under heavy taxes and assessments, though he began by being the most independent of men. . . . To speak dialectically, it is not the negative which constitutes an encroachment, but the positive. (*CUP*, p. 5)

Kierkegaard here criticizes the process of canon formation and intellectual reification at the heart of a romantic idealism that is secretly structured as an economy. The contingency of subjective truth is what makes it flexible. It is something Kierkegaard guards jealously, against a visionary company that encourages what he caustically describes as "fellowship, and . . . support from the other shareholders in the enterprise" (*CUP*, p. 62).

The idea of a personal commitment similarly applies to us. The reader, too, must take a stand in relation to the text and cannot take refuge in being reduced to a semiotic gram. Yet the position we assume will always harbor its own secrets, for becoming present to the text inevitably involves becoming represented in it. Toward the middle of the *Point of View* 'Kierkegaard' suggests that the desired reader of his texts is one who will approach them as a lover (*PV*, p. 62). The metaphor of love seems innocuous, a common romantic metaphor for understanding. But like the hermeneutic tradition that it encapsulates, it opens rather than resolves the problem of reading. As lover, the reader will have to become involved in the text, and not take refuge in a spectatorial scepticism. 'He' will be committed to understanding it, specifically to enacting a lyrical rather than critical reading of Kierkegaard's authorship. But the image of the reader as lover cannot be disentangled from its double, the image of the reader as spy. We have only to remember Kierkegaard's discussion of dialectical reduplication, where the text is figured as a coy woman yielding to her lover, to recognize that love also has its secrets. The questions that arise as we explore the intricacies of the metaphor are endless and suggest something of the complexity of even a constructive reading. Whether love is to some extent seduction is one question. Likewise, there is the problem of whether the text will yield to its lover or continue to play with 'him.' The woman, we have been told, will yield to the 'true' lover. But we might well ask whether there is a 'true' reader without his own subterfuges, who can make the text yield its truth rather than play with the metaphors within his attempts at truth. To what extent is true love simply a name for the lover's will to certainty? To what extent, on the other hand, is the notion of a will that compromises everything it does simply a name for a fear of commitment?

Reinscribing Authority: Schleiermacher

The reappearance of the writer distinguishes the *Point of View* from *The Concept of Irony* and seems to bring Kierkegaard closer to the second tendency discussed with reference to a redefined hermeneutics. But Kierkegaard's writer remains a reader who offers a point of view, and the hermeneutic that emerges from this text does not require us to make contact with the author who wrote the works. It requires us simply to follow the example of the writer who now reads them, and to take a stand toward the problem of relating the aesthetic and religious voices. The emphasis, in other words, is more on applicative than on psychological reading, and the reading process does not pretend to be an archeological one, but simply requires an existential choice on guard against its own possible secrets. Romanticism, however, can be a powerfully archeological movement, as it emerges in such poems as *The Prelude*, *The Triumph of Life*, and *The Fall of Hyperion*, in which the narrative act is a return to personal or cultural beginnings. It is not that the return is successful. Indeed, it functions paradoxically, generating from the very failure to find an origin various supplementary acts of understanding that provide new points of origin in the present, points that give us access not to the past but to the past as it survives into the present.[5] But if this sounds suspiciously like the deconstruction of reading as an archeo-

[5]I draw on J. G. Droysen's attempt to redefine rather than dismantle the idea of origins: "The seed first became a tree by growing . . . . It is of no use to deny the existence of the tree because the original seed can no longer be traced or because one is uncertain whether this, that, or a third point is the actual beginning. If one were to dig down to the roots . . . in order to find the original germ seed, it would no longer be there. Its beginning only repeats itself through its fruit": "The Investigation of Origins," in Kurt Mueller-Vollmer, ed., *The Hermeneutics Reader: Texts of the German Tradition from the Enlightenment to the Present* (New York: Continuum, 1985), p. 124.

logical act produced by Kierkegaard, there is a difference. The archeological form taken by the attempt at understanding in these texts reshapes the failure to find an unequivocal origin that is their content into a new origin. In other words, the hermeneutic form of these texts, though deconstructed by what happens in them, simultaneously reconstructs what happens in them into an event, a (dis)closure. It thus converts the supplementary acts of understanding that ensue into moments of origination in which the act of reading, of trying to understand, is once again something author(ized) and not (as in Kierkegaard's *Point of View*) purely speculative. To put it differently, where Kierkegaard renders all psychological reading essentially applicative, Schleiermacher makes all applicative reading ultimately psychological.

In returning to Schleiermacher's writings on hermeneutics, we are struck by their archeological form. The later version of the *Hermeneutics* proceeds from grammatical, through technical, to psychological interpretation, as though moving from surface to depth. The introduction to the dialogues of Plato is part of a romantic renaissance that corrects previous commentary so as to recover the 'true' Plato. These archeologies, however, succeed in a very different way from that intended. Articulating how they succeed through a 'divinatory' reading of insights that Schleiermacher himself did not systematize is the main task that faces us. Such divinatory readings seem justified not only by Schleiermacher's own principles of interpretation but also by the form of his work, much of which comes to us from his students because he himself preferred not to fix it in writing. D. F. Strauss was to criticize Schleiermacher's preference for the lecture over the essay.[6] But as will become apparent from Schleiermacher's discussion of speech and writing in Plato, the choice of a medium that is more fluid and dialogical than writing is meant to create openings for both author and reader, "compelling the mind of the reader to spontaneous production of ideas" (*IDP*, p. 37). At the same time, this very fluidity makes it dangerous to attribute a definite position to Schleiermacher. A relevant instance is the later version of the hermeneutics, where he distinguishes psychological from technical interpretation. It is by no means clear here whether the psychological is simply concerned with a more organic and inward version of the achieved, formalized unity of the text accessible to technical interpretation, or whether it provides insights into something less coherent, whether it provides access to a work or to a process. In order to pick out and develop one strand in Schleiermacher's writings, this discussion proceeds as though it is the second alternative that has authority. But it

[6]*The Christ of Faith and the Jesus of History: A Critique of Schleiermacher's The Life of Jesus*, trans. Leander E. Keck (Philadelphia: Fortress Press, 1977), p. 12.

would be more accurate to speak of certain ambiguities in Schleiermacher's theory. A tension between the formalist and the phenomenological has already been observed in various versions of the hermeneutics, where it is unclear whether psychological reading complements or supplements grammatical reading. There is also a further tension between a phenomenology oriented to the recovery of an original meaning, and a disseminative or deconstructive phenomenology that does indeed posit something more primal than writing, namely, discourse, but does not necessarily associate this with unity. Again, this discussion proceeds as though Schleiermacher is committed to a phenomenology that discloses truth as plural, and again it is important to point out that this is only a tendency in his writing.

Four texts are crucial to this discussion: the lectures on the life of Jesus, the commentary on Luke, the account of psychological reading in the later lectures on hermeneutics, and the introductions to the dialogues of Plato. Not surprisingly, as theologian Schleiermacher has a greater need for cognitive theism than as classical philologist. Revolutionary for his time in describing some of the ways in which the synoptic gospels disrupt the unity of effect that creates the illusion of a fixed meaning, he is also conservative in projecting onto the Gospel of John a hermeneutic certainty of which he cannot wholly convince himself. *The Life of Jesus* remains committed to a formalism of incarnate meaning, in which the successful text (the Gospel of John in this case) can be wholly understood through a combination of grammatical and technical interpretation. But at the same time, it introduces a need for a more phenomenological approach, in that it sees three of the gospels as 'imperfect' texts that can be understood only by going beyond the requirement of technical and formal coherence. In his study of the Gospel of Luke, Schleiermacher does indeed move in a more radical direction. This also holds true for the later version of the hermeneutics, where the subdivision of psychological interpretation into technical interpretation and psychological interpretation proper concedes the limits of a purely formalist analysis. But whether psychological reading simply deepens technical reading or whether it illuminates a kind of text that the latter cannot penetrate is left unresolved here, since the *Hermeneutics* does not deal with specific problems in practical criticism. Finally, in the introductions of the dialogues of Plato, Schleiermacher tackles the problem of interpreting disjunctive texts, apparently under the guise of finding in them a more inward coherence, but actually in order to argue for a disintegration of both formal and organic unity that makes the reader a constitutive element in the life of the text.

The Life of Jesus is unusual in that its subject, the gospels, are texts but are also readings of the life of Jesus. It is therefore concerned both with norms for the writing of texts, and with the kind of reading that seems most satisfactory. Schleiermacher's goal is to grasp the life of Jesus as history rather chronicle, to know "the inner quality of [Jesus'] life" rather than its external details (*LJ*, p. 3). The distinction between chronicle and history corresponds to the one between grammatical and psychological levels of reading. History is a method of writing that allows the reader to grasp its subject from within, whereas chronicle remains exterior and episodic, thus preventing us from moving beyond the grammatical, in order to understand the whole and not simply the parts. The Gospel of John, it seems, provides the most history-like representation of Jesus and is therefore to be preferred to the synoptic gospels, which frustrate access to the inwardness of Jesus' life by disrupting the grammar of narrative. Schleiermacher's ideal in these lectures is a form of representation that reveals the inner man, but he does not feel this can be done if the textual surface is fragmented. The Gospel of John achieves that history-likeness whose decline is lamented by Frei, and which can occur only if the close unity of inner and outer meaning has not been broken. It does so because its narrative is continuous and therefore seems to come from "one who narrates what he himself had experienced" (*LJ*, p. 159). Lacking such authority, the other gospels are unable to grasp their subject from within, to make it present within the text. The norms that Schleiermacher assumes for writing are in turn a function of what he thinks will make the practice of reading a comfortable one: the disjunctive text is inadequate because it does not yield itself to psychological reading.

In these lectures at least Schleiermacher takes an orthodox position. He is committed to texts that create the illusion of incarnate meaning by following classical principles of decorum, and he does not develop strategies of accommodation to salvage the authority of fractured texts.[7] But what is interesting is his description of the ways in which texts can fail as acts of representation, and his awareness that such texts exist even among the scriptures. Among the deficiencies of the synoptic gospels is their narrative discontinuity: their composition from separate narratives that were later joined together (*LJ*, pp. 223, 158), which gives the impression that the author is groping after a truth not fully contained in the text. Modal ambiguity and shifts in voice can also play a role in unsettling the authority of a text. The intermixture of a lyrical or dramatic element in the gospels, for example, may cast doubt on the historical character of the narrative, and so too may uncertainties about whether a narrative is interior or exterior, literal or metaphoric (*LJ*, p.

[7]Schleiermacher does suggest, however, that insofar as we read the synoptic gospels, it must be in the light of the more 'complete' version by John.

49). These descriptions of the synoptic gospels are extraordinarily accurate as accounts of the compositional method of someone like Blake, and as explanations of why his texts jeopardize a transcendental signified. Aggregational and stylistically heterogeneous texts exhibit what De Quincey calls a "mechanology of style." Where style "maintains a commerce with thought" and is "modified by thoughts," it is organic; but where "words in combination determine or modify each other" and where "words act upon words," it is mechanic.[8] In these texts narrative segments or presentational modes act upon each other, so that the signifier reflects upon itself instead of transparently reflecting the signified.

Although Schleiermacher tends to dismiss the synoptic gospels, from the admission that such texts exist in large numbers it is but a short step to the sense that they may have some legitimacy. The revaluation of the fissured text can lead in two directions: to a sentimental use of the reading process as a way of reversing the fall into writing, or to a redefinition of writing and reading as activities whose power lies precisely in their dissemination of meaning. It should not surprise us that these two very different developments manifest themselves indecisively or that they are often intertwined in the work of individual theorists. *The Life of Jesus* places itself before the flood by identifying a normative text that achieves linguistic stability and makes reading unproblematic. But a wide gulf separates Schleiermacher from those predecessors of his who similarly resist the decline of history-likeness in narrative. For he recognizes that the 'fragmented' quality of the synoptic gospels issues from the flux of the oral tradition behind them and cannot be argued away as a technical failure. If he tries to reestablish a fixed meaning through the Gospel of John—something for which Strauss criticized him[9]—he does so as if aware that his project is illusory. For one of his most intriguing concessions is that a connected presentation of the life of Jesus is in fact impossible, because John itself presents the appearance of continuity only by being highly selective (*LJ*, p. 43): "because it has a definite tendency, what it narrates as the content of a period is just as full of gaps as the other Gospel accounts" (*LJ*, p. 159). Thus the psychological coherence of John emerges as an effect of grammar. In marginalizing the synoptic gospels and requiring that they be corrected by a text whose unity has already been shown as a stylistic illusion, Schleiermacher simply brackets a problem that he knows he must address: the problem of what their fragmentation says about the status of representation itself.

[8]Thomas De Quincey, "Style," in *De Quincey as Critic*, ed. John E. Jordan (London: Routledge and Kegan Paul, 1973), p. 83.

[9]*The Christ of Faith*, pp. 36–37, 42–43.

But Schleiermacher does not always set aside this problem. Already in the protected field of biblical interpretation, in his *Critical Essay on the Gospel of Luke*, the formalist norm is seriously challenged. Beginning with the variations between the synoptic gospels, he argues against Eichhorn's attempt to construct a stemma by positing an original gospel that then became corrupted (*GL*, pp. 1–7). He suggests that Matthew and Luke often draw on different sources for the same event, that there is no original source, and indeed that there is a "plurality" of sources (*GL*, pp. 57, 7). He thus avoids the temptation to create an ideal text by a process of subtraction, implicit in the "comparative" method of eliminating what is not common to all the gospels and then selecting the most "concisely expressed" common denominator so as to produce "a still more meager original Gospel" (*GL*, pp. 17, 8). His commentary traces in microscopic detail the disintegration of unity at both the grammatical and technical levels. But contrary to expectation, he does not uncover a hidden coherence behind either level. Luke is seen simply as a compilation of narratives from different sources, which are sometimes themselves compilations rather than eyewitness accounts. Moreover, the parts of Luke's text are not unified by a pervasive cultural spirit, because they are often irreconcilable. What Schleiermacher makes of the discrepancies in and between the gospels is unclear. Sometimes he provides mechanical explanations for them, related to the biographical circumstances of the writer or compiler. But often the completely different emphases given an event reflect the fact that something is perceived in substantially different ways (cf. *GL*, p. 67). Events are repeated in "wholly different associations" (*GL*, p. 101), perhaps because the truth is originally complex. Like so much of his other writing, the form of Schleiermacher's commentary is itself open to theoretical constructions that it refuses to turn into dogma. For as he points out, what he offers his reader is an essay whose parts follow an "inartificial connexion," not a polished work the argument of which has been reduced to unity (*GL*, pp. ii–iii). He avoids an overview of Luke and provides only a part-by-part analysis of the organization of the text, thus giving his reader space to think about the implications of its polygenetic textual history for meaning and language in general. Readers are left free to conclude that some of the variations in the gospels are of merely pedantic importance. But we may also conclude that the process of variation sometimes has a bearing on the nature of meaning itself, as something unfixed both in the history and also in the future of the text.

What emerges from Schleiermacher's reading of Luke is a profound suspicion of closure, whether representational or phenomenological, whether in or behind the text. The archeological form of his inquiry, which in this case traces the historical rather than psychological emergence of the text, does not lead back to a single source, but rather to the experience by which the collective mind tries to understand and reconstruct that absent origin. At the origin of the Bible is an oral tradition inhabited by relativity rather than governed by inspiration. Closer to us are the first eyewitness narrators and their auditors who committed to writing their special but discrete insights (*GL*, pp. 12–13). Closer still there are the compilers who collected these sources and created texts that only seem more encyclopedic than the original detached narratives, but in fact avoid the use of writing to confer on themselves the canonical status we associate with the Bible. The compilations, of which the synoptic gospels are simply larger versions, do not offer themselves as "regular book[s] with a beginning and conclusion," and their "public authority" derives precisely from the fact that they are not "closed" to additions and revisions (*GL*, p. 15). Like Plato's dialogue form, they are written attempts to recapture the flux of the oral tradition, and thus the process of thought and inquiry. In moving back toward them, we are moving beneath the text to the discourse that subtends it. The role of the interpreter thus involves a deconstructive hermeneutic. We must show that the gospels are not books but compilations; we must paradoxically disintegrate them in order to recover their openness.

The *Introductions to the Dialogues of Plato* similarly address those problems of internal discontinuity in texts and canons set aside in *The Life of Jesus*. Schleiermacher observes that Plato's writings do not fit into either of the received genres of philosophy: the fragmentary and empirical, on the one hand, or the clearly systematic, in which the parts are "regularly built up," and in which "however weak the foundations of these structures often are, and their compartments taken at random, they have still an attractive look of firmness and arrangement" (*IDP*, p. 6). Plato's texts do not form a canon, and yet they have the extensiveness of one. Ostensibly, Schleiermacher attempts to establish the unity of the Platonic oeuvre, against arguments that the texts are so many different fragments that do not add up, and against the contrary argument that their true meaning must be esoteric, "sought for in secret doctrines which he as good as not at all confided to these writings" (*IDP*, pp. 7–9). The problem of the hermeneutic circle that arises through the discrepancy between part and whole at the level of the collected texts is repeated in individual texts like the *Phaedrus* and the *Protagoras*, which are also made up of parts that have little in common, and which appear to fail as acts of conceptual representation. Refusing to go beyond the language of the text to some private meaning, Schleiermacher also refuses to ignore the problem of texts that do not fit into the canon, as he does in *The Life of Jesus*. He is thus faced with the dilemma that the unity of these texts cannot be sought outside them and yet is not clearly given within them.

The radical nature of Schleiermacher's solution may not be apparent because he continues to speak of the Platonic oeuvre as though it possesses a conventional unity, and reverts to a metaphor that he had earlier criticized, that of the building systematically arranged (*IDP*, p. 42). He further describes the text as a kind of macro-dialogue, a progressive universal text "comprehending every thing in it" (*IDP*, p. 19).[10] But despite these habitual formulae he does not create a center for the canon, but rather makes discontinuity a constructive principle by replacing the idea that language has a referent with the idea that the referent is the linguistic process itself. An "analytical exposition" of the dialogues, though helpful as a scaffolding, neglects the fact that in Plato "form and subject are inseparable" (*IDP*, p. 14). The eccentricities of Plato's form, moreover, prevent the reader from coming to rest in what Plato says and instead force him to "an inward and self-originated creation of the thought in view," indeed to the "spontaneous production of ideas" (*IDP*, pp. 17, 37). Among the heuristic tools Plato uses are digression, the "frequent recommencement of the investigation from another point of view," the "concealment . . . of the more important object under one more trifling," and "the dialectic play with ideas" (*IDP*, p. 37). All of these counteract the passivity induced in the reader by "long and continuous discourses" (*IDP*, p. 16), by the philosophical equivalent of history-likeness. This idea that gaps at the grammatical level are actually stimuli to the reader informs Schleiermacher's interpretation of particularly problematic dialogues. The *Phaedrus*, for instance, falls into two parts, one concerned with love and the other with rhetoric. Instead of unifying the text by making one part the appendage of the other, Schleiermacher argues that the text does not contain a meaning but catalyzes the reader into creating one: "we are driven from an outer to an inner, and as this last does itself in turn soon become an outer, we push still onwards even into the innermost soul of the whole work, which is no other than the inward spirit of those higher laws . . . [of] dialectics" (*IDP*, pp. 57–58). Thus in Platonic dialogue what is communicated is not a series of concepts denoted by the words but an activity (*IDP*, p. 17). In a neat allusion back to his critique of a hermeneutics that searches for esoteric meaning, Schleiermacher argues that there is indeed an esoteric and an exoteric meaning in Plato's work: the exoteric being "writing," and the esoteric being "immediate instruction," the dialogue of the mind with itself, not

[10]Against this formulaic insistence on the wholeness of the canon we must set Schleiermacher's concession that when he began work on Plato, "I had the same impression of incompleteness, . . . of short-coming as regards the understanding of himself and others, as I have now after the most mature acquaintance with his writings": *The Life of Schleiermacher as Unfolded in his Autobiography and Letters*, 2 vols., trans. Frederica Rowan (London: Smith, Elder, 1860), I, 301.

something outside language, but the very process of words acting upon words.

Crucial to Schleiermacher's analysis of Plato is a distinction between writing and speech that parallels the one in the Compendium between text (*Schrift*) and discourse (*Reden*; O, p. 1). The distinction, however, is not the opposition attributed by Derrida to Rousseau, between a writing inhabited by the trace and a speech immediately linked to the voice of the soul. For while preserving a characteristically romantic contrast between the material and spiritual aspects of language, Schleiermacher reinscribes this distinction so as to associate discourse with something akin to 'difference.' The word 'akin' seems appropriate, since Schleiermacher's distinction is not thoroughgoing. Indeed, his concept of speech or discourse, like its source in Plato's *Phaedrus*, vacillates between unitary, dialectical, and dialogical concepts of language. In a passage that Schleiermacher cites, Plato seems at first to condemn writing because it places the author's words in a wider circuit of communication: "Words once written down . . . are tumbled about anywhere among those who may or may not understand them, and know not to whom they should reply, to whom not: and, if they are maltreated or abused, they have no parent to protect them; and they cannot protect or defend themselves." But as against this sense that writing makes the word an orphan by estranging it from its original meaning, Plato also seems to condemn writing because it is too single-minded: "writing is unfortunately like painting; for the creations of the painter have the attitude of life, and yet if you ask them a question they preserve a solemn silence. And the same may be said of speeches. . . . if you want to know anything and put a question to one of them, the speaker always gives one unvarying answer." At first glance it seems that oral discourse is dialectical rather than dialogical and therefore yields a meaning that is ultimately if not originally unitary. The living word of knowledge "graven in the soul of the learner" is one that can "defend itself," and that utilizes question and critique to consolidate its position.[11] Yet the notion of dialectic as a logocentric mode is itself questionable, not only in the light of Theodor Adorno's *Negative Dialectics*, which restores the link between dialectic and language elided by Hegel,[12] but also in view of the romantics' image of Socrates, which includes the Socrates of Kierkegaard as well as of Nietzsche. Of particular relevance to the idea that dialectic may result not in the defense of an initial proposition but in the development of its further ramifications is another passage that seems to welcome the au-

[11]Plato, *Phaedrus*, in *The Dialogues of Plato*, 5 vols., trans. Benjamin Jowett (London: Oxford University Press, 1871), I, 485.

[12]Theodor W. Adorno, *Negative Dialectics*, trans. E. B. Ashton (London: Routledge and Kegan Paul, 1973), p. 163.

tonomy of the author's words in the circuit of reception. The dialectician "finding a congenial soul, by the help of science sows and plants therein words which are able to help themselves and him who planted them, and are not unfruitful, but have in them a seed which others brought up in different soils render immortal."[13] The surrounding metaphors are different because they imply fertility rather than suspicion. But the underlying idea is not unlike Kierkegaard's notion that dialectical discourse harbors secrets that provoke the reader to produce and change what is said, so that it is "the same and yet not the same" (*CUP*, p. 64). Shelley will also use the image of the seed as part of a disseminative view of creation and reception, in which dissemination enhances authority. The first plant to grow from the seed is perhaps one that the writer envisages. But as that plant in turn produces a seed, and as the seed is transplanted to other soils, what happens in the process of reception is farther and farther removed from the paternity of the author.

Like Plato, Schleiermacher seems ambivalent abut the precise nature of that dynamism that distinguishes "oral instruction" from writing, and the exact consequences for the relationship between author and reader. At times the greater openness of dialogue to the reader seems to do no more than involve the reader who has "the figure already before him in his own mind" in filling in the gaps as planned by the author (*IDP*, p. 18). But at other times the method excites the reader to "spontaneous origination of ideas" (*IDP*, p. 43). As in the reader-response theory of Wolfgang Iser, there is a reluctance to pursue the more radical implications of a phenomenological approach and to abandon the idea of an implied author. A divinatory reading of Schleiermacher's practical criticism, however, can see him moving toward a theory in which the understanding of the 'theme' articulated by the various parts of a literary structure is increasingly inadequate and in which the reader must grasp the process out of which the text originates by recognizing writing as no more than a "remembrance" of the activity that produced the writing (*IDP*, pp. 16–17). Writing, as Ricoeur says in commenting on Plato, captures only "the 'said' of speaking" and not "the event of speaking."[14] To grasp this event the reader avoids being held captive by a merely technical reading, resists the tendency of writing to fix meaning, and goes beyond the written text to a 'work' now reconceived not as an intentional unity but as continuous labor. But this work is no longer a conception unfractured by expression: it is the very process of thinking itself and therefore of language. To recover the work the reader must deepen the "analytical exposition" of the text's parts produced through

[13]Plato, *Phaedrus*, I, 486.
[14]Ricoeur, *Hermeneutics*, p. 199.

technical reading, by the "supplementary process" of psychological reading, which "restore(s) to their natural connection those limbs, which without dissection, usually appear so very deplorably involved one with another" (*IDP*, p. 14). Interestingly, exposition (the reader's equivalent to *Schrift*) provides an anatomical clarity without which the reader would be confused. But this clarity is an artificial procedure, in grave danger of dismembering rather than remembering the body of the text. The reader must also return to that diacritical interimplication, that deplorable confusion of the parts of both text and canon, that discloses the structurality of expository structures.

This heuristic theory of reading works out hints that exist in Schleiermacher's theory as well as his practical criticism. In the last chapter we assumed that psychological reading was aimed at the recovery of an originary meaning. And indeed there is much in the *Hermeneutics* to suggest that where the technical appreciation of an achieved totality is impossible, divination discerns such a unity by understanding authors better than they understand themselves. It does so by finding a point of inception (*Anfangspunkt*), which is also the work's center in that it unlocks its *arche* and *telos*, and thus allows the reader to grasp it as a totality. Terms like 'unity' and 'inner coherence' are pervasive in Schleiermacher's writing, and by them he means something more than mere connectedness. The term 'unity' is sometimes accounted for in terms of the 'theme,' and sometimes in terms of the "writer's motivating principle" or "the work's overall subject as its motivation" (O, pp. 12–13). In any event, it conveys the sense of a phenomenology that is essentially a deferred formalism.

Yet a more careful reading of the later lectures suggests that psychological reading is also the unraveling of form. What distinguishes the psychological from the technical is precisely its tendency to disseminate rather than center meaning. Thus Schleiermacher points to a

> distinction between the indefinite, flowing thought-process and the completed thought-complex. The former, as in a river, is an unending, unfocused intermingling of one thought with another, without necessary connection. The latter, in finished discourse, has a definite goal, to which everything refers, one thought defines the other with urgency, and when the goal is reached, the series has an end. (*HK*, pp. 155–56)

Distinguishing for the first time between psychological and technical reading, he suggests that the latter attends to the finished thought complex, whereas true psychological interpretation concerns itself with the more inchoate thought process itself (*HK*, p. 157). The psychological "relates more to the rise of thought out of the wholeness of the life-moments of the individual," whereas the technical "is more a reduction to a definite mode of thinking and will to representation, out of which sequences [of thought] develop" (*HK*, p. 159). Technical reading is thus concerned with two processes, meditation and composition, by which a direction and then a formal shape are given to the thought process (*HK*, p. 161).[15] But psychological interpretation is concerned with the recovery of all those associated thoughts that are eliminated by the will-to-representation and the choices it makes. Given this description of the psychological ground behind the text, it is difficult to envision a reading that can extract a clear point of inception from what seem to be several points of inception. Nor is it clear why an awareness of subtextual and collateral thoughts (*Grundgedanken* and *Nebengedanken*) should focus rather than complicate what is being conveyed. Schleiermacher sometimes insists that the psychological and technical interpretations lead in the same direction. Yet clearly they are complementary only in a dialogical way. The technical reading is a logocentric one: it reduces the multiple to the linear (*die Reihe*). The psychological reading, by contrast, is concerned with the diacritical surplus that technical analysis cannot reveal. Its emphasis on collateral thoughts sensitizes it to what Derrida calls those "syntheses and referrals which forbid at any moment, or in any sense, that a simple element be *present* in and of itself."[16] At the psychological level thoughts are interwoven in such a way that each is constituted on the trace of other elements in the thought complex. This interconnectedness is indeed a version of what Dilthey will call *Zusammenhang* or organic coherence. But if it allows the recovery of what is most organic in discourse, it does so precisely at the cost of not reconstructing the thought process into a unity.

The "Academy Addresses of 1829" further help to clarify the revisionary direction in Schleiermacher's thinking. By 1822, when he wrote the "Draft for the Presentation of the Second Part" of the *Hermeneutics*, Schleiermacher was beginning to feel that his treatment of psychological interpretation in the 1819 Compendium was too simple. The section entitled "Technical Interpretation" did not respond to the complexities of psychological interpretation as described in the "Introduction," and it was possible that technical and psychological interpretation were not identical. Accordingly, he began to plan a more elaborate account of psychological interpretation that presumably formed the core of the lectures Lücke heard in 1832–33. In the 1822 draft he introduces a distinction between the "objective train of thought" leading to the com-

[15]Schleiermacher defines meditation as "the genetic realisation" of the thought process and composition as its "objective realisation" (*HK*, p. 161).

[16]Jacques Derrida, *Positions*, trans. Alan Bass (Chicago: University of Chicago Press, 1981), p. 26.

position of the text and the "subjective train of thought, the secondary representations" (*H*, p. 154). This distinction anticipates the division between the technical and the psychological, between *logos* and *differance*, around which reading will later be constructed. Interestingly, Schleiermacher concedes that leading and secondary representations may be "interwoven" and that it may not always be possible to establish a hierarchical relation between the two, but he is still enough of a formalist to describe such texts as "confused" (*H*, p. 155). Nevertheless, he recognizes that there are texts where the leading idea "has degenerated into secondary ideas" or has "occasioned them," or where the author has "yielded to a free train of thought" (*H*, p. 156). Surprisingly, the "Separate Exposition of the Second Part" (1826–27) does not develop these hints at a psychological interpretation distinct from the technical and seems strenuously committed to finding the unity of a text. But by 1829 an interest in the psychological emerges more strongly, tentatively decoupled now from the notion of unity. Given that in 1832 he will still see the technical and the psychological as parallel readings, it is significant that Schleiermacher here sees form as restrictive: "an interpreter who does not see correctly how the stream of thinking and composing at once crash[es] against and recoil[s] from the walls of its bed and is diverted into a course other than it would have taken by itself cannot correctly understand the internal movement of the composition" (*H*, p. 189). Apparently, language at a certain level does not express the movement of language itself, of thinking and composing. In the same vein the second address is at least partly a critique of Ast's concept of the hermeneutic circle as a way of grasping the totality of the work. Schleiermacher points out that almost every work contains secondary thoughts, "parts that cannot be fully understood in relation to the overall organization of the text" (*H*, p. 201). Although these parts have their own unity, which is not generic and formal but related to the author's "individuality" (*H*, p. 201), it is difficult to see why anything other than the fear of calling these texts aesthetically inferior would lead Schleiermacher to use the term 'unity' to describe what are really organic discrepancies in the text.

Although it is the final lectures that develop the crucial distinction between the technical and the psychological, it is thus clear that they are not the first to complicate the archeological movement of understanding. Already in the 1819 Compendium Schleiermacher concedes that the movement from text to voice may not resolve anything because this voice itself may require further interpretation (O, p. 8). Nor is he able to convince himself that meaning is fixed even at the grammatical level of a formally perfected text, for although he struggles to affirm that we can "identify the true and complete unity of a given word," he also speaks of "an infinite, indeterminate multiplicity," a "multiplicity . . . already . . . present in the unity" of each word (*H*, pp. 121–22). By 1832 the grammatical, with its elusive promise of lexical definiteness, has ceased to engage him. The new material focuses entirely on the psychological as the site of a multiplicity already present in the unity of a text's origin. That the later *Hermeneutics* contains in embryo a disseminative theory of intention is highly significant, because it might otherwise be objected that Schleiermacher's discovery that discourse is plural occurs only in relation to a certain kind of text that has no romantic equivalent. The synoptic gospels have what McGann would describe as a "polygenous" or polygenetic textual history.[17] They are transcribed and compiled by several people over an extended period of time. The dialogues conceal a similar though less radical polygeny. Plato is in some sense the compiler of Socrates' various reflections; the original author Socrates, as Kierkegaard recognized, is no more available to us than the original gospel posited by Eichhorn. This raises the question of whether the deconstruction of a simple origin is unique to manuscript cultures as opposed to print cultures, in which we do have a point of origin in the author. Or, to put it differently, to what extent are the models generated by studying manuscript cultures and the "pre-autonomous" works that Jauss finds characteristic of them irrelevant to a hermeneutics of texts produced in terms of a romantic ideology of the self?[18] Thus it is significant that in the *Hermeneutics* Schleiermacher transfers to the individual psyche the polygeny explored in connection with composite texts. This is not to say he describes a self that is polygenous because it is constructed out of various social texts. But if Schleiermacher is romantic in remaining resolutely psychological rather than social in his approach, the romantic ideology is clearly not for him an ideology of the unitary self but rather of the intersubjective self.

What emerges, then, from both Schleiermacher's theory and practice, is that understanding involves a movement to a depth that is not a ground. Sometimes this movement is described as being from *Schrift* to *Reden*. It would be wrong, however, to translate *Schrift* as 'writing' and *Reden* strictly as 'speech' rather than 'discourse.' The writing/speech dis-

[17]My discussion of polygenous and monogenous texts and of the influence of the 'romantic ideology' on the textual criticism of monogenous texts obviously draws on Jerome McGann's *Critique of Modern Textual Criticism* (Chicago: University of Chicago Press, 1983), pp. 15–49.

[18]On the role of the author in oral and manuscript cultures, see H. R. Jauss, "Theses on the Transition from the Aesthetics of Literary Works to a Theory of Aesthetic Experience," in Mario J. Valdes and Owen J. Miller, eds., *Interpretation of Narrative* (Toronto: University of Toronto Press, 1978), pp. 144–46; Gerald Bruns, *Inventions: Writing, Textuality, and Understanding in Literary History* (New Haven, Conn.: Yale University Press, 1982), pp. 44–59.

tinction is perhaps the clearest form that this distinction assumes. But from the fact that the object of both technical and psychological interpretation is described as *Reden*, and from the fact that hermeneutics is not exclusively concerned with the oral, we can infer that 'text' and 'discourse' are modalities rather than forms, ways of using and understanding language that cut across the formal distinction between the written and the oral. By 'text' it meant that which elicits grammatical understanding *of* a lexical system. By "the discourse of a text" (O, p. 1) is meant that which elicits a more profound understanding of the process behind the finished product. This process, however, is not something private. For discourse is "the mediation of shareable thought," (O, p. 2), and it is precisely its communality that constitutes it as a process, as the interchange rather than the fixing of meaning. Discourse will remain an important concept in modern hermeneutics, and its presence in Schleiermacher's work helps to suggest why Gadamer is wrong in claiming that he denies the linguisticality of understanding, as well as how this linguisticality is connected to a certain referential openness.[19] Characteristic of discourse, according to Ricoeur, is the fact that it is addressed to another person and is constituted by an exchange of questions and answers, whether implicit or explicit.[20] Discourse is thus oriented to other possibilities that enter it as collateral and subtextual thoughts. To understand the 'discourse of a text' is to grasp the dialogism that underlies even its most single-minded utterances. Moreover, there is no point at which the creative mind is not already part of the world of discourse, for even thought is essentially intersubjective and "becomes complete only through interior discourse" (O, p. 2). Or more precisely, there may be an originally monologic stage of thought, but it is of no importance: "original thoughts" remain unfulfilled until they have been transformed into discourse (O, p. 2).

Paradoxically, then, it is the view that has seemed to set the romantics apart from the present—the view that understanding is the recovery of a discourse/speech behind writing—that constitutes what is particularly modern in their contribution to hermeneutics. The romantic period has long been recognized as favoring speech and such written forms as approach it. But this 'speech' is itself a complex concept, partially at odds with the naive logocentrism attributed to Rousseau by Derrida. The

[19]See Gadamer, "The Problem of Language in Schleiermacher's Hermeneutic," in Robert W. Funk, ed., *Schleiermacher as Contemporary* (New York: Herder and Herder, 1970), pp. 68–84. James Edie points out that Gadamer's concept of linguisticality is limited by being somewhat structuralist and thus refusing the title of language to anything not "independent of the subjective intending of consciousness." Given a different view of language, a phenomenological view for example, the psychological and the linguistic are not incompatible (pp. 89–91, 93).

[20]*Hermeneutics*, pp. 197–99, 145–46.

problem is complicated by the fact that the association of voice with a self-identical meaning is something we do indeed find in much romantic literature. But at the same time speech is often conceived as force rather than form, as inherently shifting. Humboldt, for instance, defines language as *energeia* rather than *ergon*, and as an "eternally productive medium." Though he dismisses writing as "an incomplete, mummified preservation" and sees speech as closer to life and breath, it would be wrong to see the opposition he constructs as essentialist or idealist. For the fundamental characteristic of speech is variability or difference. Language itself develops rather than translates thought, and what it communicates is developed further by the listener.[21] The consequence of Humboldt's refusal to abstract thought from the intersubjective activity of language is a concept of speech as disseminative that is close to what Derrida chooses to associate with writing.[22] At the same time it is significant that it is speech and not writing that Humboldt and Schleiermacher place at the site of difference, for if the romantics anticipate modern theory, they do so in their own way. They preserve the opposition between speech/discourse as organic and text as mechanical while subverting its implications. In other words, by preserving the terms of the opposition Derrida attributes to them but resituating within it the attributes of identity and difference, they compel the historian looking for romantic counterparts of modern theory to reconceive the very nature of 'difference' itself. As an element now associated with speech, or with the discourse of the text, genuine difference no longer has to involve a distance from origins and a corresponding loss of contact with truth and meaningfulness. Difference is refigured as actually closer to life and therefore to truth.

Schleiermacher is often identified with Dilthey because of the latter's pioneering work as his biographer and publicist. But Dilthey has no interest in an underlying discourse of texts, as distinct from the written documents or 'life-expressions' themselves. Correspondingly, he has no interest in psychological reading as Schleiermacher envisages it.[23] Though he argues that interpretation always involves the grasping of an inner meaning, he also insists that it is wrong "to identify our knowledge

[21]Wilhelm von Humboldt, *Linguistic Variability and Intellectual Development*, trans. George Buck and Frithjof Raven (Coral Gables, Fla.: University of Miami Press, 1971), pp. 27, 34–37.

[22]At times Humboldt absorbs his perception of linguistic variability into a Hegelian teleology in which differences are part of a developing identity. But the dialogue of this Hegelianism with a disseminative theory of speech is, as it were, the 'discourse' underlying Humboldt's 'text.'

[23]It could be argued that Dilthey's aesthetics, briefly discussed in the tenth chapter, is closer to Schleiermacher than is his hermeneutics.

of this inner side . . . with psychology."[24] The inner form is for him the "mental structure" or thought complex rather than the more inchoate thought process that precedes it. The object of critical study is not "the processes in the poet's mind but . . . a structure created by these processes yet separable from them."[25] In other words, Dilthey is not interested in the psychological as something distinct from the technical. By contrast, it is Schleiermacher's interest in the psychological that is responsible for much of what is radical in his approach. Where Dilthey abandons a psychological in favor of a technical hermeneutics because the former does not yield a 'truth,' the later Schleiermacher is interested in the psychological for precisely that reason.

With Dilthey and Droysen there begins a tradition in philosophic hermeneutics that is structuralist rather than (de)constructive, conservative rather than sceptical. Insofar as he is not interested in structures abstracted from life, Dilthey is a structural hermeneuticist rather than a pure structuralist. But he anticipates structuralism in his deemphasis on the individual, who is "only the crossing-point for the cultural systems and organisations into which his existence is woven." And he also anticipates it in assuming that the resulting interstructure is systematic, even going so far as to use a linguistic model in comparing its logic to that of syntax and grammar.[26] If Dilthey parts company with the Hegelian and metaphysical tradition in ways that bring him closer to Schleiermacher, he also parts company with the latter in ways that mark Schleiermacher as fundamentally romantic. Unlike Hegel, Dilthey questions the possibility of metaphysics and argues in a historicist variation on Kant that we can know the categories that the mind uses to structure life but cannot know what is behind life itself.[27] Though he does not dismantle metaphysics as a form of desire,[28] he abandons the claim to find a transcendental signified behind the interconnections constructed by the mind. This rejection of a transcendental ground may seem to ally him with Schleiermacher's emphasis on the linguisticality of understanding. But language (or rather semiotics, since Dilthey does not confine himself to

[24]Wilhelm Dilthey, *Pattern and Meaning in History: Thoughts on History and Society*, ed. and trans. H. P. Rickman (New York: Harper and Row, 1961), p. 69.

[25]*The Essence of Philosophy*, trans. Stephen Emery and William Emery (Chapel Hill: University of North Carolina Press, 1954), p. 34; *Pattern and Meaning*, p. 70.

[26]*Pattern and Meaning*, pp. 93, 168.

[27]See Theodore Plantinga, *Historical Understanding in the Thought of Wilhelm Dilthey* (Toronto: University of Toronto Press, 1980), p. 80. See also Dilthey, *Pattern and Meaning*, p. 125.

[28]Wilhelm Dilthey, *Dilthey's Philosophy of Existence: Introduction to Weltanschauungslehre*, trans. William Kluback and Martin Weinbaum (New York: Bookman Associates, 1957), pp. 39–40, 73.

written or spoken language) is not for him what it is for Schleiermacher. Dilthey's is a structuralist and not a philological hermeneutics. He concentrates on larger unifying structures and does not engage in the close analysis characteristic of Schleiermacher's reading of Luke, which reveals slippages and discontinuities not perceptible in an overview. It may seem unusual to link Schleiermacher's sensitivity to textual difference with his interest in philology, given the way the discipline was practiced by precursors like Ernesti. But Schleiermacher's philology is often closer to Neitzsche's description of it as *ephexis* than it is to any traditional philology. As important, Schleiermacher, unlike Dilthey, shares in the post-Kantianism of the romantics: though he questions the idea of a transcendental signified, understanding is for him a process of recognition, and not simply of cognition or knowing how we know.

What has emerged is that Schleiermacher's major tools, philology and psychology, produce results radically at odds with the promise they hold out, while nevertheless constituting this process of autodeconstruction as foundational. In this respect they are aspects of that larger 'archeological' impulse in his work that distinguishes him from Kierkegaard. Obviously, given his conception of psychological reading, Schleiermacher's hermeneutic is not archeological in any literal sense. Nevertheless, if the term 'archeological' is metaphoric, the metaphor is constitutive and not just fictional. Its presence in Schleiermacher's writing as a containing form for the work as a whole reconstitutes the failure to find a ground as itself a ground from which interpretation can begin and makes Schleiermacher's hermeneutic very different from Kierkegaard's theory of reading. For Schleiermacher, the dissemination of meaning is a function of writing and thinking and not just of the belatedness of reading. That means that readers, in discovering the secrets harbored by the 'truth' they recover, are not just making contact with their own limitations but with something intended by the author. Their reading, in turn, even as it fails to recover a single truth behind the text, does in some way unveil the text and invest itself with a certain authority. But it is not an authority that precludes further reading, since what is uncovered is the process and not the meaning of the text.

PART II

A. *Reading, Culture, History*

CHAPTER FOUR

The (Un)Persuaded Reader: Coleridge's Conversation with Hermeneutics

Coleridge seems the most appropriate figure with whom to begin our examination of specific texts because of his familiarity with developments in German hermeneutics and with their consequences for literary authority. But it is not my intention to survey his writings on the Bible, not only because that task has been undertaken by others,[1] but also for strategic reasons. With occasional exceptions, critics have assumed that to look at Coleridge's poems in the framework of his biblical hermeneutics is to grant the latter the status of metastatement. The distinction between the biblical writings and the texts has not only kept religion outside psychology but has also, by analogy, located the aesthetic and philosophical writings on one side of a protective boundary that Coleridge crosses in *Biographia Literaria*, where his prelude to a religion of the imagination is produced inside the story of his life. To preface an analysis of the conversation poems by a discussion of the *Biographia* is thus to look at them through a theory that has become the scene of its own reading. Rather than keeping theory and text hierarchically separate, I shall suggest that in both the *Biographia* considered as textualized theory and in the conversation poems hermeneutic authority emerges as problematic. And in both cases the source of this uneasiness is the difficulty of translating a traditional hermeneutic protected by its association

[1]Elinor Shaffer, *'Kubla Khan' and The Fall of Jerusalem: The Mythological School in Biblical Criticism and Secular Literature, 1770–1880* (Cambridge: Cambridge University Press, 1975); A. J. Harding, *Coleridge and the Inspired Word* (Montreal and Kingston: McGill-Queens University Press, 1985); Jean-Pierre Mileur, *Vision and Revision: Coleridge's Art of Immanence* (Berkeley: University of California Press, 1982).

with the Bible into a secular context whose psychological and social complexities are harder to ignore.

Theory as Text: Scriptural and Secular Hermeneutics

The biblical writings do nevertheless provide a context for the hermeneutic desires of the *Biographia*. Coleridge had read extensively in the controversy over the discrepancies between and within the gospels on such questions as the circumstances of Jesus' birth and the events after the crucifixion. For Schleiermacher, whose essay on Luke he found too radical,[2] it was possible that the gospels could not be made identical with themselves: that there was a blend of fact and fiction, not as a result of later corruptions, but in the apostolic accounts themselves. Seeking a compromise between a view that believed in the literal truth of the Bible and one that eventually (in the work of D. F. Strauss) reduced it to myth, Coleridge distinguished in *Confessions of an Inquiring Spirit* between a doctrine of "revelation" that made the text infallible and a doctrine of "inspiration." The Bible was historically and not just metaphorically true, but at the level of the spirit rather than the letter. Discrepancies between the "letter" and the "word" were to be reconciled in terms of the spirit of the work, in effect through the psychological reading of a traditional hermeneutics that did not bind the work to accidental disfigurations at the grammatical level. As A. J. Harding explains it, Coleridge believed the reading of the Bible to be an act of commitment on the part of the reader to understanding the gospels as approximations constructed by human beings who were doing the best that they could.[3] Transferring this relatively undialectical view of the reader's role to the understanding of secular scripture, Coleridge in the *Biographia*, *The Friend*, and "To William Wordsworth" asks us to treat writers as sources of inspiration if not of revelation, and thus to credit them with an authority to which the reader must remain sympathetically subordinate.

But whether this balance between a hermeneutics of faith and a hermeneutics of suspicion can be simply maintained is open to question. It is important for Coleridge that the Bible be given the sociohistorical body that it loses if it is seen as myth: "Christianity must have its history—a history of itself, and likewise the history of its introduction, its spread, and its outward becoming."[4] The texts of Wordsworth and Coleridge

[2]Harding, *Coleridge*, p. 84; see also Coleridge's comments in MS Notebook HM 17299 (p. 51) in the Huntington Library.

[3]*Coleridge*, pp. 8–10, 58–59, 91.

[4]Coleridge, *Confessions of an Inquiring Spirit*, ed. H. St. J. Hart (Stanford, Calif.: Stanford University Press, 1967), p. 40.

create such a history for the romantic vision by placing it (as *Prometheus Unbound* does not) in a circle of real people and actual places such as Tintern and Nether Stowey. But as we shall see, such localization also marks the texts as ideological: they emerge as part of an insular tradition running from Nether Stowey to Howard's End and Little Gidding. Coleridge also assumes that to read sympathetically is to grasp the author as an unconditional unity. Yet long before Nietzsche, the Humean and associationist psychology about which he is so anxious in the *Biographia* had made it possible to conceive of the "subject as multiplicity."[5] It is the differing impulses that go to make up the creating subject which result in texts that do not quite cohere, mixtures of fact and fiction in which the figurative elements are unsettled by the possibilities they trope or efface. To read these slippages sympathetically does not mean obliterating them, as Coleridge supposed. His theory of reading, in other words, emerges at precisely the threshold inhabited by traditional hermeneutics: by introducing considerations of history and psychology for reasons that have to do with organicism rather than philology, he compromises the very authority he is trying to protect.

That Coleridge had difficulty preserving the 'inspired' text from interpersonal difference is nowhere more evident than in his often critical relationship with Wordsworth. But it is significant for his desire to repress disbelief that his approach to reading literary texts is modeled on an approach to reading the Bible rather than the reverse. One of the figures crucial to this analogy between sacred and secular is that of reading as conversion, with its accompanying distrust both of a selfhood that must be overwhelmed by 'truth,' and of a truth that needs to short-circuit rational persuasion. In *Biographia Literaria* Coleridge represents his shift from Hartley to post-Kantian idealism as a conversion (I,134) and frames his theory of imagination with a letter that asks readers to approach the text as if they were in a ruined church. In the conversation poems the accession of a resisting self to the 'other' point of view is confirmed by a benediction that marks its similarity to religious conversion. Steven Knapp has described the role of conversion in Coleridge's conception of the relationship between individual and corporate truth. Viewing the empirical self as grounded in error, Coleridge saw it as necessary to efface himself before a larger collective belief. When the self reasserted itself, he attributed this obstinacy to "a certain obscurity in the relation of the personal will to the suprapersonal reason."[6] Conver-

[5] *The Will to Power*, trans. Walter Kaufmann and R. J. Hollingdale (New York: Vintage Books, 1968), III:490.

[6] *Personification and the Sublime: Milton to Coleridge* (Cambridge, Mass.: Harvard University Press, 1985), p. 46.

sion is a response to this errancy: a submissive act that perilously wrests a positive hermeneutic from an act of self-negation. But the figure of understanding as conversion, even as it marginalizes interpersonal difference as errancy, also reinstalls a resistance in the self that must be overwhelmed. At times it becomes difficult to sublimate the violence of conversion, as in Coleridge's uneasy comparison of Wordsworth to a conqueror who must have "triumphal wreaths/Strew'd before thy advancing!" ("To William Wordsworth," ll. 81–82, *STC*).

Coleridge's anxiety about the traditional hermeneutic he promotes is evident in different ways in the *Biographia Literaria*. Coleridge's critical Prelude is best approached as what Friedrich Schlegel described as 'symphilosophy': a combination of philosophy and literature in which the text includes an account of its own genesis and a reflection upon itself. Where a conventional text might separate these elements into preface, text, and notes, *Biographia* interweaves them so as to place metastatement within a self-reflexive structure. The *Biographia* is not just Coleridge's theory of imagination but a theory of how to read that theory. We approach it in three ways: referentially for what it says, hermeneutically for the elements that lead us to reconstruct what it has not quite succeeded in saying, and reflexively because of the way the hermeneutic elements complicate themselves.[7] At its center is the theory of imagination as a synthesizing faculty that creates unity out of multeity so as to bring about the self-construction of the subject in a personal version of the Eternal Sum or I Am. As the guarantor of poetic identity, imagination is also the antidote for an associationism that seems the equivalent in psychology to poststructuralism in semiotics. Coleridge, of course, gives us only a representation of his 'theory,' in two paragraphs that barely conceal an aporia.[8] The odd mixture of autobiographical narrative with the plagiarized theses from Schelling that provide the philosophical underpinning for the theory is supposed to fuse philosophy and life but

[7]Kathleen Wheeler's *Sources, Processes and Methods in Coleridge's Biographia Literaria* (Cambridge: Cambridge University Press, 1980) is an example of the second kind of reading: one that is hermeneutic but not reflexively so. Treating *BL* as process rather than product, she performs a psychological or inward reading and sees philosophic discussions of such matters as the subject-object relationship as signals to us to perform such a reading (pp. 86, 98). According to Wheeler, "Coleridge's comments throughout his writings on depth versus surface and inwardness versus outwardness, are emblematic of the problem of reading the *Biographia*. The *Biographia* is perceived as surface only, by those whose imaginations remain inactive. Its inwardness and life are hidden from the inactive mind as the inwardness and depth of the 'material' world remain outwardness and surface to the unreflective" (pp. 89–90). Wheeler's traditionally hermeneutic reading, in which the reader must "restore or supply [links] in order to reconstruct the winding staircase" (p. 99) stands in contrast to Jerome Christensen's chapters on *BL* in *Coleridge's Blessed Machine of Language* (Ithaca, N.Y.: Cornell University Press, 1981).

[8]I refer to a tension between monism and dualism that surfaces in the description of imagination. On the one hand, Coleridge sees poetic and divine creation as analogous,

marks the theory as existing in the gap between assertion and experience. Because of the liminal character of this theory, we move to a hermeneutic reading in which we must understand the author better than he understood himself. The autobiographical setting now becomes crucial, inscribing theory and philosophy in life, so as to convince us of their necessity. Coleridge's narrative has the form of romance and thus of wish fulfilment: there are 'bad' characters like Hartley, Hume, and Descartes who divide the self from itself and its world, and there are 'good' characters like Kant and his successors. There is a period of intellectual errancy followed by a desired return to the hiding places of power. The confessional nature of the text excuses the fact that it does not quite cohere as an act of logical or narrative representation. For the grounds on which it seeks to persuade us are affective, logic being no more than a gesture made in the voluminous philosophical apparatus. The *Biographia*, moreover, is a conversion narrative. Conversion often occurs in advance of persuasion, its very force being a sign that the position embraced is still external, a mask that the convert has not quite learned to make into a face. On a hermeneutic level, then, the narrative asks us to take it on faith, to recognize but bracket the intentional structure of all conversions, Coleridge's and ours.

The hermeneutic structure of the *Biographia* is highly complex, falling as it does into two parts. In the first part, which reaches its climax in the letter from the 'friend' who tells Coleridge not to publish his treatise for lack of the right audience, Coleridge is in the position of the author seeking for sympathetic readers. Many of the apparent digressions serve a strategic function in this search. Accounts of his own literary errors and his misguided liking for the poetry of Bowles represent Coleridge as still growing, a chrysalis that may not yet have become a butterfly, to use his own image (*BL*, I,57). They also help to establish notions of literary historical development and to place Coleridge's thought within the grand march of intellect. 'Symbolic' in Hegel's sense, his work is one whose 'Idea' has not yet been sufficiently clarified to achieve adequate embodiment and must be found in unassimilated portions of the text. At the same time a number of chapters describe the difficulty that writers from Plato to Southey have faced in finding appropriate readers, and they thus make us responsible for dealing with the apparent disjunctiveness and difficulty of the text (see *BL*, I,161). Perhaps the most interesting of the many comments on reading comes in an account of Kant

---

such that the imaginative and objective worlds must be consubstantial. On the other hand, he describes imagination as "essentially *vital*" whereas objects are "essentially fixed and dead" (*BL*, I,202). As many have noted, this uncertainty as to whether imaginative life is created by the act of perception or is found in nature runs right through Coleridge's work.

where Coleridge, confronted with the fact that Kant does not quite say what he wants him to, attributes to the author an esoteric meaning that the reader must grasp by piercing through the "symbolic husk" (*BL*, I,100).

In the second half of the *Biographia* Coleridge attempts just such a divinatory reading of Wordsworth's *Lyrical Ballads*. Claiming to understand Wordsworth better than he understood himself, he purges the poems of those flaws that divert them from their 'true' project of making the real ideal. The two parts of the *Biographia* can be treated as complementary so that the text, as a theory and an enactment of reading, reaffirms the commitment in Coleridge's biblical hermeneutics to a unitary interpretation achieved through sympathy and divination. But the very conflation of 'sympathy' and 'divination' is unsettling. If we are really concerned to read the author sympathetically, should we be reading Kant against the grain and finding in the scepticism he does articulate an idealism to which he does not give voice? And if such reading is legitimate, is Coleridge not giving the reader a mandate to differ from the author at odds with any simple concept of sympathy? The text raises such problems because of the asymmetrical relationship between its parts, in which Coleridge occupies first the position of author and then of reader, so that authority is displaced with the interchanging of the two positions and the blurring of the boundary between them. To put it differently, the contradiction between the reader Coleridge constructs in the first part and the reader he becomes in the second makes it clear that concepts of reading in the *Biographia* are by no means settled.

The asymmetry between the two parts provides a context in which we can consider the asymmetry between individual readings and scenes of reading within the *Biographia*. Foremost among these is the letter from the friend, which defers to the future hopes for the right audience and which sketches in the friend a reader prepared to receive Coleridge's theory sympathetically despite its obscurities and despite the friend's own interpretive inadequacies. This section has the status of a model, although generated around an absent text and cast in the provisional and intertextual form of a letter. If its positive hermeneutic is relatively simple, we must remember that the friend does not have to provide any specific interpretations because the text itself is conveniently fictitious. Against this self-fictionalizing model we must set its implementation in specific readings that disclose the complexities of the relationship between author and reader. Viewing Kant in the light of the post-Kantians, Coleridge argues that he is more complex than he seems: that he cannot have simply thought of the thing-in-itself as unknowable, and that the categories cannot simply be mental constructs but must correspond to an external world consubstantial with the mind. "In spite therefore of his own declarations, I could never believe, that it was possible for him to have meant no more by his *Noumenon*, or THING IN ITSELF, than his mere words express; or that in his own conception he confined the whole *plastic* power to the forms of the intellect, leaving for the external cause, for the *materiale* of our sensations, a matter without form" (*BL*, I,100). This is a very 'romantic' reading concerned with what Godwin calls the 'tendencies' of a text as they emerge at a later stage in the intellectual history to which they have contributed. But if it were not so idealistic, we might also describe it as a deconstruction in which Coleridge reads Kant against the grain. The question it raises for us is whether there is a form of deconstruction compatible with sympathy, and whether psychological reading (which is clearly what is meant by piercing beyond the "symbolic husk") cannot on occasion go beyond the author's self-representation.

The reading of Wordsworth raises different problems, though it similarly entangles positive elaboration with negation. Coleridge represents himself as Wordsworth's interpreter and 'protects' Wordsworth from his critics and his own flaws by wishing away a small number of offending lines in the *Lyrical Ballads*. Rescuing the butterfly from the chrysalis, he performs for Wordsworth the kind of reading he desires from us. Yet it is also clear that this is a culturally marked reading. Its simplification of Wordsworth begins with Coleridge's decision to see the former's "matter-of-factness" as an aesthetic flaw and thus to dispossess *Lyrical Ballads* of its political radicalism. Much of the analysis centers on Wordsworth's failure to observe a distinction between poetry and prose that would keep poetry in the realm of the timeless and universal (*BL*, II,33,36–43). Amalgamating disjunctively the prosaic and the poetic, realism and idealization, Wordsworth's texts violate Coleridge's canons of an organic unity reflected in stylistic seamlessness. Though Coleridge concedes that a poem may not consist purely of 'poetry' (*BL*, II,11), he protects the poetry in the text by short-circuiting the grammatical reading of what the poem actually says in favor of a psychological reading of what it meant to say. Again, this is a very romantic reading, but the paradox is that it is curiously unsympathetic to Wordsworth. A typical comment is the one on "The Idiot Boy": "the author has not, in the poem itself, taken sufficient care to preclude from the reader's fancy the disgusting images of *ordinary morbid idiocy*, which yet it was by no means his intention to represent. He has even by the 'burr, burr, burr,' uncounteracted by any preceding description of the boy's beauty, assisted in recalling them" (*BL*, II,35). In assuming that Wordsworth wanted to idealize the boy, Coleridge ignores the possibility that he might also have wanted to question a 'poetic' discourse that buries the disruptiveness of idiocy in the myth of a common humanity. Stylistic seamlessness would have naturalized the romanticization of the idiot boy, where Wordsworth's habit of mixing up the literal and the poetic defamiliarizes his own sentimentalism.

Yet it would be all too easy to substitute for Coleridge's middle-class elision of socially subversive elements in Wordsworth's diction a reading of the poems that makes them politically correct in today's terms. Whether Wordsworth's interest in the language of the common people is 'romantic' or 'radical' is as unclear as whether the interest in marginal cultures and other worlds begun by Herder and the Humboldts involves a concern for unity or for diversity. Perhaps Coleridge is right to the extent that Wordsworth did share his desire to homogenize the issue of class but displaced the idea of a transcultural culture from the middle class to the 'people.' Perhaps in misreading *Lyrical Ballads* he nevertheless locates in that displacement an uneasiness in Wordsworth's attitude to the 'people' that makes it difficult for us to correct the misreading without creating another one in the process. What is clear is that the discussion of Wordsworth raises a plethora of issues about the differences between reader and author, about their legitimacy, and about their relationship to differences within the text. The importance of the *Biographia* lies not so much in anything it says about reading as in the spaces within and between its readings and in the asymmetry between its theory and practice. If the interpretation of Kant allows reading to open up an ambiguity within the text, the interpretation of Wordsworth cautions us that the way we specify that ambiguity may have to be situated culturally. If the first part assumes that the author can construct the reader, the second part discovers that the text may be the ground of differences between them.

Text as Theory: The Conversation Poems

As my focus on the discussion of Wordsworth suggests, the pressures that led to the unraveling of a traditional hermeneutic are not only vertical and historical ones but also horizontal ones caused by social and cultural differences between people. In the chapters that follow I am therefore concerned not simply with the supplement of reading but also with the beliefs enabled and complicated by it: with what Jerome McGann calls "the romantic ideology."[9] Bearing in mind Hegel's distinction between 'theme' and 'execution,' we can isolate in most of Coleridge's texts a thematic nexus that affirms (at least as desire) a providential economy in experience. To persuade both himself and his readers of this ideology is the project of these texts. But their execution is extraor-

[9]*The Romantic Ideology* (Chicago: University of Chicago Press, 1983).

dinarily complex because Coleridge uses hermeneutic forms like the conversation poem, the gloss, the fragment, and the miscellany. Eliciting the cooperation of the reader, these forms are not simply the medium for a message but place ideology, however reluctantly, in the space of interpretation.

At first these texts seem to contain a hermeneutic code that asks us to approach them in terms of the traditional models outlined previously. Such models underlie many of the readings that in our own time have left the romantic ideology unquestioned. But the 'hermeneutic form' of Coleridge's texts is paradoxically responsible for a dialogizing of their values. The *Biographia* again provides an example. It is just as possible to read the relationship between the two parts reflexively as confirmatively. At a thematic level the text is obviously committed to many of the concerns of high romanticism: to the idea of a consubstantiality between the internal and external worlds, to the notion that one's thoughts and also the events of one's life form an organic unity, and to the idea that imagination is the faculty that makes such unity possible. At a metathematic level its disjunctive form combined with its addresses to a reader ask us to let reading confer identity on an ideology that exists only as an intentional structure. But cutting across our desire to make the thematic and metathematic aspects of the text continuous is the reversal of Coleridge's role from author to reader in the second part. Having first assumed the position of an author who needs the right reader to complete his project, Coleridge then becomes a reader in search of the appropriate author to embody his intentions. This double deferral calls into question the status of the *Biographia*'s theme in the text's economy of supplements. If the first part sketches the author's need for a prophetic reader, the second part introduces precisely that reader and raises the question of whether the 'author' is not a construction of the reader. The text's ideology is withdrawn from 'Coleridge' and reinvested in 'Wordsworth.' But this imaginary Wordsworth is uneasily different from the Wordsworth of the *Lyrical Ballads*, and that difference reinscribes the Coleridgean project of imagination in a space no longer defined by Coleridge alone. Composed out of what Coleridge dismissed as a "multitude of small poems"[10] spoken from different perspectives, the collection resists the uniformity of the philosophic poem, which "struggles to idealize and to unify" (*BL*, I,202). As we shall suggest in the next chapter, it situates in a social text that universalizing imagination that Coleridge wanted to see as transcending cultural distinctions. Because of the metathematic structure of the *Biographia* as a continuous transfer of

[10]Quoted in Jared Curtis, *Wordsworth's Experiments with Tradition, The Lyric Poems of 1802, with Texts of the Poems Based on Early Manuscripts* (Ithaca, N.Y.: Cornell University Press, 1971). See Curtis's discussion, pp. 6–13.

authority between author and reader, Coleridge's reading of Wordsworth so as to project through him an identity for himself must in turn be read by the *Lyrical Ballads*: that text which once invited him to be its coauthor but now allows him to enter it only as a reader. What happens in the intricate arrangement of the *Biographia* is thus a constant displacement of ideology by its shifting hermeneutic inscription. As constructed by the author, the ideology is troubled by the possible absence of receptive readers. As constructed by the reader, it comes up against its own failure to find an author, to become one with the texts in which it is invested. Nor are the metathematic complexities of the *Biographia* confined to its second part. If Coleridge's attempt to read his identity into Wordsworth meets certain cultural resistances, his attempt to find it in Kant meets similar philosophical resistances.

The next two chapters focus on the conversation poems and the *Lyrical Ballads* as modes of engagement with the romantic ideology. At first the two seem radically different. Where conversation, paradoxically, strives towards a universalized monologue, Wordsworth's ballads assembled in a heteroglossic collection submit an idealizing hermeneutic and the credo it protects to intercultural reading. Nevertheless, the conversation poems are by no means culturally unspecific. Writing for a pastoral circle to which as a city dweller he does not quite belong, 'Coleridge' constructs for himself an identity that is other than his own and sets himself uneasily at odds with his own desire. We can see the poems as paradigms for the way a traditional hermeneutic, when pushed to explore its own interior distances, opens into a kind of dialogical self-reading. The compatibility between dialogism and hermeneutics stems from the latter's antiformalist interest in contextualizing literary works in their life situations, both biographical and intellectual. This interest in the circumstances of the text's creation is fruitfully at odds with the idealizing and transhistorical tendencies also characteristic of traditional hermeneutics. We find in the conversation poems a similar conjunction of tendencies: the desire, figured as 'conversation,' to arrive at universal truths, along with an intricacy of biographical and psychological detail that opens these truths to the subtextual and collateral thoughts they would exclude.

In approaching these poems I am guided by a sense that the romantic ideology was profoundly alien, though profoundly attractive, to Coleridge. Its specular structure is evident in the way it is almost always invested in some other person (Wordsworth or Asra) who has experienced the plenitude of nature in a way that the city-bred Coleridge has not. This alienation of ideology through its representation as mimetic desire defers its persuasiveness and allows the actual reader to stand back from it. For its displacement from self to other marks ideology as an image in the mirror not of mimesis but of speculation. Equally interesting is the way Coleridge constructs these poems as hermeneutic dramas, so as to regain our assent for the creed he has displaced. For he anticipates the doubts of a reader excluded from the visionary company of high romanticism by placing himself at the other end of the hermeneutic circuit, in the position of someone who must imaginatively grasp an experience he has not had. Many of the conversation poems unfold as acts of understanding in which 'Coleridge' does succeed in grasping this experience, and they model a decorum of reading in which we, too, must transcend our own prejudices. Nevertheless, the very emplotment of these poems as dramas of understanding marks Coleridge's uneasiness with a vision that needs to be understood, with a hermeneutic unity constituted on the trace of cultural difference.

As a genre the conversation poem is obviously meant to dramatize a traditional hermeneutic in which reception renews the authority of representation.[11] A sub-version of the loco-descriptive poem, it adds to the former's projection of a unity between mind and nature a community between author and reader figured in the address to a silent auditor. Seemingly minor and preliminary, the loco-descriptive poem with its commitment to abolishing the difference between inside and outside does nevertheless configure the larger romantic project of creating a world that objectifies desire. In their own muted way the conversation poems take this project into the social world and imagine the abolition of differences between self and other in a community of friends whose cleansed perceptions speak for the public utility of romantic pastoralism. The loco-descriptive poem has been analyzed by M. H. Abrams and Earl Wasserman, who see the first generation romantics as advancing the correspondence between mind and nature from analogy to identity, and also by de Man, who points to the uneasy survival of analogical language as a hidden articulation within the symbolic totality of the romantic project.[12] The conversation poem responds to both lines of interpretation. Committed to the vision described by Abrams, it tries to sublate the fear that its own language may place this vision under erasure, by introducing a listener whose presence reminds us of the limits of analyzing the text on a purely linguistic level. In this sense the genre is a microcosm of the theoretical tensions surveyed in this book and of the

[11]See my discussion of the role of the auditor in these poems in *Dark Interpreter: The Discourse of Romanticism* (Ithaca, N.Y.: Cornell University Press, 1980), pp. 212–31.

[12]M. H. Abrams, "Structure and Style in the Greater Romantic Lyric," in F. W. Hilles and Harold Bloom, eds., *From Sensibility to Romanticism: Essays Presented to F. A. Pottle* (New York: Oxford University Press, 1965), pp. 527–60; Earl Wasserman, "The English Romantics: The Grounds of Knowledge," *Studies in Romanticism* 4 (1964): 17–34; Paul de Man, "The Rhetoric of Temporality," *Blindness and Insight: Essays in the Rhetoric of Contemporary Criticism*, rev. ed. (Minneapolis: University of Minnesota Press, 1983), pp. 187–208.

emergent focus on the reader as a way of resisting certain pressures of derealization within texts.

Although we associate the conversation mode with Coleridge, it is Wordsworth who provides a 'naive' version of the form: a poem that elides the difference between author and implied reader, by figuring the listener as a sister. "Tintern Abbey" exposes its figurative structure only to inscribe a positive hermeneutic that makes the reader a bridge between intention and actuality. Like other poems of this genre, it begins with the absence of an experience it is trying to represent and never quite succeeds in making its visionary communion with nature descriptively concrete. At first memory seems to hypostatize this experience as existing in the past and thus to eliminate any need for a reader. But slowly we recognize that the past may itself be representation rather than origin, and that the mode of memory may be a way of figuring what is really a performative utterance as having a constative status. The shifting verb tenses in the poem are the first site of this recognition. Beginning with a particularized description of the landscape which does not yet contain the poem's inner 'meaning' (ll. 4–18, *LB*), Wordsworth shifts to a more compelling past that is definitely lost ("when like a roe/I bounded"—ll. 66ff., *LB*). "That time is past" (l. 84, *LB*) and the "elevated thoughts" (l. 96, *LB*) that now emerge as the true import of the poem are of a different order. These thoughts are located in an indefinite past ("I have learned," "I have felt") that insensibly slides into the present in a blurring of temporal and ontological boundaries. But it is not clear whether these thoughts are ones to which Wordsworth can return as to a place in his past, or whether (more unstably) they are thoughts he now has because he cannot revisit those earlier thoughts. Are these thoughts, in other words, produced by the presence of something in the past or by the absence of something in the present articulating itself as a representation of the past? "Tintern Abbey" offers itself as a spot of time. But contrary to the particularizing intention behind this subgenre, Wordsworth's experience cannot easily be located and thus given factual solidity. Associating it with a place does not explain it, since the feelings described are occasioned as much by the absence as by the presence of that place. Indeed, the return to the place seems at first to block the articulation of those feelings, which do not come back till Wordsworth imaginatively removes himself from Tintern and returns to those "lonely rooms" where absence, not presence, had generated the representation of a landscape that was more psychological than spatial (ll. 23ff., *LB*). On the other hand, the Tintern experience cannot really be located in time either. For it is unclear whether it is something that happened in the past and that Wordsworth cannot quite recapture in the poem, or whether it is something that happens in the writing of the poem and that is then attributed to the past so as to make it seem an effect of events rather than of representation.

In line with this blurring of the temporal and topographical precision promised by the title is the poem's language, which is full of abstractions or of phrases like "a *sense* sublime," "something . . . interfused" (ll. 96–97, *LB*). Two words are often used instead of one, as in "A motion and a spirit" (l. 101, *LB*). These words, moreover, lack precise physical or conceptual referents, so that the content of the poem is less semantic or cognitive than affective. But this is not to say that the poem fails to communicate an experience. For if its vagueness exposes memory as a figure, this very vagueness also redefines the process of reference so that it requires a correspondence no longer based on mimesis but rather on affect. "Tintern Abbey" succeeds more as an act of persuasion than as an act of representation, and its emergence as hermeneutic discourse is already implicit in its use of affective language. This shift from a mimetic to a hermeneutic view of truth is made explicit in the concluding turn toward Dorothy, toward a listener who must understand the poem and apply it in her own life. Moreover, by making the implied reader a younger sister, Wordsworth not only avoids representing reception as the site of difference, he also insures a continuity between past and future, in which the future is a return to the past, and in which past modes of perception are renewed rather than outmoded.

The emotional landscape of this poem is also a network of figures and deferrals in another sense. As Marjorie Levinson has argued, Tintern was a coal-mining town and thus part of the economy of the industrial revolution. As a victim of Henry VIII's dissolution of the monasteries, the ruined abbey also marked the loss of an ideal corporate community refigured by Wordsworth as a private unity with nature.[13] The effacement of both town and abbey from the text that bears their names makes Wordsworth's poem itself a reading dependent on the consent of his listener. But it is questionable whether we *can* read the poem otherwise, as long as we treat it as an autonomous lyric apart from the *Lyrical Ballads* and as long as we respond to it within the hermeneutic economy of the conversation poems. For that economy protects itself against questioning by making its readers part of an intimate circle. Placing itself in the public domain by offering itself to a reader, the conversation poem recomposes that domain as private space.

In Coleridge's poems the figures that articulate that space are uneasily defamiliarized, and in the *Lyrical Ballads* conversation itself is situated within a larger social economy. The Coleridge poems project a 'roman-

[13]*Wordsworth's Great Period Poems* (Cambridge: Cambridge University Press, 1986), pp. 14–57.

tic' vision of a world in which no sound is dissonant that tells of life. Thus in "This Lime-Tree Bower" the poet begins by feeling that nature has deserted him but ends by reversing the paradox of the title and finding a bower within his prison. The mildly dejected mood of the opening becomes a stimulus to creativity: the poet imagines the route taken by his friends from the unsunned dell to the "many-steepled tract magnificent" (l. 22, *STC*) and makes their journey an objective correlative that produces a change in his own mood. He is thus able to construct a figurative economy in which "waste" serves a purpose: absence produces the representation of presence, and being "bereft of promis'd good" becomes a blessing in disguise (ll. 64–67, *STC*). By a series of analogies between the microcosm of the friends' walk and the macrocosm of the journey through life, an occasional poem becomes the basis of an argument for design. This argument is more precisely located in a landscape than in "Tintern Abbey." But precisely because Coleridge is clearer, the way his argument bases itself on a series of metaphorical contrivances is also more evident. It is here, we might argue, that the conversation poem's positing of a reader becomes important. For clearly the poem has no depictive authority. Where "Tintern Abbey" relies on a language of affect, "This Lime-Tree Bower" is openly rhetorical in constructing its vision through tropes and claiming for itself a persuasive rather than strictly performative status.

By including an auditor, Coleridge's poems move beyond the exposure of their own figurality and inscribe what one might call the 'hermeneutic' function in the text: they ask us to project beyond the limits of the poem and to enact imagination in experience. But the inscription of reading in the text is more complex than it is in "Tintern Abbey." To begin with, there is the fact that Coleridge defers the imagining of communication by picturing the addressees of his poems as silent or absent. The child in "Frost at Midnight" is asleep; Lamb in "This Lime-Tree Bower" is somewhere else and Coleridge only 'deems' that they have seen the same rook (ll. 70–74, *STC*). As significantly, whereas Wordsworth can claim the authority of experience for his poem, Coleridge must derive a sense of providential design from another, as one does when reading about something. Beginning with the sense of an absolute barrier between himself and Lamb, who is enjoying his walk while Coleridge is inside, Coleridge tries to enter what Dilthey describes as a "quite alien individuality" through a process of reexperiencing (*nacherleben*). The situation of the poem reproduces in miniature the problem of hermeneutic distance: of understanding someone the structure of whose experience is radically different from one's own. This is likewise the problem that Wordsworth represents Coleridge as facing when he makes him the reader of *The Prelude*. Coleridge, however, models the hermeneutic process for us, not by addressing the reader as Wordsworth does in his role as author, but rather by showing us the responses of a reader within the poem. Moreover, the reader does not interpret a text that is already written, for the figure of Lamb as an original genius engaged in imaginative excursions is itself a construction of his 'reader,' who 'deems' that Lamb has had certain experiences. The reader, in other words, constructs an authority so as to figure his own activities as recuperative. Thus, where the hermeneutic function in "Tintern Abbey" enacts writing through reading, in Coleridge's conversation poems it also results in reading's becoming a form of writing.

Coleridge's poem, to put it differently, generates more than one model of reading because of the way it conflates and exchanges author and reader functions that in "Tintern Abbey" remain stable. The simplest of these models is the positive hermeneutic implicit in the conversation form, which depicts the poem as an intentional structure that assumes a sympathetic reader. As rhetoric, the poem can make its figurative construction explicit without putting itself in jeopardy. Somewhat more complex is the model, still traditionally hermeneutic, that emerges from Coleridge's depiction of himself as Lamb's sympathetic interpreter. Through a psychological reading that reconstructs Lamb's state of mind, Coleridge also reads the book of nature so as to divine a metaphysical pattern in the physical landscape. Although it is interpretation that seems the focus of the poem's narrative, this representation of the hermeneutic process authorizes interpretation by making Lamb a neo-Wordsworthian figure of excursive genius. Yet, on a third level it is also hard to forget that Coleridge is the author of the poem, a fact reinforced by the curious absence of Lamb from the material space of the text. The uneasy displacement of authority between Lamb and Coleridge, and our inability to place Coleridge as entirely reader or author, raises a further possibility: namely, that the scene may figure imagination as a form of reading and reading itself as something that occurs in the absence of a source. The extraordinary complexity of this poem stems from the fact that it is not simply a conversation poem but also a poem that thematizes reading. Thus, the first model is simply part of a horizon of expectations called up by the genre. But the poem generates further models, constructing and deconstructing the figures of a traditional hermeneutic so as to leave us with a palimpsest of possibilities.

The displacement of 'Coleridge' from author to interpreter is even more prominent in "Frost at Midnight." Correspondingly, the poem no longer outlines understanding as recovery and moves instead toward a divinatory hermeneutics perilously on the threshold between the positive and the negative. Here again, the intention of the poem as persuasive argument is greatly complicated by the fact that reading is not simply part of the poem's generic frame but also its subject. We may begin, however, by outlining what seems the poem's rhetorical form as a dialectical spiral in which the concluding image of the frost marks the last verse paragraph as an answer to the first. At the beginning the poet is cut off from his world by the coldness of the season and fluctuates restlessly between "Abstruser musings" and unfulfilled daydreams (l. 6, *STC*). At the end the emotional climate has changed, and the child inhabits a paradisal world in which all seasons are equally sweet. Where the solitary poet of the opening yearns for a companionable form, the child, curiously without human friends, has found companionship in a nature whose solitude is not vacancy. At the beginning the poet's world seems reduced to random atomistic phenomena: a film that flutters aimlessly on the grate, the frost that is credited in the word "ministry" with healing and religious powers but whose operations are "secret" (l. 1, *STC*). At the end the lakes and crags are reflected in the clouds and the outer world corresponds to the inner world of the child's feelings, in a nonhierarchical version of the great chain of being. Most importantly, the frost no longer seems alien. Its ministry reveals itself as artistry, making it a medium for the primary imagination, which organizes landscape as order. The poem, in other words, traces for us a typically romantic movement toward a landscape of the mind that no longer harbors vacant spots or existential waste. The signs that initially populated this landscape—shadows and films, surfaces and other empty signifiers—have been grounded in a transcendental source. They now reappear as a reflexiveness in the landscape—clouds imaging crags—that confirms the presence of design.

The circular closure of the poem is of course deceptive, for it is produced by an act of reading that projects metaphysical meaning into phenomena. It is thus useful to see how the poem depicts reading in image and narrative. From the beginning, Coleridge seeks in his surroundings signs of something more profound. He tries to 'interpret' the random motions of the film on the grate (l. 21, *STC*). He makes it a symbol of a companionable form, whereas it does no more than allegorize his desire. The first stanza is built around this contrast between the frost, agent of an obscure creativity, and the flame and film, which seem its nearest equivalents on this side of the looking glass. "Unhelped by any wind" (l. 2, *STC*), the frost simply is what it is: it becomes for Coleridge the symbol of a primary creative authority whose being is in no way derivative, because its essence coincides at every moment with its existence. This authority is, however, inaccessible, existing as it does on the other side of a glass. The glass may be a window into reality, or it may be a transparent barrier that allows the speaker to gaze into the imaginary, marking the specularity of the authority he constructs and yet defers by letting the frost guard its own secrets. The figure of the frost is repeated and (dis)figured on this side of the glass by the images of flame and film, which disjoin the functions combined in the frost. The flame, typically an image of creativity, is a shadow of what it originally was and needs some outside agent to fan it into activity. But the film, which becomes an image of Coleridge himself trying to construct meaning from the shadows that futurity casts upon the present (ll. 15–23, *STC*), never becomes any more than a disjoined residue of this shadow. Seeking to recapture some source that will ground its flutterings, the film randomly constructs shapes that refer to nothing outside itself. Between them, the flame and the film project not creation and its interpretation, but a somewhat desultory desire for those activities.

The first stanza thus constructs itself as a scene of reading. The scene contains not only a character engaged in 'reading' the world he sees through his window but also figures for the creative and interpretive activities, so that it both projects Coleridge's desire for understanding and reflects on the tropology of that desire. Locating itself in the convention of the *paysage moralisé*, the poem suspends that convention by using the clear surface of the glass to stall the commerce between inner and outer, interpretation and authority. The world beyond the glass is instinct with some kind of motion and spirit. But are "the numberless goings-on of life" (l. 12, *STC*) equivalent to the 'One Life' posited in "The Eolian Harp"? Or are they akin to what Kristeva calls the semiotic: that prelinguistic play of forces associated with the infant or pre-Oedipal phase? For Kristeva the semiotic is made up of unorganized rhythmic "pulsions" that survive inside language. They surface in moments of absence, silence, or meaninglessness, and they disrupt in this case both the rigidities of the symbolic order associated with urbanization and self-consciousness, and the imaginary landscape Coleridge will later construct by rewriting the world outside as the book of God. The cold world outside the window contains intimations of a higher meaning, but it is insistently sensory, a world of surfaces whose flatness may indicate the withholding of an interior or its absence. Given the setting, one could say that Coleridge's attempt to read meaning into the landscape emerges as an act of empty figuration, consumed by its own reflections, "every where/Echo or mirror seeking of itself" (ll. 21–22, *STC*). And yet the impact of the stanza exceeds its concluding image of interpretation as a space composed of echoes and reflections. For the frost is there and has a kind of presence that the flame and film lack. More than a construction of the mind (though the mind can know it only through its own constructions), the frost contains a phenomenological promise: it is real, and yet its reality may be nothing more nor less than its appearances.

From the perspective of the last stanza we can see Coleridge in this stanza beginning to read the landscape in terms of a fusion of Christian sacramentalism and romantic theories of a *natura naturans* that writes what Schelling sees as the unconscious poetry of nature.[14] This romantic metaphysic, however, is no more than an implication, and the thematization of reading neither sanctions nor disallows it. In the second stanza Coleridge again constructs a scene of reading. Remembering his past, he pictures himself inside a schoolroom, prevented from conversing with the natural world. His vision of a meeting with his soul-mate occurs through a blotting out of what he is actually reading and has an immediacy that the idle interpretations of the first stanza lack. As Coleridge recollects his youthful dreams, he adds to the first stanza two other elements that will go into shaping the romantic myth of the conclusion: that of a psychology freed from self-consciousness, and that of friendship and sympathy as forces that make nature into a human presence rather than the creation of some distant divinity. He imagines himself meeting a stranger who is also his psychic twin, moving out of the protected recesses of his own consciousness without being displaced from identity with himself (ll. 41–43, *STC*). The image of the sartorial twin, abstract and ungendered since it may be townsman or sister, uneasily crystalizes a typically romantic figure: the desire for an experience transcending the imaginary, one that is intersubjective but presocial, presymbolic. Curiously, the twin is "clothed alike," but not described in any more inward way, leaving open the possibility that s/he is clothed in the poet's own metaphors.

Coleridge stops the inner camera at the threshold of his meeting with the stranger. This cameo vision of a meeting that either transcends or never results in conversation emerges as the product of an activity very much like 'interpretation.' Once again Coleridge looks at the film on the grate and sees it as heralding the arrival of the 'stranger.' He makes the elements of his immediate surroundings into signs of something else, traces of a memory in which is stored, not an actual experience, but further traces, "Most like articulate sounds of things to come" (l. 33, *STC*). The track that Coleridge's daydream follows mimes the elusive path of a divinatory reading displaced between past and future. What the reader of signs conjures up is a futuristic vision uneasily hypostatized by being summoned up from the depths of the past and the collective unconscious. It does not yet exist, and yet its absence, by being located in the past, is given a shadowy presence as a desire that has already existed. Oddly absent and present, the imaginary meeting with its penumbra of romantic associations is constructed by Coleridge through an act of vi-

[14]*System of Transcendental Idealism*, trans. Peter Heath (Charlottesville: University Press of Virginia, 1978), pp. 230–32.

sion that obliterates the literal signs Coleridge is reading in his schoolbook, along with their links to self-consciousness, urbanization, and socialization. The reading of signs depicted here parallels the representation of divinatory reading in other texts like *Prometheus Unbound* and *Hyperion*. Such reading bypasses language: Asia reads Prometheus' written soul in Panthea's eyes, Keats replaces the Titans' inconclusive dialogue in book II with Apollo gazing into the eyes of his muse at the end, and Coleridge here puts dream in place of reading. But he also makes us aware of the negative structure of divinatory reading: its psychotropology of denial, its negation of what is in order to posit what is not. Uneasily allowing that vision may be daydream, he places visionary reading on the threshold between the positive and the negative that we have seen it inhabit in the history of hermeneutics itself.

Thus in the first two sections of the poem Coleridge shows himself trying to construct meaning and also reflects on that process. This double movement does not deconstruct reading as a way of grasping something that is true. To write a book and then to withdraw it, as Kierkegaard suggests, is not equivalent to not writing it in the first place. Nevertheless, reading does not emerge unproblematically in these stanzas. The third stanza is different, for it gives us only the vision with no reference to how it is produced. At the end it is the naive figure of the child which is in the foreground, unhelped by Coleridge, who has tactfully faded into the past. Like the frost, the child is autonomous: it is free of human entanglements and wanders "like a breeze" (l. 54, *STC*), an excursive genius in a world of correspondences. But the child has also absorbed Coleridge's function as reader: it reads the alphabet of God in the natural world. Reading, moreover, has been transformed. In striking contrast to his father, who was taught by a stern preceptor, what the child reads are not textual signs but an "eternal language" of natural signs (l. 60, *STC*). In the ideal world reading is no longer divided by its obliquities, but is linked immediately to truth.

The scene that Coleridge imagines is of course an ideal one. But because the child is an older version of the actual child who now slumbers beside him, one could accuse Coleridge of insensibly sliding from the imaginary to the real, were it not for the concluding image of the frost. This return to the frost can be seen as a progress that rounds off the poem:

> . . . whether the eave-drops fall
> Heard only in the trances of the blast,
> Or if the secret ministry of frost
> Shall hang them up in silent icicles,
> Quietly shining to the shining Moon.
>
> (ll. 70–74, *STC*)

But the grammatical and logical status of the last clause as an afterthought not quite encompassed within the convention of the four seasons, and the shift from the transparently sacramental language of the third stanza to the imagist mode of the final lines also suggest that at the end the poem may simply circle back into its own enigmatic hiding places. Imagism, with its antimetaphysical emphasis on the particular, but on one detail picked out and framed as though it must have some special significance, promises and withholds ultimate meaning. On a formal level, then, the image of the frost has a displacing effect. In addition, it once again images in problematic ways the interchange between the creative and receptive functions and the art thus produced. The frost is no longer unhelped but needs the moon in order to make visible its natural sculpture. The snapshot of the child, transcendentally free to set the terms of his own life, has been subtly replaced by this picture of something that must again be defined in terms of something else. The frost creates icicles that "quietly" shine "to the shining moon." The icicles borrow their light from the moon, but then the moon itself is not a source of light, being a reflection further reflected in the icicles. One could say that the frost creates the icicles but needs the moon to make them shine. Or one could say that the moon creates the icicles as works of art through its light, which is not its own light. The last line displaces the creative function between frost and moon but also makes creativity an effect of some absent source whose existence is posited only because effects are produced. The effects of light and temperature are strangely beautiful, but because they can be grounded in nothing, they appear and disappear. In the third stanza a world of reflections had been stabilized by being referred to a divine author(ity). Here we are back in a world where figuration occurs in the interchange between reflections: as a phenomenological event whose authority is metaphysically uncertain.

This uncertainty emerges in retrospect as the subtext of the frost's initial autonomy. To be "Unhelped by any wind" is perhaps to be unlinked to any authorizing breath of inspiration, and thus to be radically different from the child who wanders like a breeze in a world of continuities. The concluding image of the frost takes us out of that world and puts us back in a reflexiveness that makes a toy of thought. In contrast to the world of flame and films, the child's world is a world of symbolic or tautegorical language. In distinguishing the analogical or tautegorical from mere metaphor or figure, Coleridge in *Aids to Reflection* argues that in analogy, vehicle and tenor are gradations of the same power, whereas in metaphor or similitude they are linked only by arbitrary resemblance.[15] Because they are images of each other, the clouds

[15] *The Complete Works of Samuel Taylor Coleridge*, ed. W. G. T. Shedd, 7 vols. (New York, 1884), I, 235.

and lakes are neither mere images and copies nor transcendent essences abstracted from a material body. They are synecdochic fusions of the representative and semantic functions: the image and what it represents are different gradations of the same power. But the frost discloses the concavities of this symbolic landscape in which our uncertainty as to what reflects what had been troped into a source of reassurance. The clouds and lakes that image each other and thus contain the proliferation of reflections become the frost and moon, whose interchange keeps displacing the source of the light that makes it possible to see design. The signs that had become things in the sacramental landscape of the future revert to their present opacity, as natural phenomena become signs of something that the poem has not quite been able to capture. In retrospect, this interchange between frost and moon comments on the similar displacement of origin between father and child, past and future.

The last lines of "Frost at Midnight" thus defer the divinatory reading by acknowledging a certain hermeneutic opacity. But even within the section on the child, who is obviously the focus of the poem's themes, a fusion of horizons between text and reader remains suspended because of the child's abstraction from the world of human interactions. To put it differently, Coleridge, who has hitherto modeled the reader's role for us, is nowhere present in this section. His absence introduces a problem that becomes increasingly troubling in the later conversation poems: that of self-negation. For Coleridge, in order to read the book of nature correctly, must admit that his own experience has no applicative validity and must turn instead to his child. Self-negation may be too strong a word to use of "Frost at Midnight." Here we may simply be witnessing an act of negative capability in which the speaker withdraws from the poem so as to let a vision of life very different from his own speak unhindered. The fact that this vision speaks within the speech of someone who is passing on to his son a legacy he has never enjoyed introduces a note of regret into a voice that wants to be uncomplex and speak only this other, truer vision. Nevertheless, the renunciation of selfhood and thus the silencing of the dialogue so crucial to understanding is a paradox tactfully maintained. Perhaps that is because the very metaphor of silence in this poem has connotations of mystery rather than suppression. Perhaps it is because the voicing of a romantic ideology impossibly desocialized and thus protected from dialogical intrusions is taken back into the space of the figurative by the poem's concluding image.

Self-negation, however, becomes increasingly a problem in two later conversation poems: "Dejection" and "To William Wordsworth," which widen the distance between 'Coleridge' and the figure in whom authority is invested. "This Lime-Tree Bower" had accommodated the interrelationshp of identity and difference in the hermeneutic experience by constructing the figure of authority in a complex way. Because Lamb's unfortunate life (his mother's murder by an insane sister) placed him closer to the public persona of Coleridge than of Wordsworth, identification with him had not required 'Coleridge' to repudiate his own experience. The replacement of Lamb with increasingly simplified figures in the later poems reflects Coleridge's growing alienation from the Wordsworth circle. More and more, positive understanding occurs through the reader's negation of his own experience and is constituted on the trace of what it excludes. But this is not to say that the poems dismantle their own affirmations. For their status as autobiographical conversation requires that we reconstruct the situation of utterance in all its psychological complexity. It may be that Coleridge's alienation reflects an inadequacy in the Wordsworthian ideology. But 'alienation' may also be Coleridge's disguised refusal to converse with Wordsworth and to see beyond his own experiences without representing his insight as forced on him. Guilt over what he recognizes as his own closed-mindedness produces an over-idealization of authority figures that perpetuates this failure to converse, deferring conversation to the reader. The issue of what these poems say is unusually complex because their narratives of misunderstanding are set in a context of friendship and conversation. In conversation negations always have the potential of becoming contraries. The friendship of Coleridge and the Wordsworths, perhaps never a 'true' friendship because it never allowed opposition, also cannot be refigured as an opposition that brooks no reconciliation.

"Dejection," which follows the same plot of reading as "Frost at Midnight," is radically different from the latter. In quantitative terms, far more of the poem is given over to self-analysis: indeed, until the last stanza, the romantic vision is produced only negatively through a self-chastisement that intertwines it with the resistance it meets from Coleridge's own experience. That the poem was originally a verse-letter and is directed to a reader, that it concludes with a benedictory address, and that it is concerned with the role of imagination and the relationship between subjective and objective worlds are all features that mark it as a variation upon the conversation genre. In this poem, too, a romantic ideology in which the poet wishes to believe is placed in the framework of understanding between decisively separate people: Coleridge and Sara Hutchinson. The poem's desires are most clearly voiced in the last stanza, where images of circulation and eddying associate Sara with a vision of the One Life in which everything that lives is holy. But nothing in this stanza describes Coleridge's own experience of unmitigated depression. At first he argues like Wordsworth in the "Intimations Ode" that the capacity for joy is one that nature gave him at his birth and that has been damaged by experiences left deliberately vague so as to deny them any authority (ll. 76–86, *STC*). But as the curious image of hope as a vine suggests, a positive outlook on life may already have been something that Coleridge felt he ought to feel:

> For hope grew round me, like the twining vine,
> And fruits, and foliage, not my own, seemed mine.
> (ll. 80–81, *STC*)

Locating the romantic ideology of joy in the Wordsworth circle and then in Sara alone, Coleridge cannot finally depict it and must reappropriate it through an act of understanding in which he transcends his own 'prejudices.' What the poem enacts is not so much its credo as the hermeneutic necessary to grasp that credo, and the possibility of understanding despite conditions in one's life that resist it.

This account, however, describes only what the speaker intends to do. Throughout the poem the figures used to sustain the romantic economy have kept producing a darker side, thus suggesting a pattern in which figures of thought always disable themselves. In "This Lime-Tree Bower" an analogy between outer and inner worlds had been used to make a landscape that harmoniously combined dark and light yield a similar pattern in the poet's experience. Here it is precisely this analogy that is the source of the poet's dejection, as a change in the weather produces a disintegration of Coleridge's hopes. The collapse of figures of reciprocity and correspondence leads Coleridge to substitute for them the figure of endowment, arguing that "we receive but what we give (l.47, *STC*). Yet projection, too, has its darker side, as is evident in the penultimate stanza, where the poet hysterically acts out a pathetic fallacy in which he turns the wind into a mad lutanist. The benedictory conclusion once again uses the figure of endowment, as Coleridge gives joy to Sara in order to receive it back, hoping to generate from an act of projection the reciprocity whose absence has made that act necessary. Yet unlike "This Lime-Tree Bower" where the conclusion, however fictive, grows out of the poem's figurative logic, the "simple" (l. 137, *STC*) affirmation of joy in the last stanza defies that logic, which had suggested that figures of thought are not simple and tend to undo themselves. To put it differently, the conclusion necessarily participates in the psychotropology that governs the rest of the poem. The poem's stanzas are structured as a chain of substitutions in which the collapse of one figure leads to the construction of another. The conclusion, too, is part of this chain, a fact that qualifies its status as resolution.

The poem concludes by figuring understanding as an act of generosity that is able to set the self aside and give itself to the thoughts of another. The achievement of this understanding gives authority to the poem's final assertion and provides a model of reading for the actual reader. But this 'understanding' occurs in the context of an estrangement between Coleridge and Sara that makes it disturbingly one-sided. It requires, moreover, that Coleridge deny the role of his own experiences in furthering 'conversation,' thus bringing to a crisis the self-rejection that has pervaded the poem. At the same time this rejection is unsettled by our desire to sympathize with the speaker of the poem. It is not simply that the biographical subtext displaces the actual reader from the position assumed by 'Coleridge' in the hermeneutic plot. It is also that the relation of Coleridge to the authority he constructs is reversed by our relation as readers to Coleridge as author of the poems. Obliged by the poet's authority to concur in his idealization of Sara, we are also compelled by that authority to sympathize with Coleridge and to read the margins of his self-effacement.

This undoing of the hermeneutic model is implicit in the model itself. It is because the poem is about understanding that we feel a need to understand Coleridge as well as Sara. The dialogical nature of conversation makes us aware that understanding cannot simply posit something by negating something else, but is made up of differences. But as importantly, it is made up of differences within each act of understanding that prevent us from simply substituting one act of sympathy for another. The benedictory embrace of joy at the end emerges diacritically as a response to a dejection that Wordsworth and his circle find troubling. It emerges not as an autonomously positive gesture but as a deferral of criticism from others that contains its own criticism of a joy that cannot understand the other side of life. At the same time, the poem can no more be an ode to melancholy than a hymn to joy, because it is caught in its commitment to conversation. That commitment, soliciting as it does the understanding of those Coleridge admires, has continually produced a sense of frustration with his own dejection. In short, the use of hermeneutics as a supplement to the romantic ideology not only puts the latter in circulation, pleading conservatively for our understanding, it also becomes the site of a certain scepticism about a creed in which Coleridge passionately wants to believe, and of a reflection on that scepticism itself.

Nowhere are the self-complicating tendencies of the hermeneutic model clearer than in Coleridge's last conversation poem "To William Wordsworth." Ostensibly, Coleridge as reader of *The Prelude* once again commits himself to the hermeneutic plot. In actuality, the poem shows that the credo it promotes can be embraced only by negating the reader's experience in ways to which 'Wordsworth' seems sublimely insensitive. This insensitivity balances Coleridge's self-effacement, creating a complex psychological dynamic that unsettles the myth of understanding by implicating it in relationships of power. For Wordsworth's ability to command Coleridge's submission is the other side of a certain anxiety about this reader he needs but shuts out. It marks the dialogical construction of 'Wordsworth' in relation to an otherness within himself, making it difficult for the actual reader to accept Coleridge's acceptance of Wordsworth's authority.

At first sight, "To William Wordsworth" promises to confirm the hermeneutics of friendship that subtends the conversational mode. Written in response to another conversation poem, *The Prelude*, it acts out the fiction of interchange projected in "The Nightingale," where the birds in the grove continue each other's song, or in "The Eolian Harp," where instruments diversely framed participate in a single symphony. It seems to enact, in other words, the hermeneutics of *The Prelude*, where Coleridge is chosen as implied reader precisely because he is so different from Wordsworth and can thus be used to affirm the common substratum of human nature underlying social and psychological difference.[16] Yet this ideal is troubled by the poem's psychological undertow, the site of the poem's uneasiness with itself being precisely the trope of friendship. In those intertexts in which each figures the other, Wordsworth and Coleridge are always 'friends,' disturbingly different and uneasily, not comfortably, similar. If their differences make complete sympathy impossible, their friendship makes it difficult to recast difference into a binary opposition and implicates each psyche within the other. The representation of Wordsworth and Coleridge by each other occurs in a large number of texts, including this poem, "Dejection," *The Prelude*, and *Biographia Literaria*. Whoever tells the story, Wordsworth has always retained his identity through the agency of imagination, whereas Coleridge has gone astray in the wilderness of metaphysics. This configuration of selves is in turn due to a difference in backgrounds which somehow constructs only Coleridge's urban experience as deviant. The traces of this intertextual configuration traverse even poems that the two men did not address to each other. Coleridge's conversation poems constitute themselves in terms of their inability to be like "Tintern Abbey" and recreate epiphany through memory rather than imagination. Wordsworth in poems like *The Excursion* represents himself as having overcome Coleridgean tendencies toward dejection. In broader terms, the Wordsworth-Coleridge relationship comes to stand for a proper as opposed to an improper romanticism, an English closeness to nature in contrast to a European self-consciousness. Yet the friendship of the two challenges the autonomy of this properly romantic ideology, marking it

[16]Wilhelm Dilthey, "The Rise of Hermeneutics," trans. Fredric Jameson, *New Literary History* 3 (1971–72): 244.

as articulated in relation to anxieties about its other side. Precisely because they are friends, Wordsworth may not be as different from Coleridge as both poets wish. One might say that they are related as convex and concave. A willing participant in Wordsworth's script—both biographical and hermeneutic—Coleridge by his very attempt to play his role exposes that script to its own concavities.

These concavities are apparent even when Coleridge seems simply to be summarizing *The Prelude*. He describes how Wordsworth sought to expand his phenomenology of spirit from the private to the social arena (l. 27, *STC*), and how his hopes were struck down by the French Revolution, forcing him to retreat in a direction described as "homeward" (l. 39, *STC*) but also represented as "the dread watch-tower of man's absolute self" (l. 40, *STC*). Curiously, this is the end not of *The Prelude* but of Coleridge's reading of it. For despite Wordsworth's attempt to make the revolution a parenthesis, it is this that emerges for Coleridge as the most pivotal event in Wordsworth's psychic history, in that it gives his affirmations their anxious shape as a resistance to history and an evasion of his own experience.

Wordsworth's distance from history is further registered in the poem as a distance from his audience. From the beginning it is unclear whether he is romantically intimate with or Miltonically removed from his listeners. On the one hand, Coleridge describes Wordsworth as making contact with him through "vital breathings secret as the soul / Of vernal growth" (ll. 9–10, *STC*). On the other hand, he speaks as though there is no intuitive understanding between authority and its disciples, who are told what "to the understanding mind" is "revealable" (ll. 5–8, *STC*). Here Wordsworth's secular scripture is presented as impossibly transcendent, beyond a conversation that Coleridge, too, defers, lest it place ideology in dialogue with its other side. The alternation between immediacy and distance returns as a vacillation between tropes of voice and tropes of writing that are radically at odds with the figure of understanding as conversation. On the one hand, Wordsworth is described as making audible "a linkéd lay of Truth" (l. 58, *STC*), a truth that we know instinctively and not as intellectual conscripts, "Not learnt, but native" (l. 60, *STC*). On the other hand, he is promoted to "the choir / Of ever-enduring men" (ll. 49–50, *STC*), where he becomes a model to be imitated in terms of a dualist pedagogy. His works are placed in "the archives of mankind" (l. 57, *STC*), removed from the intimacy of the oral and filed away in a museum where they are beyond the reach of criticism and perhaps beyond any desire to reach an audience. As the poem turns from conversation to ode, the fourth stanza, with its conventional hyperboles and its formulaic tropes of Fame, conveys the sense of someone's being monumentalized and also entombed in the specular abstraction of his own reputation.

We can divide Coleridge's poem into two segments that follow the procedures typical of romantic hermeneutics: an account of *The Prelude* itself and an account of the reader's response to it. But in fact the poem calls into question the models of psychological and applicative reading that it struggles to follow. Even as he is summarizing *The Prelude*, Coleridge is reading it. Moreover, that reading, which stops the poem before the ascent of Mount Snowdon, at its chronological rather than structural ending, is not a simple reproduction of the text but a misreading that turns it toward its own empty spaces. The psychoanalysis of 'application' is even more obvious. Repeatedly, Coleridge describes the failure of his attempt to pay Wordsworth the supreme compliment of being like him as well as reading him. But the authority he attributes to the Wordsworthian ideology is belied by the images he uses to describe its effect on its audience. The poem is like life returning to a drowned man, bringing in its wake not healing but a painful consciousness of the differences between author and reader, or else reducing Coleridge to the helpless position of a "babe" (ll. 62–66, *STC*). Its pastoral vision is like flowers "Strewed on my corse, and borne upon my bier" (l. 74, *STC*). Most disturbing of all is the description of Wordsworth as a conqueror:

> That way no more! and ill beseems it me,
> Who came a welcomer in herald's guise,
> Singing of Glory, and Futurity,
> To wander back on such unhealthful road,
> Plucking the poisons of self-harm! And ill
> Such intertwine beseems triumphal wreaths
> Strew'd before thy advancing!
> (ll. 76–82, *STC*)

Coleridge says these lines as if to take responsibility for the failure of conversation by attributing it to his own pathology. Yet one might ask how the 'wreath' of conversation can be woven without 'intertwine.' Can a text that relies upon application for its authority persuade us, its actual readers, if it has no more than an antithetical application to the life of its designated reader?

On the surface the poem fulfils its hermeneutic project, returning at the end to the conversational conventions of an intimate circle and a benedictory close. But in the process Coleridge (conquered and infantile) creates a reader with whom it is difficult for us to identify and thus displaces us from the position in the poem's economy of responses that he also asks us to occupy. The description of his conversion is curiously impersonal: "The tumult rose and ceased: for Peace is nigh / Where Wisdom's voice has found a listening heart" (ll. 87–88, *STC*). The absence of personal pronouns from a process occurring deep in Coleridge's heart and their replacement by capitalized abstractions allegorizes this process as intention rather than experience. The penultimate stanza traces, in a series of (an)aesthetically beautiful images, the fading away of 'Coleridge' from the poem. Figured as a "devout child" (l. 95, *STC*), he then becomes a sea that gives off "momentary stars of my own birth," which turn out to be no more than "foam" "darting off into the darkness" (ll. 98–100, *STC*). Finally, he disappears completely, producing neither stars nor foam and becoming an empty mirror: "a tranquil sea, / Outspread and bright, yet swelling to the moon" (ll. 100–101, *STC*). These last lines recall the ending of "Frost at Midnight," where icicles are created from the reflexive interchange of frost and moon. But here nothing is created: the sea remains outspread, but the mirror is finally empty of images.

The dismantling of the poem's hermeneutic verges on the deliberate. It is as though Coleridge means to "import . . . blame" to Wordsworth (l. 86, *STC*) by reenacting but hollowing out the fictions of understanding so crucial to the romantic ideology. Yet the desire for understanding is powerfully present, and the evidence of misunderstanding emerges only despite considerable resistance from Coleridge. This resistance is fraught with ambivalence. One part of Coleridge does seem to feel that his own limitations prevent him from truly appreciating Wordsworth. Yet we are also meant to read beyond this unreciprocated generosity and to articulate the criticisms that 'Coleridge' is too decent to voice on his own. 'Resistance' itself has a figurative and substitutive structure. Coleridge's resistance to criticizing Wordsworth stands in place of a sympathy he cannot feel unconditionally and is not the same thing as sympathy. But it is also not the same as the repressed hostility on which it sometimes verges.

The most challenging reading of this poem to date is that of Jean-Pierre Mileur, who tries to save the text from its own deconstructive impulses by arguing that Coleridge uses them to humanize *The Prelude* and to make himself into Wordsworth's prophetic reader. According to Mileur, the poem's tacit criticism of Wordsworth is necessary if Coleridge is to make us treat with understanding that "defensiveness in the prophetic stance that prevents the prophecy, if not from being heard, from being read right if accepted on its own terms."[17] Yet it is hard, given his passivity, to see Coleridge as a demythologizer who amends

[17] Mileur, *Vision and Revision*, pp. 126, 124.

Wordsworth. It is also hard to ignore the biographical context: the traces of resentment that keep surfacing and that make the pleas for Wordsworth signs of stifled dissent. Somewhat too anxious to make the poem posit something, Mileur's analysis has a dialectical value as a caution against pushing too far the autodeconstruction of the poem's hermeneutic. It is more the case that Coleridge's reading of Wordsworth produces a lack of conviction about the identity he so desperately wants to accept, but also produces it as an insecurity about the personal basis for this doubt that leads him protectively to exalt Wordsworth. The psychoanalysis of both reader and author stimulated by this text is characteristic of the hermeneutic process as seen by theorists like Gadamer, for whom reading is not only the understanding of the text but also of its dialectical role in the self-understanding of the reader. Thus, the poem does not proclaim Wordsworth's irrelevance, nor does it confidently mediate for us a prophecy about which too many doubts have been raised. The prayer with which it ends defers to some reader outside the text the task of making peace between the conflicting voices that traverse Coleridge's reading of Wordsworth and his reading of himself through Wordsworth.

How the poem stages reading is complicated by a biographical setting that cuts two ways. On the one hand, the poem's claims for a hermeneutics of identity are contextualized in a real situation at odds with those claims. On the other hand, the biographical context also limits the paradigmatic authority of 'Coleridge' by making us aware that the distance between author and reader in this poem is the product of a personal falling out. How we should read this falling out is far from clear. Is Coleridge's generous persistence in seeing Wordsworth's side of things a sublimation of the self-rejection required as the price of belonging to the Wordsworth circle? Or is self-sacrifice itself a figure for a certain narrowness that cannot genuinely see the other side of things and must portray open-mindedness as forced on the self by the authority of others?

By extension we, too, are implicated in a scene of reading that raises the broader issue of what Gadamer calls 'prejudice.'[18] Prejudice, the aspects of our own background that make us resist certain culturally marked aspects of the text, functions as a mirror that refracts the historicity of the text. What Coleridge is conditioned to see as illegitimate, Gadamer has taught us to see as a constitutive part of interpretation, particularly since differences between reader and text are related to differences within the text's own ideology. At the same time, 'Cole-

[18]Hans-Georg Gadamer, *Truth and Method*, trans. Garrett Barden and John Cumming (New York: Seabury Press, 1975), pp. 238–40.

ridge's' struggle against his own prejudices reminds us that there is something wrong about prejudice. From Poulet to Gadamer the hermeneutic tradition tells us that part of the experience of reading is opening ourselves to the horizon of the other. As we apply the poem's biographical situation to our own lives, we are also led to probe the limits of the specifically contemporary fashions that make us resist the 'romantic' ideology figured in 'Wordsworth.'

Perhaps more than any form, the conversation poems crystalize for us the aspirations and problems of a traditional hermeneutic. At first, they seem committed to a philosophy of identity that inhibits the voicing of difference. "Tintern Abbey" assumes a conversant almost identical with the speaker. Coleridge's poems construct different positions but then minimize the distance between them. Yet the very notion of conversation makes us aware that the poem is dialogically shaped by the other (often the speaker himself), whom it must persuade. In other ways, too, the poems displace the hermeneutic project. Part of their strategy is the autobiographical setting, which asks that we understand texts in terms of the life situations in which they are created and received. Yet 'life' is not some metaphysical abstraction, and it is precisely the contextualization of literature in life so important in hermeneutic exegesis that complicates the ideals of self-identity and of unity between different persons. Commenting on Schleiermacher's interest in Plato's dialogues, Dilthey unwittingly suggests why dialogue, as the paradigmatic expression of hermeneutics, is also an example of the tensions that mobilize the hermeneutic project: "Philosophy is here actual life, life intermingled with conversation, and its literary representation is only a way of setting it down for further reference. So it had to be dialogue, and a dialogue of such a carefully constructed kind that it forced its readers to re-create the living transactions between the thoughts." Dilthey goes on to speak as if these transactions take on a unity that allows us to grasp "the innermost intentions" of the author.[19] But the crucial phrase is "transactions between thoughts": a phrase that suggests not a totalizing order but local connections of such micrological complexity that their retrieval will disclose a network of possibilities rather than a single intention. The very form of the conversation poem—as the transcript of an intersubjective process that cannot be fixed in writing—causes us to go beyond grammatical and technical reading to what the later Schleiermacher called 'psychological' reading. But in such reading we recover not one but several subtexts: texts that are opened up and qualified by their own subtexts. As a representation of what is really conversation, the written text is not a finished product but a heuristic stimulus to the reader to

[19]Dilthey, "The Rise of Hermeneutics," p. 242.

recreate and continue those transactions, composing from thoughts other thoughts, to use Shelley's phrase.

Coda: Later Poems and the Suppression of the Hermeneutic

The interest that the conversation poems hold for this study is that they reveal the impossibility of a traditional hermeneutics without dismantling the larger premises of hermeneutics. For the contextualization of poetry in life makes us aware of the psychic investment we (and the figures who represent us in the text) have in making and even deconstructing signs. But there are other poems, particularly later ones, that lend themselves more clearly to the thematics of poststructuralism, including its questioning of reading as a process that can make a difference. These poems are beyond the range of this study, and I mention them only to provide a point of contrast. Sometimes, as in "The Blossoming of the Solitary Date-Tree," they actually recapitulate the strategies of hermeneutics. This curious 'poem' is not about anything except perhaps the state of mind that prevents it from being written as a poem. A disjointed mixture of prose and verse, it is accompanied by a preface that asks the reader to accept its fragments as a "substitute" and perhaps to restore them to their "original integrity" (l. 28, *STC*). Yet the effect is to reduce reading to a trope known as delusive before it is ever undertaken. In contrast to the conversation poems, this poem, which is also about the desire for a companionable form, enjoins rather than enacts understanding. Moreover, the body of the text (the six stanzas) stands in the way of our enacting the hermeneutic injunction. For the plea to the reader is put in a preface, placing it outside a text that from within speaks of the impossibility of finding a companionable form. This division of textual space into an outside and an inside that is opaque and disjointed marginalizes the reader, who is involved only to be locked out of a despair that he or she cannot share, because the lack of faith in our receptiveness prevents the poem from expressing it coherently.

What I call a failure at expression, evident in the writer's reluctance to work the prose into poetry or to link the stanzas together, is more accurately described as the poet's failure to converse with himself. In "Dejection" we are given narrative or genetic accounts of how Coleridge came to feel as he does and, by implication, of how things could be otherwise. The importance of these accounts is not that they successfully explain anything, but that they show that willingness to see the other side that is at the heart of dialogue. In this poem depression is simply presented stubbornly as a fait accompli that bears no further discussion. The six stanzas retrieved from the rag and bone shop of Coleridge's heart are attempts at genetic statement. They collapse, however, into laments that whatever the poet's state of mind, it is there to stay and is not worth much expenditure of creative energy. The first stanza is riven with contradictions. It accuses the world of being unreceptive, using an image of sun and frost:

> Beneath the blaze of a tropical sun the mountain peaks are
> the Thrones of Frost, through the absence of objects to reflect
> the rays. 'What no one with us shares, seems scarce our own.'
> (ll. 30–32, *STC*)

The image does not make complete sense because the frigidity of the terrain must be due to its geographical position more than to the absence of objects. The writer therefore provides a gloss on the image, authoritatively placed within quotation marks, and proceeds to look for another image that proves to be even more at odds with the gloss:

> The presence of a ONE,
> "the best belov'd, who loveth me the best,"
> is for the heart, what the supporting air from within is for the
> hollow globe with its suspended car.
> (ll. 33–36, *STC*)

It is, to say the least, curious that the absence of a responsive other is compared to the absence of support from within. Yet the problem of whether the poet's dejection is the fault of the world or is due to some inner lack is simply elided in a general accusation whose rhetorical decisiveness masks a real and unexplored inconclusiveness:

> Deprive it of this, and
> all without, that would have buoyed it aloft even to the seat
> of the gods, becomes a burthen and crushes it into flatness.
> (ll. 36–38, *STC*)

This is only one example of how the text repeatedly overrides on a tonal level the intellectual complexity that might elicit understanding between the reader and a poet who is trying to understand himself. The poem in fact is profoundly unhermeneutic. Its exclusion of the reader, evident in its deployment of textual space, is also crystalized in the motif of the absent companion. For the companion is like the reader: bearing responsibility for her absence, she also cannot be present because her presence has been dismissed in advance as a trick of the poet's desire.

A more common version of the postconversation lyric is the allegory, a form that Coleridge uses in "The Pang More Sharp Than All," "Love's Apparition and Evanishment," and "Time Real and Imaginary," to name but a few.[20] Often these poems replay the conventions of the romantic ideology. The third stanza of "The Blossoming of the Solitary Date-Tree" provides a bored catalogue of Wordsworthian motifs:

> Imagination; honourable aims;
> Free commune with the choir that cannot die;
> Science and song; delight in little things,
> The buoyant child surviving in the man.
> (ll. 48–51, *STC*)

Less abstract but still allegorically distant is "The Pang More Sharp Than All." In many ways the poem recalls "Frost at Midnight." There is a child, associated with a flame:

> He too has flitted from his secret nest,
> Hope's last and dearest child without a name!—
> Has flitted from me, like the warmthless flame.
> (ll. 1–3, *STC*)

In his absence he is replaced by two 'playmates,' Esteem and his sister Kindness. There is a glass through which the poet sees "The magic image of the magic Child" (l. 37, *STC*): this time not a window into reality but an enchanter's glass, regressively associated with the imaginary. At the heart of this poem, then, is one of the most powerful figures in romantic myth: the child, with its associations of spontaneity and companionship, of a present that opens out toward the future, and of growth based on continuity. This figure is associated, again typically, with the glass of imagination that makes beautiful that which is distorted through an idealization that claims mimetic status. But it is as though Coleridge is retracing his earlier poem so as to decompose it. For the poem is not about what the imagination creates but about the process by which it creates. Projecting from the absence of the child a series of epiphenomenal abstractions that take the place of what was itself a figurative supplement, the poem traces imagination as a series of substitutions generated by, not simply intertwined with, a primal lack.

The figures produced by the imagination are all quaintly antique personifications: Esteem, Kindness, the child himself described as an "Elfin Knight" (l. 6, *STC*), and the 'Hope' that produces him. Similar personifications populate other late poems by Coleridge. One could argue that

[20]Rajan, *Dark Interpreter*, pp. 236–47.

these texts present abstractions that the reader is called upon to animate. But it is more the case that they reduce romanticism to a set of faded figures. It is as if the poet has withdrawn from his desire and allows the reader to watch it as it plays itself out in mechanical and predictable patterns. That desire has once existed is marked by the abstract residues that name its absence on any personal level and disengage the reader from concretely experiencing it. Coleridge's allegories, moreover, are not narrative allegories like those of Blake and Shelley, but are composed like emblems around stationary figures. The allegorical figures of eighteenth-century poetic diction, as Steven Knapp has said, are "figures whose signifying functions absorb their personalities, virtually without remainder."[21] It is in this stationary exclusion of personality that we can locate what makes these poems renunciations of the hermeneutic project. Allegory is not only an atemporal mode that shuts out that historical dimension of reading crucial to the opening of what now seems closed. As Coleridge uses it, it is also profoundly unnarrative. The conversation poems have hermeneutic consequences because they contain narrative elements, and specifically because they contain characters to whom we relate in combinations of identification and difference. Narrative elements are not the same thing as the hypostatized version of them that has come to be known as 'narrative,' or more properly plot, and that has been dismissed by deconstructive and Marxist criticism alike for its logocentrism. The conversation poems can scarcely be said to have plots. It is because they give us only fragments of plot (a single episode from Coleridge's domestic life) that the (re)constructive imagination of the reader is called into play and that the option of reading otherwise arises. Still, the conversation poems are far from the monological extreme of pure lyric or emblem, where nothing happens and there are no characters (assuming character to be an intersubjective construct). It is the possibility of identification with the characters that allows us to get involved in the text, and it is the intersubjective construction of characters in relationships of simultaneous likeness and difference from each other and from us that allows us to get involved in such a way that we do not simply identify with one character but read beyond and behind the positions staked out in the text. These readings take form as speculative narratives different from the one emplotted in the text, narratives that play out other versions of the text's central situation. Narrative elements, in other words, are crucial to the functioning of form as hermeneutic. They set in motion the dialectic of understanding, by asking us not only to understand the poem's characters, but also to understand ourselves through characters who do not quite represent us in the mirror of the text. In

[21] *Personification and the Sublime*, p. 12.

understanding ourselves as similar yet different from the text's characters, we also understand them differently. We understand something else about them that they have not understood—which is to say that the differences produced by reading do not simply function deconstructively but produce new insights into identity.

CHAPTER FIVE

The Eye/I of the Other: Self and Audience in Wordsworth's *Lyrical Ballads*

Written at about the same time as the conversation poems and even incorporating two of them, the *Lyrical Ballads* initially seem an expansion of the former to include people from all walks of rural life in a community of sympathetic conversants. Wordsworth's project can be paralleled with that of Dilthey, who begins with a sense of hermeneutic difference but who concludes that a common substratum of human nature allows us to understand the other by translating what is external to us out of our "own sense of life." Many of the poems represent people who differ in terms of age, class, or occupation talking to each other. The preface in effect announces a hermeneutic program: in turning to a popular form purged of poetic diction, it seeks to bind such people together by creating a common language based on the "elementary feelings" that we share (*LB*, p. 245). In other words, it enlists poetics in the service of hermeneutics by arguing that poetry can facilitate understanding across social boundaries. More specifically, it expands hermeneutics in a social direction by making the sharing of feelings the foundation for the establishment of transcultural values. Not only does the preface develop traditional hermeneutics in an explicitly ideological direction; the poems themselves seem to work out, through such hermeneutic figures as 'tradition' and 'circulation,' the cultural mechanisms necessary to universalize that ideology.

Yet it is significant that for Wordsworth the hermeneutic project emerges at a linguistic site: that the ideal of complete understanding is linked to an awareness that language must be purged of its social markings for such hermeneutic transparency to occur. Coleridge was later to question whether Wordsworth had succeeded in this goal (*BL*, II,30–

31). But because of its heteroglossic inclusion of different voices, the *Lyrical Ballads* itself inscribes its project in a social text that causes us to reflect on romantic ideals of sympathy and community. The creation of a social hermeneutic thus becomes implicated in a social dialogic that makes us aware of how our languages diverge.[1] This awareness develops logically from Wordsworth's stated interest in "the fluxes and refluxes and refluxes of the mind" (*LB*, p. 247) and from a radicalization of the romantic concern with perception. Such a concern survives conservatively in later arrangements of the short poems according to faculties like imagination and affection and stages of life like youth and old age. The 1815 classification naturalizes perception by explaining it in terms of universal psychological categories. But instead of grouping poems of one type in a self-confirming series, the *Lyrical Ballads* juxtaposes different types of poems so as to sensitize us to the issue of sociolects, of how discourses are formed and cultural texts constructed. The collection thus becomes the scene of its own reading, eroding further the protective boundary between the conversational and the dialogical. Incorporating poems like "Tintern Abbey," it also situates them, so that conversation is no longer their operative mode but is itself a figure of understanding.

The Ballad as Mirror-Stage

The motives that precede and emerge from Wordsworth's experiments with the ballad compose something of a palimpsest. Because of its simplicity and its association with folk tradition, the ballad seems closer to the unadorned truth than more cultivated forms. Thus Wordsworth talks of using "the real language of men" and of choosing "Low and rustic life . . . because in that situation . . . our elementary feelings exist in a state of greater simplicity" (*LB*, pp. 241, 245). Written in a 'real' language that denies the represented status of the text, the ballad provides an anthropological authority for the truths it conveys by linking them with a return to origins: the nature that precedes culture, the feelings that precede literary expression, and the popular forms closest to beginnings. But against the truth claim made by the ballad we must also set its association with the topical. Lennard Davis reminds us that ballads and novels are linked with the new and with the transmission of

[1]This chapter owes a considerable, if unspecific, debt to Don Bialostosky's fine book *Making Tales: The Poetics of Wordsworth's Narrative Experiments* (Chicago: University of Chicago Press, 1984), which uses a Bakhtinian approach to the shorter poems. In general, the use I make of Bakhtin is more oriented to the social than Bialostosky's appropriation of him.

'news,' and it is well known that the broadside ballad constituted an early form of journalism.[2] Characteristic of such ballads is a concern with events that are not simply recent, but that potentially touch our own lives so that we are "both object and subject, both reader of events and participant in those events." This immediacy can be seen as part of the ballad's claim to authenticity, as Davis argues. But on the other hand the rapid dispersion of news gives it a certain ephemerality, for as Davis also argues, from the late seventeenth century onward it is print and not orality that is associated with legitimation. Broadside ballads, while printed, are printed in a loose-leaf form that is vestigially oral and thus makes their authority merely provisional.[3] Upon issue, they enter the space of dissemination, an unprotected space very different from that of literary patronage, the conversational circle, or institutional reception into the archives of libraries. As important is the fact that ballads have no authors, an aspect of the genre that Wordsworth and Coleridge preserved in issuing the *Lyrical Ballads* anonymously. What stands behind the ballad is not an authorizing figure whose credentials we can trust, but 'tradition': something amorphous, indicating survival but not in any classical sense, because what is transmitted through the generations is partly hearsay, superstition, legend.

We can best describe the status of *Lyrical Ballads* by saying there are tensions embedded in the ballad genre that both invite and problematize the project of the collection. Whether the *Lyrical Ballads* introduced a new poetic form has been much debated. But what seems unique about them is their inclusion not only of traditional and broadside ballads, but also of personal lyrics like "Tintern Abbey" and the Lucy poems, which relate not to legend but to Wordsworth's own experience. These lyrics are quite distinct from the lyric 'songs' that coexist in collections of folk poetry with narrative ballads,[4] since they are in no sense communal. They are often what Geoffrey Hartman calls 'credal lyrics' that enunciate the poet's values: his sense of a 'one life' that links man to nature, his respect for a common humanity, and his advocacy of a 'wise passiveness'

[2]Lennard Davis, *Factual Fictions: The Origins of the English Novel* (New York: Columbia University Press, 1983), p. 48. On the subject of the ballad as journalism see also Albert Friedman, *The Ballad Revival: Studies in the Influence of Popular on Sophisticated Poetry* (Chicago: University of Chicago Press, 1961), pp. 46–49; M. A. Shaaber, *Some Forerunners of the Newspaper in England, 1476–1622* (Philadelphia: n.p., 1929), pp. 196–97.

[3]Davis, *Factual Fictions*, pp. 73, 139–45. Broadsides were often discarded after reading: see Leslie Shepard, *The Broadside Ballad: A Study in Origins and Meaning* (London: Herbert Jenkins, 1962), p. 23.

[4]On Joseph Ritson's distinction between 'song' and 'ballad' see S. B. Hustvedt, *Ballad Criticism in Scandinavia and Great Britain during the Eighteenth Century* (New York: American Scandinavian Foundation, 1916), p. 254.

that achieves culturally unmediated contact with the forms of nature.[5] They do not always project experiences of communion with a pantheistic nature. What they share is an insistence on private feeling as a value in itself. Deriving from the sentimental tradition as opposed to the documentary tradition of the novel as news, the credal poems center on personal moments, desocialized and arrested in a crystalline space as *spots* of time, registers of change that have been *placed* and tranquilized. Although this poetry of the sentiments is at its purest in the personal lyrics, the same voice is present in more dialogical poems like "The Old Cumberland Beggar" and "The Idiot Boy," trying to wrest a lyrical epiphany from situations that a novelist might have rendered very differently. The impulse behind the collection is thus the naturalizing of a poetics of subjectivity: a poetics that would otherwise seem a romantic imposition on a world already encroached upon by the new discourses later developed by thinkers like Marx. Ordinary experiences from the poet's life (a conversation with a landscape, the death of someone whose importance was felt only by him) are set beside experiences in the lives of other ordinary people. These personal myths, instead of being enshrined as Keats says "in some untrodden region of the mind," then pass into the realm of the collective and are "incorporated with the . . . permanent forms of nature" and human nature (*LB*, p. 245).

The desire underlying the *Lyrical Ballads*, then, is to legitimize the discourse of the feelings that Wordsworth was beginning to develop in working with "The Ruined Cottage," by associating it with the communal form of the ballad. The difficulties of such legitimation can be considered in terms of the related problems of place and audience. For the politics of reading implied in this desire is both more ambitious and more dangerous than the one contained in the conversation poems. The *Lyrical Ballads* includes a wide variety of modes from romance to irony. It aims at being a *Gesammtkunstwerk*, crossing historical and class boundaries rather than boundaries between the sister arts, so as to create a universal community constituted around respect for the feelings. This community joins the pantisocratic middle class of the conversation poems to a rural middle class of shepherds whose strong sense of place is occupational and pragmatic rather than literary, and it tries to absorb various displaced people like the female vagrant and the Cumberland beggar. We might thus describe the project behind *Lyrical Ballads* as 'localization.' In his local poems, whether they deal with numinous spots in nature or with people who are strongly a part of the region where

[5]*Wordsworth's Poetry, 1787–1814*, rev. ed. (New Haven, Conn.: Yale University Press, 1971), p. 157.

they live, Wordsworth tries to 'place' his own discourse by creating a real world for it. Discussing the social phenomenology of art forms, Wilhelm Worringer associates abstraction with a sense of not being at home in the world and the realistic attention to detail with the opposite.[6] But in Wordsworth's poetry from 1798 onward we have both styles of awareness: the prosaic attention to facts that Coleridge criticized in the *Biographia,* as well as a language of abstract pantheistic generalization asserted rather than grounded in the particulars of experience. Because the two coexist, Wordsworth's realism emerges as a form of desire. This displacement of realism is evident in his sense that he does not quite belong in the small rural community where most of the poems are set. For Wordsworth often represents himself as Coleridge describes him: namely, as a spectator *ab extra* seeking instruction on local lore from the natives of the place. His dislocation is symptomatically related to a curious interest in displaced people quite unlike himself: in beggars, women, and old people, who are likewise on the margins of this tightly knit community. As displaced figures, the two are linked in the rhetorical economy of the collection: to find a place for one alien discourse is to legitimize the other. On the question of whether these people can find a home in Wordsworth's imaginary community depends the question of whether he must encounter the prospect in his mind as a human community or whether he must live it as uneasily displaced from its own center by the consciousness of what it excludes.

Related to the problem of place is that of reception. Wordsworth's use of the ballad genre is uneasily eclectic, drawing as he does on both traditional and broadside forms. In imitating eighteenth-century ballad collections that haphazardly combine the two forms,[7] Wordsworth may not have been initially aware of the differences between the two types and may have been attracted by what seemed an ageless and classless form. Nevertheless, the two kinds of ballad are aimed at very different audiences, and in conflating them, he creates a palimpsest in which the genre's claim to classlessness overlaps with a sense of the audience as a site of social differences. The traditional oral ballad, though popular, is not addressed to any particular class, nor are its concerns social or political. It may well express archetypal experiences that can be translated into the high mimetic modes of the romantic and heroic ballad as well as into low mimetic narratives of the folk. Broadside ballads, however, were

[6]*Abstraction and Empathy: A Contribution to the Psychology of Style,* trans. Michael Bullock (Cleveland and New York: Meridian Books, 1967), pp. 4–25.

[7]On the differences between the traditional and broadside ballad see Friedman, *The Ballad Revival,* pp. 11–63. The marginalization of the broadside ballad is characteristic of theories that, like F. B. Gummere's theory of the ballad as expressive of a communal spirit, 'romanticize' the genre.

a later form developed within a literary economy with greater class differentiations. They were sold to an audience that was not essentially a reading public, and in the course of the nineteenth century became more and more a lower-class genre.[8] As precursors of the cheap paperback, their concerns were quite diverse. They dealt with news, with melodramatic stories that admittedly turned social history into potboiler, and on occasion they became purveyors of radical politics.[9] Often the experiences they described were ones produced by the class system, not ones that transcended it. We have only to turn to other writers like Scott and Keats to recognize that Wordsworth was unusual in drawing more on the broadsides than on the traditional ballads, and that his interest in the genre is social, not antiquarian. Although it is unlikely that the actual readers of the *Lyrical Ballads* included beggars and vagrants, since the poems were not issued on broadsheets, what concerns us here is the implied audience of the collection as a reactive or dialogical constituent of individual texts. Wordsworth's collection uneasily inhabits a split between two audiences from which the credal voice is likely to encounter very different receptions. The presence of these two audiences accounts for a hermeneutic anxiety in the collection, evident in the fact that so many poems are concerned with someone's telling a story to someone else or trying to convince someone of another point of view.

The polygenous reception history of the ballad makes it a convenient paradigm for problems that are more generally present in first-generation romantic poetry. Most of these poets still sought patrons and to a limited degree had them. But as Wordsworth complains, they also had to support themselves through publication.[10] A system involving circulation within an intimate circle thus coexists with one involving distribution to a much wider audience. That the values even of a middle-class audience may be different from those of the poet is evident from Peacock's not entirely ironic account in *The Four Ages of Poetry* of the outmoding of 'poetry.' Because of its heteroglossic genre, the *Lyrical Ballads* becomes the scene of a discovery profoundly at odds with the assumptions of romantic hermeneutics: that 'audience' is neither a stable nor a homogeneous category.

Our remarks so far suggest that the ballad functions as a psychic screen on which desires having to do with ideological authority and

[8]See S. B. Hustvedt, *Ballad Books and Ballad Men* (Cambridge, Mass.: Harvard University Press, 1930), pp. 197–98; J. S. Bratton, *The Victorian Popular Ballad* (Totowa, N.J.: Rowman and Littlefield, 1975), p. 137.

[9]Shepard, *The Broadside Ballad*, p. 26; Bratton, *The Victorian Popular Ballad*, p. 137.

[10]See John E. Jordan, *Why the Lyrical Ballads? The Background, Writing, and Character of Wordsworth's 1798 Lyrical Ballads* (Berkeley: University of California Press, 1976), pp. 24–25.

hermeneutic community are projected and analyzed. The contrary pulls to which Wordsworth becomes subject in using the genre have to do with its complex archeology and long history. But in this respect it is simply one instance of the tendency of genres to become cultural palimpsests inhabited by the traces of more than one ideology. Perhaps the tendency of *this* genre to function as mirror and mirror-stage stems from the fact that the literary revival of the ballad coincides with its scholarly recovery. One example of the problems raised by scholarship is the debate over the popular minstrels whom Percy romanticized, and whom Ritson saw as little short of vagabonds.[11] On their position hinged not only the authority of the minstrel ballads, but also the ideal of a feudal society with a literature that bridged the gap between popular and aristocratic forms of consciousness. To what extent was this idea of a multeity in unity, of a pluralist society that had classes but without class divisions, simply a romantic fiction? At the time Wordsworth was writing, the career of Thomas Chatterton, who not only passed off modern inventions as ancient discoveries but fabricated historical documents from the 'Rowley world' to buttress his case,[12] must have cast further doubt on the anthropological and archeological legitimation of romantic norms. The editing of the ballads raised other problems, not clearly articulated till the mid-nineteenth century, but having to do with concepts fundamental to traditional hermeneutics like 'author' and 'origin.' For the ballad poses a challenge to the myth of the author as a locus for a fixed meaning, a myth that Wordsworth himself was to promulgate in his account of his early years as a prelude to his assumption of post-Miltonic authority. Ballads have no authors and do not exist in fixed versions. Although they may not be heuristic texts, they are instances of what H. R. Jauss calls a pre-autonomous literature that functions heuristically for us in allowing later readers to question a substantialist conception of literary works.

Research on the ballad participated in that larger movement that Lee Patterson describes in terms of "the analytic dissolutions of historicism,"[13] a movement that reluctantly prefigures the theoretical dissolutions of deconstruction. Like the textual criticism of *Beowulf*, ballad criticism did not actually dispense with the idea of an original text until the mid-nineteenth century. In 1847 Svend Grundtvig, drawing on a principle urged twenty years earlier by the Scottish editor William Motherwell,

[11]Friedman, *The Ballad Revival*, pp. 215–19; Hustvedt, *Ballad Criticism*, p. 191.

[12]See Donald S. Taylor, *Thomas Chatterton's Art: Experiments in Imagined History* (Princeton, N.J.: Princeton University Press, 1978), pp. 44–78.

[13]"The Logic of Textual Criticism and the Way of Genius," in Jerome J. McGann, ed., *Textual Criticism and Literary Interpretation* (Chicago: University of Chicago Press, 1985), pp. 76–79.

published an edition containing multiple versions of ballads and assigning them equal authority. But Percy still believed in a stable, original text corrupted into a babel of versions by the errors of transmission.[14] Nevertheless, ballad scholarship was entwined with the far more advanced line of Homeric scholarship that culminated in F. A. Wolf's *Prolegomena ad Homerum.*[15] Wolf's careful research disintegrated the notion of the Homeric poems as created by a single intention and saw the extant texts as authorially composite writings made up of layers of altering, editing, and imperfectly disguised attempts at unification. Wolf's empirical findings were far more remarkable in their impact than the traditional hermeneutic that led him to short-circuit them through a stemmatic theory that posited a lost original. For those findings led to a certain desacralization of ancient texts, a fear that the recreation of the spirit behind them might not prevail against the analytic dissolutions set in motion by textual study.

How closely Wordsworth knew the new philology is not crucial.[16] The point is that its problems are so deeply embedded in the ballad genre that they will emerge in any serious (as opposed to exotic) recreation of the form, whether academically through editing or fictionally through imitation. Wordsworth may have approached the ballad with a mystical concept of a folk authorship that was collective but unitary, open enough to provide a home for his own very different voice, yet sufficiently homogeneous not to relativize it in a collage of discourses. His assumptions about the ballad may have been those of F. B. Gummere, who later argues for a ballad tradition that is "Unwritten, just as ordinary experience is unwritten," and defines the ballad as "a narrative lyric handed down from generation to generation of a homogeneous and unlettered community".[17] What Wordsworth would have found, however, was a culture that was heterogeneous, a fabric of texts. The philological problems that arise as ballad scholarship becomes more sophisticated are homologous to hermeneutic problems that Wordsworth encounters as he reads the social text and his own position in it. To begin with, there is the marking of the text as text that occurs when a body of writings is submitted to scholarly scrutiny. Then there is the challenge to author(ity) that stems from the fact that ballads are relayed rather than originated. Percy's romanticized theory of the minstrel, so influential on

[14]Hustvedt, *Ballad Criticism*, pp. 3–7, 227.

[15]Friedman, *The Ballad Revival*, pp. 251–55, 172.

[16]There was presumably some awareness of the problems raised here among romantic writers. Thus Jerome McGann argues that Blake would have known the new developments in textual studies through the work of Alexander Geddes: "The Idea of an Indeterminate Text: Blake's Bible of Hell and Dr. Alexander Geddes," *Studies in Romanticism* 25 (1986): 303–24.

[17]F. B. Gummere, *The Popular Ballad* (1907; rpt. New York: Dover, 1959), p. 43.

poets like Beattie, seeks to deflect that challenge by positing a minstrel who is spokesman for his culture. But Wordsworth's narrators do not afford us this panoptic gaze, being shepherds and sea-captains who do not understand the full import of what they are saying and whose stories are already within an interpretive chain. Finally, there is the problem that ballads exist only in versions. There are no original texts of the ballads, nor does tradition, as Gummere argues, function in place of the author by "effacing" variations and forcing the different versions into a historical consensus.[18] Providing us only with versions of truth, Wordsworth's ballads force us to attend to the slight variations that mark the different ways stories are told in different sociolects.

The Hermeneutics of the Personal Voice: Inscription, Tradition, and Circulation

Wordsworth's project, as we have suggested, is the legitimation of a personal voice that believes in a community based on the feelings and that lyricizes narratives of loss and destitution so as to make them sublimatory preludes to vision. It seems appropriate to speak of 'voice' before we speak of 'form,' partly because this voice is an intention that cannot but be displaced in its articulation, and partly because it takes more than one form, and our understanding of it develops in the gap between these forms, and finally because in attempting to understand it as something that never successfully takes form, we recognize that it is never a unified voice. In giving voice to a romantic ideology, Wordsworth, like Coleridge, makes use of a positive hermeneutic, according it a social role as a way of binding people together and cleansing the doors of perception. But unlike Coleridge, he represents this voice and its strategies of legitimation as already under erasure. While the reflexive reading of the conversation poems is an aftereffect generated by their attempt to function hermeneutically rather than referentially, Wordsworth's choice of the collection rather than the autonomous lyric already situates his hermeneutic in the scene of its own reading. For the *Lyrical Ballads* initially impress us with their heterogeneity, and any attempt to unify them under the rubric of a 'project' is thus a psychological reading based on the articulation of this project in the preface or in other poems. That we must find it outside the poems themselves, that this project is in a sense *our* hermeneutic construction, makes these poems fundamentally different from Wordsworth's extended conversation poem *The Prelude*. For it marks his recognition that this project is supplementary, and that

[18]Ibid., pp. 287, 321.

the subject who pursues it is not the transcendental subject (author or reader) of traditional hermeneutics, but is already within the social text that he tries to rewrite by inserting himself into it.

The personal voice and the positive (rather than dialectical) hermeneutic that it promotes are fundamentally conservative. David Sampson notes that Wordsworth's almost obsessive interest in the rural poor does not translate into a concern with the "social and political implications" of their situation."[19] More approvingly, Robert Langbaum argues that "Wordsworth alludes to social class only to show its unimportance for the kind of spirituality he is portraying."[20] The elision of the political takes the form of a reduction of narrative to lyric tableau that constructs the world in terms of feelings rather than events or situations. Thus a poem like "The Old Cumberland Beggar" focuses on the pleasure that individuals derive from acts of charity rather than on the economic conditions that lead to beggary. The emphasis on feeling perpetuates and is supported by a *hermeneutics* of sentimentalism. For the tradition of sentiment, as James Averill describes it, deemphasizes narrative to focus on response: on the telling of a sad story to a listener whose reactions draw the reader into the community of those who feel for others.[21] Sentimentalism, stressing as it does what unites rather than what separates us, is linked to an elision of those differences that make a more dialectical hermeneutics part of a political project. But those differences are inscribed in the very genre Wordsworth chooses. As we consider his displacement of the conservative social hermeneutic he tries to legitimize, we shall focus on such things as the figures he uses to establish it, the audience as a dialogical constituent of the texts, and the forms assumed by the personal voice as displacements of the intentionality behind it.

The rural setting of *Lyrical Ballads* is an important figure in the representation of Wordsworth's responses as 'natural.' But other strategies are used in legitimizing the discourse of the feelings, among them what we shall call 'inscription,' 'tradition,' and 'circulation.' These hermeneutic figures are by no means unproblematic. The first of them, inscription, involves an anxious textualization of another metaphor of epistemic authority, incorporation. Wordsworth introduces this figure in the preface, when he speaks of feelings that are "incorporated with the . . . permanent forms of nature" (*LB*, p. 245). Often nature will give substance to a character's feelings by seeming to embody them in a specific place.

[19]"Wordsworth and the Poor: The Poetry of Survival," *Studies in Romanticism* 23 (1984): 50.

[20]"Wordsworth's Lyrical Characterisations," *Studies in Romanticism* 21 (1982): 320.

[21]*Wordsworth and the Poetry of Human Suffering* (Ithaca, N.Y.: Cornell University Press, 1980), p. 24.

In "The Brothers" she incorporates the boys' devotion to each other in the "brother fountains" and then incorporates the violent prematurity of James's death by destroying one of the fountains (ll. 139–46, *LB*). Behind incorporation is the powerful trope of the book of nature, which underwrites our moral construction of the world by creating a correspondence between words and things. The metaphor of inscription both continues and problematizes this figure by writing, not embodying, personal myth in the public domain. The clearest instances of inscription are the poems on the naming of places, but several other poems added in 1800 testify to what is almost an obsession with the mode.[22] Moving beyond the occasional status of the mode in neoclassical poetry, Wordsworth's poems colonize an imaginative terrain so as to further the project of localization. For even though they *are* occasional, as the only poems in the collection that are accorded their own advertisement, the poems on the naming of places make the more ambitious claim of a literary cycle. Experiences from personal life are associated with specific places so as to render them permanent, part of a spatial rather than temporal order, while also recreating various un(re)marked spots through the mythmaking of the ordinary imagination: "By Persons resident in the country and attached to rural objects, many places will be found unnamed or of unknown names, where little Incidents will have occurred, or feelings been experienced. . . . From a wish to give some sort of record to such Incidents or renew the gratification of such Feelings, Names have been given to Places by the Author and some of his Friends (*LB*, p. 217).

What Wordsworth describes here as "naming" is linked in the note to the second poem with the greater antiquity of inscription, which literally writes such experience onto the rocks of Cumberland and Westmoreland. Yet naming is not inscription, and inscription itself is the textual imposition of meaning on the natural scene. As attempts to create a new fund of communal lore that will take its place among existing traditions, these poems have an anxiously recent quality. They transplant the circumscribed circle of the conversation poems into a community curiously void of local people, except for some mandatory "shepherds" (l. 42, *LB*) and a vicar who is allowed to speak thirteen words (ll. 23–24, *LB*). With the exception of a meeting with a leech-gatherer, the experiences inscribed do not transcend the realm of private allusion. The longest poem, "To Joanna," vaguely commemorates "affections old and true" (l. 81, *LB*). Abstract as they are, the poems do not accomplish their project

[22] I refer to "Inscription for the Spot where the Hermitage stood on St. Herbert's Island, Derwent-Water," "Inscription for the House (an Outhouse) on the Island at Grasmere," "Lines Written with a Slate-Pencil upon a Stone, &c.," "Lines Written on a Tablet, in a School," and "A Poet's Epitaph."

of carving out a place for themselves in regional literature, but rather name, in a circular way, the inscriptive function itself. This is not to suggest that they are textually self-conscious poems, but rather that they explicitly mark for us a trope that functions less visibly in other poems, and thus lay the groundwork for the self-critical playing out of that trope that occurs in a more complex poem like "Lines Left Upon a Seat in a Yew Tree."

In this poem literal inscription is deliberately criticized so as to displace the inscriptive authority claimed by the text itself. The solitary who has trained the tree "to bend its arms in circling shade" (l. 11, *LB*) has written into nature his own self-encircling withdrawal, "tracing here /An emblem of his own unfruitful life" (ll. 28–29, *LB*). Because he is now dead, a monumental writing closed to the complexities of life is tacitly associated with entombment. But Wordsworth's response to the solitary's inscription is equally closed in its moralizing complacency. As far as he is concerned, love of nature leads unproblematically to love of humanity, in ways that are merely asserted. The insecurity of Wordsworth's creed is evident in the fact that he addresses the poem as much to himself as to the traveler, dividing himself into instructor and pupil and speaking as resolved soul to another self that is still traveling. The speaker of the poem concedes the provisionality of his own response in merely pinning some lines to the seat rather than inscribing them, a gesture that is of paradigmatic significance for the status of Wordsworth's creed in the collection as a whole. These lines lack the epigrammatic closure of the traditional inscription and take form as a much longer text that exhibits the fluxes and refluxes of his mind and is thus subject to further reading. They also lack the impersonality of the inscription. Spoken in a distinctly personal voice, transcribed on paper rather than carved in rock, and left there for an unspecified 'Traveler' to read, they allow the reader to affirm, reject, or simply situate them.

If incorporation and inscription claim an identity between discourse and truth, tradition and circulation are figures of communication that create a transhistorical audience for this discourse. Tradition, so crucial to the ballad, facilitates the transmission of communal wisdom through the generations and thus the ratification of this wisdom by time. Among the traditional ballads are those that simply map a rhetorical space. "Ellen Irwin," for instance, is there to make the point that the regional tradition includes antique ballads as well as more recent ones like "Ruth" and thus to allude to the endurance of the past and present into the future. Tradition is subtly conservative, eliding the socioeconomic specificities of a poem like "Ruth" by suggesting that tragic love tales are archetypical. Its horizontal equivalent is circulation, the passing around rather than the handing down of shared insights. Jon Klancher has described the conservatizing role of reading in the economy of circulation, whether it occurs through readings and conversations in coffeehouses, or through periodicals and memberships in circulating libraries. The orderly circulation of material through such groups was meant to unite its members within "a knowablc community of discourse." Drawing on Arthur Young's *Travels in France* written during the French Revolution, Klancher distinguishes between "circulation" as an activity designed to draw new groups into an existing consensus, and "dissemination," the propagandistic issuing of texts to anonymous readers at the other end of a polarized social spectrum without the safeguards of an intimacy between author and reader.[23] "Tintern Abbey" like other conversation poems dramatizes the ideal of circulation, the transmission of insights within an intimate circle of friends. But Wordsworth himself uses the figure and expresses the hope that his poems might "circulate" among the people: a hope that is figured in his many representations of himself in dialogue with humble people. Circulated rather than disseminated, Wordsworth's texts claim to share their insights with others rather than to dispense their wisdom from a position of authority. They are passed around without the impersonality of dissemination and thereby hope to avoid dissemination in its more contemporary sense of a critically different appropriation by a reader who is not obliged by fictions of intimacy to accept the authority of the text.

Tradition and circulation are figures of transmission that assume that because of our common humanity, we can bridge the distances between people. Wordsworth speaks elsewhere of how a writer must create the taste by which he is to be enjoyed,[24] and these figures are clearly part of his attempt in *Lyrical Ballads* to make his own audience. But as we have already suggested, Wordsworth's real and desired audiences were not identical, and the discrepancy is reactively felt as an uncertainty even as to his desired audience. Thus he sometimes indicates his desire for an audience wider than that of the conversational circle: "I have many a time wished that I had talents to produce songs, poems, and little histories, that might circulate among other good things in this way, supplanting partly the bad; flowers and useful herbs to take the place of weeds. Indeed some of the Poems which I have published were composed not without a hope that at some time or other they might answer this purpose."[25] But as the natural-cum-political word "(sup)plant" implies, the

[23]Jon Klancher, *The Making of English Reading Audiences, 1790–1832* (Madison: University of Wisconsin Press, 1987), pp. 20, 28–35.

[24]Wordsworth, "Essay Supplementary to the Preface," in Paul M. Zall, ed., *Literary Criticism of William Wordsworth* (Lincoln: University of Nebraska Press, 1966), p. 182.

[25]Letter of 5 June 1808 in E. de Selincourt, ed., *The Letters of William and Dorothy Wordsworth: The Middle Years, 1806–1820*, rev. Mary Moorman and A. G. Hill, 2 vols., 2nd ed. (Oxford: Clarendon, 1969–70), I, 248.

legitimacy that a popular audience confers may involve an act of usurpation. However much Wordsworth hoped to have his poems circulate among the people, the fact is that they were initially printed as a volume and sold to an educated public. Thus one is never sure if the poems are aimed at the middle class or the people. If they are intended to challenge the discursive categories of an urban middle class, their new ways of shaping reality through language are representations constructed by a writer who is still part of the class from which he departs. If they are aimed at the people, we can question whether they did indeed meet their goal. *Lyrical Ballads* sold reasonably well, and some of its poems were reprinted in periodicals.[26] A very few were reprinted on broadsheets, and because broadsheets were read aloud in pubs, it is possible that they reached a different class. But as H. D. Rawnsley reminds us, Wordsworth's real audience probably remained circumscribed. Rawnsley quotes the comments of an old Westmoreland cottager: "He wozn't a man as said a deal to common folk. But he talked a great deal to hissen."[27]

The point is not that Wordsworth would have been a better poet if he had written in the idiom of the common people. Nor would he have been more honest if he had recognized with Coleridge the impossibility of speaking the language of real people. The point is rather that Wordsworth was involved in an ambitious semiopolitical project that is better understood as emergently self-critical than as an instance of either middle-class hybris or naïveté. It is noteworthy that he does not assume the mantle of original genius in describing his poems and instead calls them an "experiment" (*LB*, pp. 8, 241).[28] *Lyrical Ballads* is an experimental performance of its own project. The split nature of Wordsworth's desired extramural audience registers both hope and anxiety as to how universal his new discourse can indeed be. At the same time in intramural terms this ambivalence is intensified by the ballad's composite social origins and thematized in scenes of textuality and communication within the poems. For the collection already anticipates the gap between its desired and 'real' audience as a discrepancy within its characterized audience. These discrepancies, we shall go on to suggest, are related to discrepancies in Wordsworth's voice. For 'voice' is not some essence that we abstract by bracketing the external world, as classical and preexistential phenomenology would have it. At its origin it is intentional, related to some aspect of the external world, addressed to someone, and reactively shaped by what is outside it.

[26]Jordan, *Why the Lyrical Ballads?* p. 113; Robert Mayo, "The Contemporaneity of the *Lyrical Ballads*," *PMLA* 69 (1954): 518–20.

[27]"Reminiscences of Wordsworth among the Peasantry of Westmoreland," quoted in D. D. Devlin, *Wordsworth and the Poetry of Epitaphs* (London: Macmillan, 1980), p. 3.

[28]On this point see also Averill, *Wordsworth and the Poetry of Human Suffering*, pp. 149–50.

We can therefore expect the very figures that promote a traditional hermeneutic to be the site of its questioning. A case in point is the thematization of tradition in "Hart-Leap Well." The poem falls into two parts: the first is a straightforward telling of a story about a valiant animal who eludes his aristocratic hunter in death, and the second is a dialogue about the story in the present. But the poem is not just about the survival of a story from chivalric to modern times. It is about the changing frame of values in which that story has survived and thus the historicity of discourses. The bold device of separating the story from the response makes it clear that the poem is about interpretation. Told to Wordsworth by a shepherd whose identity is revealed only in the second part, the story at first comes to us decontextualized, without a characterized narrator or audience. From the perspective of Wordsworth's own time, it seems to reveal the callousness of an aristocratic culture of the hunt. That judgment is implicit in the surrounding context of stories about ordinary people into which this museum-piece is inserted. For though the knight is affected by the animal's death, he is moved not by the wantonness of that death but by its heroism, which allows him to compensate for the fact that the hart has finally eluded his hermeneutic grasp in death by repossessing it as the egotistical self-projection of his own values. He remembers the animal by building a pleasure-dome which is more for his own use than for purposes of commemoration, and he continues to visit the site with his paramour. But because the story initially lacks a rhetoric of fiction, we are uncertain how to read it. We wonder whether we should trust our own judgments or reconstruct the responses of the original audience, and we are increasingly aware of differences in the possible discourses of reception. We can imagine at least three such discourses: a morally critical response; a response from the knight's peers that praises him for his chivalrous recognition that a mere animal has proved his match in gallantry; and an 'aesthetic' response, a simple absorption in the telling of a tale of suspense and adventure. The vacuum in which the story is relayed forces us to reflect on how we draw the boundaries between story and discourse, and on how much of what we take to be "in" the elementary language of the story is actually figurative. In other words, the fact that this tale is relayed rather than authored by someone who takes responsibility for it makes us reflect on the status of ballads themselves as empty schemas into which different people project their own values.

When the narrator is identified in the second part as a shepherd rather than a minstrel, we discover 'how' to read the story, which now assumes its place among Wordsworth's credal poems, confirming the belief that we should love all things both great and small. We realize that the pleasure-dome was the sign of a culture autocratically imposed on nature. By allowing it to decay, nature 'incorporates' a sadness that the point of the hart's story has been missed. Finally, the poet Wordsworth explicitly proclaims this point and brings the poem to a conclusion.

But because of its complicated temporal and hermeneutic framework, the poem asks that we do more than simply extract a message from it. Functioning within the distinction that Godwin was later to articulate between the 'moral' or original intention of a text and its 'tendency' or historically developing meaning, Wordsworth asks us to realize that it is the progress of time that allows for the emergence of his more enlightened reading of the story as didactic pastoral rather than adventure story, as lyric rather than narrative. But to recognize that historical shifts (such as the decline of the feudal aristocracy) produce new modes of understanding is also to situate the understanding that 'Wordsworth' himself achieves. For the scene of the romantic poet reading the chivalric tale internalizes in the poem the situation of a future reader reading Wordsworth's poem. Moreover, Wordsworth is not the teller of the tale, and despite pronouncements to the contrary (l. 162, *LB*), there is just enough difference between his responses and those of the shepherd to unsettle our assent to his didacticism. The shepherd very simply describes the blight that has descended on the place where the hart died. He reacts to the story by sympathizing with the animal but does not extract general principles from it. For Wordsworth, embarrassed that the shepherd's 'simplicity' and lack of social power make him accept suffering, there is the assurance that things will return to normal through some process for which the responsibility is mystically deferred to 'nature.' Elements of both responses can be located socially. Wordsworth's meliorism and didacticism are functions of his social superiority. At the same time his insistence on a nature that is more than just helplessly sympathetic masks his own fear that he, too, may be able to do nothing but listen. On the other hand, the responses of the shepherd, much more tentatively phrased, bear out (though one might do without the condescension) Coleridge's contention that the rustic conveys "*insulated facts*, either those of his scanty experience or his traditional belief; while the educated man chiefly seeks to discover and express those *connections* of things, . . . from which some more or less general law is deducible" (*BL*, II,39). Dialogue and narrative retelling make the poem a site for the intersection of cultural discourses and compel us to ask what tradition is. Tradition itself emerges as self-revising rather than confirmative: an agreement to tell the same stories but not a consensus about what those stories mean.

The trope of circulation proves similarly complex as poems cross the fine line between dramatizing figures so as to confirm them and thematizing them so as to question them. A case in point is a poem with the cumbersome title: "Lines written at a small distance from my House, and sent by my little Boy to the Person to whom they are addressed." The carpe diem stand taken in the poem is a familiar one. Wordsworth addresses Dorothy and asks her to "Put on with speed your woodland dress, / And bring no book, for this one day / We'll give to idleness" (ll. 14–16, *LB*). The communicative framework of the poem recalls that of the conversation mode: a letter from Wordsworth is sent to his sister by way of the child, urging her to apply what she reads in the letter to her own life, and allowing the poem's 'message' to circulate among a small, intimate community. Yet the elaborate title conspicuously intersects the enthusiasm of the poem itself. At the risk of seeming literal-minded, we may ask why Wordsworth, who is only a short distance from his house, sends Dorothy a letter, the writing of which will surely rupture his bookless communion with nature. And what, we might ask, will be the reaction of Dorothy on reading a letter that exhorts her to stop reading? Such questions make us aware of the artifice involved in the simple life and of the social artifice involved in limiting a plea for rustic indolence to those who are leisured enough to read about not reading. The voice of the poem is a didactic one, though in a light-hearted way. It is obvious enough that writing this voice places its credo in a hypothetical space, especially given that there is no answer from Dorothy. In a larger sense, the replacement of direct speech by letter writing thematizes the position of Wordsworth's lyrics and ballads as a whole: those "songs, poems, and little histories" that he wrote to supplant the "straggling papers" on broadsheets, and that are addressed from a distance to people whose response he does not know. From the inscription of an implied reader in the person of Dorothy arises the troubling question of actual readers, raised by the collection itself as it attempts uncertainly to carry out Wordsworth's dictum that a poet must create his own audience. Who are the audience(s) of nugatory effusions like this one, consisting of lines tossed off hastily and delivered by a child rather than of verses deliberately thought through and distributed by a publisher? Because of the context of this collection, Wordsworth's restriction of his audience to an intimate circle is troubling, at once protective and honest. Perhaps it is no accident that in 1798 this poem comes immediately after "Goody Blake and Harry Gill," a poem about a woman who is too poor to afford firewood, and that in 1800 it is immediately followed by "The Female Vagrant." Stylistically seamless if taken by itself, the poem's framing representation of its textuality becomes the site of its reluctant insertion into the interdiscursive network of the collection, which combines middle and low styles so as to map not simply a prospect in the mind, but a social text. Audiences, as Jon Klancher suggests, "are not simply distinct sectors of the cultural sphere. They are mutually produced as an otherness within one's own discourse."[29] To read Wordsworth's lines by themselves would be to let them exist in a distinct cultural sector. Though such a reading is not precluded, we also cannot stop at it. For the issuing of the poems in a collection is a socially symbolic act: a material and visual sign that perceptual spaces are both separate and part of a collectivity, both privileged and relative.

Center and Periphery: Modes of the Personal Voice

The sense we have that Wordsworth situates his own discourse, rather than claiming for it the bardic authority uneasily appropriated in *The Prelude*, comes partly from the way he sketches in his function in speaking and listening situations. As we move between the poems, Wordsworth himself moves between center and periphery, between authority and its displacement. Personal lyrics such as "Tintern Abbey" are spoken in a humble version of the egotistical sublime. But Wordsworth the author is often a character in the poems and thus a figure in his own text. As character, moreover, he is often a questioner, a visitor, a returning traveler who must elicit information from some local shepherd or sea captain. His intermittent presentation of himself as an outsider marks with a certain tangentiality those poems like the "Lines Left Upon a Seat," where he addresses other travelers such as ourselves from the position of someone who knows the legends and people of the place. If he is not literally an outsider, he is an observer, as in "Old Man Travelling," where the entry of the old man's voice into the monologue suddenly puts Wordsworth outside what he has been observing. For the literal positioning of himself as an outsider in some poems raises the figurative problem of his being outside what he seeks to colonize through his discourse. Again, Wordsworth will often present himself as naive: as an adult who knows less than a child in "We are Seven" or "Anecdote for Fathers," and conversely as a child who may know less than an adult in "The Fountain." Not only does he constantly take away the authority he confers on himself, he also plays different roles (adult and youth, insider and outsider) so as to suggest that 'Wordsworth' himself may be a shifting position, a self existing only in relation to other selves and changing as those other selves and future readers change.

But we should not conclude that the interweaving of irony and authority makes understanding illusory. In "The Pet-Lamb" the ballad that Wordsworth sings about the child and her pet lamb is only half hers "and one half of it was mine" (l. 64, *LB*); and this ballad in turn is about

[29]*English Reading Audiences*, p. 12.

the girl's attempt to imagine what the lamb might be feeling, across the recognition that the feelings of animals, even pets, are somehow closed to us. The sense that the languages of adult, child, and lamb can never quite connect is balanced, however, by the sense that the hermeneutic stories we construct to bridge such distances do sometimes produce insights:

> "Nay" said I, more than half to the Damsel must belong,
> For she look'd with such a look, and she spake with such a tone,
> That I almost receiv'd her heart into my own.
>
> (ll. 66–68, *LB*)

Crucial to the survival of the hermeneutic project are the various dialogue poems: "Anecdote for Fathers," "We are Seven," and the four Matthew poems. "We are Seven" is a conversation between a cottage girl and an adult male. The child organizes her world imaginatively so as to elide the difference between death and sleep. Convinced that her dead siblings are simply sleeping in the earth instead of in their beds, she is innocent in Blake's double sense: unrealistically lacking in adult sophistication, but also able to see something that is missed by the literal-minded 'Wordsworth,' who uncharacteristically invokes a male logic in addressing the poem not to Dorothy but to "dear brother Jim" (l. 1, *LB*). Constructed around impasses of various kinds, Wordsworth's dialogue poems differ from Marvell's in making us aware of the cultural origins of perception and thus rendering differences relative rather than paralyzingly absolute. They do not simply enunciate positions as economically as possible, but focus on the process by which these positions are conveyed: the characteristic turns and displacements of a person's language. They also differ from Marvell's Manichaean confrontations in their hermeneutic form. They are conversations between people rather than between positions or abstractions. And they are texts that point beyond their own impasses by gesturing toward a reader (dear brother Jim), or placing themselves, as in "The Two April Mornings," in a temporal continuum in which the past is seen from the present and thus the present from the future. Although these poems dramatize the misunderstandings that occur because we speak different languages, they are a powerful enactment of the fact that we do talk in spite of, and perhaps because of, our differences.

We have spoken so far of how Wordsworth relativizes the personal voice by replaying it in ways that raise questions about its authority and reception. But its situatedness is also apparent as a difference within the voice itself and in the forms it assumes. The Wordsworthian discourse is often seen as lyrically withdrawn from social commitments. This lyricism, however, must be understood as intentionality rather than achieved form. The first question to ask is how the personal voice is "composed": both in the sense of being made out of composite elements, and in the sense of claiming a composure that elides its interdiscursive composition. For there are at least two modalities of this deceptively unified voice: the voice of personal feeling and the didactic voice. In a poem like "She Dwelt Among the Untrodden Ways," no attempt is made to go beyond the overwhelming feeling of loss caused by Lucy's death. In a poem like "Lines written at a small distance," surrender to the joys of the moment is assertively generalized into a creed. Often the two modes are intertwined, as in "The Old Cumberland Beggar," where absorption in the movements of the beggar abruptly gives way to an assertion of his social utility. In the context of this intertwining, both sentimental absorption and didacticism cease to be positive terms and disclose themselves through the differences between and within them. Credalism emerges as an anxious response to the helplessness of simply contemplating suffering or the hedonism of a "wise passiveness." Pragmatic and ethical, the didactic voice sometimes guiltily takes the place of a social activism that would ameliorate rather than simply watch suffering, but then defers amelioration from man to nature. Sometimes this voice responds to an implied criticism of romantic sensibility, the almost aestheticist absorption in feelings or landscapes for their own sake, as being without larger social utility. Inevitably, the didactic voice is complicated by the undercurrents of what it does not say. But the sentimental voice does not achieve ideological autonomy either, since its very passivity marks it as a voice of retreat that concedes the impossibility of changing conditions that the contemplation of suffering makes us want to change.

Divided at its origin into active and passive modes, the personal voice also takes up residence in forms that are curiously mixed and that keep rereading themselves. Often the *Lyrical Ballads* are seen as subordinating a situation to the feelings it arouses so as to convert narrative, with its implication in the world of events and social change, into a spot of time sealed in lyrical stasis. Wordsworth himself speaks of how the feeling developed in these poems "gives importance to the action and situation and not the action and situation to the feeling" (*LB*, p. 248). But the antinarrative elements in poems that are also part of a developing tradition of regional realism give the ballads as much affinity with the short story as the lyric. The short story can be seen as a frustrated lyric. It shares with the lyric an abridgment of time and a transcendental impulse evident, for example, in Joyce's epiphanies, which suddenly switch the reader from a despairingly realistic frame of values to one that is symbolist or anagogic. But because empirical details are more insistently present in the short story than in the lyric, the voiding of the realistic dimension seems more evasive. The truncation of plot registers as paralysis, suspending the form between the inability to place an episode in a connective framework that will explain its ugliness and the desire for a visionary transcendence that will abrogate the need for such explanation. An example of the poem as short story is "The Thorn," which focuses obsessively on the spot where an unwed mother is said to have disposed of her child. Taking form as a series of anxious rhetorical questions, the old captain's monologue pivots on a single traumatic scene, a scrap from a sensational tabloid. In his attempt to place this fragment, he desperately lyricizes it. He reduces Martha Ray's story to the feelings it arouses, and he makes the scene with which he associates her into a symbolic landscape in which the thorn weighed down by lichens embodies the harshness of life. Visionary dreariness, however, is constantly interrupted by the obsessive factual details about the dimensions of the thorn that so annoyed Coleridge, and that make lyricism seem like a symptom of the narrator's dislocation rather than a successful transmutation of trauma. The flood of questions and the framework of the poem, in which a story is being told rather than a mood created, militate against any reduction of Martha's life to a spot of time and leave us wanting to know more about what happened and the community where it happened.

Though they displace lyrical intention, Wordsworth's "short essays," as he described them (*LB*, p. 247), do not always deconstruct lyric as avoidance. In "The Idiot Boy" the effect is more that of a palimpsest. The idiot boy never does come back with the doctor, but he eventually returns with the statement "The cocks did crow to-whoo, to-whoo, / And the sun did shine so cold" (ll. 460–61, *LB*). On a realistic level the poem troubles us with what might have happened to Johnny and Susan, and with the isolation of these two old women who have no one to depend on but a retarded boy. Superimposed on the realistic details of the story, which are all too familiar from ballads about the poor, is the narrator's emphasis on the feelings of anxiety and pride aroused in Betty Foy and the epiphany experienced by Johnny, both perhaps unfamiliar to a middle-class audience who can only look at the poor 'realistically.' Yet we are not entirely convinced that the almost tragic story can be comfortably reread on the plane of feeling as in pure lyric. For one thing, Johnny's ephiphany, expressed in two lines that may be proto-imagist or merely prosaic, is oddly flat. We are thus unsure whether the epiphany is his or ours, the product of a guilty humanism that makes us want to attribute value even to idiots. The poem hovers uneasily between lyric and realism, suggesting that each is a compensatory response to the other, and each is a mode of reading that is partially true.

Because the heterogeneity of *Lyrical Ballads* foregrounds the issue of discourse, the poems must be read not just for what they say but also as exhibiting self-critically their own forms of awareness. A brief example is "Old Man Travelling." Obviously a dress rehearsal for "Resolution and Independence," the poem moves closer to making the old man a mere occasion for poetic insight in the 1815 revision, in which the last six lines are eliminated. Many critics have been embarrassed by the 1798 version's rude interruption of its visionary mood, as the old man tells 'Wordsworth' that he is not tranquilly living in the eye of nature but is journeying to see his dying son in a hospital. But it is clear that the original poem is deconstructed around the discrepancy between lyrical and narrative frames of value, so as to play the one critically against the other in a way that makes it a paradigm for other discursively complex poems in the collection. Wordsworth's description of the poem as a 'sketch' already makes us aware that its sentimental characterization of the old man is hesitantly brief. A sketch is not a realistic portrait: it provides outlines rather than interiors and reflects the casual perceptions of the artist rather than objective truth. Sketching is, moreover, a leisure-class activity. From the assumption that the situation of the old man is less important than the feelings it arouses in the spectator, 'Wordsworth' moves quickly to humanize the possible absurdity of the man's life through an existential romanticism that makes the aimlessness of life's journey less significant than the responses that occur in our mental travel and that are their own reward. The shift from 'Wordsworth's' lyrical meditation to the old man's short, bare account of where he is going makes us abruptly aware of the gulf that separates their two discourses: the one privileged in being able to attribute value to life by displacing detail from the literal to the symbolic level, and the other not necessarily more 'true' but excluded from metaphysical consolation. In the old man's statement there are only facts, no feelings:

> —I asked him whither he was bound, and what
> The object of his journey; he replied
> "Sir! I am going many miles to take
> "A last leave of my son, a mariner,
> "Who from a sea-fight has been brought to Falmouth,
> And there is dying in an hospital."
>
> (ll. 15–20, *LB*)

These lines are indeed "uninteresting," in Robert Langbaum's phrase,[30] in the sense that they provide no personal insight into the old man. But they convey a troubling social insight, namely, that feelings may not be shareable. Perhaps in the old man's sociolect, feelings are not important: perhaps one has them but does not express them, because what one shares is information. Or perhaps the old man feels that information is

[30]"Wordsworth's Lyrical Characterisations," p. 330.

all that can be shared across the boundary dividing him from 'Wordsworth.' That the poem ends with this uncertainty is significant for the hermeneutics of feeling so crucial to this collection. 'Wordsworth' could have responded to the old man and generated a conversation in which the man would have expressed his grief over his son or his indignation over the war. Such a continuation would have punctured 'Wordsworth's' view of the old man as content, but only to replace one feeling with another, since the two men would still have been bound together in the shared feeling of an inconsolable loss. But instead 'Wordsworth' awkwardly drops the conversation. That the author in the original version puts the old man's speech in quotation marks is also significant, for the old man thus remains unappropriated into 'Wordsworth's' discourse. But already in 1800 the effacement of difference begins. The old man's account is now conveyed as reported speech, located in the past as a spot of time and thus placed, psychologically as well as orthographically, within 'Wordsworth's' own language.

"The Old Cumberland Beggar" and "The Brothers"

Poems like "Old Man Traveling" which deliberately plays one language against another, sensitize us to the duplicities in texts whose rhetoric is more seamless, and encourage us to read symptomatically the hermeneutics of sentimentalism that frames so many of these poems. We conclude by looking at two poems that seem to support the ideology of the personal voice but that also reproduce (not always deliberately) some of its tensions. The more obviously political of these poems is "The Old Cumberland Beggar." According to the Fenwick note, it was written to defend the individual rights of beggars against the political economists who threatened to sweep them away into state-run poorhouses. In place of such collective solutions the poem describes a conservative, community-based welfare in which the beggar makes his rounds from house to house, and the process of alms-giving remains personal rather than commodified. So old that Wordsworth remembers him seeming just as old when the poet was a child (ll. 22–23, *LB*), the beggar is a local tradition and circulates among the local people, becoming the occasion for a social hermeneutic:

> While thus he creeps
> From door to door, the Villagers in him
> Behold a record which together binds
> Past deeds and offices of charity
> Else unremember'd.
>
> (ll. 79–83, *LB*)

The poem at many points echoes the conversation poems, in its evocation of "A life and soul to every mode of being / Inseparably link'd" (ll. 78–79, *LB*), and most of all in its benedictory conclusion (ll. 155–189, *LB*). As a poem about a beggar, it is thus crucial to Wordsworth's project of moving beyond coterie poetry and claiming universality for the conversational vision. Were the text to consist only of the poem, we might well see it as affirming this social hermeneutic, though unconvincingly. But "The Old Cumberland Beggar," as it now comes to us, breaks up into three repetitive intertexts. The text itself consists of a headnote that defends individual rather than institutional solutions to poverty, and a monologue oddly divided between meditative and propagandistic voices, between aesthetic and political defenses of this solution. To this amalgam of discourses we must add the frustrated Fenwick note of 1843 whose attack on political economists has no clear referent, since it seems to expose the commodified structure of the philanthropy advocated in the poem, in the very process of criticizing the system of socialized charity that is about to displace such philanthropy. The redundancy of the poem's structure, combined with the need years later to supplement the headnote with an explanatory footnote, gives the impression of someone who does not quite know what he is saying, in the midst of the various discourses that speak through him. Composed as it is of texts that displace rather than satisfactorily comment on each other, "The Old Cumberland Beggar" enacts Wordsworth's attempt to place the old beggar within various discourses, each anxiously positive, and yet each produced partly as an otherness within the discourse it rejects.

The simplest of the intertexts is the headnote, which laments the passing of a system in which local communities look after their own, and in which the philanthropy attacked by Blake in "The Human Abstract" really does seem consistent with a respect for the beggar's autonomy. Yet in the poem itself, which breaks up into two divergent sections, respect for the beggar's individuality and the attempt to integrate him into an economy of sentimental values seem curiously at odds, in ways that make us uneasy with both rhetorics. The poem begins with a detailed description of the beggar already divided in the effect it produces. The description is not so much sentimental as aesthetic: every detail of the old man's activity is observed with a negative capability that makes no attempt to fit him into any moral scheme. Like some character in a Beckett novel, he arranges his "scraps and fragments" and scans them "with a fix'd and serious look / Of idle computation" (ll. 11–12, *LB*). In the context of the headnote we see this non-judgmental recording of his most trivial motions as respectful of his right to exist as he is. At the same time, the meticulous painting of the beggar turns up a plethora of troubling details that make us suspect a certain callousness in this respect for the beggar's individuality. His hand is so palsied that he drops the crumbs of his meal and inadvertently shares them with the little birds (ll. 16–21, *LB*). He is so bent that he sees only what is on the ground and scarcely knows what he sees (ll. 45–51, *LB*). As the careful observation of the beggar proceeds, it generates two overlapping perceptual frames: a romantic perception of everything that lives as holy, and a materialist awareness that these are after all the signs of poverty and that "Beauty is truth, truth beauty" may not be all we need to know. The long section beginning "But deem not this man useless" (l. 67, *LB*) arises as a way of eliding the uneasiness that Wordsworth feels, by assuring us that something *is* being done to help the old man and that he can be helped without removing him from "that vast solitude" where he is able to roam freely in all seasons (l. 156, *LB*), an aged version of the child in "Frost at Midnight" and a token that the romantic vision of the one life survives even in poverty.

The nervous verbosity of this section reminds us of the insincerity in this typically sentimental form of charity, in which people give alms to the poor in order to watch themselves being compassionate. But what is equally interesting is that Wordsworth in the Fenwick note unwittingly converts an attack on the other into an attack on himself. He begins by criticizing the reification of charity: "The political economists were about that time beginning their war upon mendicity in all its forms, and by implication, if not directly, on Almsgiving also." But he continues by attacking a system of voluntary charity which could well refer to the philanthropic chain praised in the poem:

> This heartless process has been carried as far as it can go by the AMENDED poor-law bill, though the inhumanity that prevails in this measure is somewhat disguised by the profession that one of its objects is to throw the poor upon the voluntary donations of their neighbours; that is, if rightly interpreted, to force them into a condition between relief in the Union poorhouse, and Alms robbed of their Christian grace and spirit, as being *forced* rather from the benevolent than given by them; while the avaricious and selfish, and all in fact but the humane and charitable, are at liberty to keep all they possess from their distressed brethren. (*LB*, p. 306)

What is puzzling here is that Wordsworth attacks the state for throwing the poor "upon the voluntary donations of their neighbours": in other words for reinstating precisely the system it is accused of eliminating. Brought back as a response to the poor laws, voluntary charity no longer seems attractive or even voluntary. But the reinscription in bad faith of what Wordsworth himself advocates discloses an uncomfortable sense that voluntary charity may always have contained traces of commodification. Granted that the poem describes charity given "with Christian grace." Nevertheless this charity is a matter of "habit," of "The mild *necessity* of use" (ll. 91–92, *LB*; italics mine). Moreover, it is difficult to deal with Wordsworth's second objection without running afoul of his first one. One cannot invent a form of charity that includes "the avaricious and the selfish" in that participatory bonding necessary to a sense of community without some system of taxation that would impose a collective will on the individual. Where the headnote simply contrasts two ways of dealing with beggars, one humane and the other callous, the Fenwick note confuses our sense of a right way to deal with social problems by suggesting that all economic solutions to poverty are divisive and devalue the individuals they are meant to serve.

The intertextual effect of the Fenwick note is a curious one. The poem by itself might simply have provoked us to continue the progress from aesthetic to social consciousness by imagining a way of reintegrating the beggar into the community less condescendingly than the one 'Wordsworth' so blusteringly affirms. Blocking a hermeneutics of enlightenment that tries to 'improve' the poem, by inscribing such a reading in the very meliorisms it corrects, the Fenwick note makes us reevaluate the 'aesthetic' consideration of the beggar at the beginning. But this discourse reenters the interpretive field by default and can have no more than a supplementary status. The various 'economic' discourses (including our own) treat the old man as a sign, as part of a system of exchange in which he represents something to someone else. The aesthetic discourse of the beginning treats him as a symbol, as someone whose meaning is in what he is, and therefore as an end in himself. Even granting its privatism, the bracketing of all concerns about what the beggar represents to society affords us an insight into his uniqueness that is possible only within a 'romantic' discourse we too easily dismiss as dated. And yet this very insight is blind to the old man's material needs, as is apparent from Wordsworth's need to supplement it with the account of how the beggar is looked after. As the poem compels us to think about both aesthetic and economic discourses, so also it allows us to question the paternalist moral economy that 'Wordsworth' defends, but not to dismiss it. However the twentieth-century left may resolve the problems of another age, it is worth remembering E. P. Thompson's comment that "the Plebeian culture" of Wordsworth's time "is rebellious, but rebellious in defence of custom."[31] Blusteringly affirmative on the surface, the effect of the poem is actually to play one discourse against another so as to bring out how they exclude each other and yet must uneasily cohabit in a social consensus that is dialogic rather than traditionally hermeneutic.

[31]"Eighteenth-Century English Society: Class Struggle without Class?" *Journal of Social History*, 12 (1978): 154.

Our final example uses many of the figures of understanding familiar from the other lyrical ballads. "The Brothers" is the story of two orphans: the older brother, Leonard, who goes to sea at the age of thirteen to earn a living, and the younger brother, James, who is then adopted by the community but mysteriously dies. The poem consists of a dialogue between the priest and Leonard, who has returned in search of James, only to find a new grave in the cemetery and to hear that one of the 'brother fountains' with which he associates himself has disappeared. Reading the poem uncritically, we might say that it incorporates the story of the brothers' love into the natural scene and then preserves this story through tradition and conversation. Significantly, the graves are all unmarked. To Leonard's comment that such unnamed graves in no way mark the fact of death, the priest replies that the stories of the dead are kept alive orally:

> We have no need of names and epitaphs,
> We talk about the dead by our fire-sides.
> (ll. 179–80, *LB*)

Even more intriguing is his comment that for death "*we* want / No symbols, Sir, to tell us that plain tale" (ll. 181–82, *LB*). A language of facts that are unre(mark)able, the plain tales of people's lives and deaths need neither symbols nor writing, because there is no disagreement about what they mean. They simply are, and their elemental truth is reaffirmed in conversations with those who share the bond of humanity. Crucial to our own inscription in the poem's hermeneutic is the inclusion of Leonard as both participant in the tragedy and implied reader. Through Leonard, who at first seems like us a mere visitor in the poem, we, too, become spectators *ab intra*, participants in an economy that circulates and reconfirms the values of sentimentalism.

The reading described here depends, however, on our investing the "homely Priest of Ennerdale" with the same authority ascribed to the pastor in *The Excursion*. Yet the poem opens with a lighthearted interlude between the priest and his wife Jane, in which he mistakes Leonard for a tourist. He never does recognize Leonard as one of the brothers whose story he tells, and we are left wondering why Wordsworth presents him as mildly obtuse if we are supposed to accept his responses. The question is best approached by asking what exactly the discourse is that the priest creates out of the brothers' story and how he is characterized as reader. Being hermeneutically naive, he is not conscious that he is doing any more than tell a story or that its 'lesson' is not similarly part of the order of mimesis. The world is "a great book" (l. 270, *LB*) made by God, and in it he reads the message of this story, which is that the brothers' mutual devotion shows a touching 'piety' (l. 271, *LB*). The priest's account of the parents' death and of why Leonard went to sea is relegated to prefatory segments of the narrative, and his emphasis is on the virtues that were thereby brought out in the boys: the fraternal love that made Leonard leave to earn money for his brother, and the loyalty that made James pine for his brother to the point of sleepwalking and 'accidentally' falling to his death. The possibility of suicide is elided, because such an un-Christian death might raise the question of whether a pietistic discourse is the right framework in which to read this story. The priest, in other words, uses the story to create a discourse built around virtue. Because of the lyricizing emphasis on feeling, and because the story unfolds entirely in the past, being told rather than dramatized, we have a distancing sense of fatalism, a sense that things could not have happened differently.

One does not question the deep feelings that underlie the brothers' relationship. Yet there is something incomplete about an interpretation that turns the story into a spot of time associated with the place where the brother fountains once were and then treats it as a memorial relic that is circulated but never questioned. The fiction of a community that shares experiences like death and loss is troubled narratively by the fact that the younger brother, James, though he was "the child of all the dale" and "liv'd / Three months with one, and six months with another" (ll. 353–54, *LB*), never really feels at home in the happy valley after Leonard's departure. It is troubled hermeneutically by the fact that there never really is any communication between the priest and Leonard, who reveals his identity only after leaving, and then, too, his identity but not his thoughts. As unsettling is the reversal of Wordsworth's usual convention of making the hearer of the tale a spectator *ab extra* who is initiated into communal lore by a native of the place. Because Leonard, the apparent outsider, turns out to be more within the story than the priest, and yet because he asks questions but never tells his story, we are left wondering whether we have indeed got inside the story. As in so many of these poems, the socioeconomic context has been curiously muted though not entirely omitted. We wonder why the boys' parents both died, and what led to the failure of a farm that had been in the family for five generations. The latter is presented as an isolated occurrence in a valley that has otherwise remained the same. But given that Walter Ewbank worked hard, is it credible that his failure is not part of some larger economic crisis elided from what the priest says? Leonard's reticence in front of the priest clears a space in which the reader can begin to tell the story differently. For the point about the genre of social history as opposed to sentimental narrative is that although the story itself does not change, the responses do. The lyricizing discourse of the feelings naturalizes tragedy: "For accidents and changes such as these, / Why we have a store of them!" (ll. 147–48, *LB*). Memory, its principal agent, can be a profoundly conservatizing force, because it composes the details of an experience in one particular way and then seals it in the past. The more materialist and historicist idiom that culminated in the Marxist rearticulation of temporality as history finds causes for social calamity and looks for solutions. We never really know whether Leonard's concluding silence marks his consent to the poetry of human suffering or his failure to find different words: his restless and still unformed sense that his family's tragedy did not have to happen after all.

At the heart of the poem's ambiguity is its invisibly symbolic mode, which is curiously at odds with the priest's claim, "We have no need of . . . symbols." For the interpretation of the poem as a spot of time that incorporates the virtues of loyalty and brotherhood among the forms of nature is dependent on a symbolic connection between the brothers and the 'brother fountains.' Yet the meaning of the fountains is far from clear. We can read the disappearance of one of the fountains two years after the death of one of the brothers as nature's sanctification of their relationship and her admission that the death of such a special person does make a difference. But the event that causes the fountain to disappear (the rending of a huge crag by lightning) is cataclysmic, hardly of the same order as the plowing and spinning with which the priest compares it. Perhaps the event means that the suicide of one so young is a breach in nature, something the community could have tried to prevent. The epitaphs and tombstones absent from Ennerdale serve the pragmatic function of identifying the dead that Leonard attributes to them. In a more profound sense, however, they encrypt the dead: they make the lives of the dead cryptic rather than transparent. A tombstone marks the fact of representation by creating a boundary between the presence and now the impenetrable absence of the dead, and our attempts to represent them. On the other hand, the unnamed graves are like the effaced coin in Nietzsche's famous discussion of truth and lie. Claiming as they do to tell a plain tale, these graves express the will of a community that has effaced not only the faces of the dead but also the metaphors that inhabit its own consolatory truths. For the unnamed graves, by making death commonplace, elide the scandal of the individual death. They permit the unquestioned circulation of stories that place particular deaths and that thereby keep in being the values that sustain a conservative psychic economy.

As an act of circulation itself, the poem is powerfully committed to uniting text and reader in a pathos that overwhelms any desire to ask questions. But on another level it also divides that pathos, causing it to speak its own silences. For one thing, the constant references to emblems, symbols, and tales encourage us to read the poem on the level of the signifier. As already suggested, the discrepancy between the priest's claim to be telling a plain tale and the poem's symbolic mode intimates a larger uneasiness with plainness: with the collection's project of an elementary language that is beyond representation because it achieves an exact equivalence between what is said or felt and what really is. This uneasiness emerges as an awareness of the customary origins of the languages we speak, of the language that the priest speaks, perhaps on behalf of Wordsworth himself. For where pure lyric is unsituated and thus universalizes its language, the opening domestic sketch of the priest marks his language as socially generated, and the dialogue format gives the reader a vantage point outside this language. One final factor is even more significant in making the text the site of the reader's dialogue between the poetry of human suffering and the prose of the world, and that is Wordsworth's realism: that attention to detail which Coleridge criticized as matter-of-factness, and which tells us how long the family had owned the farm and how great the age difference between the brothers was. The combination of precise factual detail with a certain vagueness about facts acts as a heuristic stimulus that provokes us to ask practical questions that we would not ask of a poem like *Adonais*, while making us wonder whether such an irritable reaching after fact does not miss the point. This intertwining of lyric and realism, in other words, dislodges us from comfortable tenancy in the discourse of the affections, a discourse whose power to move us must be balanced against its tendency to make feeling an end in itself.[32]

This discussion of a lyricizing romantic discourse that deflects social consciousness has obviously benefited from the work of Marxist and new historicist critics on the romantic repression of history.[33] My emphasis, however, is different. For one thing, the displacement of the reader that makes such a discussion possible does not result in the replacement of Wordsworth's desired reader with a real reader able to dismiss lyric as a form of repression. We cannot determine what Wordsworth's real audience was, and if we could, that would not establish what his real au-

[32]On a thematic level, too, Wordsworth seems critical of the affections, and suggests that they contain a destructive element, as Frances Ferguson argues: *Wordsworth: Language as Counter-Spirit* (New Haven, Conn.: Yale University Press, 1977), pp. 48–49. He is critical, too, of the imagination. "The Brothers" comes immediately after "There Was a Boy," and the description of the "feverish passion" with which Leonard on his travels sees the landscape reflected in the water and projects into it the uncertain heaven of his native valley recalls the final lines of the lyric on the Boy of Winander.

[33]See the work of Klancher and Levinson already cited; James Chandler, *Wordsworth's Second Nature* (Chicago: University of Chicago Press, 1984); Alan Liu, *Wordsworth: The Sense of History* (Stanford, Calif.: Stanford University Press, 1989).

dience *is*. Such a determination, moreover, would oversimplify the 'real' by assuming that it is a positive essence rather than a differential relation between antonyms such as 'desired,' or 'ideal.' Though reader-response theory is often accused of approaching the reader in an insufficiently materialist way, literalizing the notion of audience by identifying it with a specific historical group is equally essentialist and has value more as a corrective than as truth. There are advantages to defining 'audience' as a blank that can be filled in more than one way, while defining the audience-oriented text as an unstable compound of voices that can never quite be fixed. Where Marxist criticism might fix the text once and for all as a flawed product of its times, the historicizing of hermeneutics that *Lyrical Ballads* ultimately invites sees the very nonidentity of the text as one of the factors that makes it a productive stimulus as well as 'situating' it.

Second, it is incorrect to speak of repression, given that the 'romantic discourse' is never anything more than a project. Eschewing monumental writing, the Wordsworth of the prelaureate years allows his lyricizing of plot and situation to be caught within a contrary movement toward the novelizing of lyric. Embedded in the broadside ballad are traditions of populism, of political concern and social protest that Wordsworth effaces in the 1815 rearrangement but calls into play in this collection. A lyrical ballad is not a lyric: it is a composite form that is the site of heuristicially productive tensions. These tensions do not emerge through a later and more enlightened reading but are built into the poems themselves. Wordsworth does indeed want a world where different social selves cohabit, rearranged in an order that is horizontal rather than hierarchical, but in a rural rather rather than urban world that is tolerant because it is also spacious. But the collage of discourses collected in the *Lyrical Ballads* does not finally, as Jon Klancher argues, shade "into the Romantic poet's pluralist blending of differences."[34] As importantly, these differences do not simply undermine the discourse of the private self. Ultimately because of its focus on how we constitute the world through perception and because of the perspectival format of a collection composed of poems spoken in different voices, *Lyrical Ballads* asks us to accept the romantic discourse as no less legitimate than any other, though incapable of being insulated from what it deflects and always a differential rather than a positive term.

[34]*English Reading Audiences*, p. 148.

CHAPTER SIX

Wollstonecraft and Godwin: Reading the Secrets of the Political Novel

The genre of political fiction seems inhabited by certain formative disjunctions. To cast political theory in narrative or dramatic form is to disclose the fictions used in the political world. But on the other hand, the presence of political themes in a literary text assumes an extratextual referent and demands that we confront the problem of how texts are related to the world. The dialectical use of the form as a mixed genre is not inevitable. But the novels of Wollstonecraft and Godwin, in contrast to those of Thomas Holcroft, for instance, cross a particularly 'romantic' threshold in the history of the genre, in that they raise the problem of the textuality of political writing.[1] We are aware that Holcroft in a novel like *Hugh Trevor* is constructing a textual world in which characters are invented to fill plot functions, events are related to 'themes,' and captions at the head of each chapter instruct us on how to read. But the purpose of these devices is rhetorical rather than self-reflexive. In constructing an internally coherent paper world, Holcroft simply uses fiction to illustrate ideology and render it persuasive. Wollstonecraft and Godwin, however, use fiction self-consciously to make us aware of reality as a 'text' or system of misrepresentation, but also of ideology as a form of textual desire. As in much romantic literature, the problem of textuality proves inseparable from its ramifications for action and application, but the very notion of application is itself enmeshed in that of representation.

[1]My sense of what makes the political novel 'romantic' is different from that of Gary Kelly, who assumes that Jacobin novelists become 'romantic' at the point where they turn from the political to the domestic: *The English Jacobin Novel, 1780–1805* (Oxford: Clarendon Press, 1976).

Insofar as these texts raise the question of their reading, reading itself emerges as the site of a constant crossing between textuality and referentiality. This chapter accordingly traces the inscription of reading in three texts that compose a critical though not a chronological series. Mary Wollstonecraft's first novel, *Mary: A Fiction*, is of interest as a point of contrast. Unaware of itself as a text, it neglects the historicity that is part of both writing and reading, and reifies a view of the feminine character that is part of a system of representation. *The Wrongs of Woman or Maria*, by contrast, raises textuality to thematic prominence. Structured as a series of attempts by people who are literally or metaphorically imprisoned to communicate to those who might be outside, the novel raises the question of reading as a way of cleansing the doors of perception. Through the child, to whom Maria addresses her memoir, it introduces the possibility of a prophetic reader who will complete the text from a later vantage point in the historical process. This model is similar to the one later articulated by Schleiermacher and Hegel, and more specifically by Schelling, who 'divines' the truth behind appearances through negation. But already the teleological historicizing of reading is cast in doubt by our uncertainty as to whether the child exists. In *Caleb Williams*, finally, the subtext of a divinatory hermeneutics is explicitly explored. For Godwin's novel is not simply a memoir addressed to a future reader by someone who has himself tried to correct past misreadings of the truth. It is also a novel that psychoanalyzes reading so as to implicate readers in the strategies they use. It is the story of how Caleb becomes a spy in order to 'divine' the truth, and it thus creates an infinite regress in which his 'truth' is necessarily suspect, subject to a reading that will make it, too, disclose its hidden secrets.

The previous chapters approach the interaction between text and reader synchronically. But we must also consider the diachronic insertion of the text into future history, if the dialogue between hermeneutics and culture is not to be suspended in aporia. Godwin's own interest in a divinatory hermeneutics emerges in his essay "A Choice in Reading," where he distinguishes between the 'moral' and the 'tendency' of a text. The moral is "an ethical sentence to the illustration of which the work may most aptly be applied," where the tendency is "the actual effect [the text] is calculated to produce upon the reader and cannot be completely ascertained but by experiment."[2] Or put differently, the moral is the

[2]Godwin, "A Choice in Reading," *The Enquirer: Reflections on Education, Manners, and Literature*, 2 vols. (Philadelphia: 1797), I, 109. I am indebted to David McCracken's essay "Godwin's Literary Theory: The Alliance between Fiction and Political Philosophy," *Philological Quarterly* 49 (1970): 113–33. McCracken does not place Godwin's aesthetic theory in relation to the hermeneutic tradition. But his article provides a thoughtful analysis of some of the tensions in Godwin's essay.

authorial intention, whether original or final, whether established before the process of writing or in retrospect through a series of rationalizations and subterfuges.[3] The tendency, on the other hand, is an intersubjective and historically developing significance, generated by the interaction of intention and its representation and subsequently of the text and its reading. Thus authors "show themselves superlatively ignorant of the tendency of their own writings," which "has often lain concealed for ages" from their "most diligent readers."[4] Unlike Wordsworth, who similarly relates the text to its future in his "Essay, Supplementary to the Preface," Godwin frees the reader from an auxiliary role and makes history the site of difference rather than of an atemporal vindication of authorial identity. It is clear that for Godwin, who criticized Holcroft for his didacticism, meaning is shifted by its articulation in language,[5] and that is why the reader cannot be governed by the announced moral, but must read actively, doing more than simply reproducing the text. For by making writing the production rather than the reflection of an anterior meaning, Godwin also makes reading the production, through 'experiment' or experience, of a text that is still in process. At the same time, he is reluctant to give way to a complete relativism. Hence, his historicizing of intention takes the form of a divinatory hermeneutics, which imposes a teleological direction on the history of reception, consistent with his own notions of perfectibility. He uses the metaphor of recovery and speaks of a truth that has "lain concealed." He assumes a prophetic reader who will uncover the "genuine tendency" of the text,[6] and whose principles will coincide with those of Godwin himself. For instance, Nicholas Rowe's *The Fair Penitent* may have been written as a critique of illicit love, but despite itself, what it does is to expose the limitations of certain attitudes toward women. Like Shelley's reading of Milton, Godwin's reading of Rowe goes beyond the moral discerned in a merely grammatical reading, to a deeper tendency that becomes evident only through the enlightened reading that historical progress makes possible; and like Shelley, Godwin seems to regard this second reading as definitive.

But clearly this theory of reading calls into question the very model that it introduces. For in shifting from a mimetic to a hermeneutic view of the text, Godwin, like Hegel and Schelling, also historicizes the pro-

[3]Godwin, "A Choice in Reading," p. 107.

[4]Ibid., p. 106.

[5]For instance, Godwin argues, "If the moral be invented first, the author did not then know where the brilliant lights of his story would fall, nor of consequence where its principal power of attraction would be found. If it be extracted afterwards he is often taken at a disadvantage, and must extricate himself as he can" (ibid., p. 107).

[6]Ibid., p. 106.

cess of interpretation. He thus allows for the divinatory model itself to be read as a peculiarly 'romantic' construction: romantic in the way it reimposes the desire for unitary meaning on a deference to the reader that disestablishes both author and authoritative meaning. If Godwin's intention is to propound a divinatory hermeneutics, the tendency of his essay is to promote an 'historical' reading whose status is heuristic rather than traditionally hermeneutic, because it recognizes that the truth one divines is always the representation of a particular ideological will. For one thing, the concept of the text as tendency is much more open than a divinatory hermeneutics can allow: the word 'tendency' does not suggest anything determinate enough to ground meaning. Just as in Godwin's view the writer who tries to impose a final intention on his text scrambles belatedly to simplify what has become complex, so, too, readers who attribute such an intention to the world-historical process exert their own will-to-power in reducing a tendency to a direction. This chapter therefore discusses how the political novel, instead of simply transferring traditionally hermeneutic models into the text, produces the heuristic tendencies of Godwin's aesthetic theory. In doing so, it draws on Kierkegaard's displacement of traditional hermeneutics but also on descriptions of textual structure borrowed from contemporary Marxism. This is not because the analysis offered here is specifically Marxist. Rather, it is because Marxist reading itself develops from the hermeneutic tradition, specifically from Hegel's *Aesthetics*, which re-visions dissonances between the "idea" and its "embodiment" from a later vantage point. Inasmuch as earlier Marxist theory shared the tendency of a traditional hermeneutics to explain the text from a later vantage point and to desire (if not to achieve) its closure, more recent Marxist criticism can be used in reverse to refigure its parent tradition and decouple it from the nostalgia for closure.

Reading beyond the Ending: From *Maria* to *The Wrongs of Woman*

Wollstonecraft's prerevolutionary first novel provides a good starting point, not so much because it thematizes its status as fiction as because it fails to do so. For *Mary: A Fiction* presents itself as an imitation of reality, without much awareness that this reality is itself written by literary and social conventions, and therefore without much awareness of a reader who might read its story otherwise. Rachel Blau DuPlessis has pointed to the predominance in novels about women of plots ending in the marriage of the woman and her assimilation into the male system of values, or in her death and in the implied failure of her search for an autonomous identity.[7] It is the second version of this cultural script that is played out in *Mary*, where at the end the heroine waits to die. Given that the very conventions of narrative seem ideologically infiltrated, the problem for the woman writer becomes one of using narrative structures against themselves so as to stimulate the reader to think beyond them. "Writing beyond the ending," as DuPlessis defines it, involves "the transgressive invention of narrative strategies, strategies that express critical dissent from dominant narrative."[8] Such strategies invite us to go beyond a purely grammatical reading of what is said in the text, to an articulation of what Macherey calls its absences and silences. Far from being uniquely feminist, reading beyond the ending is essential to any political reading—whether divinatory and utopian as in Hegel or more cautiously historical as in Macherey—and political reading is itself a development of the hermeneutic tradition. But it is precisely such reading that *Mary*, on a formal level, resists.

The closed form of *Mary* is consistent with Wollstonecraft's other writings of this period. *The Female Reader*, a series of moral and religious readings for young women, differs markedly from *A Vindication of the Rights of Woman* in assigning women to the domestic sphere and in refusing to see social psychology as something historically produced. Its instructional form assumes the anterior presence of universal truths, without raising the question of their representation. Didactic prose does not usually call into question its status as truth. But *the Cave of Fancy*, a fragmentary philosophic tale begun in 1787, is similar in its epistemology. The title suggests a neoplatonic framework that associates truth not with history but with a higher realm. The sage Sagestus watches over a purgatorial cave where potentially virtuous spirits come to be reeducated. The text was to consist of a series of autobiographies told by the spirits in order to educate a child the sage had rescued from a shipwreck. The only one of these to appear in *Posthumous Works* concerns a woman who marries for duty, sublimates her love for another man, and eventually concludes that it would have been neglect of God to indulge this love.[9] Stories are passed on from generation to generation here, but the model of transmission remains one of passive absorption. In keeping with this view of truth as fixed are the parabolic form and exotic oriental setting of the tale, which posit a truth that is esoteric rather than imme-

[7]Rachel Blau DuPlessis, *Writing beyond the Ending: Narrative Strategies of Twentieth-Century Women Writers* (Bloomington: Indiana University Press, 1985), pp. 1–4.

[8]Ibid., pp. 5, 7.

[9]Wollstonecraft, "The Cave of Fancy," in William Godwin, ed., *Posthumous Works of the Author of a Vindication of the Rights of Woman*, 4 vols. in 2 (Clifton, N.J.: Augustus M. Kelley, 1972), II, 154.

diately accessible, but that is also universal and (by virtue of its setting) culturally despatialized.

Where these other texts involve the reader rhetorically if not heuristically, *Mary* seals itself against even our passive participation. The story is a conventional one, as if written ventriloquistically by the various cultural voices for which 'Wollstonecraft' is a gathering point. Yet it is offered to us as an "artless tale" in which "the soul of the author is exhibited" (*MWW*, p. xxxi) and in which there is therefore no need to read beyond what is said. At the beginning Mary seems significantly different from her mother Eliza, a "mere machine" (*MWW*, p. 1). But her 'identity' proves largely vicarious and consists of attempts to define herself through philanthropy, through her unsatisfying friendship with Ann, and through her love for the dying Henry, a person even more sickly than herself. Throughout the novel we are aware of an inner void that cannot be filled by others, of an excessive sensibility that verges on narcissism. Her one attempt at an independent identity, her decision to work, is quickly forgotten. By the end of the novel, Wollstonecraft's attempt at representing a new woman and the protagonist's attempt at self-representation have both collapsed. Resignedly, Mary adopts a voice of religious deferral, as she anticipates "hastening to that world *where there is neither marrying*, nor giving in marriage" (*MWW*, p. 68). The oddly critical and irritated attitude toward Mary, who is initially supposed to provide a model of the new intellectual woman (*MWW*, p. xxxi), seems written by the reaction against the cult of sensibility in which Wollstonecraft's middle-class pragmatism forces her to share. Yet at the same time, and despite the fact that Mary is derivative and formed by a "fondness for reading tales of woe" that her sensibility causes her to live out (*MWW*, p. 6), her author is also attracted to the tradition of sensibility, because it offers her the only available discourse that values feminine qualities. This double deformation of the novel's emotional identity, in which neither the protagonist's style of awareness nor the voice that criticizes it rings true, creates a gap in the text that stimulates us to read beyond the languages in which it is constrained to speak. But it is precisely such reading that the novel, through its closed and unreflexive form, discourages. Its terse style, consisting of short chapters in which plot dominates character, creates a sense of inevitability and allows the reader no space in which to think beyond the design imposed on her by the plot. Monologically unified, the novel lacks the exploratory distractions and alternative turnings provided by subplots and stories within stories. As important, it does not thematize the problem of reading through characterized readers or scenes of reading that mark the possibility of reading otherwise. Maria in *The Wrongs of Woman* makes desperate attempts to communicate to others who inhabit 'realities' different from hers. But the only thematized form of communication in *Mary* is the heroine's diary (*MWW*, p. 51), a narcissistic medium that offers her no exit from the forms in which she is conditioned to represent herself.

Mary, in short, institutionalizes a representation of women as doomed to fail because of their sentimental nature. Yet this "nature" is itself developed within a social text that assigns women the genre of sensibility. Although the actual reader may read beyond the novel's end, however, the text itself does not write beyond its ending by explicitly thematizing the historicity of its representations. With *A Vindication of the Rights of Woman* Wollstonecraft begins to view the condition of women historically. She provides a polemical rereading of *Mary* and ironically echoes its last sentence,[10] resituating her first novel and arguing that excessive sensibility is an effect of society's denying women an independent professional and financial identity. This rereading continues in *The Wrongs of Woman*, which rewrites *Mary* so as to turn it in a more revolutionary direction. The protagonist's name, Maria, is similar and there is a parallel love triangle: Maria has been married to Venables but falls in love with Darnford; Mary, too, had been married to a husband she did not love and had formed a Platonic attachment with the dying Henry. The differences in plotting are, however, much more striking. Mary's husband, Charles, is inoffensive and allows her to stay away from him for long periods, during which she meets and then tends Henry. George Venables, by contrast, forces Maria to give him her property, tries to make her into a prostitute for the gratification of his business associate, and finally imprisons her in a private asylum. Moreover, the problem of sensibility is now specified as socially caused: "In a life of such seclusion," the narrator comments, "the passions gain undue force" (*MWW*, p. 91). Not only does Maria's incarceration in a literal prison externalize a psychological or biological condition as a social one. Its manifest injustice also provokes the reader to revolt against the prison of things as they are. Other changes likewise contribute to this rewriting of a fatalistic novella as a radical novel. Henry Darnford is less sickly than Henry and initially represents Wollstonecraft's hope that a change in male attitudes is not always already doomed. Maria is given a child and made to seem more mature, oriented toward the future rather than the transcendent, and capable of the fruitful relation to life she is denied. Anne, the consumptive friend whom Mary helps and accompanies to Portugal, is replaced by Jemima, who introduces into the novel the particular problems faced by lower-class women.

As important is the greater structural complexity of the novel, which

[10] *A Vindication of the Rights of Woman* (New York: Norton, 1967), p. 68.

does not consist of a plot that imitates an action, but of Maria, Jemima, and Darnford telling each other their life stories. The result is to foreground the issue of (self) representation: to shift attention from what happens to how people narrate what happens. Maria's story, for instance, is cast in terms of the sentimental novels she is fond of reading. As she tells her tale of male oppression and expresses sentiments of feminist radicalism, she continues to look to men like her uncle and Darnford for help: she plays out her life in terms of romance conventions such as the ideal lover who will prove to be a knight in shining armor. Jemima's story is similarly formulaic, but according to the conventions of the jaded and fatalistic working-class realism we also find in some of Blake's *Songs*. Significantly, these stories are full of hiatuses and subject to awkward interruptions, like the "indistinct noise" that abruptly terminates Jemima's story (*MWW*, p. 118). As Mary Poovey observes, Wollstonecraft breaks off the characters' stories because she senses that the reader is being drawn "into stories that are patently not true and whose aesthetic closure would artificially resolve whatever politically effective emotions the stories might arouse."[11] What the emphasis on stories brings out is the way narrative and life mutually articulate each other, the power of narrative over life, and the need to read beyond the way we write ourselves.

It is no accident that these stories are all replayed in the setting of a prison. Through Maria's sentimental rhapsodies and her autobiographical memoir, writing is repeatedly thematized not only as a substitute for action (*MWW*, p. 82) but also as a confining repetition of the past. But if the narcissistic sensibility of the memoir recalls Mary's diary, it also differs from the latter in being addressed outside the self, in being an intent at communication as well as self-expression. Moreover, reading and communication are associated with an attempt to transcend one's own condition. Crucial to the implication of the reader in the text is the exchanging of stories among the three main characters, which marks their attempt to move beyond the imprisoning roles they write themselves into and also functions as a hermeneutic signal that invites us to read beyond and between the lines of their stories. Through Maria the text, as we shall see, sometimes thematizes the wrong kind of reading. But Jemima, her jailer who in her own way is equally oppressed, reads to educate herself (*MWW*, pp. 112–13). It is through reading that Maria and Darnford begin to know each other: she by reading the marginalia he has written in books he loans her, and he by reading her memoir,

[11]Mary Poovey, *The Proper Lady and the Woman Writer: Ideology as Style in the Works of Mary Wollstonecraft, Mary Shelley, and Jane Austen* (Chicago: University of Chicago Press, 1984), pp. 106–7.

which is to be passed on to Jemima. However limited the success of these characters may be in reading each other, their exchanging of textual and narrative materials sets up a circuit of communication which can be projected beyond the text itself and in which Wollstonecraft's novel then takes its place. By placing itself in this circuit, the novel suggests that writing is not the reproduction of a fixed meaning assumed in *Mary*; rather, it is an occasion for reading, and for a meaning yet to be produced.

This is not to suggest that reading is represented unproblematically. Indeed, the novel questions the fiction of a transparent reading put forward when Darnford seeks to know Maria by reading her memoir, or when we imagine that we know Mary Wollstonecraft because her editor has "give(n) to the public the words, as well as the ideas, of the real author."[12] When Maria reads, she reads Dryden, Milton, and Rousseau, at least two of them authors whom Wollstonecraft repudiates in *A Vindication*. Maria's reading of *Heloise* is particularly pernicious because it encourages her to become the sentimental heroine in search of an "ideal lover" (*MWW*, p. 89), and thus to play out the melodramatic version of Rousseau's romance script by becoming the betrayed mistress of the concluding fragments of the novel. How then can we hope to grasp the true Maria by reading her memoir, when the way she represents herself is itself shaped by *her* reading? The dangers of a merely passive reading are intimated by Wollstonecraft herself when she describes how Maria looks for "tale(s) of fictitious woe" that bear a "resemblance to her own" (*MWW*, p. 81) and then allows herself to be coopted back into what she is trying to escape.

But almost unobtrusively, the novel suggests a second model of reading. For Maria also reads the marginalia written by Darnford in the books he lends her. Though she herself does not reflect on the ramifications of what she is doing, what she brings out is that the activity of reading occurs in the margins and between the lines of the text. Given that writing, even when it is constituted as criticism, is still a reproduction of ideology that can do no more than display its gaps, reading must do more than also simply reproduce what is said or intimated. It must articulate what is not said or what is said only through those "determinate absences which twist [the text's] various significations into conflict and contradiction," to quote Eagleton.[13] The answer that the text seems to provide to our question of how we are to grasp the true Maria is that we cannot simply read her memoir or even the novel in which it is contained. The true self is still liminal, written in the margins of other

[12]Godwin's preface to *Posthumous Works*, I, n.p.

[13]Terry Eagleton, *Criticism and Ideology: A Study in Marxist Literary Theory* (London: Verso Editions, 1978), p. 89.

people's texts. The kind of reading that the novel elicits, then, is neither a surface reading that confirms it as a tale of woe, nor a deeper but still positive reading that acts upon the desire intimated in it: the desire for a sentimental ending in which Maria is united with Darnford. Rather, we are invited to practice a negative reading that unfolds a meaning shadowed in the text but not yet contained in it as either manifest or latent content.

Crucial to the negativity of the text is the way it fragments narrative to prevent us from settling into any single story of how things are. Each of the characters' stories negates itself as a historically limited misrepresentation. The result is that the meaning of the text does not seem to inhere anywhere in it but remains to be produced.[14] In keeping with the relationship it establishes between reading and negativity, the novel is careful not to identify the true practice of reading with any of its own characters. As a reformed version of Venables, Darnford projects the potential for change within a male audience and seems Maria's desired reader. But although Darnford and Maria meet obliquely by exchanging marginalia and memoirs, the distance of reading is never quite overcome. Their conversations are repeatedly interrupted, as if to inhibit us from settling into a fiction of transparent communication. Moreover, Darnford comes across as a shifting plot function rather than as a personality. His character is not fully worked out: the events of his life history are flat and clichéd, as if inserted to fill a space, while his role in Maria's life is left vague. It is never clear whether they have met before their imprisonment (*MWW*, p. 93), nor is it clear how he behaves after they leave the asylum. This refusal to specify Darnford's character raises but defers the possibility of a hermeneutic reading. It holds before us the possibility of true understanding, but without anchoring it in any particular person or social group. The figure of an appropriate reader is similarly constructed and deconstructed through the child. Never actually materializing in the plot, announced as dead toward the middle of the novel, and then ambiguously brought back in one of the endings, the child functions as a floating hermeneutic signifier. Like the child in Coleridge's "Frost at Midnight," it allows the text to point beyond the present and to represent a change that may actually have to occur through rupture in the reassuringly predictive terms of genesis and filiation. But because the child, unlike Hartley Coleridge, is entirely outside the text, the un-

[14]Poovey's otherwise excellent discussion treats Jemima's story as having more authority than Maria's and as leading us toward the repressed content of the novel. Her reading typifies the tendency of a Marxist historicism to see the text as limited by the historical circumstances of its production. My own reading, by contrast, does not allow us to settle into a Marxist dismissal of the novel by arguing that it contains a true meaning that it represses and the critic uncovers.

derstanding it promises and the application of that understanding to life cannot be identified with anything achieved in the novel. The possibility of reading beyond the present remains disembodied, deferred to a reader who exists only as a shadow.

The (de)construction of the reader allows for no definite terminus to the negativity of the text. But we must distinguish between the way the text actually functions and the reading 'Wollstonecraft' inscribes in it. Logically, the process of negative reading cannot reach a positive conclusion. The text, as Eagleton points out, is "never at one with itself. . . . It is, rather, . . . an attempt to overcome the problem of itself, a problem produced by the fact that the text itself is the production rather than the reflection of an ideal 'solution.'"[15] Because reading is similarly a production of ideology, it, too, is never at one with itself. Up to a point 'Wollstonecraft' uses this negativity as the propulsive force behind her text, and uses it even at the end to disengage us from a reading too identified with the figure of Maria. But in the chancery scene she also imposes a premature closure by positing a correct reading: an ideological key to the text, furnished in *A Vindication* and activated in this novel through a hermeneutics of reversal. In this respect she follows the pattern typical of a negative hermeneutics such as that of Schelling, who explores what is unsaid only to turn around and build a positive statement on it through a dialectical reversal of the unsaid into the said. We have seen in the case of Kierkegaard how this romantic impulse toward closure is reopened, how he explores the subtext of negative hermeneutics through a form of negative reading paralleled by developments in contemporary Marxist and psychoanalytic theory. In displacing negative hermeneutics into negative reading, Kierkegaard reads beyond Schelling's residual impulse toward Hegelian closure: he takes the latter's attempt to end the negation of external surfaces by deciphering the metaphysical unconscious and reads the unconscious (which Kierkegaard calls the Governance) as itself a text. It seems similarly true to the novel's political unconscious to reopen the strategies of reading that Wollstonecraft herself inscribes in *The Wrongs of Woman.*

But first we must describe the way 'Wollstonecraft' tries to make the reader wrest a positive meaning from the climax of what was intended to be part II. For there is little in the way the story unfolds to suggest that *The Wrongs of Woman* is any less fatalistic than *Mary*. The first part ends with the memoir as it breaks off on a note of despair, with Maria now in the asylum. In the second part, sketchily outlined in the last three chapters, Maria escapes and lives for a while with Darnford, though not in "uninterrupted felicity" (*MWW*, p. 192), and then fails to obtain a di-

[15]*Criticism and Ideology*, p. 89.

vorce. The fragments printed by Godwin in the conclusion sketch various versions of the third part, and with one exception the saga continues from bad to worse: among the woes still in store for Maria are an award of damages to her husband, pregnancy, miscarriage, and suicide. The structure of the novel, however, is such that its meaning is contained not in the narrative itself but in the interaction between the text and its future reader. By the end of the chancery suit several features have combined to elicit a reading based on a hermeneutics of reversal. To begin with, there is the pairing of the novel's title with that of Wollstonecraft's political treatise, which suggests that 'enveloped' within the wrongs of woman are the rights of woman, which can be unfolded through the model of counterreading articulated by Schelling. The resolution of the chancery suit, moreover, is highly melodramatic, with the judge tyrannically refusing Maria's request for a divorce and the right to her own property, even as he concedes that the decision might be different in a different court (*MWW*, p. 199). This naked assertion of prejudice is inflammatory, and the text thus provides an antithetical stimulus to the reader to transfer the venue of the action to the court of public opinion. Melodrama is, after all, a demonic form of romance, and its plots call for imaginative reconversion into what they should be. Peter Brooks has pointed out how nineteenth-century melodramas often include the character of a mute.[16] Silenced by society and forced into a nightmarish reality, the mute is a radicalizing figure with a specific rhetorical function. In the courtroom Maria has been muted and feels compelled to present her case in a paper that is read out. Our desire as readers is to give her a voice once again, to restore to her the power to act as well as to write through her words.

But the text does not simply call for an inversion of its plot, in which Maria is granted a divorce and lives happily ever after with Darnford. Maria has been silenced at a more significant level than simply not speaking in court, and the problem of the novel is not solved simply by reinvesting her text with the power of speech and action. We have already commented on the melodramatic, almost gothic, quality of the novel with its tale of imprisonment in an "abode of horror" and its brutal male villain, more sociologically specific but as nightmarish as Radcliffe's Montoni. The interest of women writers in the gothic, as several critics have suggested, derives from its ability to suggest an experience of frustration and confinement, a world that is internally disordered and split with no possibility of transcendence.[17] The *Wrongs of Woman* is a form of

[16]*The Melodramatic Imagination: Balzac, Henry James, Melodrama, and the Mode of Excess* (New Haven, Conn.: Yale University Press, 1976), pp. 56–75.

[17]For various points of view on the subject see Juliann E. Fleenor, ed., *Female Gothic* (Montreal: Eden Press, 1983).

political gothic which retains the gothic setting as a socially imposed metaphor so as to exhibit critically the emotional excesses of the form and its complicity in the attitudes of patriarchy. For another feature of the gothic is that it is nightmarishly unreal. It twists reality so as to make us question whether what we are reading is really happening. Because the gothic deformatively produces archetypes as stereotypes, it bears out Nancy Miller's claim that "the plots of women's literature are not about 'life' and solutions. . . . They are about the plots of literature itself."[18] The fraudulent and fabricated quality of the gothic romance has, in this novel, the effect of a double negation. It is as if the actual ending of Maria's story, in which villainy triumphs, is projected onto a screen, theatricalized, and replayed as a cultural nightmare. But at the same time the happy ending for which Maria pleads is similarly made to seem like a cinematic dream. Maria's political radicalism is only a thinly veiled disguise for her sentimentalism, union with her lover being simply the dream equivalent for the nightmare of imprisonment by the villain. The fact that the chancery scene is not yet about solutions but about plot, about the power that imposes narratives or the desire that produces them, compels us to read beyond Maria's defense as well as the legal decision. In its polemical tone Maria's defense resembles *A Vindication*, but the differences are fundamental. Her plea for divorce is simply a plea to reenter the matrimonial system over again, whereas Wollstonecraft is concerned with establishing psychological and therefore economic autonomy for women. Maria's defense is still represented as a text, and we must read its margins to bring out what she has not found a social language to articulate. However, as the pairing of the titles indicates, reading the social text as a negative transparency is not in Wollstonecraft's view an endless process. In order to unfold the rights that are 'enveloped' within the wrongs of woman, one turns to *A Vindication*, which specifically treats what is occluded from Maria's manifesto: the problems of sensibility, of female autonomy, and of the need for feminism to include a critique of society that will study the intersection between gender and class. The reader is encouraged to turn to *A Vindication* because Maria's text, though still a form of writing and therefore of repetition, is emergently different from her memoir and effusions. It at least adopts the language, if not yet the content, of a political critique grounded in a materialist analysis.

Were the novel to end with the trial scene,[19] reading it would not be

[18]Nancy Miller, "Emphasis Added: Plots and Plausibilities in Women's Fiction," *PMLA* 96 (1981), p. 46.

[19]I assume here that the author's text concludes with the chancery scene and that the fragments are part of the editor's text. But the question of where we draw the boundary between the text and its editing is a difficult one, as is the question of Wollstonecraft's

endlessly complex. But the various projected endings appended by Godwin force us to map the territory between present and future, between the judge's response and the just society we are provoked into constructing in our minds. Two detached sentences, based on Wollstonecraft's own experience with Imlay, raise the possibility that Darnford may prove disloyal. If so, then the hope that there exist some progressive men falls apart, and it is this hope that helps us to believe that the rights of women can be vindicated, even though power is exclusively vested in the hands of men. Of the "scattered heads for the continuation of the story," most mention Darnford's treachery and consist of brief point-form formulae whose predictability makes us question whether Maria will not automatically fall back into a male script. These endings re-inscribe *The Wrongs of Woman* in the feminine fatalism of *Mary* and make it once again into a tale of woe. But the most fully worked out of the paragraphs is different. It shows Maria having tried to kill herself by taking laudanum and deciding to live for her child, whom Jemima has found. This scenario, in which Darnford does not appear, and in which the daughter is a figure for a resurrection of hope based on an exclusively feminist society, interested Wollstonecraft enough for her to develop it at greater length than the others. Where the chancery scene has a revolutionary effect, the various endings are self-canceling, though not necessarily in a hopeless way. None of the endings involving Darnford is elaborated in sufficient detail to acquire any mimetic authority, and all of them are too based on clichés to ring entirely true. Their fragmentation and mechanization is a way for the text to write beyond itself, to exhibit the conventionality of the systems of representation it is forced to use, even as it stops short of overturning them or replacing them. Paradoxically, the manner in which these endings base

---

'intention.' On the one hand, there is 'Wollstonecraft's' text, which ends with the chancery scene. This text is more of an aesthetic whole than the one we have, on a hermeneutic if not on a formal level. Ending with a provocative crisis, it seems to have been cut off by the author's death, and the pathos of this 'fact' leads us to vindicate Maria and complete her moral-political education. But this text, if it existed for us, would be Godwin's text as much as Wollstonecraft's, because it would exist only through Godwin's decision to suppress a part of what his wife had actually written. We can speak of this text as the one Wollstonecraft intended because it seems to be in accord with *A Vindication*, and on some level she probably did intend it. But the Wollstonecraft who intended it is also a 'figure,' a figure perhaps constructed by Wollstonecraft herself in a radical mood. On the other hand, we have spoken as if the text that results from the printing of the various fragmentary endings is Godwin's, and indeed it is unlikely to have been the text with which Wollstonecraft, had she lived, would have presented us. But who is to say that it does not represent her intentions on some other level, on that level explored by Schleiermacher when he discusses a psychological reading that does not yield a unified meaning because it includes subtextual and collateral thoughts? The circumstances of the text's publication necessarily blur the boundary between Wollstonecraft and Godwin, between text and apparatus, author and editor.

themselves on Wollstonecraft's own life also limits their authority, by making too personal the repetitive and compulsive replaying of the author's anxieties. As importantly, Wollstonecraft does not incorporate them into the novel and does not thereby prevent us from reading the story otherwise. They are transmitted to us by Godwin as possibilities we must play with, probabilities we must think beyond, cultural anxieties that may continue to haunt our attempt to move beyond them. On the other hand, if the perfunctoriness of these endings reduces their authority, the greater length of the hopeful ending does not make it more realistic. Maria's final cry, "The conflict is over!—I will live for my child!" (*MWW*, p. 203), is conventional in its own way, its melodrama the sign of some voice that still remains muted and requires further reading. In practical terms we may wonder how feasible an isolationist society built around Maria, Jemima, and the child will prove to be, and that doubt is registered in Wollstonecraft's suggestion that the child itself may be a mirage: "A new vision swam before her. Jemima seemed to enter— . . ." (*MWW*, p. 203). Moreover, it is clear that the resolution projected here is still reactively shaped by the psychorhetorical systems it resists. If Maria's decision to live is an assertion of female autonomy, there is in her decision to live for her child and not herself a trace of the desire to bury herself that was evident in her attempt at suicide.

The editorial presence of Godwin adds yet another layer to the novel, distancing us from the author's voice and presenting both Wollstonecraft and her fiction to us as a text. For Godwin's introduction, interpolations, and conclusion must be considered part of the text, with the result that in this novel fictional mimesis is always already implicated in hermeneutic problems. Put differently, since *Mary* was issued by its author, it speaks to us in a historical present that reifies its truths as timeless. But since *The Wrongs of Woman* is an edited text, it speaks to us from the past and allows us to see how both Wollstonecraft's imitation of reality and the strategies she uses to make us reconstitute that imitation are historically produced and therefore subject to further interpretation. Taken without Godwin's additions, the second novel is already different from the first in making the process of signification hermeneutic rather than directly referential. Though the plot of the novel moves ineluctably toward a catastrophe, the thematization of reading and the polemical link with *A Vindication* encourage a divinatory reading that will liberate the true significance of the text from the prison of things as they are. Godwin's additions further complicate the text by bringing out its historical and heuristic tendencies. For in surrounding the novel with reminders of his wife's death, Godwin takes the future she has inscribed in the present and places it, too, in the past. His mediation creates a space in which we become aware of the historical forces behind a divinatory reading: the post-Enlightenment, even postrevolutionary optimism that allows Wollstonecraft to invest her hopes in the future, and the historically feminine tendency to defer the realization of her project to a reader, even as Maria reposes her hopes in her child and Mary trusts in God. In placing the text within history, Godwin encourages us to read beyond the simplicity of a divinatory reading while also conserving something of that reading. For a posthumous collection has a phenomenological structure similar to that of an epitaph. Because it commemorates and monumentalizes its subject, it asks us to sympathize with her goals. But the very fact of a tombstone, of an inscription, makes personality into something that must be read and situated, so that the epitaphic mode encrypts as well as enshrines.

We must be clear about what it is that Godwin, as his wife's editor and first explicit reader, does not do. His treatment of Wollstonecraft is sympathetic and respectful. But he does not grant her the privilege of prosopopeia or prophecy, and thus enlist the reader into a visionary company. Mary Wollstonecraft is presented not as an unacknowledged legislator like the visionary in *Alastor*, but as someone whose work was unavoidably incomplete, perhaps in substantive as well as formal ways. Godwin's additions consist only of a brief preface, an 'advertisement' placed between chapters 14 and 15 that outlines the projected plan of the whole, and a conclusion explaining the state of the fragmentary endings. Although these additions do not direct our interpretation, they place a frame around the text and locate us outside it. They create a historical space between author and editor, editor and reader, which becomes constitutive in our experience of the text. Across this space both Godwin's preface and Wollstonecraft's own preface remind us of the author's political project, and the epitaphic mode of a posthumous collection elicits our cooperation in taking it further. A divinatory reading forms part, but not all, of this cooperation. For Godwin's additions implicitly suggest two models of reading that we are likely to intertwine. In the editorial bridge between chapters 14 and 15, he provides an outline of Wollstonecraft's plan to write the novel in three parts, suggests that the "broken paragraphs and half finished sentences" are "sketches" on the verge of receiving the "finishing touches of her genius," and asks us to complete the text through a traditional hermeneutic (*MWW*, p. 186). But in the conclusion he insists on the ephexis, the undecisiveness, of philological accuracy and lays before the reader every last fragment of the projected endings. He thus elicits from us a nonrecuperative reading that culturally situates the anxieties and desires that produce various attempts at closure and that outlines these attempts against their silences. Such reading is akin to what Terry Eagleton describes as criticism: "Criticism is not a passage from text to reader: its task is not to redouble the text's self-understanding . . . [but] to show the text as it cannot know itself, to manifest those conditions of its making (inscribed in its very letter) about which it is necessarily silent."[20]

From the interchange between divinatory and critical readings arises a process best decribed as dialectically combining historical and heuristic reading. On the one hand, in divining the work Wollstonecraft intended, we also recognize the psychological and cultural conditions underlying that work and grasp it critically as a conflictual site. In that respect our reading is historical. On the other hand, we are still concerned with the project of the work or with our heuristic continuations of that project. To continue the past into the present, to allow the text a transhistorical function instead of limiting it to the moment of its production, is to conserve at least part of the impulse behind divinatory reading. For a Marxist 'criticism' assumes that the text's meaning is fixed once and for all by the original circumstances of its production,[21] and this meaning can be recontextualized only through a hierarchical separation between the culture-bound text and its more enlightened modern reader. But the kind of reading proposed here questions this identification of the text with its moment of production and recognizes both that the effects of the text cannot be reduced to its origins and that these effects, in a complex way, are part of an 'intention' evident at least in this text's refusal of closure. Macherey's criticism of Umberto Eco's idea of an 'open' text will help to clarify where an approach oriented toward the reader diverges from a (post)structural Marxism. "If the book does not produce or contain the principle of its own closure," he argues "it is nevertheless definitively enclosed within its own limits. . . . The work is finite because it is incomplete."[22] To recognize that the gaps in a text open it to the participation of a future reader is to see the text as both contained within and transcending its historical moment.

Caleb Williams: Metafiction and the Hermeneutics of Suspicion

It is partly because Wollstonecraft herself did not superintend the publication of the manuscript that we can, to borrow Macherey's important distinction, read *The Wrongs of Woman* as "produced under determinate conditions" rather than "created by an intention,"[23] and hence as

[20]*Criticism and Ideology*, p. 43.

[21]I am indebted for this point to my former student Anne Todkill in her unpublished dissertation, "The Historicity of the Text: Recent Theories in Marxist and Rezeptionsästhetik Literary Criticism" (Queen's University, 1985).

[22]Pierre Macherey, *A Theory of Literary Production*, trans. Geoffrey Wall (London: Routledge and Kegan Paul, 1978), p. 80.

[23]Ibid., p. 78.

available for historical reading. The circumstances of the novel's publication of course simply foreground a feature of all texts: namely, that they are the property of their readers as well as their authors. Nevertheless, there are writings in which the status of the text as production is something that emerges in the process of its transmission, and ones that deliberately question a substantialist ontology of the text. *The Wrongs of Woman* falls into the first category. Godwin's *Caleb Williams*, by contrast, is a work of political metafiction that explicitly raises the question of the relationship between writing, reading, and political action.

To begin with, Williams is employed as Falkland's secretary and librarian, with the task of reading books on Falkland's behalf and preparing "an analytical survey of the plans of different authors, and conjectural speculations upon hints they afforded, tending either to the detection of their errors or the carrying forward their discoveries" (*CW*, p. 6). Moreover, in the later part of the novel he is himself the subject of tales and misrepresentation, and his memoir (Godwin's novel) is therefore addressed to a future reader who must similarly detect error and forward discovery. It is not until Godwin revised the ending, however, that the novel became truly metafictional, making the final courtroom confrontation into a scene of reading rather than a battle of wills, and retrospectively making reading the object of the novel's scrutiny as well as the mode of its operation. The original novel relies on an almost crude hermeneutics of reversal to convert things as they are into things as they should be. It raises reading to a certain level of thematic prominence in the book because the reader is the means by which the vindication of Caleb is to be effected. But Godwin, as is well known, conceived his novel backward, beginning with the third section and the original ending, and ending with the first section. The middle and opening sections are concerned with the "analysis of the private and internal operations of the mind" and employ a "metaphysical dissecting knife in tracing and laying bare the involutions of motive" (*CW*, p. 339). As Godwin wrote, the opposition between Caleb and Falkland began to collapse, and an ending based on that opposition must have come to seem a repression of the novel's moral complexities. For if Falkland and Caleb are not simply antagonists but also doubles, the fact that the novel is a first-person narrative by Caleb can no longer hinder us from applying to his text whatever methods of reading he applies to Falkland's representation of himself. The revised ending takes account of the disturbing kinship beween the Promethean Caleb and his Jovian opponent and makes this kinship the dialectical ground of a reconciliation, which comes too late for the characters in the story but not too late to have an impact on the reader. The greatest difference between the endings is that the first version concludes not with Caleb's mistrial but with his return to prison, and therefore with the figure of imprisonment which is simply the rhetorical reverse of a simplistic and utopian desire for liberation. The new version ends with a much more complex court scene, in which the legal trial becomes entwined with Caleb's confession, with a trial of the inner self. And in substituting trial for imprisonment as the novel's final hermeneutic figure, Godwin turns the novel back on itself, placing not only Falkland and Caleb but also his own ending on trial.

The original novel is a pessimistic inversion of *Political Justice,* which shows the triumph of evils the Jacobins were fond of indicting: the potential for tyranny unleashed in Tyrrel and even the once noble Falkland by their rank and wealth, the corruption of the law, the greater goodness of outlaws like Gines, and the injustice of the prison system. But from the beginning Caleb's memoir is put forward not simply as a description of things as they are but as an address to future readers with the "faint idea that posterity may by their means be induced to render me a justice which my contemporaries refuse" (*CW*, p. 3). The terminus of the novel is therefore not in Caleb's imprisonment and madness, but in its effect on us. One can of course say this of most satire, and it is simply that the role of the reader gains greater prominence in *Caleb Williams* because of the way reading emerges as a motif in the text. From the beginning it is presented as that which brings the truth to light. The first section consists largely of Collins's narrative, which purports to explain the gothic melancholy of Falkland. It tells of the excesses and mysterious death of Tyrrel and attributes Falkland's tempestuous gloom not to the possibility that he is guilty of the murder and the hanging of the Hawkinses, but to his fine if extreme sense of honor, which causes him to feel that Tyrrel's death has cheated him of the chance to avenge publicly his humiliation by the latter. Collins's acquittal of Falkland accords with what we know of Falkland's character, and his story at first has what Caleb claims for his own narrative: "that consistency, which is seldom attendant but on truth" (*CW*, p. 3). But once we proceed to the second section, Collins's narrative, along with the letter from Hawkins and the secret contents of the trunk, become texts to be read for their lacunae and hidden depths (*CW*, p. 101). Through Caleb as reader, Godwin inscribes a model of reading as the unearthing of truth and the correction of past misrepresentations. In finally becoming to Caleb what Caleb has been to Hawkins, we recover a truth of a different kind: the truth of what should rather than of what really did happen. Like *The Wrongs of Woman*, the original version ends with a trial scene, and it is the blatant unfairness of the judge's decision in favor of Falkland that causes us to replay the scene correctly in the theater of our minds. For the pervasiveness of theatrical metaphors in this text (pp. 90, 3, 79) has made it clear that Caleb's trials and persecution are predetermined by a social script, while Caleb himself has introduced the metaphor of his text as evidence to be laid before a court of readers rather than judges (*CW*, p. 106).

Added to the rhetorical effect of Caleb's mistrial and imprisonment is the pathos of his subsequent madness, which makes him into something of a martyr and gives to his testimony a kerygmatic and more than ordinary dimension. The figure of madness serves as a form of mystification, finally disengaging Godwin's ideology from any articulation within the order of social representation and allowing it to address us from the inner sanctum of feeling. The metaphors of testimony and trial have been analyzed by Paul Ricoeur, who suggests that they are analogous, respectively, to revelation and hermeneutics in interpretation.[24] In the situation of a trial the inner truth of testimony is subjected to a reading that may treat voice as text, analyzing rather than being persuaded by it. One could argue that the coupling of testimony and trial deconstructs the priority of a revelation that precedes its interpretation and discloses truth as a moving army of figures. But it is not until he rewrites the ending and removes the suggestion of martyrdom that Godwin will make the trial into a genuine scene of reading and deny ideology the status of a secular scripture. In the present context, where 'trial' has eschatological as well as judicial connotations, interpretation is perceived as a mistrial to be rectified by a future reader. The submission of inward testimony to the court of current public opinion recognizes the contingencies of the historical process but also condemns this process as a betrayal.

In a curious way the original version, despite its bleak ending, supports Godwin's dictum that sound reasoning and truth, when adequately communicated, must always be victorious over error.[25] But the revolution effected remains abstract because it depends entirely on a future reader. Godwin's revision of the ending seems intended to make things as they should be into an evolution from and not simply a refutation of things as they are. In the new ending Caleb, instead of being defeated and going mad, comes prepared to accuse Falkland only to find him most "dreadfully reduced" (*CW*, p. 319). He is moved not only to pity but to a scrutiny of the selfish motives that have impelled him to destroy Falkland to save himself. His long speech is therefore an indictment not only of Falkland but also of himself, for having been insensitive to Falkland's virtues. Though suspicious at first that Caleb is using "a pretence of liberality and sentiment, to give new edge to [his] hostility" (*CW*, p. 324), Falkland is finally so moved that he confesses and in his turn

[24]*Essays in Biblical Interpretation*, ed. Lewis S. Mudge (Philadelphia: Fortress Press, 1980), pp. 123–53.

[25]Godwin, *Enquiry Concerning Political Justice and Its Influence on Morals, and Happiness*, ed. F. E. L. Priestley, 3 vols. (Toronto: University of Toronto Press, 1945), I, 85–92.

lavishes praise on Caleb. The death of Falkland shortly thereafter and the condemnation of Caleb to a life of remorse make a happy ending impossible. But the project of reconciliation is offered to the reader as one that we can continue. The new ending appears to serve the purposes of political justice far more effectively than the old one, being more dialectical and less rhetorical. For one thing, the reader of the original version might have been uneasy at being used to vindicate Caleb's character, given that Caleb's voyeuristic curiosity makes him the mirror image of Falkland: equally compulsive, and desirous of a power that is simply more passive and secretive than the power exerted by Falkland. By moving beyond the black-and-white claims of the original ending, Godwin makes Caleb's self-justification seem less hypocritical but also makes the possibility of reform more real, since Falkland's conversion is spontaneous and since the old order that he represents is admitted to have some good in it. At the same time, he makes the scene of reconciliation at the end no more than a tendency, an intention. He thus passes on to us the task of applying in our own lives an insight that comes too late to help the characters, unlike Holcroft in *Hugh Trevor*, where the Macchiavellian Wakefield is converted and lives happily ever after with the virtuous Hugh. For in having Falkland die and deferring an effective reconciliation beyond the narrative itself, Godwin creates a temporal separation between the old society and the new. Unlike Holcroft, he avoids the contradiction of creating the new order within a narrative world he has spent several hundred pages castigating and also avoids making perfectibility into perfection by literalizing a conversion that still requires much moral work.

But as we have suggested, it is really much more than just the ending that is changed. In rereading its previous ending and making the cancellation of the moral Godwin first intended into the dialectical ground for the positing of a new tendency, the text has become a work of political metafication, concerned as much with interpretation as with ideology, and recognizing how the process of writing backward has itself become a process of reading. Narrative and reading thus become subjects of the text. There are numerous references in the book to the construction of "narratives" and "tales," from which one gathers that for Caleb, as for a contemporary critic, narrative is associated with a will to closure, with an internal consistency, that gives the appearance of truth and causality (*CW*, pp. 3, 106, 4). But reading is to some extent a deconstruction, and not simply an amplification of narrative. It is worth quoting Caleb's description of what happens when he is no longer listening to Collins's narrative, and instead is considering it as a text:

> At first I was satisfied with thus considering every incident in its obvious sense. But the story I had heard was for ever in my thoughts, and I was

> peculiarly interested to comprehend its full import. I turned it a thousand ways, and examined it in every point of view. In the original communication it appeared sufficiently distinct and satisfactory; but, as I brooded over it, it gradually become mysterious. (*CW*, p. 107)

In the first version of the novel the model of reading described here is applied only to Collins's narrative, and not to Caleb's own story, which is apparently to be read in its obvious sense. The second version probes the secrets behind Caleb's own self-representation as well. Thus in its concluding textual somersault the novel has Caleb discard his memoir as "a half-told and mangled tale" (*CW*, p. 323) and suddenly puts in its place another story, the "plain and unadulterated tale" of Caleb's remorse and confession (*CW*, p. 326). By now, however, the reader has learned to suspect the narrative consistency that gives the appearance of truth. After all, when Caleb had first heard Collins's narrative, he had found "a connection and progress in [it], . . . which made it altogether unlike the little village incidents I had hitherto known" (*CW*, p. 106). Yet Collins's tale had been mined for its buried secrets. There is no reason why Caleb's own tale of remorse and conversion should not similarly prove to contain things it has not said.

At first, it seems that we are meant to take at face value Caleb's remorseful outline of things as they might have been. His last speech is in the form of a confession, and to confess is finally to tell 'the truth.' Moreover, Caleb and Falkland have moved beyond the ambiguity of reading and are present to each other, in a situation where the spoken word seems to carry "conviction to every hearer" (*CW*, p. 324). In *Cloudesley*, a much later novel where the protagonist Danvers has a similar guilty secret but is made to live up to his remorse by his former employee Cloudesley, the conversion of Danvers occurs when Cloudesley gives up writing letters to him and finally confronts him. Godwin relates the spoken word to the dialectical generation of truth: "A letter is a dead and powerless pleader. All that it says is already put down, and the man that answers it pronounces a decision where there is no one near to dispute or remonstrate. A personal conference . . . is a very different thing."[26] But already in the case of Collins's narrative, which is persuasive when first heard but full of gaps when reexamined, Godwin has raised the question of speech as a text. Moreover, as Paul Ricoeur has argued in discussing our culture's explanation of the origin of evil, the confession of sin is itself a complex tissue of fiction and truth, a meaningful action that must be considered as a text.[27] To confess is to invent a

[26]*Cloudesley: A Tale*, 2 vols. (New York: J. and J. Harper, 1830), II, 46.
[27]*The Conflict of Interpretations: Essays in Hermeneutics* (Evanston, Ill.: Northwestern University Press, 1974), pp. 272–86.

cause to explain a series of effects that may elude such explanation; it is also to exchange responsibility for power, to admit guilt for the way things are in order to claim the ability to change them. Confession, in other words, is part of an economy, a system of representation and exchange, in which nothing is simply what it is. Because Caleb's confession is made in the context of a trial, it is not simply the way that Falkland and Caleb have hitherto represented themselves that is subject to cross-examination, but also Caleb's current representation of himself that is on trial. Behind this self-representation is an entire ideology: a 'romantic' ideology of truth and love in which opposites are reconciled through the dialectic of experience, and in which evil is simply error. In the last scene Caleb puts on a highly theatrical performance: a performance so effective that it asks us to listen to this ideology, but also so melodramatic that it asks us to listen for its silences. The ideology of *Political Justice* can perhaps explain how a not indecent person like Falkland is trapped by errors characteristic of his class into perpetrating evil and using power to protect himself. It cannot explain the motiveless malignity of Tyrrel, a thing of darkness whose psychotic temperament precedes his use of power to safeguard himself. Moreover, Godwin's ideology is equally silent about an issue he will explore in *St. Leon*: that of how an individual conversion like Falkland's is to change social structures that are larger than any individual, without itself being changed by those structures.

What occurs between the first and second versions of *Caleb Williams* is somewhat like the development traced in the history of hermeneutics itself. Godwin begins with an almost naive model of reading, in which our role is to reverse the grammar or plot of the novel so as to actualize a psychological meaning (the triumph of truth) that is quite clearly present in the text as desire. In the second version he actually acts out a complication of this model which is more genuinely akin to a divinatory hermeneutics: he invites us to reverse the plot of the novel in order to grasp the tendency behind its psychological meaning, the desire for honesty based on reconciliation that underlies Caleb's defensive desire for vindication. But this divinatory reading becomes in turn a narrative that is subject to reading, a way of arranging and simplifying the evidence. It is a curious coincidence that the reader in this novel, Caleb himself, is figured as a spy. In casting the reader in the role of spy, Kierkegaard will later effect an uncanny displacement of divinatory reading, with its hermeneutics of perfectibility, and will make the process of reading potentially endless. For the spy is a kind of diviner, a reader of other people's secrets, but the spy also possesses secrets, personal motivations for reading a certain way. In an early essay P. N. Furbank suggests that *Caleb Williams* is "a highly dramatised symbolic picture of Godwin himself in the act of writing *Political Justice* . . . . Caleb

Williams is clearly Godwin himself, Falkland the ancien régime, and the opening of the trunk is the writing of *Political Justice*."[28] But as a text that allegorizes itself, Godwin's novel does not simply culminate in the triumphant issuing of *Political Justice*. It inescapably associates ideology with narrative, and thus with the reading of narrative: reading in the double sense of bringing to life and probing what is hidden.

St. Leon: Reading as History

To apply theory to life without discovering its hidden articulations and fragmentations is perhaps impossible. Indeed, it is these fragmentations that generate new tendencies and thus make reading a vital part of the economy of political fiction. The symbiotic relation between political desire and its deconstruction emerges strongly in Godwin's next novel *St. Leon*. *St. Leon* does not explicitly thematize the problem of reading. Instead, it thematizes its own historical status and emphasizes the relativism of any moral it may appear to urge. The shift from textuality to historicity as a mode of hermeneutic self-reflexiveness is significant, because it brings out the life as well as the intentionality of signs. It results in a deconstructive pragmatism that uncovers the secrets harbored within political and social fictions while allowing them a real and not just a hypothetical viability. The later novel deals with a sixteenth-century aristocrat who gambles away his fortune and submits to a virtuous poverty, until through a compact with a mysterious stranger he acquires the philosopher's stone, which confers immense wealth on him, but at the cost of alienating his family and making him an object of suspicion and persecution. The novel is historical in two ways: it is set in the past and its action covers a considerable period of time, thus registering changes in socio-intellectual values. During the first half St. Leon utilizes his secret for purely personal ends. His use of power is feudal and ostentatious. His attitude to his family is hierarchical, not only in that he does not confide his secret in them (which he has sworn not to do), but also because he wants the satisfaction of being their sole support, despite the fact that his wife Marguerite has from the beginning been an equal economic partner. But the death of Marguerite, St. Leon's imprisonment by the Spanish Inquisition, and his miraculous escape from execution mark a turning point in the novel. To escape detection, St. Leon takes the elixir of youth, becomes forty years younger, and begins a new life as Chatillon, the benefactor of postwar Hungary. His power is now used for political and social justice. He does not set himself above those

[28]"Godwin's Novels," *Essays in Criticism* 5 (1955): 215–16.

he is trying to help as a philanthropist motivated by a desire for fame, but tries to be as inconspicuous as possible (*St.L.*, p. 374). Moreover, he realizes that he cannot change things through a magical and authoritarian transfusion of wealth that will allow him to bestow his largesse while keeping power in his own hands. In a striking anticipation of Marx's critique of money as alienated representation, he tries to use economic power in ways that are not external to the structures they seek to alter:

> I easily saw that, if I would confer a substantial benefit on this unfortunate nation, I had scarcely any other means for the purpose, than that of reviving among them a spirit of industry. I was aware that, in the strictness of the term, money was not wealth; that it could be neither eaten nor drunk; . . . It was my purpose to stimulate and revive the industry of the nation: I was desirous of doing this with the least practicable violence upon the inclinations and freedoms of the inhabitants. (*St.L.*, pp. 372–73)

In this half of the novel one's sympathies increasingly shift to St. Leon. Marguerite's moral purity had seemed a desirable if pastoral luxury. But her patriotic and honest son Charles, who condemns the impostor Chatillon for not allowing Hungary to starve and for thus strengthening the Turkish occupation, seems inflexible. And if we are inclined to admire anyone, it is St. Leon, "an equivocal character, assuming different names, and wandering over the world with different pretences" (*St.L.* p. 475).

From the opening pages of the novel, systems of perfectibility are linked to the rather dubious practice of alchemy. Predictably, St. Leon's motives in trying to improve his family's lot and later the economy of Hungary are submitted to a merciless scrutiny, and the base materials out of which his gold is compounded are exposed. But the metaphorical equation of alchemy with ambition is not used unequivocally to condemn him. In this respect the novel resembles another work of Godwin. In his *Lives of the Necromancers* he demythologizes magic and sees it as a historical phenomenon, a discourse in Foucault's sense. Magic is the form taken in superstitious ages by a will-to-power that would now express itself through scientific experiment. The Faustian condemnation of alchemy as unhallowed emerges as a historically situated rhetoric, and magic itself as a set of metaphysical practices generated by resistance to that rhetoric, and therefore participating in its assumptions.[29] The historical perspective makes Godwin aware of a certain legitimacy in the (nec)romantic impulse that earlier ages could not discern, but also allows him to see it as something that is a product of its ethos and is not simply in advance of its time. The result is neither an orthodox condemnation

[29]Godwin, *Lives of the Necromancers* (London: Fred Mason, 1834).

of magic nor a romantic and Promethean elevation of it. Rather, Godwin engages in a historical reading of necromancy, in which he sees it as the sign of a more profound impulse, but without falling into an essentialism that abstracts tenor from vehicle, because the form assumed by this deeper impulse is for the moment part of its nature. His reading is best described as historical and heuristic rather than grammatical or divinatory, because it tries to get at what is behind certain cultural practices, while constituting this deeper will as a constantly shifting political unconscious rather than a transcendental signified.

This treatment of necromancy is inconceivable apart from the historical relativism that accompanies the hermeneutic movement. As Godwin in *The Lives of the Necromancers* uses methods emerging in biblical hermeneutics to reread the practice of magic and draw out its value for the present, so, too, in *St. Leon* he turns the historical novel into a heuristic form so as to make his readers separate the moral from the tendency. Because the tale is set in the sixteenth century but addressed to a later reader, we are encouraged to think beyond a moral framework that would either condemn St. Leon for choosing power over value or yield fatalistically to the series of calamities that seems the price of Faustian heroism. But we are not really placed in any other framework and so are not encouraged to convert the tendency into the signified by reading the novel typologically as a story of Jacobin radicalism and its persecution. Whatever social experiments St. Leon performs are, after all, placed behind us as the past and not in front of us as the unheralded future. They become the subject of analysis rather than the object of hope. The historical form, in other words, creates a double displacement and forces us to inhabit the gap between a grammatical reading that accepts the dated moral framework of the original tale and a divinatory reading that might appear to unlock its 'true' revolutionary significance but would also create a different set of lies in the process.

This displacement occurs not only because of the historical distance between text and reader, but because of the historical dimension within the text itself. Critics have disagreed radically about what the novel means. According to B. J. Tysdahl, alchemy "is presented . . . as a symbol of those aspects of society which Godwin wants to criticise," and St. Leon is associated with the false Burkean ideals of honor and chivalry earlier identified with Falkland.[30] According to Gary Kelly, alchemy is associated with a curiosity "which is also the essence of dissent and intellectual progress," and St. Leon's secret practices remind us that by "several important anti-Jacobin propagandists the French Revolution had been attributed to the thought of the Enlightenment working through

[30]*William Godwin as Novelist* (London: Athlone Press, 1981), p. 86.

secret societies such as the Freemasons and Illuminati."[31] But the novel is not summed up either by a mimetic and grammatical reading that assumes there is no more in it than the condemnatory moral it appears to urge on us, or by a divinatory reading that makes a tendency in it into its ultimate meaning. The novel is, as we have suggested, self-historicizing. Because he possesses the elixir of youth, St. Leon lives through more than one period and becomes the vehicle of a world-historical spirit that evolves and changes and cannot be subjected to a single moral evaluation. The moral that dominates the first half, where personal power causes St. Leon to neglect his common humanity, is unsettled by the revolutionary tendency of the second half, where he begins to use his power for the social good. But as St. Leon puts the beneficial potential of alchemy into practice, the radical tendency of the novel is submitted to an intense scrutiny. St. Leon finds that money does not have an intrinsic value but is part of a system of representation, and that by using political alchemy to increase the supply of precious metals he inevitably produces an inflationary situation (p. 379). When the populace turns on him for his failure to work miracles, he is, moreover, forced to the un-Godwinian recourse of asking for the help of the occupying Turkish government to protect himself and the commodities he is trying to dispense. What St. Leon discovers is that power always participates in an economy, that it is involved in substitutions that make its structure disjunctive. Yet knowledge is indissolubly linked to power, articulated and facilitated by it, as thought is linked to language. The symbiotic relationship of power and knowledge puts this novel at a considerable distance from the optimism of other Jacobin writers. But this is not to say that the second half ends by confirming the cautionary moral of the first half, as the novel's repetitive rhythm might suggest. Instead, because the Hungarian experiment is historically localized, the reader is again invited to think beyond its failure, to imagine further continuations of the novel's project.

The unfolding of the political novel parallels developments that occur over a more extended period in the hermeneutic tradition itself. The political novel becomes 'romantic' at the point where it crosses the threshold between rhetoric and hermeneutics, making the reader more than simply the recipient of a text that is to be read for its moral. By involving the reader in the making of the text, it releases us from the text of things as they are. At the same time, because such novels create a form in which meaning does not have to be embodied in the text, they avoid the contradiction characteristic of Holcroft's novels, where an idealized ending is superimposed on the real world and made to claim mimetic

[31] *The English Jacobin Novel*, pp. 212–13.

authority. But the introduction of the reader is an ambiguous blessing, because the text that relies on reading to produce its meaning is always under the arrest of further interpretation. What follows is not so much an endless abyssing of meaning as a recognition that if reading is to remain a productive activity, it must be historical and critical rather than prophetic. Like *Hyperion* and *Christabel, The Wrongs of Woman* is broken off at a crisis, and the effect (whether intentional or not) is to elicit a divinatory completion. But the editorial frame that Godwin adds to the novel allows us to 'situate' the hermeneutics of the broken text. Likewise, Godwin's revision of *Caleb Williams* makes interpretation the very subject of the novel and thus translates the divinatory reading that it stages into the ground for a further critical reading. The development described here finds a parallel not only in the way Kierkegaard opens up and complicates Hegelian hermeneutics, by making the reader as diviner into the reader as spy, it also finds a parallel in what was happening in biblical hermeneutics, where the imperialism of the Christian eschatology from which Hegel's secular scripture derives was coming into question. In the work of Schleiermacher the rationalization of gaps in scriptural ideology through typological reading had given way to a disintegrationist reading in which these gaps were attributed to the composite authorship of the Bible. In classical philology F. A. Wolf had similarly argued that the Homeric epics were composite pieces made over a long period of time. Though the early philologists neither intended nor developed the theoretical implications of their research, they laid the groundwork for a reading that would no longer consider texts as revelations, and, more importantly, they left the reader free to interpret the text as produced under determinate conditions rather than as created by a transcendental intention. It is unlikely that Marxist criticism of the modern scriptures could have happened without what Lee Patterson calls the "analytic dissolutions of historicism,"[32] and it is in this tradition that Godwin places himself when he publishes his wife's novel, figuring himself as editor and philologist as well as scribe and prophetic reader. This tacit displacement of the hermeneutics of perfectibility had been anticipated in *Caleb Williams* by the demystifying figure of the reader as spy. Finally, in *St. Leon*, where the figure of action as alchemy parallels that of reading as espionage, Godwin incorporates his earlier insights at the level of the fiction itself. Instead of thematizing the problem of textuality, he develops a genuinely heuristic form, that of the historical novel, which generates a dialectic between ideology and its reproduction that makes it possible to act within history as well as read through it.

[32]"The Logic of Textual Criticism," in Jerome J. McGann, ed., *Textual Criticism and Literary Interpretation* (Chicago: University of Chicago Press, 1985), p. 78.

PART II

B. *Canon and Heresy: Blake's Intertextuality*

CHAPTER SEVEN

Untying Blake's Secular Scripture

Blake criticism, under the aegis of Frye, has until recently assumed the coherence of his work by composing it according to the hermeneutic code of his later system. The system is not a synchronic entity, and indeed that is why we have had recourse to a hermeneutic in order to find it in texts where it is not clearly present. In line with the divinatory readings developed by post-Kantian idealists like Schelling and Hegel, the 'mature' Blake represents his early texts as shadowy types of the later work and figures the latter as still evolving. The dissenting energies of some of the early texts are thus bound within the stubborn structure he was trying to build as he proceeded from a multitude of small poems, through the antechapel of the minor prophecies, to the philosophic poem that he alone among the romantics actually approximated.

Insofar as Blake himself encourages canonical reading, while at other times stimulating resistance to it, his work is centrally involved in the dissemination of a traditional hermeneutic. The figure of the canon brings together the cultural ambitions of the hermeneutic tradition as we have traced them in the three previous chapters. Not only does it employ reading synchronically to claim consensus, as Wordsworth tried to do, it also develops the diachronic dimension of hermeneutics by using the supplement of history both to claim future authority and to contain textual contradictions within a teleological narrative. The Bible, which Blake described as the great code of art, has been the model by which both we and he have read his secular scripture. Assembled out of the writings of many men and conjoining two distinct cultures, it provides analogies not only for a unification of the authorial canon but also for a hermeneutics of cultural history that we may now see as imaginative imperialism. In the reading of the Bible, radically different texts are made to advance a narrative that becomes clear only later in history. In actuality, the Bible is not an eschatological narrative, but a collection of writings that inscribes the holoscopic impulse in an intertextual field. When we refer to it, however, we refer to an *editorial* activity supervised by the institutional church. This activity produces a cultural paradigm that typologically absorbs difference into unity: a paradigm in which all religions are made to be one.

In the later prophecies Blake experiments with a self-canonization that submerges those differences from himself that he dismisses in *The Everlasting Gospel* as "Self-Contradiction" (E520; l. 92). But the system is a later supplement, and the presystematic texts are very different from the late ones. We must remember also that the Blake who used the biblical paradigm to limit reading was profoundly influenced by gnostic heresies that questioned the authorized version.[1] Gnosticism rather than Protestantism made possible Blake's radical humanism as well as his anti-institutional belief in the individual as the source of gnosis. This emphasis on the individual challenged belief in a single scriptural canon or a single reading of it. For as Elaine Pagels suggests, the gnostics, though they sought one truth and were not relativists, regarded all doctrines and myths including their own "only as approaches to truth."[2] Given the existence of the heresies, the forming of a scriptural canon had for centuries been the scene of a struggle in which doctrinal questions were entwined with political issues such as the status of women and the democratization of the structures by which religious knowledge was transmitted.[3] Like Wordsworth, Blake inherited these issues as part of the archeology of his chosen genre. As he composed his secular scripture, he was forced to consider whether there were not voices and perspectives excluded by the activity of canon formation and thus to assess the legitimacy of his project.

These chapters will be concerned with Blake's heresies against his own system. The work of Damrosch and Mitchell, as well as the essays collected in *Unnam'd Forms*,[4] have already made us aware of a nonsystematic Blake. Drawing on such studies but focusing on texts in the larger context of Blake's corpus and on the canon itself as a cultural form, I try

[1]On the general provenance of gnosticism in the romantic period, see James Rieger, *The Mutiny Within: The Heresies of Percy Bysshe Shelley* (New York: George Braziller, 1967).

[2]*The Gnostic Gospels* (New York: Vintage, 1981), p. 137.

[3]See ibid., pp. 49, 70–74, 125–28.

[4]Leopold Damrosch, *Symbol and Truth in Blake's Myth* (Princeton, N.J.: Princeton University Press, 1980); W. J. T. Mitchell, *Blake's Composite Art: A Study of the Illuminated Poetry* (Princeton, N.J.: Princeton University Press, 1978); Nelson Hilton and Thomas Vogler, eds., *Unnam'd Forms: Blake and Textuality* (Berkeley: University of California Press, 1986).

to reconceive what might otherwise become scepticism or aporia as generating a revisionary hermeneutics in which intertextuality replaces canonicity. For the early Blake did not simply write poems that failed to resolve themselves into a system. He created a counterpractice that encourages us to reflect on the very processes of interpretation and institutionalization, though one that is still a 'hermeneutic' in that it involves writer and reader in a process of cultural self-understanding. Accordingly, the present chapter is a theoretical one, which plays traditional arrangements of Blake's canon against an admittedly heuristic remapping of the textual field into three 'sectors.' In keeping with our convention of beginning with theoretical paradigms developed by the writers themselves, it treats *Milton* as a fictionalized elaboration of the hermeneutic on which canonical readings rely, while using *The Marriage* as a 'source' for the early Blake's counterpractice. This counterpractice finds expression in a writerly use of form that is phenomenological rather than postmodern and that therefore generates a perspectivism that is not relativism. Focusing on Blake's early texts, the subsequent chapters deal with two sectors of his work as perspectives from which to view the canon he subsequently constructs. Thus, the earliest poems allow us to view experience from an individual rather than systematic perspective, and by inviting intertextual rather than teleological reading, they question any narrative into which we might fit them. In the brief epics that are the subject of the third chapter, Blake begins the construction of a narrative to contain individual episodes, but in a manner that calls for constant rereading.

The Early Texts and the Displacement of the Canon

Any description of how Blake displaces his canon must begin with the differences between the early and late texts. For not only does the shared use of biblical patterns make the two seem continuous. Sometimes editors further emphasize this continuity by divisions into 'minor' and 'major' prophecies, in which poems like *Thel* that are in no sense prophetic are typologically absorbed into the category of minor prophecies so as to blunt their dissenting force.[5] One area of difference is suggested by Leslie Tannenbaum, who argues that while the Lambeth books, like the Bible itself, compose a secular scripture from "a number of disparate books," the later prophecies fuse "biblical prophecy with the

[5]I refer here to the popular edition by Northrop Frye, *Selected Poetry and Prose of William Blake* (New York: Random House, 1953).

epic mode, casting the entire vision of the Bible in a single work."[6] Although he is arguing for the unity of Blake's oeuvre, the early use of what we shall call 'segmented' form generates questions about the epic totality later developed to sublimate the differences embedded in the great code itself. These questions may well persist in later texts whose totality is not explicitly under erasure but which, as David Clark has shown, turn out on closer inspection to be "self-displacing."[7] Nevertheless, the two groups of texts are vastly different as frames through which to view the textual field. The whole in the epics claims a rhetorical precedence over the parts; in the earlier texts it is the parts that precede their assemblage into wholes that may be no more than interpretive constructions.

Perhaps more accurate than a genetic arrangement that marginalizes the earlier texts as 'minor' is a division of Blake's work into three 'sectors': the early poems (such as the *Songs, Visions,* and *Thel*), the brief epics from *The Marriage of Heaven and Hell* to the Lambeth period, and the longer prophecies, which most clearly articulate the system. The differences between the earliest and final texts are the most striking. Although the former contain characters and symbols later absorbed into the system, they are not yet part of a macro-poem that Blake, as medium for the world-historical spirit, is involved in constructing. They connect with each other, but dialogically rather than anagogically. Their perspective is not yet cosmic: like the *Lyrical Ballads,* the *Songs* are spoken by a heteroglossia of individual voices, whereas *Thel* and *Visions* provide inside views of the experience of one character. Told as they are from an individual perspective, they suggest to us that experience or experiment may have priority over any preestablished system. In the longer prophecies it is precisely this emphasis on experiment that disappears, as particularized symbolic characters are replaced by mythic characters with whose selfhood the reader is not supposed to identify, and who are therefore sketched in structurally as actants rather than phenomenologically as selves. These characters function allegorically, not in the sense that they stabilize reference in a system of one-to-one correspondences, but in the sense that their referent is an argument (however self-complicating), and not an 'inside,' a personality. Gone also is the conspicuous assemblage of texts in terms of short, monad-like sections. This method of presentation had created a certain resistance to totalization, being a structural marker of the recognition that the whole is always less than the sum of its parts.

[6] *Biblical Tradition in Blake's Prophecies: The Great Code of Art* (Princeton, N.J.: Princeton University Press, 1982), p. 7.

[7] "Auguries of Difference: Indeterminacy and Displacement in Blake's Prophetic Texts" (Ph.D. dissertation, University of Western Ontario, 1986), p. 71.

Somewhere in between these two poles are the brief epics. For though they share with the earliest texts a composition in terms of disjunct, mobile parts, they also share with *Milton* and *Jerusalem* the project of a secular scripture. The holoscopic intentions of the brief epic are described by Barbara Lewalski, who sees it as sharing with epic a proposition or invocation, a rising action that moves toward victory, and a hermeneutic claim to provide a compendium of all knowledge.[8] *Europe* and *America* clearly have rising actions, and the various introductions and preludia of the Lambeth books occupy the structural position of propositions, whether or not they provide a key to the action. Unlike its longer cousin, the brief epic concentrates on a single episode and does not begin in medias res so as to unfold the story of things archeologically and teleologically from an event that is made the metaphysical center of a phenomenology of spirit. But the totalizing effect created in the larger form by the text's ability to move forward and backward in time is supplied in the brief epic by the use of typological symbolism, which enhances the "epic dimension" by giving the particular episode a paradigmatic significance.[9] Blake's system, we can argue, similarly functions as an "abstracted typology"[10] that transposes the episode from diachronic and historical to synchronic and mythic time. Also characteristic of the brief epic, as Lewalski points out, are spectacular scenes:[11] a series of tableaux whose melodramatic or apocalyptic staging inhibits complex response and asks us to see events in black and white patterns. Spectacle, to put it differently, subordinates event to rhetoric rather than allowing experience to complicate argument.

In contrast to the early texts, the force that drives the brief epic is a totalizing one. Moreover, where dialogue and counterpoint dominate the early texts, speech in these poems has become oratorical. Nevertheless, Blake's brief epics are also sites at which this totalizing impulse is challenged. To begin with, the brief epic is, in de Man's sense of the word, 'intentional': it inscribes epic as desire. The Lambeth books are only preliminary sketches for Blake's global vision, and their very brevity suspends their claim to finality. Thus, in *Europe* the poem breaks up into a series of flamboyant happenings that leave us uncertain whether its climax is central or peripheral, an episode or a paradigm. Moreover, although we feel in the poem what Mitchell calls a "pressure for resolu-

[8]*Milton's Brief Epic: The Genre, Meaning, and Art of Paradise Regained* (London: Methuen, 1966), pp. 21, 26, 31.

[9]Ibid., pp. 64, 45.

[10]Paul Korshin, "The Development of Abstracted Typology in England 1650–1820," in Earl Miner, ed., *Literary Uses of Typology from the Later Middle Ages to the Present* (Princeton, N.J.: Princeton University Press, 1977), pp. 147–203.

[11]*Milton's Brief Epic*, p. 83.

tion,"[12] the precise meaning of the resolution is far from clear in this text whose claim to be a 'prophecy' can only refer to how it is spoken and not to what it says. The liminal structure of the poem, which takes us to but not across a threshold, collapses the encyclopedic perspective of eighteen hundred years into a sense of the text as an episode. This marking of the text as installment is even clearer in *Urizen*, which begins by reminding us that we have read only the first book. As the installments accumulate, but without following a pattern of advance or decline, 'epic' increasingly comes to seem transcendent, a matter of the formal covering rather than of the inward content, which remains, in Hegel's term, "indeterminate." As in Hegelian hermeneutics, these poems invite us to resolve the gaps between theme and execution through a divinatory reading that constructs the whole into which they fit. But such resolutions are constantly suspended by the tension between epic rhetoric and brevity of form. Related to the problems of brevity and indeterminacy is the use of the spectacular, which emphasizes appearance at the cost of what lies behind it. Spectacle, though powerfully oratorical, is uncertain in the truth-claim it makes. Hyperbolical in its structure, spectacle is a mode of excess that hovers between overstatement and apocalyptic wisdom.

The totalizing impulses of the early prophecies are similarly arrested by the form they share with the early poems. Briefly, Blake uses a modular form organized around juxtaposition rather than continuity. The early texts are made up of discontinuous discursive segments, sometimes spoken by different voices. Though we encounter them in a certain order, they do not simply unfold into each other: they function as mutually reflecting mirrors that make the reading experience recursive. Perhaps the most extreme example of this disjunctive structure is *The Marriage of Heaven and Hell*, which combines poetry and prose, aphorism, logical discourse, fantasy, and prophecy. More common is a conjunction of preludium, narrative, and a further preface or motto: a form we find in *Thel*, *Visions*, *Europe*, and *Urizen*. Often, the meaning of these components is less clear than their structural function, so that there is a defamiliarizing of this function in which the text's form becomes its content. Thus, mottos do not simply provide guidance but raise the question of whether there *is* a key to the text's meaning. Introductions do not simply lead into the narrative but make us reflect on whether the narrative is shaped by the point at which we enter it. The resulting reflection on perspective is encouraged by the relative spatial autonomy of these segments. The parts are foregrounded in a radical challenge to the hermeneutic circle with its organicist notion of a correspondence be-

[12]*Blake's Composite Art*, p. 107.

tween part and whole. The 'whole,' instead of being what the parts fit into, is a perpetually shifting effect of the (part)iculars through which we view it.

Segmented construction characterizes even the texts whose plates are in a relatively fixed order. But Blake also makes his parts movable by varying the order of the plates and leaving them unbound. He thus creates what Barthes calls a 'writerly' text which the reader cooperates in making.[13] The writerly text denies to itself a canonical form and makes us aware of its truths as a field of metaphors that we structure by inscribing in it our own further metaphors. The order of these texts is not infinitely variable, because a poem like *Thel* will often have page numbers. Nevertheless, Blake did not paginate components like mottos, frontispieces, and tailpieces, and thus provided a heuristic stimulus to the reconception of the text as flexible rather than dogmatic. Leopold Damrosch, one of the few critics to recognize that the transferability of parts calls into question an organic conception of the text, sees this extraordinary use of form as creating a synchronicity characteristic of myth.[14] But although it is true that an open form unbinds us from the mimetic claims of chronology and allows for visionary rearrangements that defy historical limits, mobile forms open windows into eternity only as part of a perspectivism that reinscribes vision in a field of relations. These relations are necessarily cultural and experiential. Refusing to make the poems embody what Damrosch calls "a single and inevitable form,"[15] Blake does two related things. He opens his text to the fact that readers (including Blake himself as reader of his texts) see things differently depending on who they are and when they live. He also opens us to the fact that psychological and historical constructions of the self are not forms of determinism but 'states' that we temporarily inhabit.

The field of possibilities which constitutes such a text is generated not only by the shifting relations between its parts but also by the relationships between poems that cite and revise each other. Blake's patrons made their own relationships between texts, binding certain poems together and thus constructing different 'canons.' The intertextual structure of these poems obviously qualifies any claim by the prophetic mode to provide a divinatory reading of cultural history. Thus, the relatively hopeful prophecy of *America* is accompanied by a preludium whose dark virgin recalls the shadowy female of *Europe*. The ambiguity of this seg-

[13]There is some debate over whether the various orders in which the plates survive were sanctioned by Blake. But as Robert Essick points out, his method of printing allows that readers do different things with texts, and that the text may be partly constructed by the accidents of transmission. "William Blake, William Hamilton, and the Materials of Graphic Meaning," *ELH* 52 (1985): 841, 868.

[14]*Symbol and Truth in Blake's Myth*, p. 351.

[15]Ibid.

ment, which may suggest that this revolution, too, will produce a fruitless implosion of energy, is compounded by a further segmentation in which Blake covers up in some copies the lines that depict the bard breaking his harp. The position of this segment, whether the bard is "asham'd" (E52; 2:18) of the doubts expressed in the preludium or of the hopes expressed in *America* itself, is likewise unclear. The indeterminate relationship of the poem's segments generates further questions about the relationship of Europe and America in Blake's cultural narrative. The fact that the preludium was added later may make it a European revision of American optimism in the light of experience. Or it may limit the authority of the preludium by suggesting that its mood was colored by the writing of *Europe*. The point is not to choose between these interpretations, but rather to recognize the implications of Blake's structure for a substantialist conception of the text. The spaces between segments are spaces in which readers must think about the cognitive categories they use to relate these segments. Moreover, in constructing our own version of the relationship between the segments, we also become aware of critical sub-versions in relation to which our own (current) version can do no more than maintain itself as a diacritical possibility.

Most of Blake's early and middle texts are composed of movable segments that make us think about structure and perspective. This method, though still present in later works, is less conspicuous because the main narrative takes up so much more space in relation to the prefaces and preludia, and because the densely packed print of *Jerusalem* is less interrupted by full-page designs. The segmented construction of individual texts carries over into the macro-poem Blake may have been trying to assemble out of them in his middle phase. Stationing ourselves at the beginning of that project, we become aware of how the secular scripture is assembled out of parts that do not make a whole, produced if not by different authors at least by different 'Blakes.' We can read a poem like *The Song of Los* as a frame for *America* and *Europe*, so as to make the assembled structure into a narrative that proceeds from creation to apocalypse.[16] As the poems are written, however, the 'frame' is consciously supplementary in the way it telescopes beginning and end together in a separate text, without being able to integrate them with the middle from which the end must grow if it is to be persuasive.

In fact, Blake's canon bears an uncanny resemblance to his great code. The early texts and brief epics are his old testament. Written in vastly different styles, they are poems of exile and experience whose liminal hero Orc is a god of wrath as much as of energy. Where these texts are

[16]Tannenbaum, *Biblical Tradition in Blake's Prophecies*, p. 7.

scattered episodes from a story that does not yet exist, the longer prophecies are parallel versions of that story, told in *Jerusalem* on a cosmic scale and in *Milton* on an individual scale. In their coherence of purpose they are much more like the gospels, which they resemble in substituting Los for Orc, the order of mercy for that of wrath. But if the Bible provided an imaginary identity for Blake's texts within a typological series, the genre of secular scripture also functioned as the ballad did for Wordsworth, as a mirror-stage. Blake was aware of the new developments in biblical hermeneutics, and specifically of the detailed philological work that called into question the authority of the Bible as the product of a creative spirit with a single purpose.[17] Schleiermacher was shortly to take the radical view that discrepancies in the synoptic gospels could not be explained as later accretions, that they constituted layered readings of indeterminacies in some of the pivotal events of the Christian story. In some sense Blake was drawn to the scriptural analogue precisely because it was dangerous as well as reassuring. The fundamental indeterminacy of those primal cultural scenes that 'explain' the human condition is something he encounters repeatedly, and it is such indeterminacies that generate the multiple perspectives from which the texts read themselves.

Reading the Vortex: *Milton* and the Reconstruction of a Canon

Although these chapters attempt to unsettle a canonical reading of Blake, that reading is one that he himself later inscribes in his work. In *Milton* Blake begins the task of creating a canon by imagining a scene of reading that will contain previous errors: his own and those of cultural history generally. As a writer who returns from the dead to become his own reader, Milton limits the disseminative potential of the writerly mode by modeling it for us. He becomes his own prophetic reader: he reorganizes the chaos of his past from a higher perspective, by unearthing from it that subtext that made him a member of the devil's party without his knowing it. His divinatory reading takes form as repentance, as a hermeneutics of charity that finds value in errors that become the impetus for truth. As a figure for the stable interchange of writing and reading functions, Milton is also Blake as his own reader and Blake's desired reader. He acts out a way of organizing a text like *The Four Zoas*, which was a workshop where Blake drafted material for the final prophecies and stored what he could not yet assimilate. Sublated into *Milton*, Blake's unengraved epic is his first attempt to construct a

[17]Cf. Jerome McGann, "The Idea of an Indeterminate Text: Blake's Bible of Hell and Dr. Alexander Geddes," *Studies in Romanticism* 25 (1986): 303–24.

whole out of the parts into which it kept collapsing. *The Four Zoas* is in turn a synecdoche for the earlier poems, with their oversignification of part over whole.

Milton also humanizes for us the abstractions of Christian hermeneutics, by coupling them with an interiorized self-exegesis remarkably like psychoanalysis, though protected from the latter's tendency to deconstruct the self by its association of understanding with charity and salvation. The Puritan poet descends into his past self through a self-displacement in which the ego or selfhood stands outside the subject, who remains in heaven lying on a couch, an empty form waiting to be reinvested with a new identity. The exegesis of the "real . . . Self" (E 109;15:11) is by no means simple, but involves reversal and overturning. The famous image of the vortex, to which we shall return, is one of Blake's most striking figures for the reversals necessary to reading correctly and for the way they first impinge on us as a proliferating psychic chaos. As Milton falls like a "wintry globe" into the "Sea of Time & Space," he enters a vortex in which "what was underneath soon seemd above / A cloudy heaven mingled with stormy seas in loudest ruin" (E110; 15:39–46). This disorganized state of affairs in which the world is inverted parodies the way Milton has made the spectrous undergrowth of his warped system into a heaven of transcendent principles. At the same time, these lines have the effect of defamiliarizing Milton's perversity, of exposing his system as what Schelling calls an inverted world that demands a counterreading: a reading that takes the form of a dialectical rather than a simple reversal. Blake would not have known Schelling but certainly knew Boehme, who is the source for the latter's view that opposites are interimplicated so as to make the negative into the ground of the positive. In Blake's terms, Milton is not his negation but his contrary, and the latter's inverted world contains enabling traces of Blake's vision. Just as the fall into the vortex registers on the character Milton as an optical jolt that occurs only because he is falling and sees things upside down, so it engenders in us a desire to rectify an unnecessary distortion of vision and functions as a hermeneutic signal to make us correct what the inversion parodies. The passage is thus a mise-en-abime of the larger text, figuring as a problem in perception what is more extensively narrated as Milton's paradoxical reversal of himself: his return from the dead to a living world that turns out to be dead, his return to a past that turns out to be the future. The vertigo of these reversals, though potentially endless, is stabilized by their association with religious paradox and their anchorage in a hermeneutics of conversion.

In retrospect, we must take this scene of reading as narrating our own mental travel through the inscape of Blake's corpus. The weeds of death in which Milton becomes entangled as he falls into the sea recall the

Urizenic chaos of Experience. In the early texts Blake had shaped that world into the "wintry globe" he describes here. This process of 'conglobing' or 'englobing' in which Blake images a fallen creative activity that is both constructive and constrictive is also described at the beginning of *Jerusalem*: "There is a Void, outside of Existence, which if enterd into / Englobes itself & becomes a Womb" (E144; 1:1–2). The globe, visually associated in *Urizen* with the globule of blood, is the aborted fetus created by the poet, who is a spectral and misguided version of Urthona. In a very different way Blake's early texts also conglobe a miscreated vision: a vision bitterly critical of Milton but, as we shall see, capable of negating only Milton's system of salvation and not his vision of the fall. That criticism, Blake now insists, can be seen not simply as harrowed by the anxiety of influence but as the self-disintegrative prelude to the major prophecies. That the early Blake could only reinscribe Milton, and that Blake's *Milton* revisits the site of his own early work, is marked by the fact that it begins with a reduced repetition of *The (First) Book of Urizen*, announcing itself as the second or perhaps third book of *Urizen*, now seen from a higher point on the spiral of understanding (E96; 3:1–43). We are also reminded that Milton is Blake's redeemed specter by the doubling of the two in a circular exchange in which Blake reading Milton sings the bard's song, which inspires Milton to reread himself so that he can enter Blake's left foot and enable him to write.

Milton is, in other words, Blake's poetic equivalent to Schleiermacher's Compendium. In it he not only stages the *agon* of reading as a process in which truth must be arrived at through negativity, he also begins to articulate rules of exegesis to limit the dissemination of meaning in his canon. These have to do with both detail and structure, and the rules that govern detail must be understood in the context of structure as a process rather than a static system. At the level of detail, one of the more prominent strategies of interpretive containment is the organization of the canon in terms of binary oppositions such as the distinction of contraries from negations, or the division of people into three classes: the 'redeemed' and the 'reprobate,' on the one hand, and the merely negative 'elect,' on the other. Although the notion of contraries is present as early as *The Marriage*, it is not opposed to the category 'negation,' which allows us to segregate as irrelevant whole areas of experience with which the early Blake engages in ways that threaten the closure, if not the intellectual vigor, of his dialectic.

The division into classes likewise limits ambiguity. Thus the uncomfortable proximity of the 'organized' innocence projected in the Lyca poems to the 'unorganized' version of the *Songs of Innocence* in which they were first included can be rationalized in terms of Bloom's characterization of the bard as merely 'redeemed,' unable to imagine an Eden that does not relapse into Beulah.[18] As the redeemed speaker occupies the uncertain ground between reprobate and elect, so, too, his idea falters between the organized and the unorganized without really calling into question the possibility of organized innocence. Blake's binary oppositions, as this example suggests, are tenuously woven into a more complex field of three or sometimes four terms. Intertwined in the notion of classes is a third term that unsettles the opposition of the reprobate and the elect and a binary opposition that tries to restructure the triad by making the 'redeemed' a contrary aligned with the 'reprobate' and completely separate from the negation constituted by the 'elect.' As we try to read Blake's texts in terms of the grammar he provides for them, they keep slipping away from us. Satan in *The Four Zoas* "never can be redeemed in all Eternity" (E380; viii.381), and in *Milton* Satan or the Spectre is a negation (E142; 40:34). Yet Milton, surely an imperfect (redeemed) version of Urthona, identifies himself with Satan or the specter (E139; 38:29). It is unclear whether the Spectre, whom Los tyrannically puts to work at his forge, is Los's contrary as Reason is the outward circumference of energy, or whether he actually negates the creative project. In all probability 'negations' and 'contraries' were themselves states that Blake passed through, feeling sometimes that his art was self-consuming, and at other times that he must enter the heart of his own darkness to make the void a womb.

The fact that Blake's classifications are states that he moves through rather than the '*langue*' that governs particular narrative articulations suggests that they have only a heuristic status. Yet once again *Milton* tries to contain the disseminative implications of turning Blake into his own reader by making his rules provisional resting points in a hermeneutics of process. The text introduces a historical perspective committed not to relativism but to a progressive, universal poetry in which poet and reader are joint laborers in the teleological revisioning of earlier texts. Contradictions are an inevitable part of forging this coherence. Like Hegel, Blake sees the structure of his system as immanent and emergent rather than synchronic. Perhaps the best model for this notion of structure is the paradigm assumed by Goethe in his analysis of anatomical structure and developed by Dilthey into an analogy for the reading of literary structures and canons. When he made the discovery that people as well as animals had an intermaxillary bone, Goethe found that a component which served a particular purpose in one kind of structure could be adapted to a different structure as the species evolved. For Dilthey, Goethe's discovery was a crucial part of the intellectual climate that shaped hermeneutic assumptions about the relation between part and

[18] *Blake's Apocalypse*, pp. 130–32.

whole. It "established a case in which a uniformity of structure given in the original design may exist in contradiction to the requirements of the completed structure; so the structural part in question had to be adapted to these requirements through a later coalescing of parts which originated separately."[19] The authorial canon may seem composed of parts that pull in different directions, and the individual text may similarly contain unassimilated surpluses. But Dilthey's paradigm gives us a way of reconceiving discrepant elements within the ongoing process of the text's structure. Blake's familiarity with the model would have come from its use in the increasingly vexed area of biblical hermeneutics, as an explanation of how a canon that lacked a single author(ity) could still be an authoritative whole. *Milton* is, in fact, an enactment of the paradigm. Beginning with a text that exceeded its own bounds in being of the devil's party, it adapts Milton to the needs of a later structure; gathering up parts of Blake's own corpus that originated separately, it struggles to idealize and unify them.

For strategic reasons the later prophecies will not be our concern. Although we have read *Milton* hermeneutically, it is clearly possible to uncover in it asymmetries between the mimetic, hermeneutic, and reflexive levels similar to those discussed in the *Biographia*. For instance, as Milton's prophetic reader, Blake reinvents him, but instead of transferring the power of re-vision from author to reader, he has Milton enter his body so that Blake can derive his authority from what he has created as reader. This displacement of power between Milton and Blake can be seen as the symptom of an uneasiness about the prophet's power, which has no origin and for which one must therefore create a genealogy that produces power as effect rather than source. The same structure of displacement unsettles the status of Blake and Milton as historical 'figures' outside the text and characters inside it. Thus, it is entirely possible to see the late prophecies as the work of a less than resolved soul. Nevertheless, thematic and unreflexive readings of these poems have given them a place in the critical canon which now needs to be questioned. Emphasis on *Milton* and *Jerusalem*, in other words, has naturalized a hermeneutic reading of the earlier texts because it seems to be what Blake 'finally' wanted. To see the corpus from the perspective of these earlier texts is to recover the heuristic potential of the texts as a whole. Such a shift of terrain will unsettle the paradigmatism of part and whole implicit in the hermeneutic circle of the canon. It will allow us to see the parts as having a certain autonomy from the later whole, and to see the whole as inscribed in the parts rather than as transcending them.

[19]Wilhelm Dilthey, "The Schleiermacher Biography," *Dilthey: Selected Writings*, ed. H. P. Rickman (Cambridge: Cambridge University Press, 1976), p. 62.

The Cubist Whole: Blake's Perspectivism

The foregrounding of part over whole characteristic of Blake's early works is best summed up by the term 'perspectivism.' This description of Blake's technique is by no means new. It is often pointed out that in *Milton* we see the action from Milton's point of view as he descends into Generation. But his immortal self simultaneously sleeps on a couch in heaven, so that we also see things from the perspective of eternity. Not surprisingly, discussions of Blake's perspectivism generally assume a synchronicity of part and whole that is, at best, relevant only to *Milton* and *Jerusalem*. Perspectives are aligned in terms of the hermeneutic schema of single to fourfold vision that Blake later developed, and are seen as parts of a totality. Susan Fox thus associates Blake's layered organization of multiple perspectives in *Europe* and *Milton* with a simultaneity that substitutes visionary for linear time. Perspective, according to her, is an angle of deviation, to be measured in relation to "the comprehensive criterion of eternity."[20] But in the early texts perspectives are juxtaposed rather than cinematically superimposed, the bard's song being counterpointed against Earth's answer and not hegemonically placed above it. The fact that we pass through various perspectives serially, and that we cannot occupy them at the same time, suggests that we need a new perceptual vocabulary to describe the perspectivism of the early Blake.

It may be more accurate to see Blake's perspectivism as cubist than as visionary, and thus to recognize its nonhierarchical nature. Albert Gleizes and Jean Metzinger point out that their aim is not to make the spectator juxtapose the six faces of the cube so as to recompose them into an organic whole: "An object has not one absolute form, it has several. . . . As many images of the object . . . as minds to understand it."[21] Abandoning the concepts of an absolute space and time constructed from a fixed point of view, cubism sees things as existing in relation to each other and as appearing differently from different perspectives. Wylie Sypher describes the cubists as breaking open "the volumes of things by spreading objects upon shifting interrelated planes . . . planes which give an illusion of closure and depth but which are always moving and readjusting themselves to one another."[22] The incomplete contours and the conspicuous use of surfaces so as to restate three dimensions in two remind us that 'reality' is known as a series of appearances, that volumes (as we perceive them) are surfaces that we

[20]*Poetic Form in Blake's Milton* (Princeton, N.J.: Princeton University Press, 1976), p. 9.

[21]"Cubism," in Robert L. Herbert, ed., *Modern Artists on Art: Ten Unabridged Essays* (Englewood Cliffs, N.J.: Prentice-Hall, 1964), p. 13.

[22]*Rococo to Cubism in Art and Literature* (New York: Vintage, 1960), pp. 267, 270.

endow with depth. It is to such a use of surface rather than to mythic stylization or to an allegorical deferral of meaning beyond the temporal world that we can attribute the lack of interiority of Blake's early characters and the flatness of his narrative world. His 'outlining' of characters like Oothoon and Thel does not give us, as in abstract art or for that matter archetypalism, the essential form of the character, but rather its appearance. On the other hand, it does not reduce character to surface, as if there were no inside to be constructed. For surfaces, as the outward bound of volumes, invite us to construct those volumes that the text does not wish to fix in writing. Such a use of surface is phenomenological, in that reality is not denied but does not exist as a transcendental signified.

The analogy is of course inexact, since cubist compositions are quietly removed from the social arena, concerned with perception and not with moral commitments. Blake, on the other hand, is also a poet of melodrama and climax, of spectacular cultural battles that promise decisions, as in nineteenth-century historical painting like that of Delacroix. The will to understanding and power inherent in Blake's metaphysical and historical subject matter is engaged in a passionate struggle with a method of construction that constantly situates it. Cubism does, however, provide a suggestive analogy for understanding, on a technical level, Blake's departure from realism. It stops short of the radical antirealism of abstract art, which is essentialist and structuralist in positing a world of pure mental forms outside phenomena. Cubism is also quite different from symbolism, which denies the empirical reality of the world and makes it into a forest of symbols that are yet to be decoded rather than allegorically transparent. It sees reality as present in appearances that are partly constructed by the eye, such that the ground of this 'reality' can never quite be located in fact or fiction.

It is this phenomenological construction of 'reality' as the shifting conjunction of outside and inside that seems most relevant to the early Blake. Allowing as it does for the role of perception in (re)covering reality, the cubist aesthetic lends itself to a writerly element in texts. Wylie Sypher argues that "the cubist object has . . . a plural identity apparent only as a passage between thing and idea, fact and fiction."[23] To put it differently, cubism is perceptually self-critical: it denies us a point of view and juxtaposes different perspectives in a space where they must know their own margins. It neither takes 'reality' inside a single mind, nor does it see things from some omniscient perspective that naturalizes point of view as objective. Rather, the cubist camera is objective in taking in several perspectives, but it does not organize the field of

[23]Ibid., p. 288.

vision in an optical hierarchy that lets the viewer come to rest in one of them, nor does it claim the omniscience of encompassing several perspectives.

Blake's own phrase from "The Mental Traveller" best describes the perceptual structure he creates. "The Eye altering alters all" (E485; l.62) does not proclaim an idealist recomposition of reality by the inward eye, but suggests a complex phenomenological interchange between inside and outside in which the verb 'altering' describes both what the eye does to the object and what happens to the eye in the process. The eye is constantly moving, seeing things in new ways, but being altered by those perceptual shifts so that it must keep reenvisioning what it 'sees.' As the punning use of the word "eye" suggests, this process situates the subject as an effect of its perceptions, so that the 'I' is always already a reflexive instrument: an eye that looks at itself. The diacritical account of eye and object as mutually altering applies to the relationship between reader and text as well as to the author-text relationship, thus generating, as we suggested earlier, a writerly text. Just as the text is the site of intersections, mutually opening and disruptive, between the author and 'things,' so, too, it is also the shifting ground on which reader and author keep exchanging positions.

Perhaps closest to this view of the text as perspectival is Donald Ault's discussion of transformational structure. In *Visionary Physics* Ault had discussed Blake's use of an 'anti-Newtonian' narrative form in which causal and linear relationships between events were disrupted, as a way of replacing chronological with visionary time. By contrast, his recent discussion of *The Four Zoas* sees nonlinear narrative as antimetaphysical and thus incompatible with the grasping of a transcendental signified, however fluid.[24] To say that "the Eye altering alters all" is not to claim that one must see 'through' and not 'with' the eye. Rather, it is to acknowledge that 'with' and 'through' are intertwined, because the eye is not just a window through which one sees into eternity but also a mirror that reflects itself. Thus for Ault, Newtonian or conventional narrative would assume that "behind the text lies a single unified field" that appears different at different times only because we have not fully grasped it. Correspondingly, it would assume a "rigid subject-object division" between reader and text, in which the narrative is *in* the text, and the reader's function is to understand it. For the notion of an underlying world "that supports the details of the surface narrative and is signified by them," Blake substitutes "a deep structure that is a transformational

[24] *Visionary Physics: Blake's Response to Newton* (Chicago: University of Chicago Press, 1974); "Re-Visioning *The Four Zoas*," in Hilton and Vogler, eds., *Unnam'd Forms*, pp. 105–40. Ault does not situate himself in relation to contemporary theory, but this is what I take him to be doing.

process" generated "by the operations of the poem's narrative surface." The consequence is an intertextual process in which the narrative is a "transformative agent through which reader and text mutually alter and revise one another."[25] A related phenomenon has been noted by Thomas Frosch, who argues that although the components of Blake's imaginary landscapes "singly offer the eye no difficulty," their "interrelations and the transitions from one to another" are too rapid for us to visualize.[26] Though Frosch sees this decomposition of the visual surface logocentrically, as recentering the text at the aural level of prophecy, it is equally possible to see it as deconstructing stable representation by making us aware of how the text shifts even as we try to visualize it.

The coupling of Blake with perspectivism is likely to be troubling to those who think of him as a strenuously affirmative writer. But as Alexander Nehamas has observed with reference to Nietzsche, perspectivism does not have to be relativism. It is simply an admission that one's own point of view is not uniquely privileged and that there is no synoptic point of view one can adopt to attain that privilege. This renunciation of authority comes from the recognition that different points of view cannot be "smoothly combined" because they do not necessarily bear on the same object. That we differ from each other because we are talking about different aspects of the object, and that there is no 'object' apart from its appearance in discourse, is the surest obstacle to the creation of a common language that needs no further rereading. Thus, as we shall see in *Thel*, the positions of the cloud and of Thel's final speech cannot be reconciled or hierarchized, because they are not really talking about the same thing except in a superficial sense. But this does not mean that perspectives are completely disjoined from one another, for that would lead to a hegemony of the subjective in which partial vision is re-privileged as the only alternative to an impossible total vision. Each approach, as Nehamas argues, "is capable of correcting itself, and many can incorporate new material. . . . What is not possible is that at some point we can incorporate 'all' the material there is into a single approach."[27]

One consequence of a transformational view of the text is a decoupling of perspectivism from nihilism. Perspectivism need no longer paralyze (intellectual) action, as is assumed by so many who see political and deconstructive criticism as incompatible. The undecidability of the text is paralyzing only if we make difference a negative hypostasis of logocentr-

[25] Ault, "Re-Visioning *The Four Zoas*," pp. 106–8, 129.

[26] *The Awakening of Albion: The Renovation of the Body in the Poetry of William Blake* (Ithaca, N.Y.: Cornell University Press, 1974), pp. 111–12.

[27] Alexander Nehamas, *Nietzsche: Life as Literature* (Cambridge, Mass.: Harvard University Press, 1985), pp. 49–52, 51.

ism by assuming that there *is* some truth about which we can only write texts. But by making the text a transformational field, Blake gives up any notion of an absolute truth and creates a form sensitive to the historicity of the text as the site of individual and cultural exchange. This view of the early Blake is obviously very different from that of Jerome McGann, who sees Blake's decision to be his own author, editor, and publisher as an attempt to privatize production and reception.[28] But resistance to corporate technology, though obviously a 'romantic' position, is not necessarily a retreat from political engagement. Blake's method avoids a mass consumerism that would absolve his readers from the need to put things together for themselves. This resistance recognizes that the lion and the ox do not "see alike" and is thus potentially an openness to other points of view. For Blake, too, must keep putting things together differently, avoiding the homogenized vision of a text finalized for commercial publication. Blake's method of production is in fact an attempt to avoid the alienation of labor: both ours and his. In creating a text that is open to revision from its readers, he also tries to avoid the alienation of the *author* from the dissemination of his text: the death of the author whose resistance to reappropriation makes him irrelevant and thus creates a dualism of past and present in which reading becomes a reification of the text as cultural error.

It is useful to return to the concept of writing as 'work,' both to specify the nature of Blake's perspectivism and to qualify charges of privacy. The extraordinary coherence of the early texts at the level of the issues they address allows us to speak of Blake's "work" in the sense of labor. But their stylistic diversity complicates any attempt to naturalize perspective by abstracting what is said from how it is said, and thus to make labor yield a "work" in the classic sense of a finished product. The figure of labor can be set against the image of mental fight, dramatized in battles between zoas and their specters that promise some kind of epic resolution. Depictions of characters as laboring at a forge, weaving, or tilling suggest a more complex participation in an economy, a semiotics of exchange. The metaphor of labor helps to distinguish Blake's poems from Yeats's "vacillations," from a dramaturgy of stylized masks that the subject inhabits rhetorically rather than existentially, and that may indeed be a form of relativism. Labor suggests an attempt to produce something, a belief in the value of what one is doing as an activity if not as something that continuously corresponds to truth. But labor does not necessarily result in progress, except in very local ways: hence the early

[28] Jerome McGann, *A Critique of Modern Textual Criticism* (Chicago: University of Chicago Press, 1983), pp. 44–47.

Blake's arrangement of his text in a nonlinear array[29] that prevents the reading process from becoming complacently teleological. The construction of the individual text in movable parts is repeated on a larger scale by the construction of Blake's work as an intertextual field: a field in which our tendency to use chronology as a way of arranging poems in an evolutionary narrative is blocked by the way Blake keeps reproducing earlier texts along with later ones, uncertainly refiguring and reinhabiting what he has 'left.'

Counterhermeneutic: *The Marriage of Heaven and Hell*

As *Milton* is the later Blake's statement of a traditional hermeneutic, so it is in *The Marriage of Heaven and Hell* that the earlier Blake's view of the text as heuristic emerges. A rereading of the Western tradition, *The Marriage* introduces what Nietzsche and Foucault were later to call a genealogical approach that entails both a view of language itself as the site of ideological (de)construction and a view of reading as the (re)generation of ideas. Genealogy locates the text as a perspective. For although *The Marriage* is the early Blake's most credal text, its mythmaking occurs at a threshold between the visionary sense of myth attributed to the romantics by Bloom and Frye, and Barthes's revisionary sense of mythologies as attempts to naturalize the cultural origins of sign systems. One can trace this second notion of mythology back to the rise of anthropology in the romantic period, and to Schelling's awareness in *The Philosophy of Mythology* that myths are historical expressions of the cultures that produce them. But where Schelling naturalizes myths within a teleological movement that sees them as progressively truer, Blake is strikingly aware of myths as linguistic constructs. Thus, his ideological criticism is conducted through a semiological deconstruction that implicates Blake himself in his own practice, in a way that the simple intellectual dismissal of his precursors would not. In a curious anticipation of Nietzsche's *Genealogy of Morals*, Blake begins *The Marriage* by focusing on the signifiers 'good' and 'evil' and their purely customary relationship to the qualities they represent in a culture that uses binary rhetoric to naturalize its morality. Such reflections on the sign clearly apply to 'Blake' himself: if energy is merely 'called' evil by Miltonic Puritanism, then who is to say that what Blake calls energy is not itself a name for something else? Genealogy studies belief as the representation of a cul-

[29]I borrow this term from McGann, "Some Forms of Critical Discourse," *Critical Inquiry* 11 (1985): 402–6.

turally interested will-to-power. Intermittently, Blake will open himself to genealogical reading, as when he leads the angel through hell in an attempt to convince him that it is really heaven, and then concedes that "we impose on one another" (E42; 20). As significant is the memorable fancy in which he traces a belief in the poetic genius back to the Hebrews, only to assign this belief persuasive rather than constative status, warning us against a visionary discourse that may be the imperialism of a small sect denied the status of capital letters: "This, [said Ezekiel], like all firm perswasions, is come to pass, for all nations believe the *jews* code and worship the the *jews god*, and what greater subjection can be" (E39; 13—italics mine).

Crucial to the text's strategy of defamiliarization is its construction of a 'genealogical' as opposed to a 'genetic' narrative: one that exposes the basis of language in power. Genetic narratives legitimate themselves through causal structures that make their vision seem natural. They move from beginning to end so that what they narrate seems to happen, either factually or psychologically. Thus, the creed of *The Prelude* 'grows' out of childhood experiences and that of *Jerusalem* arises from psychological need. *The Marriage*, by contrast, does not begin: it erupts, in an attempt at beginning whose obscurity makes us aware of beginning as a structural function. Thereafter it proceeds discontinuously, through a series of abstract propositions alternating with visionary anecdotes. The anecdotes take the place of narrative and try to show the antinomian discourse of energy as happening in the world. But because of their brevity, it is as if that attempt must happen over and over again. The abrupt shifts in *The Marriage* convey the structure of discourse as interruption or imposition rather than origination, and they expose a certain arbitrariness in these interruptions. Blake does in fact provide 'origins' for his myth in locating it as a transvaluation of Milton or an overgoing of Swedenborg, and in giving it an ancestry in the Hebrew prophets. But these tracings are genealogical rather than genetic, because they reveal the self-interest that produces an act of linguistic usurpation, or that legitimizes a discourse by giving it an ancestry that exposes its tribalism. As if to protect the reader from this usurpation, Blake deconstructs his precursors through word games that give his own counteridentity an unstably linguistic existence. An example is the criticism of *Paradise Lost*:

> Those who restrain desire, do so because theirs is weak enough to be restrained; and the restrainer or reason usurps its place & governs the unwilling. . . .
>
> The history of this is written in Paradise Lost. & the Governor or Reason is call'd Messiah.

> And the original Archangel or possessor of the command of the heavenly host, is calld the Devil or Satan and his children are call'd Sin & Death
> But in the Book of Job Miltons Messiah is call'd Satan.
> For this history has been adopted by both parties (E34; 5)

By playing Job against Milton, Blake reveals the arbitrariness of the names that Milton uses to label moral positions as real. What is Messiah to Milton is Satan from another perspective whose character as mere inversion marks it as no truer than what it replaces. But the arbitrariness of moral signifiers becomes truly vertiginous as we approach what seems to be Blake's 'solution':

> It indeed appear'd to Reason as if Desire was cast out. but the Devils account is, that the Messiah fell. & formed a heaven of what he stole from the Abyss
> This is shewn in the Gospel, where he prays to the Father to send the comforter or Desire that Reason may have Ideas to build on, the Jehovah of the Bible being no other than he, who dwells in flaming fire. (E34–35; 5–6)

Given the confusion about who Messiah is, is Blake in the spirit of the fourth memorable fancy saying that Satan or energy formed the true heaven in the abyss conventionally perceived as hell? Or is he saying, as the next proposition suggests, that Christ borrowed from Satan the passion necessary for Reason to "have Ideas to build on"? The first possibility dismisses 'reason' where the second redefines it. Generating one possibility from the other, Blake makes his ideology a transformational discourse that exceeds his various attempts at propositional paraphrase. He also defamiliarizes the names by which religious systems identify themselves. 'Messiah' and 'Satan' are simply functions in a narratology: they have been and will be differently occupied by various systems according to the self-interest of each.

Blake's willingness to grant his system an existential but not an epistemological truth is related to his unusual theory of language as difference. In his celebration of the ancient poets, he places myth at the intersection between theology and semiology, and he insists that language must remain vitally metaphorical in Shelley's double sense of the term:[30]

> The ancient Poets animated all sensible objects with Gods or Geniuses. . . .
> And particularly they studied the genius of each city & country, placing it under its mental deity.

[30]See my discussion in Chapter 10.

> Till a system was formed, which some took advantage of & enslav'd the vulgar by attempting to realize or abstract the mental dieties from their objects: thus began Priesthood.
>
> Choosing forms of worship from poetic tales. (E38; 11)

Although the opposition between concrete and abstract thinking is typically 'romantic,' mythic language, unexpectedly, is visionary but not logocentric. Blake opposes the Cartesian separation of inside and outside, and endows material objects with mental deities so as to affirm the presence of imagination in the world. But his monism does not result in an identity of mind and nature that hypostatizes mental categories. Anticipating Nietzsche, he insists that myth remains imaginatively vital only as long as it is recognized to be a moving army of metaphors. To turn it into dogma amounts to an alienation of imaginative labor in which the dualism of mind and its objects resurfaces inside an 'identity' of the two that masks a lack of engagement between the mind and its atrophied products.

Blake's theory of language as a transformational practice leads to a sense of reading as dissemination, such as we shall trace in Shelley's *Defence*. Many of the vignettes that make up *The Marriage* present scenes of rereading and play with the memorable fancies of a traditional hermeneutic. The section in which 'Blake' takes the angel through the void in order to show that the abyss is a product of distorted perception presents an early version of the vortex in which reading generates perceptual reversals so as to produce a corrected vision. The vortex is Blake's image for a hermeneutics of reversal that employs what Schelling calls irony and involution. Plate 14 likewise represents Blake's rereading of the tradition in terms of a hermeneutics of negativity in which he must unsay what has been said in order to liberate things as they should be from things as they are. It describes how he prints in the "infernal method, by corrosives, which in Hell are salutary and medicinal, melting apparent surfaces away, and displaying the infinite which was hid" (E39; 14). Although Blake in this text plays the role of reader and negates the surface of *Paradise Lost* so as to discover the infinite within it, what he also does is to give his own readers a way of interpreting texts like *Urizen* and *Europe*. But in this text at least the strategies of romantic hermeneutics are put forward with exuberant irony. Against the episodes in which he plays the revolutionary reader, revising Milton and Swedenborg from a more enlightened point on the spiral of history, we must set the anecdote in which Blake looks amusedly at the arrogance of his authorized version. In the final memorable fancy Blake describes the conversion of a resisting reader to his own perspective in a comic-strip narrative that has the angel turning blue, yellow, white, and then pink. The section is followed by the line "One Law for the Lion & Ox is Oppression," as if to remind us that oppositional reading, not angelic submission, is true friendship.

That we must guard against a hermeneutics that turns prophecy into priesthood is something Blake emphasizes in the section on the printing house in hell, sometimes placed at the end (copy E). This section is often read straightforwardly as a description of how the visionary text is produced and then received by "Men" who take the forms of books and thus embody it. But the last phase in this process is highly problematic. In the fifth chamber the propagation of knowledge is still associated with a generative chaos: "In the fifth chamber were Unnam'd forms, which cast the metals into the expanse" (E40; 15). For much of *The Marriage* Blake represents himself in intimate conversation with prophets and devils, and assumes that his readers will form a visionary company that hears his voice. Here he represents himself as a radical pamphleteer, cast out of an oral into a print culture and exposed to an economy of dissemination rather than circulation. Transmitted by unnamed forms instead of by an author who controls the circulation of meaning, the text enters a space where its identity seems at risk. But this space, described as an 'expanse,' stands in contrast to the imaginative contraction that begins with the reassertion of literary protectionism in the sixth chamber. For the bizarre image of people taking the "forms of books" and being "arranged in libraries" describes a process of reification in which passive readers become deadeningly identified with the commodities they consume.

By encouraging the independence of his readers, Blake allows us to see his myth as a perspective. But *The Marriage* is uniquely affirmative in allowing other points of view a theoretical existence without admitting them into the text. Blake marks the limits of his myth not by actually calling it into question but through a disjunctive interplay of styles that includes parody and high seriousness, dogmatic abstraction and fantasy. As Alexander Nehamas has said of Nietzsche, his stylistic pluralism

> is his solution to the problem involved in presenting positive views that do not . . . fall back into dogmatism. . . . His many styles make it impossible to get used to his presence and . . . to forget it. They therefore show that his positions are expressions of one particular point of view besides which there may be many others. They show his perspectivism without saying anything about it, and to that extent they prevent his view that there are only interpretations from undermining itself.[31]

[31]*Nietzsche*, p. 40.

Perspective is marked only through form. The individual sections of *The Marriage* do not challenge each other; rather, their brevity curtails any tendency to monumentalize their ideological constructions. At the same time, the text's proliferation of forms prevents its irony from becoming self-devouring, and results in a stylistic exuberance that makes scepticism only the outward circumference of imaginative energy. In *The Marriage* the reader plays with the possibility of other viewpoints. In Blake's other writings we begin a different kind of labor: the labor of distinguishing and combining perspectives, and of determining whether they can be combined at all.

CHAPTER EIGHT

Early Texts: "The Eye Altering Alters All"

Blake's early work, as we have suggested, approaches the relationship between text and culture in terms of an intertextual rather than canonical model. But at the same time he conceives this work as 'labor' and not simply 'dissemination.' Thus, the earliest texts are characterized by two apparently different tendencies. They invite us to see experience through the eyes of an individual subject (be it 'Blake' or someone else), and yet as intertextual constructions they make us aware that the insights thus produced are perspectives. Taken together, these tendencies produce reading as a cultural critique that is still a hermeneutic, an application of intertextual reading to the process of understanding ourselves through others. This hermeneutic requires not only that 'Blake' reread his own writing from the perspective of characters like Thel, but also that we situate our more contemporary readings by experimentally identifying with 'Blake.' The two tendencies, located in different subsectors of the early work, put reader and writer in a position like the one articulated by Kierkegaard in his *Point of View*. Though making the text a transformational surface that generates constant rereading, they do not allow intertextuality to become an impersonal semiosis in which we can evade our position as subjects in the play of signifiers. Thus the *Songs*, which bring together a multitude of small poems in a structure that suggests complete relativism, must be read in conjunction with early poems like *Visions* and *Thel*, which focus on a single protagonist. Doing so encourages us to organize them experimentally from subject positions suggested by these narratives, so as to give a direction to the displacement of one text by another. Conversely, the longer poems, which seem to bring their stories to a conclusion and to tell them from a fixed point of view, must be read with a sensitivity to an intertextual construction that puts any narrative writer or reader might construct out of them under erasure. Accordingly, this chapter looks at the earliest texts as producing intersecting cognitive structures that reshape our reading of the work as a whole. These structures in turn find an epistemological basis in the early tractates. For although these texts are sometimes seen as evidence of uncompromising idealism,[1] in their emphasis on "experience" and "experiment" they come closest to Godwin's sense that meaning can be ascertained "only by experiment," to a paradoxically romantic symbiosis of empiricism and idealism.

The Collection as Intertext: *Songs of Innocence and of Experience*

To read the *Songs* is to encounter difficulties analogous to those produced by the movement earlier described from signs to propositions. Individually simple, they become ambiguous at the point where we try to connect them so as to make them yield a narrative or an argument. Instead of being an expression of the system, their very format as a collection that can be put together from more than one perspective raises the problem of system: of how parts are organized into wholes and of how evidence is generalized into explanatory structures. Indeed, the history of the *Songs* emphasizes the status of writing as 'text' rather than 'book,' and our reading becomes a further part of that history. For Blake initially included three of the *Innocence* poems in his satirical *An Island in the Moon*. He then published the more homogeneous *Songs of Innocence*, which abandons contrapuntal construction to seal the vision of innocence in the purity of lyric. But he then unbound the book of Christian pastoral by adding the *Songs of Experience* and issuing the poems in nineteen different arrangements. In adding the *Songs of Experience* and then further poems like "To Tirzah," Blake himself seems to have read his text in more than one way: in terms of the Swedenborgian pietism of *Innocence* issued separately, in terms of the antinomian radicalism of *The Marriage*, and in terms of a deeply pessimistic antinaturalism. That he continued to issue *Innocence* separately and to reproduce his early texts alongside *Milton* and *Jerusalem* suggests that he saw these perspectives as displacing and not replacing each other.

Where the form of prophecy arouses our hermeneutic impulses, the collection from the outset stimulates heuristic reading. Its title indicates an issue we can follow in our reading, but the poems are not about innocence and experience in the sense of having as their content an

[1]Martin Nurmi, *William Blake* (London: Hutchinson, 1975), p. 52.

answer to the question of how these states are related. Rather, they are about the schemas we construct to answer this question. Any book we might construct to fit the poems into a canon ('Blake's' or ours) is thus displaced by its inscription in the shifting combinatory network of the collection. Among the more obvious ways of organizing the poems is a serial reading in which experience inevitably succeeds innocence, or a static juxtaposition of matching poems which sees the two states as irreconcilable ways of looking at life. But the replacement of a linear structure by that of an array, along with the fact that the subtitle describes innocence and experience as contrary 'states' and not as successive stages of life, frees us from a mimetic submission to the way the text unfolds. It thus allows the reader to assume a more active role in producing something not actually in the collection. What we produce may be the synthesis elsewhere sketched by Blake as the culmination of a progression through contraries. But it may also be a questioning of whether reading can indeed re-form reality. Considering the poems from the subject position of 'Blake,' or from a more sceptical perspective, we are forced to recognize the limits of subjectively constructed readings. On the other hand, because of the identification with a speaking subject modeled for us in other poems of this period, this very process of intertextual displacement remains part of a hermeneutic in which different positions are experienced and not simply textualized.

We can begin with a dialectical reading of the *Songs* that generates from its static oppositions the synthesis that Blake later called "organized innocence." Such a dialectic would have five stages. Beginning with a naive reading of the *Innocence* poems as Christian pastorals that celebrate a childlike vision, we would reconsider them from the perspective of an experience, traces of which are already present in the *Innocence* poems. The disclosure of innocence as a perceptual surface would then produce, as a pessimistic counterreaction, a naive reading of *Experience* in which it is identified with 'reality.' But reconsidering the *Experience* poems through their counterparts would similarly disclose experience to be a state of limited vision. As in Platonic dialectic, the negation of our various pictures of reality would lead finally to a higher innocence that would be produced in the consciousness of the reader.

Our first reading of *Innocence* is vague and thus unorganized. Responding to the poems as songs and thus to their mood, we accept their image of a world in which we are all children watched over by guardians. The unsettling of innocence begins only with a second reading in which we realize that the poems, far from being repetitive confirmations of each other, fall into three categories. There are nonnarrative poems like "The Lamb," which seem insulated from complication by their very brevity; longer poems like "The Ecchoing Green" and "Nurse's Song," which already place innocence within the temporal cycle; and social poems like "Holy Thursday," "The Chimney-Sweeper," and "The Little Black Boy," whose transposition of innocence from country to city displaces pastoral from the literal to the metaphoric. The first two categories protect the world of innocence, though only at the price of a certain hermeneutic passivity. Thus, at first glance the world of "The Lamb" seems one of lyric simultaneity, conducive to the sacramental identity of lamb, Christ, and child. "The Ecchoing Green," with its construction in terms of receding temporal vistas that move from the children to Old John, differs in conceding the mutability of innocence. But even here we are allowed not to question an innocent aesthetic. Conventionally pastoral, these poems are instances of a form that naturalizes innocence and then absorbs its loss by suggesting that it can be recovered through memory or through its recurrence in the lives of the next generation. The figure of diurnal or life cycles in which repetition is naturally ordained becomes in turn a paradigm that naturalizes pastoral representation as a repetition in which writing makes present what is known to be impermanent. These poems are full of gaps in the representation of innocence, such as the fact that the animals in "Night" have to die in order to establish the existence of that protection which would not have been necessary if it had existed in the first place. Inasmuch as children's literature uses animals to gloss human situations, the gaps refer to gaps in the social text supported by the conservatively pietist tradition of Isaac Watts and Mrs. Barbauld on which the poems are modeled. But these gaps, instead of stimulating a critique of pietism, are seen as functions of temporality, justifying a substitution in which writing or memory stands in place of a real innocence. This supplementary use of pastoral as a form of (re)-covering innocence will emerge as profoundly repressive, perpetuating as it does a status quo that makes a heaven in hell's despite.

Dividing the poems into categories begins the work of breaking down an unorganized impression of innocence into the minute and troubling particulars that compose it. For in the social poems images from Christian pastoral are used of children in an environment beset by problems like child labor and racism, so as to disclose the role of pastoral language in an economy that depends on keeping children innocent. An innocent reading of "Holy Thursday" might take it as promising that the meek shall inherit the earth.[2] But we pass very quickly to a reading like that of Bloom, who points out that charity is a form of parasitism that perpetuates poverty to congratulate itself for alleviating it, and that the radiance

[2]E. D. Hirsch, *Innocence and Experience: An Introduction to Blake* (New Haven, Conn.: Yale University Press, 1964), pp. 194–97.

of these charity-school children is "all their own."[3] In "The Chimney Sweeper," similarly, the sense of innocence is in the way the children perceive their condition, and that perception is both touching and ominous. Dreaming of the day when he will be freed from his life as a sweep, the younger child figures the dark, narrow chimneys as "coffins of black" and imagines an angel with a "bright key" who will "set them all free" (E10). The conventional use of a figure to represent what is unpleasant (death) as pleasant (the angel) is oddly crossed here by the image of a coffin, which represents the sordid working conditions of the child in terms of something worse (his death). It is as though the literal referent buried in the first figure has resurfaced in the second, reproduced in the very process of its effacement. This reversal throws into relief the role of imagination in the social economy, unraveling as text the mythology of an afterlife that justifies present injustice.

A simple reading of the pure lyrics and pastorals is necessary to the dialectic of experiencing our own complicity in limited vision. But by organizing the poems in groups and then rereading the first two categories in relation to social poems linked to their counterparts in *Experience*, we reenter the simpler poems from a different perspective. The saccharine flatness of the pure lyrics now appears as a form of defamiliarization that allows us to focus on the semiosis of innocence. Crucial to the rhetoric of innocence is a metaphoric thought structure that confuses as well as fuses. Thus the child in "The Lamb" creates an imaginary identity between child, God, and animal by blurring the antecedents of his pronouns in a way that is foregrounded by the conspicuous repetition in the poem:

> Little Lamb who made thee
> Dost thou know who made thee
>
> . . . .
>
> Little Lamb I'll tell thee,
> Little Lamb I'll tell thee!
> He is called by thy name,
> For he calls himself a Lamb.
>
> (E8–9)

The pronoun "He" stands in place of either Christ or the child, creating a con-fusion of human, natural, and divine orders that is specifically characterized as linguistic: a product of the activity of naming. The blurring of the antecedent in turn elides an ambiguity within the open-

[3]Harold Bloom, *Blake's Apocalypse: A Study in Poetic Argument* (1963; rpt. Ithaca, N.Y.: Cornell University Press, 1970), pp. 44–45.

ing question. Seemingly a rhetorical question implying that Christ made the lamb, the question is answered in such a way as to imply the conventional answer, but only metaphorically. For Christ is present in the poem only through a pronoun that may not refer to him, and through a metaphor that seems to have no tenor: "He is called by thy name." It is as though we remain suspended in a world of signifiers in which the answer to a question is a pronoun that stands in place of something that can only be named in terms of another name. The tautologically circling way in which 'Christ' is traced into the text raises the possibility of a different answer to the child's question in which it is the child who constructs an imaginary world of innocence through the language in which he "clothes" the lamb. Metaphor and mythmaking are not pernicious here, but the poem provides a stencil of the linguistic displacements to which we should be alert elsewhere. For in a poem like "The Chimney Sweeper," where the child is again a 'lamb,' we see how the clothing of experience in innocence can substitute dream for reality while disguising an ideologically motivated substitution in what seems to the child an identity.

One of the more interesting examples of defamiliarization is "Infant Joy," which is awkwardly brief and keeps repeating the child's name in an annoyingly tautological way. The absence of significant content in the poem foregrounds its form, or more precisely its structures of predication, so as to make us aware of how a grammar can create reality. The poem begins by making the child a blank slate: "I have no name / I am but two days old.—" (E16). The attribution of language to such a child suggests that what we are witnessing is a process of cultural inscription. For the child's relative lack of character makes it clear that the writing of its identity constitutes it as a function in a social script rather than as a person. Its function is to perform the role of innocence regardless of the actual circumstances of its life. This construction of the child, moreover, takes the form of a hypostasis in which an adjective ("happy"), expressive of a momentary feeling, is conveniently turned into a substantive ("Joy"), which then becomes the child's name: "I happy am / Joy is my name,—" (E16). The endowment of the child with identity through a process that is allegorical and not mythic, not the animating of a sensible object with a god or genius, makes naming into a labeling by which identity is imposed on what may be highly complex, so as to generate an ideological product that is easily consumed. In parodying the simplicity of children's literature, thus subjecting it to a textual practice that requires readers to think for themselves, the poem subtly criticizes the marketing of popular forms for a mass consumption that encourages passivity.

A second reading of the poems, in other words, turns them in a linguistically reflexive direction. But this is equally true of a second reading of *Experience*. "Infant Sorrow" is spoken by a child who sees its swaddling bands as shackles imposed on it by society. The hysterical absurdity of this image, attributed to a child who may be no older than its innocent counterpart, draws attention to the stereotypical nature of the reaction behind it. Unlike the characters of *Innocence*, those in *Experience* are resentful and jaded. The nurse turns "green and pale" as she watches the children playing, while the chimney sweeper describes himself as wearing the "clothes of death" (E23). At first the starkness of the rhetoric overwhelms a critical reaction, as though its overstatements register the intensity with which trauma has previously been repressed. But gradually we become aware of a melodramatic quality in this rhetoric that limits its claim to truth. Melodrama has two main characteristics. As drama it is a dialogical form in which positions are staked out in relation to other positions and have no absolute validity. It shows (as lyric does not) how the emotions are generated by a social text, and it subverts its own claim to unveil a world of primal passion and absolute truth. Second, as a hypertheatrical mode given to black and white characterization, melodrama is generated by a certain imbalance between signifier and signified in which the speaker wears a mask that overstates and thus distorts what it signifies. Thus the characters of *Experience* play roles in a theater of frustrated revolt where the suppression of their uprising dooms them to a self-consuming passivity. As the curtain is raised on this primal scene, we seem to enter something more 'profound' than innocence with its veil of metaphors. But the very fact that these characters keep returning to particular linguistic strategies marks their perception of experience, too, as a representation. Many of the poems are allegories. "The Garden of Love" allegorizes the repression of the instincts in terms of the building of a chapel in Eden. "The Sick Rose" uses the flower to allegorize a process of internal corruption. The allegorizing impulse does not succeed in creating a world of simple signifieds, but rather conveys a desire to schematize, to see life in static ways. Again, many of the poems are highly graphic in the way they are built around a single gesture or image. In "London" the sweep is represented only by a cry and the harlot by a curse. This simplifying reduction of situation to tableau takes us beyond the content of Experience to the mental structuring of this content in the rigid ways that, more than anything, make experience a decadent state.

A second reading of *Experience* thus returns us dialectically to the poems of *Innocence*. Some of them have no counterparts in *Experience*, perhaps to dislodge us from the habit of rereading innocence in terms of experience. To leave the embittered children of *Experience* and return to the little black boy is to realize that we cannot just dismiss his desire to be "like" the white boy so that "he will then love me" (E9). The concluding image of his stroking the white boy's hair may show how the future he imagines replicates the social relations of the present. But it also shows his ability to believe in the potential of those who have hurt him, a capacity that may be necessary in revolutionary action if it is not to take the regressive form it assumes in the Orc myth. Trust, on the other hand, can be abused. Interplaying innocence and experience, the dialectical reader constructs an 'organized' innocence that cannot be finalized *in* Blake's text because it must remain sensitive to the details of different historical situations. Such a reading is encouraged by versions of the collection that end with "The Clod and the Pebble." Encapsulating the attitudes of innocence and experience in the malleable clod and the hardened pebble, the poem ends with an impasse in which the positions simply parody each other. The clod builds "a Heaven in Hells despair" and allows itself to be trodden on, while the pebble's cynicism creates a "Hell in Heavens despite" (E19). Both positions are defamiliarized by their association with inanimate objects, and the reader, unable to identify with either speaker, is left to find a way between the extremes.

Even as we construct a dialectical reading, however, it generates questions. One of its more troubling aspects is that organized innocence exists only in the mind of the reader. We could say that its creation through an applicative reading lends added force to it, because it emerges from our experience instead of being a merely linguistic construct. But its deferral beyond the written text also makes its achievement dependent on the reader and opens it to historical as well as internal sub-versions, such as those we have outlined in relation to the Lyca poems. Bypassing the psychosocial problems so prominent in *Experience*, these poems inscribe a simulacrum of Eden that may either serve as a dialectical stimulus to the reader to break the grip of experience, or may leave us wondering whether utopias do not always contain traces of the unorganized. They thus inscribe as a reading any use of the poems to bring about a hermeneutic completion of the *Songs*.

What has been sketched here is not a negation of the dialectical reading but a deferral of its closure. Such sub-versions are encouraged by the collection itself, for the author enters the text only through figures that do not quite represent him, like the piper and the bard. Indeed, both introductions can be seen as staging the problem of reading. At first sight the piper's song sustains an aesthetics in which writing preserves, though inadequately, the presence of innocence, and in which reading is correspondingly recuperative. The poem moves from the original vision of the child, through the piped song that can only represent him, to the song unaccompanied by music, and finally to the substitution of writing for voice as the poet's pen "stain(s) the water clear" (E7). But as in the figures of echoing and temporal repetition so frequent in the series, writing and reading are still representations of an original presence. It is possible, however, to read the poem very differently, beginning with the grammatical ambiguities of the first stanza:

> Piping down the valleys wild
> Piping songs of pleasant glee
> On a cloud I saw a child.
> (E7)

In the text as opposed to the picture, it is far from clear who is piping and whether the child or the piper is on a cloud. Either the speaker is on a cloud and sees the child piping down the valleys, in which case the child is oddly beneath the piper, as if more in touch with actuality; or else the piper is in the valley and then sees the child on the cloud, in which case the temporal relationship between the two events raises the possibility that the 'child' is brought into being as illusion by the piper's song. In both cases the piper's representation of the child lacks an extra-textual origin, for either the child is his construction or it does not correspond to his representation of it. Interestingly, the piper wants to restrict his audience to children or to his figure of them, and writes songs that "Every child may joy to hear." But the child in his final instruction no longer mentions songs and asks the piper to "write / In a book that all may read—," associating access to a wider audience with the transition from voice to writing. This transition, in turn, complicates interpretation, not only because author and reader are no longer present in the same space but also because the reading of words is a more reflective experience than the hearing of music. As the child vanishes, we stand on the threshhold of a further declension from writing done with a "rural pen" to the printing press on which Blake's poems were actually produced.

Conflating the oral and the textual as he insists on writing as something one 'hears' (l. 20), the piper resists the complexities that result from this expansion of the hermeneutic economy. But the piper's obvious anachronism in a collection that includes poems about racism and child labor is the point at which Blake casts his own songs into the expanse, printing them for all to read, and thus complicating the restricted economies of both pastoral and prophecy. For the question of restricted versus expanded audiences raised in the first introduction necessarily applies to the bard of *Experience*, who merely substitutes one form of orality for another, assuming that he can address a homogeneous entity called "Earth" and can use a single sign to represent an immensely complex referent. "Earth's Answer" raises the question (as Keats was later to say of Milton) of whether a lesser anxiety for humanity proceeds from seeing farther or from a vision limited by its very omniscience. It is interesting that Blake makes Earth female, while counterpointing her view against the presumably male voice of the bard. Earth's insistence that arguments for spiritual regeneration based on the natural cycle of night and day do not apply within the profoundly unnatural context of restrictive moral codes (E18–19; ll. 11–20) contains contradictions that might mobilize the stasis of her trauma. For instance, she ends by wanting to be freed from her bondage, although she also dismisses talk of liberation as useless. But the point is also that the bard's easy optimism may be insensitive to certain specifics of the female experience: to the fact that recognizing one's manacles as mind-forged may simply increase one's frustration if one's culture has constructed one as helpless. In this respect Earth may represent not only women but other marginal groups as well. The two introductions are a paradigm for the collection as a whole, in that they not only make the bardic voice answerable to an audience but recognize that "all" do not read alike. The counterpointing of bard and respondent creates a scene of reading which concedes that interpretation is engendered by cultural differences. But these very differences, which make closure impossible, also prevent impasses from being aporias, because they are historically specific. For the female reader may not feel bound to identify with the Earth. The Earth, for one thing, uses an archetypal language that represents her situation as perennial and thus repeats that very inability to think historically that she tacitly criticizes in the bard, but by making culture the negation rather than the contrary of nature.

To return culture to its status as a contrary is to open dialectic through its sub-version. But a further arrangement of the poems might challenge the very notion of dialectic, not only as a movement toward synthesis but even as a productivity, by replacing the dialectic between contrary states with a dialogue within each state that suspends forward movement. On returning to the *Songs of Innocence*, we again find that they fall into three categories, and that the illusion of innocence in the pure lyrics is challenged by poems that explain its vulnerability in radically different ways. In poems like "The Ecchoing Green" the loss of innocence seems part of a natural cycle. On the other hand, in poems like "Holy Thursday" it is socially caused and thus unnecessary. At first sight, the impasse created by these two alternatives seems to be mobilized by the *Songs of Experience* into a linear progression. For we enter the second state through the bard's song, which tells us that Earth has it in her power to change, and we then come upon a number of 'diagnostic' poems that tell us how to change by tracing the repressions of experience back to social codes and to the institutions they generate. Foremost among these is "The Garden of Love," in which the Miltonic view that the imposition of the law was necessary because of humanity's fall is replaced by the 'Blakean' view that it was the law that caused the fall. Picturing the fall as the erection of a chapel in a garden where there were once flowers, the speaker attributes his psychic disorganization to the institution of the church. In "London" the bard attacks monarchy, child labor and prostitution. And finally in "The Sick Rose" he diagnoses the rose's sickness as a psychosis caused by the repressiveness of sexual codes. But if these poems represent the state of experience as kept in being by mind-forged manacles, many of them also contain traces of the natural hypothesis that they seek to efface. For the *Songs of Experience* fall into two categories, and the poems that initially seem to ascribe experience to culture also turn out to imply that it may be natural. Thus "The Garden of Love" sees the binding of instinct as unnatural but describes this process through the natural image of briars growing in a garden (E26). "The Sick Rose" describes the deterioration of love through an image that is again curiously natural, that of a worm in a flower (E23). If these subtexts bitterly normalize experience, a poem like "London" arrives at the same fatalism by a different road. On a second reading "London" no longer seems to be spoken in the voice of the bardic introduction, which calls on the fallen Earth to renew herself. It seems descriptive rather than hortatory, helpless rather than prophetic, a poem whose con-text may be "Earth's Answer." It is notable that the various people imprisoned in mind-forged manacles are all powerless: children, prostitutes, soldiers rather than generals. 'Wandering' aimlessly from street to street, the speaker may realize that a diagnosis is not a remedy and that the state of experience is so widely dispersed as to elude any centralized critique. In one of the most striking lines of the poem, even the church is described as 'appalled' by the cry of the chimney sweeper: a powerful institution helplessly traumatized by its own complicity in what it claims to be fighting.[4]

In the reading process as described here, a progress in the first series of poems from the 'natural' to the 'social' hypothesis is aporetically canceled in the second series by the disclosure that even the most politically radical poems are disturbed by a certain fatalism about what is 'natural' or at least inevitable. This arrangement of the poems, chiasmic where the other one was teleological, frustrates any appropriation of the *Songs* for political ends. If the ending of the collection with "The Clod and the Pebble" (copies B, C, D, E) encourages dialectical reading, the reading suggested here is supported by versions that end with "To Tirzah" (cop-

[4]Jonathan Culler points out that critics have persistently taken the word "appals" in its secondary sense of 'to cast a pall over' rather than in its primary sense of 'to horrify': *The Pursuit of Signs: Semiotics, Literature, Deconstruction* (Ithaca, N.Y.: Cornell University Press, 1981), pp. 70–72.

ies L, K, O): a poem in which the bardic speaker answers Earth by turning away from her complexities and renouncing the optimism he proclaimed before he had really been through experience. But although Blake added "To Tirzah" relatively late as a pessimistic coda, he sometimes moved it to the middle of the collection, eroding the authority of its bitter transcendentalism by situating it among other texts and letting us read it as an overreaction to problems that only seem insurmountable. Placed in dialogue with "Earth's Answer" the male speaker of "To Tirzah" seems conveniently oblivious to the text and not to the subtext of what she is saying. Where the bard of the introduction had assumed change to be easier than it was, the speaker of this poem misogynistically argues that the "Mother" of his "mortal part" is beyond help: "Then what have I to do with thee?" (E30). Such a response fails to read the complex cultural structuring of Earth's answer. For her very insistence that the bard's advice does not apply to her conveys a desire for change along with a feeling that it is too difficult, and her sullen refusal of help is paradoxically a self-assertion: a defiant compliance with the passivity to which she has been conditioned. By setting the speaker of "To Tirzah" in the midst of other social types, Blake allows us to see his Old Testament rhetoric as out of place in nineteenth-century London. The poem in this sense is a paradigm for the way the shifting of texts leads us to reflect on the differences between readers: on the cultural engendering of the texts we ourselves construct in reading the *Songs*.

That a pessimistic reading of the collection is no more complete than a dialectical one is signaled by the fact that however many subcategories we invent in organizing it, they fail to include everything that is there. As we construct categories to account for new evidence, we also shift the meaning of texts we have already placed in an interpretive schema by putting them into new frames. Where, for example, does "The Tyger" fit in? Bloom has worked out a dialectical reading of the poem in which our naive identification with the speaker, who watches in terror as the world of the tiger invalidates that of the lamb, must be overcome through a cleansed perception of the tiger as energy rather than evil.[5] Such a reading, which paradigmatically makes the poem a contrary rather than a negation of innocence, leaves unexplored the problem of whether dialectic does indeed yield closure. Blake's ambivalence toward energy is well known, and the poem does not tell us whether the tiger forged on the anvil of imagination is a creation of Los, a Demogorgon, or perhaps a rough beast slouching toward Bethlehem to be born. Eluding a dialectical reading, the poem also thwarts a fatalistic reading that sees experience as part of the nature of things, because it forces us to

[5] *Blake's Apocalypse*, pp. 137–39.

rethink the labels 'experience' and 'nature.' It depicts a fearful symmetry in which the lamb and tiger coexist: a world beyond good and evil, but one that may be no easier to frame in terms of the values *The Marriage* substitutes for the conventional ones. This world is hardly the paradise regained of the Lyca poems, where the tiger and the child live in narcotic peace. On the other hand, it is not corroded by the decadence and repression elsewhere associated with Experience. It seems a world of paradox and tension rather than synthesis, involving a symbiosis of opposites within the economy of what is better described as 'organized experience' than as 'organized innocence.'

Perhaps the most significant aspect of the *Songs* is Blake's use of the collection to unsettle the identity of the book or the autonomous lyric. The diacritical nature of a collection registers an awareness that meaning cannot be totalized, because it is produced by relationships that are always shifting. Individual texts do not have a positive meaning: their significance changes in relation to their con-text. The shifting of contexts is encouraged not only by the fact that the *Songs* exist in different orders, but also by the history of their composition, as a diacritical complex from which Blake generated texts that were then reinscribed in the collection. This is not to say that the *Songs* ask us to renounce the idea of totalizing knowledge or reaching conclusions. Indeed, the very project of a collection, a bringing together, holds out hopes of organization if not of totality. But in contrast to a more linear form like the *bildungsroman*, a collection can be entered at more than one point and usually is not read in its entirety. Thus, the whole one assembles out of it will always be an effect of one's perspective and will always be subject to the arrest of what it excludes.

But it is not enough simply to describe Blake's work as diacritical. Both the *Songs* and the other early texts we shall consider are instances of what Kristeva calls "intertextuality," a concept that turns the play of difference toward an interaction with social texts that makes literature what she calls a "productivity." Elaborating an idea implicit in Bakhtin, Kristeva sums up intertextuality as a critical practice that "situates the text within history and society, which are then seen as texts read by the writer, and into which he inserts himself by rewriting them."[6] This definition perhaps needs to be expanded so as to include the reader as the site where our own texts are reinserted, through what Kierkegaard calls a dialectical reduplication, in histories we have forgotten. The components of Blake's intertextuality are thus vertical as well as horizontal. On the horizontal level of Blake's own textual network, his poems constitute

[6]Julia Kristeva, *Desire in Language*, trans. Leon Roudiez (New York: Columbia University Press, 1980), pp. 36, 65.

intertexts that are transcodings of shared thematic matrices. Meanwhile, the individual texts consist of mobile fragments that articulate their own structurality by transcoding each other along paradigmatic or syntagmatic axes. In *Europe*, for instance, the preludium and the preface in which Blake meets the fairy are different versions on a paradigmatic axis of a scene of origination or creativity that tries to revolutionize how we perceive the world. The prophecy itself repeats the concept of perceptual revolution as historical revolution and develops it on the syntagmatic axis of a narrative describing eighteen hundred years of European history. In the *Songs* the syntagmatic axis has more or less disappeared, there being no narrative: the individual poems rewrite each other by refiguring similar situations in the experience of different characters. So far, we have focused largely on the horizontal operation of Blake's intertextuality. But in addition, his texts function vertically in relation to previous and future history. That he rewrites the social text, in the very specific sense of analyzing how it is composed by perceptual or semiological systems, has long been recognized. What has been less discussed is the way this process reinserts his own scripts in that text which calls them into being and also marks their limits. Moreover, this process of mutual inscription is repeated with reference to future readers, in readings whose content Blake could not have anticipated but whose possibility he allows for at the level of form. This vertical aspect of intertextuality will be our concern when we come, by way of the early tractates, to *Thel* and *Visions*.

Vision as/or Experiment: The Early Tractates

Blake's perspectivism, and hence his emphasis on reading intertextually, arises from his early commitment to "experience" or "experiment." These are vexed terms, given his attacks on Bacon and Locke, and we should understand them in an existential rather than a positivist sense. For if Blake objected to empiricism for limiting us to what is known through the senses, it is not clear that he disagreed with its inductive emphasis on testing hypotheses through experience rather than interpreting experience in the light of a priori truths. Nor is his alternative a visionary idealism that bypasses experience entirely, given the opening up of the latter concept implicit in its coupling with the term "experiment" (E1). Instead, in the early tractates Blake inscribes the visionary within the empirical, articulating a highly idealistic series of propositions in a format that displaces them. Blake's re-visionary empiricism is in turn relevant to his hermeneutics, for it frees us from a theory of reading as reproduction and allows us to see reading, too, as an experiment with the text.

The first tractate "All Religions Are One" begins with the statement "As the true method of knowledge is experiment, the true faculty of knowing must be the faculty which experiences" (E1). Although it is often read ironically, we shall experiment with reading this "Argument" as an introduction to what follows. Dialectically displacing a conventional opposition between experience and the "poetic genius," Blake seems to say that imagination, not reason, is the faculty that experiences and thus accumulates knowledge, but also that imaginative wisdom is gained *through* experience and cannot be put in the golden bowl of a protected idealism. This double transvaluation of the opposed terms is summed up in the paradox from "There Is No Natural Religion": "Therefore God becomes as we are, that we may be as he is" (E3). The paradox promises an identity of opposites through the mystery of the Incarnation. But the reversals necessary to achieve that identity also raise the problem of a permanent asymmetry between the terms: the possibility that once God has been through experience, we may not be able to become gods in any conventional sense of the term.

In both tractates the choice between reason and imagination is raised in terms of the problem of perspective. Reason or the ratio of what we already know limits us to our own perspective, where imagination allows us to travel in what Blake calls "unknown lands" (E1). It is imagination that therefore provides us with experience by allowing us to project ourselves into perspectives other than our own. Moreover, in "All Religions are One" the unknown is linked to the problem of different cultures increasingly prominent in the work of Herder and the Humboldts. Difference, in the form of gender difference, will be a concern of *Thel* and *Visions*, and the tractate thus introduces problems in cultural hermeneutics relevant to these early poems. Like Wilhelm von Humboldt, who saw each language as the unique expression of its culture, Blake says that the "Religions of all Nations are derived from each Nation's *different reception* of the Poetic Genius" (E1; italics mine). Committed like Humboldt to a unity that will absorb cultural diversity, Blake is nevertheless anxiously aware that different "sects of Philosophy" are "adapted to the weaknesses of every individual" and that these perspectives are all authentic, because "No man can think write or speak from his heart, but he must intend truth" (E1). In other words, though the tractate promises a dialectical synthesis of experience and vision, what it discloses is a potential asymmetry between them. The uniformity of vision associated with the poetic genius when Blake uses the analogy of the biblical syncresis of old and new contends uneasily with a diversity allowed to 'genius' when he speaks of it in experimental rather than religious terms, as the experiencing of different perspectives. This uneasiness is present in the very title of the tract, which may reflect either the syncretism of thinkers like Jacob Bryant who expands Christian typology to the study of comparative religion and myth, or which may imply a radical perspectivism. For "All Religions are One" may mean that they all say the same thing. Or it may mean that they are equally valid, because each is produced by people thinking and speaking from their hearts.

In "There Is No Natural Religion" Blake's attitude to 'experience' is ambiguous in different ways. The text with which most of us are familiar consists of two series of propositions (one negative and one positive) and a summary (printed in slightly different orders by Erdman and Bentley). In form, this text anticipates the contrary propositions of *The Marriage*, in which two perspectives are given but one seems correct. The "Conclusion" characterizes the two perspectives by maintaining the opposition between the 'poetic' and the 'experimental' displaced in "All Religions Are One" and valorizing the former. But is it entirely clear that to desire something is to possess it (E3; b.9), and that we are wrong to doubt the existence of something we have not seen or experienced? At one time Blake undoubtedly did construct the text as a hierarchical confrontation of contraries, because he numbered the plates so as to arrange them in two paired series. Even within this structure the reader must recognize as overstatement the simple reversal of empiricism into its opposite and must try to replace inversion with something more dialectical. But what is interesting is that the Erdman-Bentley text is an eclectic version that corresponds to no extant copy and that a reasonably complete set of the positive propositions occurs in only one copy. The remaining copies all have only three plates from the positive series, and sometimes fewer. The summary is printed by Erdman as follows:

> Application. He who sees the Infinite in all things sees
> God. He who sees the Ratio only sees himself only.
>
> Conclusion. If it were not for the Poetic or Prophetic character. the
> Philosophic & Experimental would soon be the
> ratio of all things & stand still, unable to do other than repeat the
> same dull round over again
>
> Therefore God becomes as we are, that we may be as he is (E3)

But in the extant copies only the last of these summary propositions occurs with any frequency, whereas the other two occur only once. Whatever Blake may have intended when he engraved the full series of plates, it seems that he dismembered his text, that he systematically failed to print five of the seven positive propositions, and that in no surviving copy do we have the visionary humanism of the summary as impressively massed together as in the modern editions.

In the surviving arrangements, moreover, only one bound copy actually separates the plates into two series, whereas the other five intertwine both series. The specific orderings have no authority, but they suggest that Blake drew back from the defiantly visionary idealism of the text we have. The position he wants to assume is evident: the negative series of propositions is self-limiting, and the three positive plates that usually turn up (3, 4, and 12) begin the articulation of a counterphilosophy. But missing is the rhetorical force of an ideology refuted point by point and then conclusively dismissed. Those arrangements that intertwine the two series allow readers to move dialectically between empiricism and idealism, or to traverse an ellipse of perspectives in which we contemplate the alternative to a purely empiricist position and then return (though uneasily) to a recognition that humanity still may not be infinite. But most interesting of all is what happens to the three-point summary printed in modern editions. It seems that Blake had second thoughts about opposing the poetic and experimental characters, and issued the relevant plate (11) only once. It also seems that the conclusive position assigned to the paradox identifying God and human beings is an editorial construction based on a canonical reading. In six bound copies this paradox only once comes at the end of the verbal text. In that position the statement absorbs the discontinuity between finite and infinite revealed by the polarized structure of the text and constructs a paradoxical circuit that allows 'Blake' to produce the propositions of series b as a dialectical reversal rather than a simplistic inversion of series a. Displaced to the middle of the text, the paradox still promises a resolution of contraries, but one that seems more speculative, given its encirclement by the maze of contraries that a final placement allows it to transcend.

In short, the tractates disclose a writer uncertain about how we get from the finite to the infinite and unclear about the relationship between individual experience and visionary imagination. The full force of this uncertainty is held in check by the fact that these texts consist of abstract propositions unelaborated in terms of character and situation. But in *The Book of Thel* and *Visions of the Daughters of Albion* Blake will put into question the hope that all religions can be one even though we see things differently. He will likewise explore the power of imagination to bring into being the infinite. For Thel's conversations with natural entities who see eternity in a grain of sand are experiments in imaginative projection. But then so, too, is the vision in her grave plot, which likewise exceeds the ratio of what she has seen and known.

En-Gendering the System: *The Book of Thel* and *Visions of the Daughters of Albion*

If the *Songs* foreground their intertextuality, *Thel* and *Visions* provide inside views of a single subject whose experience we must live through if we are to understand it. But the identity of this subject is less clear than it might seem, for canonical readings of the texts have tended to subsume the female protagonists into the voice of the male author, or rather have used the 'experience' of the characters to legitimize the 'vision' of the author. There is, in other words, more than one 'subject' in these poems, including the reader. We shall therefore focus on those elements that make us aware that the subject is already intertextual, that 'Oothoon' has been partly written by others, and that 'Blake' cannot represent 'Oothoon' without becoming inscribed in his difference from her. In the process we shall see how a hermeneutics of identification both facilitates and impedes a cultural critique. For it encourages us to identify with perspectives different from our own, and yet it also risks concealing difference in uncritical identification.

Most readings of *Thel* identify not with Thel but with 'Blake.' Thus the poem has been read canonically in the light of Blake's later attacks on the selfhood, as a critique of its virginal protagonist whose fear of losing her identity prevents her crossing from innocence into experience.[7] In the course of the poem a lily, a cloud, and a clod of clay reassure her that what seems like death to her is, from an eternal perspective, part of a regenerative process. For those who see Thel as wrong to flee back to the vales of Har, she thus becomes a figure in the argument that the entry into experience is a fortunate fall that will lead to organized innocence. But whether the cloud and the clod adequately represent 'Blake' is far from clear, given that the latter appears in the *Songs* as a figure not just for generosity but also for naïveté. Moreover, as the personification of natural objects suggests, the cyclical construction of time that allows Thel's conversants to imagine organized innocence is linked only metaphorically to a human world that may be irrevocably linear in its movement toward decomposition.

Crucial to our sense that the poem can be read heretically as well as canonically is precisely this use of metaphor or figure as transposition, as a perspective shift that tries to transform one position into another. An initial example is Thel's description of how the lamb 'crops' the lily's flowers, a curiously gentle term for what (given Thel's identification with her) is actually the flower's death. In one sense the substitution of the cut flower for the violated person asks us to change our perspective and to

[7]An exception is Mitchell, *Blake's Composite Art*, pp. 78–106.

see what is horrible to us as natural. But in another sense metaphor suspends this cleansing of the doors of perception at the site of language, making us aware that it is safe to change our perspective only because the poem is a pastoral that constructs an artificially stylized world. And pastoral, as Blake suggests in the *Songs*, may itself be a political convention used to cloud our perception of social violence.

Some sense of a violence that exceeds the ability of Blake's system to contain it emerges in Thel's final monologue, which is the scene not only of her figures but also of ours:

> Why cannot the Ear be closed to its own destruction?
> Or the glistning Eye to the poison of a smile!
> Why are Eyelids stord with arrows ready drawn,
> Where a thousand fighting men in ambush lie?
> Or an Eye of gifts & graces show'ring fruits & coined gold!
> Why a Tongue impress'd with honey from every wind?
> Why an Ear, a whirlpool fierce to draw creations in?
> (E6; 6:11–17)

Two assumptions have informed commentary on this passage. Although the language is completely inconsonant with any she has used hitherto, we assume that the lines are spoken by a self-projected specter of Thel rather than by a collective unconscious that might lend them authority. And we assume that Thel's questions refer to her fear of 'normal' sexual experience, and that since virginity is 'wrong,' her horror can be dismissed as hysteria. But the referent of the traumatic images is far from clear, for a "thousand fighting men" may just as well refer to war as to sex. In copies that eliminate the last two lines of the passage, with their reference to the "youthful boy" and the "curtain of flesh," the lines point more directly to some amorphous form of social violence the source of which seems lost somewhere in the political unconscious. Although the poem leaves us free to think that this unconscious is another figured curtain (perhaps a screen for Thel's sexual fears), its obliteration of precise referents also raises the possibility that our dismissal of her fears may be a screen for our own fears. In other words, the passage also asks us to enter the space Thel flees and to construct what might be there that so violently negates the language of (un)organized innocence.

At the heart of this poem is a deep uncertainty as to whether there is innocence after experience. This uncertainty can be located in elements of the poem's discourse and construction that mark its indeterminacy as deliberate. For one thing, there is the division of a relatively short text into chapters that mark off different discourses from each other, a feature that limits the authority of each character to the chapter that it dominates. What results is a juxtaposition of different perspectives on the poem's central problem, rather than a continuous narrative that builds up authority for the perspective of eternity and reaches a crisis at which Thel denies that perspective. If Bogen and Erdman are accurate about the chronology of composition, Blake may actually have written the poem in segments marking his own shifts in perspective. Thus it seems that chapter III (on the clod and the worm) was executed separately from the first two chapters, and that the final chapter was composed later (no earlier than 1791) as an "'Experience' climax and commentary attached to what may in 1789 have been more purely a poem of 'Innocence'."[8] The perspectivism of the poem is further emphasized by the motto. Providing us with questions rather than moral prescripts, the motto does not valorize any one point of view. For although the eagle cannot know what is in the pit in the way the mole does, neither can the blind mole wholly see what is there. But although the eagle may see more than the mole, that does not necessarily change the mole's world, which is constituted by its blindness. That wisdom cannot be kept in a silver rod suggests, moreover, that understanding must not be codified in closed forms that provide one law for mole and eagle alike. Each speaker, including Thel, claims such closure, although the dialogical form of the poem belies it. For the lily and the cloud, having delivered their message, retreat to a "silver shrine" and an "airy throne," respectively. Only the clod invites Thel into her home, thus potentially opening herself to another perspective that she, too, avoids by disappearing from the poem thereafter.

By composing the poem in perspectival segments, Blake creates a text that exists in different 'states,' accommodating but always situating the perspectives of both author and reader.[9] As in many of these texts, variant orders for the plates are of symptomatic rather than determinate significance. The existence of offset numbers for the plates that include the narrative prevents us from literally rearranging Thel's history. But the free-floating status of the text's margins (motto, illustrations, etc.) has a suggestive function, reminding us that even fixed narrative orders can be seen in more than one way: the entry into the grave plot can be seen as a crisis in which Thel refuses wisdom, or it can be viewed as a peripeteia that exposes the hollowness of what has gone before. This sense of the poem as existing only in states is reinforced by the most noticeable variant: the relocation of the motto from the beginning to the

[8]David Erdman, *Blake: Prophet against Empire* (1954; rev. ed. Garden City, N.Y.: Doubleday, 1969), p. 131n.; Nancy Bogen, *The Book of Thel: A Facsimile and Critical Text* (Providence, R.I.: Brown University Press, 1971), p. 3.

[9]I use the term 'state' as Blake himself used it. But the term is also used in the graphic arts to denote a particular 'state' of an engraving, and so it is worth noting that Blake sold his plates in earlier states, thus allowing our philosophical and bibliographical uses of the term to coincide.

end in copies N and O. Those who see the motto as a 'moral' see it as counseling Thel to accept experience (like the mole), and not to protect herself with symbols of privilege like the rod and the bowl. Shifting it to the end would then reinforce a reading of the poem as a critique of Thel and would place a space between us and the sympathetic impact of her final speech. But we can also read the motto existentially and see it as dismissing the visionary eagle in favor of the mole, who understands that there is no 'vision' beyond 'experience.' In that case Thel, who has entered the darkness in which all transcendental consolations are dissolved, would actually have lived by the motto whose location at the end would refigure it as a confirmation of nausea. As the significance of the shifts depends on the meaning we attribute to the individual segment, so the mobile structure of the text generates a radically perspectival reading experience. Blake's new practice of reading has two unusual consequences. It creates a dialogue in which readers do not simply find an ambiguity that is *in* the text, but open up from a different historical vantage point possibilities that 'Blake' may not have entirely foreseen. But by making us aware of how we construct the text from the perspective we bring to it, it also compels us to historicize that perspective and to recognize it as constituted on the traces of other horizons of expectation inscribed in the text and its reception history.

Perhaps the most disturbing aspect of the text has to do with the deferral of authority for the credal passages. For these passages are either not spoken by the characters to whom they pertain, or are dubiously authorized by an anthropomorphism that makes voice a figure. Thus the conversation with the lily breaks up into two discursive segments, repeating itself so as to produce differences within the creed of self-sacrifice, and displacing the enunciation of that creed between the lily and Thel in such a way that it is finally spoken by no one. The lily begins by pointing out that she, too, is vulnerable, but that God watches over her, and when she "melts" in the summer (a pointedly gentle word for 'withers'), it is "To flourish in eternal vales" (E4; 1:24–25). The notion of a lily's having an afterlife is of course a pathetic fallacy, and that fact is registered in the transference of the discourse to Thel, who sustains the fiction that death is not painful, but with complications that betray an increasing anxiety. This time the lily's death is not part of a natural cycle but is produced by others: by the lamb 'cropping' her flowers (E4; 2:6). There is also no reward in eternity, nothing being posited beyond the natural world. The continued pastoralization of death masks a displacement, the significance of which Thel herself may not grasp. The consolation of 'eternity' has been dropped because it has not satisfied Thel's desire for reassurance about *this* world. And the lily has not dealt with the problem of unnecessary suffering implicit in the fact that the lamb eats the flower. In the second set of lines the lily is still described as smiling in the face of her sorrows. But then these lines are not spoken by the lily herself, but by Thel, nervously voicing what may be the conventional wisdom. When Thel asks the lily to reconfirm her aestheticization of suffering, the latter does not answer but refers her to the cloud. The cloud in fact does take Thel's suggestion for re-visioning death as mutability to the appropriately pietistic conclusion. But the cloud is also the only male character in the trio who speaks to Thel, a fact that is of significance in terms of the gendering of voices that (as we shall see) plays so important a role in this poem.

Perhaps the most disturbing of these deferrals comes in the final chapter, where the clod, a female character, seemingly confirms the cloud's wisdom. In response to Thel's identification of the worm with unaccommodated man ("an infant wrapped in the Lilly's leaf"), the clod assures Thel that God cherishes even the most ugly of things. Whether the clod's reassurance that God values the worm who will eat her properly answers Thel's fear of becoming fertilizer is not something we shall explore. But it is also notable that the worm, who lacks the cloud's airy throne and lives in a house of clay, never adds its voice to the chorus of reassurances. Instead, the clod speaks for the worm, who simply weeps. Thus, when Thel finally decides to confront experience, she does so from within a network of evasions and on the basis of what can be no more than a representation of the worm's condition as a metaphor for her own, the worm's silence marking a certain resistance to metaphor and thus to the idealizing imagination. Or it may be that the clod does not even claim to speak for the worm. It may be that because Thel has addressed herself to the worm, she *takes* the clod's reassuring words as applying to the worm and concludes that God cherishes it "With milk and oil." (E6; 5:11). But while the clod is said to bend over the worm in "milky fondness," it is on the clod's head that God pours "his oil" (E5; 4:9, 5:1). Whether the clod's words of wisdom refer to herself or also to the worm is thus unclear. And functions like reference and metaphor are in fact at the heart of this poem, which is set up as a conversation with natural objects figured as speaking, and which thus brings to the foreground the problem of how we perceive the world through language. What is clear from the way discourses are juxtaposed and characters are made to speak for each other is that in the lived world reference operates through metaphor and is thus fundamentally ambiguous. We make one situation refer, by metaphorical extension, to another. The ambiguity generated in the gap between the clod's words and Thel's understanding of them raises a larger problem about the reference of the abstract to the concrete. Can the clod's experience stand for that of the worm or for that of Thel, and can credal abstractions refer to concrete existential situations?

The poem's self-reflection on its figures, and its operation as a semiotic screen on which readers must view their figures, is mobilized around the central figure in the text, Thel. In both *Thel* and *Visions* Blake focuses on female characters and both women use a language that is highly figurative, naming their experience in terms of something else, as though lacking unmediated access to their own lives. The depiction of understanding as engendered through the intermediary of figures is particularly striking in *Thel*, where the protagonist invents three figures for herself—a flower, a cloud, and a clod—and where she often speaks of herself in the third person. The poem of course, is not about female identity in the way Wollstonecraft's novels are. Rather, it is about an aborted transition from innocence to experience that Blake *represents* through a young girl. The questions it raises thus pertain first of all to the *semiotic* status of woman in the economy of mythmaking. Or more precisely, we can read woman as both a signifier, a figure for a certain life situation, and as a suppressed referent, someone who must be figured in certain ways to construct her as the appropriate signifier. This crossing of figure and referent has the effect of interrupting the unambiguous functioning of the signifier, making it the site of a resistance to any attempt to fit it into the system. The female figure—for she is always a figure—thus becomes a mirror that reflects back the metaphors used to compose her identity. And because she is a figure in an argument that the poem puts into action but also textualizes, the text's reflection on its own mode of production has two consequences. It draws attention to the figures that support its argument, and it makes us consider the visionary arrogance of using people as figures without regard for their experience. Using woman to promote a certain relationship between innocence and experience, the poem raises the question of how we figure women, and thus allows us to question the legitimacy of the way the relationship is being constructed and evaluated.

In using a female figure to embody his 'myth,' Blake therefore chooses an overdetermined figure: one that is the site of cultural tensions, and he thus engenders a dialogue between hegemonic and oppositional readings of the myth. Blake would have been aware from Joseph Johnson's radical circle that the rethinking of female identity was being done partly in linguistic terms: that writers like Mary Wollstonecraft thought of women as constructed by language and reading, and of women writers as limited by the genres of experience available to them. By focusing on a young girl at the point in cultural history when he was writing, Blake suspends the ratification of any normative identity he or we might construct for her through the use of culturally engendered figures. It is probably no accident that the poem is called "The *Book* of Thel." The protagonist is on the threshold between innocence and experience, but also on the threshold between receiving an identity from others and constructing one for herself. As Thel proceeds through a landscape that is obviously symbolic rather than real, and thus the scene of various cultural inscriptions, she tries to read her identity in the book of nature and thus to accept as natural the identity modeled for her by others. But we are all the time aware that the book of nature is a reversible trope: that the natural may be something written. Thel's behavior is characteristically female. She does not assert her identity like the bard of *Experience*, or even like the ungendered child of "Infant Joy," who says with innocent directness, "I happy am." Instead, she asks others to tell her who she is and what she should do. This linguistic detour creates a space between Thel and the identity offered her. Her own uncertainty about accepting the prescription of the lily, cloud, and clod is evident in the fact that she must hear it three times. And because we are aware that her passivity is gender-specific, we are hesitant to ask that she identify with roles that she wants to assume yet projects as other. What is most striking about the figures who try to reassure Thel is that they are all feminine, behaviorally if not pronominally. The lily who suffers herself to be eaten by the 'innocent' male lamb follows the feminine path of self-sacrifice. The clod is associated with nurturing and pitying. Only the cloud is male, and Blake's identification of him as such, in contrast to his use of the figure elsewhere,[10] marks his desire to normalize a pattern that demands the sacrifice of selfhood. It marks, in other words, the difficulty of placing 'Blake,' who seems to raise and suppress the question of gender, who wants Thel to follow the advice she is given and who also seems sensitive to her doubts. We should not minimize Blake's own commitment to the 'message' of Eternity. Yet the very attribution of gender to natural objects suspends this message in an anthropomorphism and raises the question of whether 'eternity' itself is not a cultural construction. And paradoxically it is the fact that Blake makes one of these characters male instead of making them all female that raises the question of gender as a point of anxiety.

If this approach to the poem constructs a feminist reader, it does so partly as a paradigm for avoiding an archetypal reading that would protect the text from any insertion into history. Blake's use of a female protagonist allows him to experiment with a creed he could not otherwise promulgate. The clod could not have offered the same advice if the protagonist of the poem had been Orc. But insofar as the female figure facilitates the articulation of this creed, the interruption of figure by referent that occurs when we consider Thel as a 'real person' configures

[10]In *Visions* (iii:7–8) Oothoon is a cloud rent by Bromion's thunders, and in *Europe* the shadowy female is associated with clouds (1:12). My point is not that clouds are female, but that Blake does not always make them male.

a larger interruption of visionary argument by social and historical considerations. To put it differently, 'Blake' argues for an approach to experience that he seems to naturalize by associating it with traditional female virtues, but he does so at a point when people are beginning to question the nature of woman. He also makes his protagonist ambiguously silent in the face of the female roles offered her by the figures she finds in the book of nature. The result is that the text becomes a site for the reader to produce a genealogy of its morals: an analysis of the historicity of values that is not dissimilar from the one Blake himself performs in *The Marriage of Heaven and Hell.*

Such a genealogy involves historicizing not only the poem but also contemporary readings of it. The normalization of experience as something Thel ought to face comes from an effacement of its social dimension that makes it simply a temporal category, a stage of life. This effacement occurs through a placing of Thel's 'virginity' within a horizon of expectations that is both male and modern. Thus, one possible reading might reclaim 'Blake' as an advocate of free love by assuming the healthiness of (sexual) experience, and thus the regenerative role of all 'experience' for achieving emotional wholeness. But how the reader is to place herself in relation to Thel's virginity may well seem clearer now than it did at the end of the eighteenth century, when 'sex' was interimplicated in its social construction and had not yet been reconstructed as 'natural.' Blake often does advocate an open embrace of sexual experience, and yet the consequences of that experience in a poem like *Visions* seem to justify Thel's fears. Insofar as virginity plays a symbolic role in the economy of the poem—which we literalize in using it to prescribe Thel's conduct—Thel's desire to remain a virgin suggests that sometimes experience may be unavoidably, yet irrevocably, crippling. It does not dogmatically suggest that, however. For Blake not only focused on Thel at a threshold in her life that looks both backward and forward; he also focused on a female figure at a threshold in women's history. The semiotic function of the female figure is to be an open signifier in a way that a male figure could not have been. Because of the increasing consciousness among women writers about social conditioning, woman had become a *tabula rasa* cleansed of previous cultural inscriptions and open to new formulations of her identity. On the one hand, the liminal status of woman at this point in history allows us to see trauma itself as socially engendered rather than as a deep structure, a Freudian absolute. On the other hand, the text raises the question of whether there is such a thing as virginity, in the sense not of sexual innocence but of not yet being written on. Already Thel seems inhabited by experiences she has not had, by some collective unconscious that occupies the void of her not yet having become anything. Her sense of nightmare is generated by a temporal metalepsis in which the future is already past. And in a larger sense this metalepsis is a cultural structure that calls into question not only virginity but any form of newness or origination, be it regeneration in eternity or historical renewal.

In *Visions of the Daughters of Albion* Blake again contextualizes his reflection on organized innocence through a character whose gender raises questions of cultural inscription. The narrative begins, like *Thel*, with a dialogue between Oothoon and her figured self, in which the marigold responds to her reluctance to pluck it:" 'pluck thou my flower Oothoon the mild! / Another flower shall spring" (E46; 1:8–9). Most critics see the hopes Oothoon projects onto the flower as enshrining the poem's wisdom and assume that the world of experience will include (re)generation. Oothoon, as is well known, is raped by Bromion and then rejected by Theotormon as soiled, on the basis of a classification of woman as property. At first she internalizes the latter's standards, but then she counters them by refusing to treat *him* as property, offering instead to procure girls for him and watch them copulate (E50; 7:23–26). This generous offer supposedly marks her emotional regeneration, for she has now entered the gift economy of feminists like Cixous, and sees beyond the narrow perceptions of selfhood supposedly disdained by Blake.

Given the way he later writes her into his dictionary of symbols, some part of 'Blake' clearly does see Oothoon as achieving wholeness in a poem that authorizes its myth by claiming to be a radically feminist statement. But the early poem is also distinguished by an individual focus that makes us see the system from the viewpoint of its participants. As a mobile text that does not put wisdom in the "golden shrine" of the marigold but exists only in its reading, the poem situates 'Blake's' perspective against its own margins. These margins emerge first of all in the discrepancies between juxtaposed segments that repeat and displace each other. Thus the argument might seem to duplicate the narrative. But in beginning with Oothoon's love for Theotormon and ending with her rape, it summarizes only the first seventeen lines of the narrative. One way of viewing this discrepancy is to say that it juxtaposes the merely factual account of Oothoon's experience with the much longer inside view that focuses on what a person creates from the events that bound her life. Oothoon in the narrative deals constructively with the rape, while in the argument she simply says, "But the terrible thunders tore / My virgin mantle in twain" (E45; iii:7–8). But then the fact that it is the argument, not the narrative, that is spoken by Oothoon herself raises the possibility that the narrative does not develop beyond line 17 but continues the rape by dramatizing the rending apart of Oothoon's psyche. Discrepancy is likewise the subject of the poem's motto: "The

Eye sees more than the Heart knows." Does this mean that the reader's eye can see more than Oothoon's heart knows, and what in turn does she know? Does the heart know only the pain of rape, while the visionary eye can see beyond this experience? Or does the empirical eye see things to which the heart, with its will to vision, is justifiably blind? To interpret the motto is irrelevant, because we need to see it not as a hermeneutic key but as a grammar of understanding. As such, it provides verbs that lack predicates as well as personal subjects. It thus produces perceptual positions that can be occupied by anyone and that will accordingly change in the perceptions they generate. But it produces them in such a way that the positions are diacritically constructed, and qualify or reverse each other so as to keep the meaning of the poem open.

At the heart of the poem's indeterminacy is Oothoon as a figure for organized innocence. Damrosch is one of the few to note the Urizenic images in which her generosity is described:[11]

> But silken nets and traps of adament will Oothoon spread,
> And catch for thee girls of mild silver, or of furious gold;
> I'll lie beside thee on a bank & view their wanton play
> In lovely copulation bliss on bliss with Theotormon.
>
> (E50; 7:23–26)

"Nets" and "traps," images even in this poem of dissimulation (E49; 5:18, 6:10–12), mark Blake's awareness that there is something not quite right in the representation of Oothoon as emancipated. Significantly, several lines after she is thought to have unbound herself from Theotormon's standards, she is still described as 'reflecting' his "image pure" (E47; 3:16), as culturally constructed by what she so passionately resists. To oppose the designation of women as private property by becoming a procuress is hardly liberated behavior even in terms of the ethic dubiously described as 'free love.' Not only does Oothoon still conceive herself as an instrument of male pleasure; she also visits on other women a version of her own fate. We could (and to some extent we probably do) argue that she is only a flawed type of organized innocence. But to abstract from the material circumstances of Oothoon's response something of which it is a sign is a kind of essentialism. Moreover, it is questionable whether a woman, once she allows herself to read as a woman, would not see Oothoon's 'generosity' as a notion conveniently engendered within a male discourse. Read psychologically rather than typologically, Oothoon's solution may well be a symptom of deep trauma. One could speculate that her fantasy about other women copulating

[11]Leopold Damrosch, *Symbol and Truth in Blake's Myth* (Princeton, N.J.: Princeton University Press, 1980), pp. 197–98.

'openly' is a way of justifying to herself the enormous cost of *her* having been open to the world of experience. Thus she imagines a scene in which her openness is refigured so that it no longer opens women to male compulsion, because their entry into the economy of pleasure is voluntary. But it is significant that she does not participate in this scene, marking both a silent doubt about her fantasy and the fact that she has been emotionally crippled by the rape. Of significance here is the ambiguity raised by Oothoon's openness, as to whether she is actually raped in a legal sense.[12] Oothoon had imagined a world in which that ambiguity could not exist because there was no rape: a world in which she could be open without opening herself to exploitation. At the end she reverts to that utopia in a voyeuristic fantasy that sees exploitation as innocent openness.

The problem of how to read Oothoon's cure throws into relief the larger question of how the text's figuration of her discloses the genealogy of its own visionary morality. On one level the poem enacts a familiar Blake pattern: the story of how a fall from innocence becomes the dialectical ground for the imagining of a more genuine innocence. But it is also a defamiliarization of that pattern, a pattern that operates by substituting symbolic referents for literal referents, the spiritual story of Oothoon's suffering and regeneration for the more disturbing physical story of her rape. If the text dramatizes the power of imagination, it is significant that the 'reality' it tries to transfigure is a rape, an event whose sheer physicality thwarts attempts to read it figuratively. By figuring the Blakean paradigm through the story of a rape, the poem calls into question the very making of figures, crossing aesthetics with ethics and asking us whether it is right to use rape as a figure of something else. Blake's own complicity in this displacement is marked by the curious fact that Oothoon's rape is not simply refigured; it is never actually named in the poem. It enters the poem not only as a figure for other violations that are similarly unnamed, but also through a figure: the figure of Bromion's thunders, which Oothoon says tore "My virgin mantle in twain." Indeed, the narrator's repetition of this figure, "Bromion rent her with his thunders" (E46; 1:16), goes even further toward naturalizing the event, effacing any mention of virginity or of the violent removal of clothing. That the rape is from the beginning poeticized is what makes it possible to compare Oothoon's loss of innocence to the plucking of a

[12]Since it is Oothoon who plucks the marigold, it is not entirely clear that she is raped according to then-prevailing legal definitions of the term, though it is clear enough that Blake perceives what Bromion does as a rape, and most critics have accordingly treated it as a rape. Leslie Tannenbaum, however, is an example of someone who takes the legal interpretation, thus opening the whole issue of 'openness': *Biblical Tradition in Blake's Prophecies: The Great Code of Art* (Princeton, N.J.: Princeton University Press, 1982), p. 188.

flower. And the fact that the unnatural is uneasily represented as natural is what makes it possible to see Oothoon as responding positively to an 'experience' Thel could not see as normal.

This representation of Oothoon is in a sense a second rape: a linguistic rape that repeats the original violation even as it criticizes it, by denying Oothoon the right to speak her pain as it is. For Oothoon has not found a language to express her emotions. Trying to articulate what she *is* in her words, she also expresses that identity as something she is not through the gaps between her words, through her cries and silences. Though she speaks for most of the poem, unlike Thel who is represented by others, Oothoon's language is opaquely symbolic, as though she has lost the literal referents of her words:

> With what sense is it that the chicken shuns the ravenous hawk?
> With what sense does the tame pigeon measure out the expanse?
> With what sense does the bee form cells? have not the mouse & frog
> Eyes and ears and sense of touch? yet are their habitations.
> And their pursuits, as different as their forms and as their joys:
> . . . .
> Ask the blind worm the secrets of the grave, and why her spires
> Love to curl round the bones of death; and ask the rav'nous snake
> Where she gets poison: & the wing'd eagle why he loves the sun.
> (E47; 3:2–12)

The hysterical crescendo of questions does not clearly say anything, though valiant attempts have been made to explain them in terms of the 'system.' In the first passage it seems that Oothoon is attributing to each creature a sixth sense that makes it unique, thus asking Theotormon to see her on her own terms by perceiving her through the organ of perception unique to her. Yet the impression of a series of analogies accumulating conviction for this point of view is belied by the heterogeneous jumbling together of everything from chickens to snakes. Even as we look for the common denominator in this chaos of analogies, we are distracted by the resonances of individual analogies. Can Oothoon praise the chicken for shunning the hawk, yet also view the fact that she did not shun Bromion as a fortunate fall that allows her to see new possibilities? If the "night is gone" that closed her "in its deadly black" (E47; 2:29), why does she image her new-found identity in terms of poison and death as well as the wild ass refusing burdens? How we construe the images is less important than the pathology of their form. For Oothoon says nothing directly. Instead, she refers to chickens and bees, creatures who do not so much provide her with useful analogies as suggest that she cannot speak literally about what she feels. What she feels is not of course clear, for the distance of her language from any literal referent is symptomatic not only of a distance between conventionalized language and inward experience, but also of her alienation from herself. Allowed to name her experience only symbolically, Oothoon is cut off from her own body, not simply by a patriarchal order but also by her own trauma, which leads her to seek figurative displacements and ultimately to 'heal' herself in ways that perpetuate that order. She has, as it were, a symbolic body, a body of metaphors and metonymies that we should not too easily take for truth. And the renovation of that body projected by 'Blake' may likewise be symbolic, disembodied.

The fact that organized innocence may still be unorganized is marked for us by the movability of the frontispiece depicting Bromion and Oothoon still invisibly bound together, with Theotormon on one side of the entrance to a cave, his face averted. None of the characters face each other, and the plate thus represents the traumatized stasis produced by the rape, in which Oothoon's position is still determined by that of her oppressors. Whether the transposition of the plate to the end in one copy (A) and its repetition at both beginning and end in another (F) was an accident is irrelevant. Clearly, these shifts represent someone's sense of another way the poem asks to be read, and clearly, the way Blake produces his texts allows them to exist in more than one version. Placing the plate at the beginning seems to allow that the narrative develops beyond its initial stasis. Placing it at the end gives a certain finality to its bleak image of a psychologically frozen world. Because the plate in copy A is actually more brightly colored than in some other copies, the pessimism of the final placement is subject to revision.[13] But the point is that its movability allows the meaning of the poem to be constructed by the reader in a field of intertextual possibilities.

It would be easy to condemn Blake for imposing a male discourse on the poem, or to concur in what seems a celebration of free love. But the author in this text is self-critically evasive. David Punter has pointed out that the trauma is also Blake's: the trauma of a man who does not know how to deal with what his culture has done to women.[14] It is interesting in this context that Ortega y Gasset should relate metaphor to "the spirit of taboo." Metaphor, he says, "substitutes one thing for another—from an urge not so much to get at the first as to get rid of the second."[15] But significantly, although Blake presents the rape figuratively, he does not efface its violence. Indeed the tendency to naturalize rape is crossed and

[13]In this copy the sun is rising, whereas in others it is setting, and in yet others the spaces left for sun and sky are colored blue-black so as to efface the sun entirely.

[14]"Blake, Trauma and the Female," *New Literary History* 15 (1984): 475–90.

[15]*The Dehumanization of Art and Other Writings on Art and Culture* (New York: Doubleday, 1956), p. 31.

suspended by a desire to dramatize other modes of exploitation such as slavery and capitalism, by figuring them as forms of rape. The fact of violence structures critically the space in which Blake must move as reader of his own text. For violence constitutes its object as other, removes it from the sphere of our own experience and thus of our understanding. In dealing with someone whose experience is unutterably more painful than anything we ourselves know, the immediate response is to find analogies from our own experience that will heal the rupture created in cultural understanding. Not only must we explain an alien experience to ourselves; we must also explain ourselves to the other person, contending with an obscure sense of complicity in her pain. This complicity (which we also feel in the face of natural occurrences such as death) may not stem from anything we have done, but simply from a sense that we have hitherto been insensitive to what has now ruptured our security. Breaking the social hermeneutic in which we all thought we understood things in the same way, violence forces us to use language to reestablish a sense of shared values, but compels us to recognize the tenuousness of the bridges thus constructed. Blake is nervously aware that images of plucked flowers and thunderstorms, with their attendant promise of regeneration, are analogies that do not identify Oothoon's experience so much as refigure it as Blake wishes it were. This awareness surfaces in the imagery of nets and traps, and in the fact that the frontispiece can be relocated as a coda. It also surfaces in the poem's recourse to silence and cries. Oothoon 'howls' (E46; 2:12) and 'laments' (E47; 3:1). She is silent for periods of up to a day (E47–48; 3:14, 4:25) and is supported by a nonverbal chorus: the daughters of Albion, who echo back her "sighs" but not her words, as though her words are really circumlocutions for sighs. It is all too easy for us to read the poem instead of hearing it, as the daughters do, and thus to reduce the duration of its silences from a day to a line. But these silences manifest the gaps in the text where language cannot reach and force Blake's ideology to know its own margins.

What I have suggested is a different perspective on the poem from the visionary reading that we assume 'Blake' to want. But Blake may also be uneasy about a reading that would incorporate Oothoon into his corpus, fixing her in her symbolic body. As in *Thel*, the double reference of the poem—both visionary (to Blake's system) and historical (to specific events of the kind detailed in Stedman's narrative)—produces a crossing of figure and referent in which the typological reading of Oothoon is interrupted by a psychological and social reading that reconstructs her as person rather than sign. This crossing becomes an occasion for us to reconsider the kind of reading necessary to sustain Blake's system. Tannenbaum suggests that for Blake typology is "synonymous with the creative process itself" and that by "defining Christ as the Imagination, Blake adopts as his subject the typological process itself."[16] Or to put it differently, by placing Christ at the center of his phenomenology of spirit, Blake represents imagination as typological and demands, for that representation to be sustained, an archetypal reading that translates individual experience into a central paradigmatic story. But the early poems are too close to their social referents not to be aware of the cultural imperialism that informs such reading as a will-to-power over the text's own uncertainties. By writing for an audience composed of men and women instead of sheep and goats, Blake calls into play instead of effacing the cultural differences that the 'romantic imagination' tries to dismiss. And inasmuch as rape is a metonymy in this poem for other acts of psychic and political seizure, its resistance to being read figurally marks a certain limit to the attempt to silence other forms of social violation through imaginative transfiguration.

[16]*Biblical Tradition in Blake's Prophecies*, p. 99.

CHAPTER NINE

(Infinite) Absolute Negativity: The Brief Epics

To approach Blake's corpus in terms of sectors is to displace any genetic narrative (either of evolution or repression) that one might construct because the texts follow each other chronologically. Each sector provides a perspective on the whole that inscribes rather than anticipates or surpasses the intentions of other sectors. Thus, the earliest texts encourage us to experiment with the priority of individual experience over systematic constructs. In so doing, they open canonical reading to problems of cultural difference. In the brief epics, which more assertively begin the construction of a canon, we are encouraged to play with the absorption of difference into identity through the subsumption of present into future. But here, too, the traditional hermeneutic promoted by the later prophecies encounters metaphysical if not cultural challenges. If Blake's work differs from earlier canons, it is in the fact that his canon is not a preestablished structure but something that he must create through evidence and consensus. The texts we shall consider here are paradigms for the way the supplementary use of hermeneutics in forming canonical values necessarily stimulates a certain reflexiveness toward that project.

The brief epics differ from the previous texts in their renunciation of an individual perspective in favor of an omniscient voice that tries to see events both transcendentally and historically. Attempting to construct a phenomenology of history, Blake sometimes brings present, past, and future together in one text like *The Marriage*. But more often he deals with them separately, in a concession that history cannot yet be put together. These texts, however, are quite different from the final prophecies. They lay the groundwork for a canon by implying their own continuation in some further text and by thus making the part a sign of some absent whole. But it is not until later that Blake introduces the strategies typical of canon formation: the exclusion of certain perspectives and the incorporation of others as partial types of truth. Moreover, the early poems are prophetic in wanting to move toward the future, but this movement is hortatory rather than predictive because voice and event are not fused. If *Milton* is more grounded in a personal narrative, that is because Blake has withdrawn from the theater of history to what (superficially at least) seems the more tractable stage of the self. The early prophecies situate themselves in a historical world, that of Europe in the late eighteenth century, and the abstraction of prophecy from event or of voice from subjectivity is a concession to the unreadability, perhaps the unmanageability, of history. Not only is the realization of the vision adumbrated in *The Marriage* deferred, its central principles are also challenged: principles such as the attribution of the fall to Urizen and to his imposition of boundaries, our power to repeal the chaos we have created, and indeed the very possibility of organized innocence. The insecurity of the secular scripture confirmed through canonical reading is reflected in Blake's continued use of mobile forms that make 'omniscience' no more than a perspective. Thus, at the beginning of *Urizen* Blake assumes the stance of the Eternals, only to withdraw them from the action. The Eternals thus emerge as an intent at transcendence that Blake can do no more than inscribe in the text.

Europe: A Prophecy

Our discussion will focus on *Europe* and *Urizen*, so as to bring out how they stimulate and displace the negative hermeneutic necessary to fit them into Blake's canon. The text of *Europe* is assembled out of several pieces: the narrative itself, a preludium, a title page, a design of a Urizenic figure mapping the world with compasses, and a preface that exists in only two copies. Superficially we may be reminded of *Jerusalem*, where each chapter is similarly introduced by a combination of a preface and either a lyric or motto. But the later poem's preface draws the reader into a space of authority, by characterizing the author we must accept or reject. By contrast, the prefatory materials to *Europe* are like a series of asymmetrical frames from which 'Blake' seems teasingly absent. When he does represent himself, as the one who hears the fairy's song in the preface, it is in a whimsical way that mocks our attempts to grasp him. The text gives us its meaning as something that must be pieced together but breaks and interchanges the frames that we might otherwise use to give it its bounding outline. Its construction raises at the outset the question of interpretation, forcing us to encounter problems of structure before we hear the 'voice' promised by prophecy, and thus suspending rhetoric and the powerful responses it arouses in epistemology.

The simplest of the frames are the frontispiece and the title page. The picture of the Ancient of Days, first in all but one copy, suggests that we are entering a world of restriction. The title page with its description of *Europe* as a 'prophecy' allows us to think of that situation as open to change, a statement that things will change or that they should change. In different proofs of the title page, moreover, the figure caught in the coils of the serpent is Urizen or Los.[1] We thus enter the narrative at a threshold between the actual and the possible. The narrative itself telescopes all of Christian history into a few pages before precipitating itself toward a climax of indeterminate import:

> Then Los arose his head he reard in snaky thunders clad:
> And with a cry that shook all nature to the utmost pole,
> Call'd all his sons to the strife of blood.
>
> (E66; 15:9–11)

To follow Erdman in interpreting the 'strife of blood' as a reference to England's counterrevolutionary war against France is to read the poem as a corrective satire.[2] To see the climax as representing the revolution itself is more pessimistic, for it is not just Orc but also Los (clad in snaky thunders that recall the serpent temple of Baconian science) who is now internally bound in a cyclic entwinement with what he opposes. On the referent of this phrase, deliberately obscured like the word 'prophecy' on some copies of the title page, depends our sense of how 'Blake' reads cultural history. That the poem encourages us to reflect on how we construct a hermeneutics of history is evident in the way it interrupts its mythopoeic style with neo-Hogarthian designs such as plate 7. These designs make myth responsible to a world of historical detail and encourage us to apply it to specific events in the way that Erdman does. On the other hand, the discontinuity between realistic and visionary segments makes us wonder whether myth *can* be used to read history: whether it does not encounter an obscurity about which part of the pattern relates to which event.

At the root of our uncertainty about whether a negative hermeneutic can be used to bridge the gap between myth and actuality is the gro-

[1]David V. Erdman, *The Illuminated Blake* (London: Oxford University Press, 1974), pp. 396–97.

[2]David Erdman, *Blake: Prophet against Empire* (1954; rev. ed. Garden City, N.Y.: Doubleday, 1969), p. 264.

tesquely parodic mode of the narrative—not something we find in the original scriptures. Echoing Milton's "Nativity Ode" but making the 'secret child' Orc instead of Christ, the text turns Miltonic Christianity into a cinematic horror show whose overblown figures explode it from within. Parody obviously does not posit in any conventional sense, but whether it posits by negation and thus yields to hermeneutic reading is what remains ambiguous. Richard Poirier distinguishes between a parody that is "other-directed—by one writer against another or at the literary modes of a particular period," and a much more recent literature of self-parody that "shapes itself around its own dissolvents [and] calls into question . . . the activity itself of creating any literary form."[3] Blake himself seems to be writing both kinds of parody, for if the prophecy satirizes Milton so as to make us reverse the catastrophe he has produced, it also bitterly mocks *The Song of Los* with its celebration of Orc so as to consume what it posits through negation. Moreover, it is unclear whether we can even make Poirier's distinction. Parody is fundamentally imitation: whether one sees the imitation as cathartic satire or as obsessive repetition, there is some kind of identification between the parodic text and what it projects as other. While reducing what it mocks to a series of empty forms, the parody itself remains locked in the same hollowness, a mockery of itself. Thus we often wonder whether figures like Orc and Los provide alternatives to Urizen or simply replicate the structure of what is already a parody. At the same time parody, however self-consuming, cannot but retain the trace of a belief in truth and origins precisely because it *is* a form of imitation, although an iconoclastic one. Parody mimes an ideology that has been reduced to a formalism. Thereby constituting itself as a reflection of a reflection, it also creates by the very act of imitation the expectation of a positive source travestied by the sources it discovers. That Blake conflates in the figure of Orc elements of Satan and Christ is a thematic symptom of the ontological structure of parody as a mode in which negation is not nonbeing but the ground of coming-to-be. For the nativity evokes as an empty schema a pattern that neither Orc nor Christ fulfils, and that pattern then becomes a shadow that futurity casts upon the present, unsettling any identification of the text as a prophecy of doom. To put it differently, parody does not posit anything. But linked with prophecy, it may have the hermeneutic structure of what Kierkegaard calls infinite absolute negativity. Even as it negates everything, it may ask the reader to imagine that it does so from the standpoint of a truth that it does not yet embody.

Our first reading of the narrative is by way of the preludium, which in most copies is unaccompanied by any further preface, and which thus

[3]"The Politics of Self-Parody," *Partisan Review* 35 (1968): 339.

seems to frame the rest of the poem in the voice of the nameless shadowy female. Reading it mimetically, we might see the prophetic bitterness of the text as unable to do more than reinscribe things as they are. The "nameless shadowy female" is a will that has not yet achieved representation. She first pictures herself as an inverted flower whose roots are "brandish'd in the heavens" and whose fruits are buried in the earth (E60; 1:8–9), recalling bitterly those flowers in *Thel* and *Visions* which believed that being uprooted by experience could be joyful. Wrapping herself in a "turban of thick clouds" and a mantle of "sheety waters" (E61; 1:12–13), she seems a figure similar to the Earth of Experience. Like Earth, she sees her potential as stifled and sees life as an endless cycle in which revolutionary energy bursts forth only to be stamped with Enitharmon's "signet" in the "solid form" of things as they are (E61; 2:7–10). Her lament provides a preview of the narrative that follows and also, since she may be Blake's muse, a commentary on the poem's mode: warped and inverted, turbaned in an imperious obscurity that folds inward to an inner void, a "secret place" (E61; 2:18). To see the prophecy from the perspective of the shadowy female is to accept its parodic inversions as self-consuming rather than apocalyptic, and to deconstruct the negative hermeneutic that parody seemingly offers. Fundamentally obscure, the prophetic voice acknowledges its failure at representation in the concluding image of secrecy and involution:

> . . . I roll inward & my voice is past.
>
> She ceast & rolld her shady clouds
> Into the secret place.
> (E61; 2:16–18)

But even without the preface there are indications that a purely deconstructive reading is limited. For one thing, the shadowy female addresses herself to someone who might think differently from her. She poses self-justifying questions, asking why she should hope, given her experience so far. She asks, "who shall bind the infinite with an eternal band," thus constructing her statement of the paradox that necessarily consumes the infinite over the recognition that there may be bands that do not bind (E61; 2:13). Addressing herself nominally to Enitharmon but also to some other voice that reproaches her for her premature despair, she tacitly raises the possibility of reading the text of history differently. Like "Earth's Answer," the voice of the preludium is unsettled by its dialogical emergence in relation to a more hopeful voice that it can neither accept nor totally ignore. Moreover, the gender of the shadowy voice is significant. For in responding to it as specifically female, we become aware that oppression and helplessness are not archetypal realities, as her mythic language would have us believe, but aspects of the way women are figured and socialized. We see that the female's predicament is not preordained, and that she is a historical construction that then constructs history in a certain way. To introduce the supplement of gender is not, however, to produce a hermeneutic transfiguration of the text, since gender (like history itself) is a reflexive category. Thus, we may also recognize that what we would substitute for the female's construction of history, namely, the image of a transcendental subject able to cast off its mind-forged manacles, is equally a figure. As such, it may be unresponsive to woman's experience of being helpless, as well as to the self-doubt implicit in Blake's engendering of the prophetic voice as female.

As important as gender to the marking of limits is Blake's segmental construction of the poem. Segmentation functions somewhat like aphorism in creating spaces between texts that act as frames which "magnify the power of exaggeration within them but don't allow it to penetrate beyond their confines."[4] In other words, the preludium is stopped from functioning as the major premise in the poem's argument because its voice is placed outside the text of the prophecy. To absorb this voice into the subsequent text would be to naturalize it—a move that Blake arrests by conspicuously isolating it from the rest of the narrative. He also 'ungrounds' it, for it seems to come from nowhere, to hover abstractly like a state that we may pass through, but not to have the identity of a person whose origins we know. While the voice has interiority and thus pathos, we are displaced from an affective identification with it by the fact that it has no exteriority. It is almost impossible to visualize this shadowy female who is first an uprooted plant and then (dis)appears in a turban of clouds, who seems to originate from "out the breast of Orc" but who then brings forth from her bosom the "howling terrors" and "myriads of flames" that earlier seem to have produced her (E60–61; 1:1, 2:4,9). The paradoxical genetic relationship between Orc and the female creates a radical uncertainty as to the identity of this shadow who is known to us only as a sequence of stylized responses (deracination, turning inward, secrecy). Is her despair the inevitable consequence of Orc's destructive revolutions, or does her despair produce revolution in such a way that it must be destructive? What, moreover, is her relation to Enitharmon? She addresses her as though she were the victim of Enitharmon's machinations, as "mother Enitharmon" and thus as the origin of her woes (E60; 1:4). Yet her own role as mother of the howling terrors, which is another name for Orc, parallels Enitharmon's role as

[4]Alexander Nehamas, *Nietzsche: Life as Literature* (Cambridge, Mass.: Harvard University Press, 1985), p. 23.

mother of Orc and raises the possibility that the shadowy female and her mother are aspects of each other. The relationship between these characters who intergenerate each other takes form in what Ault calls a "causal loop," a "perspective transformation" in which temporal relationships are constantly transposed, such that something that precedes an event suddenly comes into being only as a result of the event it precedes.[5] Such loops bring to the surface of the text an undecidability that can sometimes create openings. In this case the loop makes us aware of the narrative as a transformational surface that keeps generating voices and characters to explain itself, freeing us in the process from the demonically cyclic explanation of history to which the shadowy female ascribes the involution of prophecy. In other words, it makes us aware that the narrative field of this poem is highly fluid, and that the perspective from which we structure it is capable of changing.

Nevertheless, if the preludium de-identifies us from its voice and thus from a fatalistic reading of the prophecy, it does not really give us another position with which we can identify, producing hope only negatively as a disembodied space inside despair. What radically alters the poem is the addition of the preface in copies H and K. Here Blake overhears the song of a fairy sitting on a streaked tulip, carries him home while gathering flowers on the way, and sets him down on his parlor table, where the fairy dictates *Europe*. This whimsical attempt to displace the shadowy female as the origin of the narrative begins with an account of expanded perception:

> Five windows light the cavern'd Man; thro' one he breathes the air;
> Thro' one, hears music of the spheres; thro' one, the eternal vine
> Flourishes, that he may receive the grapes; thro' one can look.
> And see small portions of the eternal world that ever groweth;
> Thro' one, himself pass out what time he please, but he will not.
> (E60; iii:1–5)

We are sufficiently familiar with passages that speak of seeing eternity in a grain of sand to assume that this must finally be the voice of Blake. Thus, Leslie Tannenbaum links the fairy to the fairies and giants in the preface to *Jerusalem* and argues that in substituting it for the traditional Christian muse Blake continues his parody of Milton through a countergenealogy of morals. He returns to the vision of the Ancient Poets in *The Marriage* who found "an immense world of delight" in the senses (E35; 7), and he dismisses as unnecessary the dualism of sense and spirit that produces Europe's woes. From the view that the poem has as its goal

[5]Donald Ault, "Re-Visioning *The Four Zoas*," in Nelson Hilton and Thomas Vogler, eds., *Unnam'd Forms: Blake and Textuality* (Berkeley: University of California Press, 1986), p. 111.

the "exposure of error,"[6] there follows a view of the preface as enacting a hermeneutic program based on a reversal of perspective. Its stylistic incongruity is part of this reversal. To read the preface as a postscript, as we do knowing that it was added to the poem, is to move from a melodramatically serious vision to a charming anecdote that suddenly turns us upside down so as to make us wonder if we are not now seeing things the right side up. Granted that a fairy does not belong in a parlor. But are not Enitharmon and Ocalythron equally preposterous (and much more harmful) concoctions? Treading a fine line between the absurd and the miraculous, the fairy asks us to see the narrative as a nightmarish fiction. For a moment he seems to be parodying *Europe* only to appear as absurd himself, but then he puts us through a further reversal of perspectives by juxtaposing pastoral and humor, Albion's fairies and eighteenth-century domestic interiors, in such a way as to open inside the ridiculous a window into the miraculous. As a hermeneutic signpost, what this poem tells us is to turn *Europe* around and around till the chinks in its cavern become windows into eternity. The cavernous form of parody, which sometimes seems to consist only of the void created by hollowing out the object of the parody, must be read in such a way. Parody in the bitter form it takes in the narrative carries us to the vortex of vision. To pass through this vortex is to revision the parodic process in another more creative form.

What the preface generates, in other words, is a dialectically intricate hermeneutics of reversal. The seeing of the vortex (as opposed to the vortex itself) is Blake's image in *Milton* for a hermeneutic that grasps 'reality' as a transformational surface. As the mental traveler enters the vortex, it contracts to a point of nonentity. As he emerges from it, he sees it in reverse, expanding behind him:

> The nature of infinity is this: That every thing has its
> Own Vortex; and when once a traveller thro Eternity.
> Has passed that Vortex, he percieves it roll backward behind
> His path, into a globe itself infolding; like a sun:
> Or like a moon, or like a universe of starry majesty.
> (E109; 15:21–25)

In the passage immediately following this one, Milton, having entered his shadow, the body of beliefs he can no longer inhabit, enters the inert Albion, and his vision contracts toward imaginative death. At the same time, the Eternals, from the other end of the narrative vortex, see Milton's "immortal Self" sleeping "on a couch / Of gold" (E109; 15:11–13).

[6]Leslie Tannenbaum, *Biblical Tradition in Blake's Prophecies: The Great Code of Art* (Princeton, N.J.: Princeton University Press, 1982), pp. 181–82.

As a figure of reading, the vortex provides a means of containing the proliferating reversals of parody. As we travel through *Europe*, the parody first generates a contracting vortex, inverting the "Nativity Ode" so as to empty Milton's corpus of life. It mocks Milton into nonentity but also restricts imaginative space so that we think of nothing except the horrors of eighteen hundred years of history. As parody takes a more open form in the preface, the fairy's song allows us to emerge from the vortex. The narrative of *Europe* is still the vortex we are about to enter. But we also know that when we return to the text's beginning, we can see the vortex roll backward behind us and can see the parody of Milton not as an inwardly spiraling despair but as "a globe itself infolding": a new world, though still limited and involuted.

It is clear that the preface expands the ways we can perceive the narrative by effecting a somersault from parody to vision. But we also cannot ignore the ambiguities of its style and placement. For its modular status and incongruous style suspend its ability to function as the major premise in a (re)visionary argument. Recalling the introduction to *Innocence*, where the piper is inspired by a child on a cloud, this poem almost seems to parody an equation of it with the earlier one by inspiring a narrative radically discontinuous with its fairy-tale world. The fairy is oddly indifferent to the content of what he dictates, as he sits in a parlor sheltered from the international warfare described in the poem. Instead, he laughs aloud to see the flowers "whimper because they were pluck'd" (E60; iii:19–21). The parlor itself is a somewhat odd place for the fairy to be. The paradoxical urban fairy is of course a parody of precisely the response sketched here. But on another level the disjunction between the preface and the narrative reminds us of a later poem: Keats's *Lamia*, where the charming story of Hermes and the nymph tells us how it is in eternity, but evaporates into anachronism as we confront the tangled world of Lycius and Lamia.

Moreover, the preface is simply not present in most copies, as if this way of seeing is not feasible most of the time. Placed before the title page and the picture of the Ancient of Days in one copy, it is placed after these plates and before the lament of the shadowy female in the other copy. What this means is unclear, except that we should not too easily settle into one view of the perspectival relationship between the preface and other segments. Perhaps by placing the segment inside the Urizenic frame, the text suggests that it is fantasy to emancipate the fairy from the laws of space and time. Or perhaps it suggests that inside this Urizenic world there is a window that looks outside it. Placing the segment outside the Urizenic frame has no positive meaning either, except as a decision not to place it inside, which itself can be viewed from more than one perspective. Depending on how we see the inner placement of the preface, its placement outside may exempt it from the Urizenic world or may simply make it irrelevant to that world.

The (First) Book of Urizen

Lacking anything like the fairy's preface, *The (First) Book of Urizen* stimulates no visionary somersaults, so that the counterreading of things as they are occurs only negatively, as in the case of *Europe*'s preludium. But if the text thereby exemplifies the tendency of a negative hermeneutics to collapse in on itself, it is also an instance of how negativity can have consequences that exceed the deconstructive. That the negativity of this poem is productive is due in large part to its intertextuality, Urizen himself being an intertextual figure whose refiguration elsewhere encourages us to re-vision this poem's deconstruction of itself. *Urizen* is Blake's most ambitious epic so far: an attempt to trace not simply the origins of European culture but of the (mis)creation itself. A first reading is depressingly bleak, unsettling any claim that the text forwards Blake's system by diagnosing the errors that have created the world of experience. The narrative begins after Urizen's 'separation' and depicts Eternity in a flashback that receives only four lines, as if the cosmos was never sufficient to have stood or free to fall. The Urizenic world—whether it arises as an act of usurpation or as a natural mutation—generates attempts at containing its disorganization which only replicate what they resist. The Eternals react to the chaos of experience by building a tent around the world (E78; 19:2–9). Los is more constructive, following the model of Christ and entering experience to save Urizen. But as he works at his forge binding Urizen, he, too, takes on the latter's functions, in Blake's first recognition that the imagination may be its own specter. Los then divides himself and fathers Orc, whom he nails to a rock in a curious disintegration of the Christian myth, which has 'Los' occupying the functions of both Christ and his destroyers. Because the plot of *Urizen* echoes but displaces the Christian story, the text seems to hollow out the positive model that it seeks to reinstall across its distortion.

Augmenting our sense of a text that deconstructs itself is the collapse of the oppositions that might make it the history of Urizen's 'error.' There is the erosion of the boundary between then and now which allows us to conceive of a world without Urizen. The Eternals claim that death enters the world after the separation of Urizen (E74; 6:9–10). But according to Urizen, death exists in Eternity whose inhabitants already feel "unquenchable burnings" (E71; 4:13). The four-line description of Eternity is too vague and abstract for us to determine whether it is indeed a weightless freedom in which the senses can be expanded at will (E71; 3:37–38) or, as Urizen claims, whether its fluidity is a chaos that requires the imposition of boundaries for its form to emerge. Clearly, what precedes Urizen's separation is inchoate, and it is only with the assertion of what Blake later called the 'selfhood' that the world we know emerges: the world of "beast, bird, fish, serpent & element" (E70; 3:16). Because the creation is coeval with the fall, the fall cannot be a dereliction as it is for Milton, though what is created is a depressingly involuted form of life. If the text blurs the line between Eternity and Experience, thus disintegrating the norms from which Urizen has deviated, it also unsettles the opposition between Urizen and the unfallen Zoas on which Blake's later system is based. As positive models, the Eternals become constructs that the poem discards. As long as they simply are, they seem emancipated from the order of time and space. But as soon as they start to act, their affinity with Urizen emerges. They produce the seven deadly sins that are also attributed to Urizen (E72; 4:49, 5:1–2, and 4:30). They stand "wide apart" from the earth in a posture of dualistic avoidance that mirrors Urizen's separation from the world of process (E73; 5:41). Significantly, their response to Urizen's separation is described in terms of a cloud rent by thunder: "Rent away with a terrible crash / Eternity roll'd wide apart" (E73; 5:4–5). The image suggests that the fall is a violent, arbitrary event. But it also implies that the separation simply potentiates the disorganization of Eternity by disclosing what lies behind the mystifications in which we cloud it. This ambiguity about the chronology of Eternity and Experience is present from the very beginning: "Lo, a shadow of horror is risen / In Eternity!" (E70; 3:1–2). The phrase "is risen" suggests an event, a cataclysmic change. But this change may not be from Eternity to the Urizenic world, for the shadow may be "in" Eternity itself.

Our sense that the Urizenic world could have been avoided is further unsettled by our uncertainty as to the chain of responsibility. From the outset, an indeterminate syntax casts doubt on our assumption that Urizen is the cause of what happens:

> Of the primeval Priests assum'd power,
> When Eternals spurn'd back his religion;
> And gave him a place in the north,
> Obscure, shadowy, void, solitary.
> (E70; 2:1–4)

Does he assume power in the sense of seizing it, or do we merely assume him to have power? The lack of an apostrophe in the word "Priests" (not "Priest's") leaves us uncertain whether the referent is singular or plural, and thus whether Urizen is the primeval priest or whether the Eternals are priests who assume the power to reject his religion, insensitive to the fact that "No man can think write or speak from his heart, but he must intend truth" (E1). We assume that it is Urizen who separates himself from the Eternals, but then he is also described as "rent from Eternity" (E74; 6:8), as if by someone else, and he is characterized as "The obscure separation" (E73; 5:40), as if he is simply an effect of an absent cause. In failing to explain how the fall occurred, the poem limits our ability to think of an origin that might have been different, leaving us simply with the fact of things as they are.

A second reading of *Urizen* would not begin with the text described here, but rather with its place in the secular scripture that Blake, by the time he engraved this poem, was trying to assemble. Such a reading would try to contain the deconstructive energies of *Urizen* and to find in the poem traces of its own later re-visioning. Constantly recalling Miltonic and biblical parallels so as to dispossess them of their positive potential, the text at first seems profoundly resistant to canonical strategies of recuperation. But in contrast to the bleakly naturalistic stories of Wordsworth's early phase, Blake's poem uses parody and grotesqueness to produce what Brecht calls an alienation-effect that prevents us from passively submitting to the plot. Parody allows us not to identify with Urizen, or not to see him as inevitable. We note how the cosmogonic decomposition that occurs as the text moves from Urizen to Los and Enitharmon to Orc is allegorized and thus dispossessed of psychic concreteness. Reason separates from the unified self, provoking imagination to bind it, but in such a way that imagination is divided by pity and produces revolution, which in turn is bound by imagination. This deeply troubling cultural deformation is then skeletalized, abstracted from our own experience, and mockingly represented through a succession of cellular fissions and incestuous births.

Dissociating us (however tenuously) from its world of distortion, parody frustrates the reader into constructing the absent norm against which distortion can be measured. Though it risks self-consumption, its instability can be appropriated by a hermeneutics of reversal that makes the negativity of the text into the ground of coming-to-be. For Blake would have found in Boehme and Paracelsus the ontology that generated Schelling's hermeneutic: an ontology in which opposites are mutually necessary and evil contains the root of good, thus generating the processes that lead to its own reversal.[7] On one level parody remains caught in what Paulson calls an anal or regressive form of revolution,

[7]On Blake's reading of Paracelsus and Boehme see Erdman, *Prophet against Empire*, pp. 12, 37.

while prophecy is more clearly progressive, an internalization of paternal authority.[8] The revolt of parody is grotesque rather than sublime, a self-revulsion. But, on the other hand, the parodying of Milton—and (through Los) of Blake himself—could be said to cleanse and make available certain functions that can be used positively: the creative function misappropriated by Urizen, the redemptive function misused by Los, the function of exodus and liberation sketched in Fuzon. A traditionally hermeneutic reading would thus proceed by negating both the world of Milton's God parodied in Urizen, and the flawed figure of Los who is as far as Blake can get in conceiving a way out of the Urizenic system. Blake himself describes the positive thrust behind his strategy of negation in *The Marriage*, where he speaks of "printing in the infernal method, by corrosives, which in Hell are salutary and medicinal, melting apparent surfaces away, and displaying the infinite which was hid" (E39; 14). In an uncannily similar passage Kierkegaard focuses on the pedagogical reasons for using negativity:

> there is a difference between writing on a blank sheet of paper and bringing to light by the application of a caustic fluid a text which is hidden under another text. Assuming then that a person is a victim of an illusion, . . . if I do not begin by deceiving him, I must begin with direct communication. But direct communication presupposes that the receiver's ability to receive is undisturbed. But here such is not the case; . . . one must first of all use the caustic fluid. But this caustic means is negativity. (*PV*, p. 40)

A hermeneutics of negativity accounts for the most troubling aspect of the poem: the fact that the Eternals provide no viable alternative to Urizen. A reading of the poem as straightforward satire would have to construct a binary opposition between Urizen and the Eternals, in which they represent a truth from which he deviates, and in which his perversity is avoidable. As that opposition collapses, so, too, does the corrective authority of satire. Satire, at least in the form of stable irony, assumes a positive origin, but it is precisely that origin which Blake denies by making the creation and the fall simultaneous. Because positive norms have never existed, the poem can only negate. Allowing it to deconstruct both Urizen and the Eternals, a hermeneutics of negativity lets the text exist in a state of infinite absolute negativity without making its failure to conceptualize positive norms a renunciation of their possibility. This negativity, though potentially dialectical, is not like the positive dialectic generated by the *Songs*, where the innocence of the children is a shadowy type of something valuable. The Eternals have no positive value and are

[8]Ronald Paulson, *Representations of Revolution (1789–1820)* (New Haven, Conn.: Yale University Press, 1983), p. 8.

not models we can emulate: they arise only as a repudiation of Urizen, who also has no absolute value as something we can avoid, being shadowy and unseen. Potentiality can thus appear only as a gap within the negative and not in any positive way. The gap is sometimes innaccessible to language: it appears, for instance, in full-page designs depicting anguished figures who resist the world they have brought about. If the plot increasingly traps the characters in cycles of repetition, the "visions of dark torment" unfolded in the designs unsettle the "words," the consciously taken positions, that dictate each character's entrapment (E70; 2:6–7). Significantly, the preludium speaks both of "words" dictated to 'Blake' and of "visions" unfolded before him, describing the two media used in this text that is more dominated by full-page designs than any other in the oeuvre. The metaphor of dictation suggests a meaning already decided: one that is transmitted to Blake and petrified in the *The Book of Urizen*, in whose codification the Eternals as sources of Blake's inspiration are also accomplices. The concept of "visions" suggests something more immediate: a form of perception in which the signified does not precede its transcription, and in which what is seen is simultaneous with its seeing, as though things are still in process. Although the designs may not be any less pessimistic than the text, they are different in the mode of perception they generate in the reader. The text records what has happened; the designs involve us in what is still happening. Urizen, who lies in a "stony sleep" in the text (E74; 6:7), is falling, weeping, struggling upward in the designs. Associating negativity with energy rather than petrification, the designs allow us to think of it as Boehme thinks of evil: as an intensifying anguish and darkness that ultimately develop a countermomentum strong enough to overcome their destructiveness. The designs stop the text and confront us with something that has not been said and can only be articulated in the cinematography of trauma. The form of their negation differs from that of the text, thus creating a gap within the text's negativity in which hope can produce from its own wreck the thing it contemplates.

As he developed his system, Blake created a context for his Bible of Hell that would enable readers to mobilize the negativity of texts like *Urizen*. But there are features unique to this text that may render such re-visioning problematic. For reading (whether hermeneutic or heuristic) occurs through levels of identification between us and the characters who represent us in the text, and through the speculative narratives that these relations of identity and difference allow us to construct. But it is not clear that the text *contains* 'characters' in the conventional sense. From the beginning it challenges its own personification of Urizen. It tells us that Urizen may simply be the name given to a mutation in the order of things:

> . . . what Demon
> Hath form'd this abominable void
> This soul-shudd'ring vacuum?—Some said
> "It is Urizen."
>
> (E70; 3:3–6)

Because 'Los' and 'Urizen' are not so much personalities as functions, we increasingly notice the plot rather than its automated agents. It is as if the plot is a machine with its own logic: an empty logic in which actants are automatically transferred from function to function so as to abort the purpose of their previous function.

One of the more confusing aspects of the poem is the way it echoes and disorganizes the Christian story. Los recalls Adam whose wife is also wrenched out of his body; but he also plays the role of Christ as well as of Christ's destroyers. Hurled into his own region in the north where he divides and reproduces himself in a series of incestuous births, Urizen recalls Milton's Satan with his progeny, sin and death. But he also recalls God who creates the world in six days and rests on the seventh (E83; 25:39–40). It is not surprising that Urizen should conflate the functions of God and Satan in a poem meant to parody Milton. But then the Eternals also recall Milton's God, who stands wide apart from the fallen Adam, leaving Christ to save him. Dividing the characteristics of one biblical character between several actants in the Urizen story and then allowing one actant from the parodic version to transit several characters in the biblical story, the text seems to generate a narrative that is profoundly unreadable. Character names and plot functions do not stay associated long enough for us to place a character or know whether we should identify with him. This unsettling of the distinctions between characters is repeated at almost every level of the text, from its syntax to the organization of its parts. Thus Blake often uses dangling participles or ambiguously situated adjectives that can be referred to more than one character. An example is "Los wept . . . for in anguish, /Urizen was rent from his side" (E73–74; 6:2–4), where the word "anguish" applies to both Urizen and Los. A larger version of this phenomenon is the transposition of full-page designs to go with different parts of the text. Thus plate 27, a picture of a figure fleeing with his back to us, comes between plates 23 and 24 in copies C and G, but at the very end in copy A. Coming after the section on Urizen exploring his dens (or in the middle of this section in B, D, E, and F), the plate seems to refer to Urizen. Coming at the end, it may also refer to Fuzon, whose exodus then becomes a turning away, a negative gesture that associates him with Urizen.

The reduction of personality to an effect of plot is further augmented by the displacement of characters in the narratological grammar of the poem. Urizen falls into a catatonic state after his speech in chapter II and appears only in genitive or passive constructions, until he briefly reemerges as the grammatical subject in chapter VIII, where he wanders through his dens in a manner that reminds us less of a tyrant than of the helpless voice of "London." Meanwhile Los, who plays the role of grammatical subject for five chapters (III-VII), simply disappears from the last two, as Urizen in the final chapter is once again transferred from the nominative to the genitive case. Characters do not seem to control events but to be produced, reproduced, and discarded by them. As the story opens, it invents Urizen so as to produce its own beginning. Failing thereby to recover an origin, it sets Urizen aside and invents Los as a way of moving toward its end. But 'Los' only allows the story to repeat itself, so he, too, is discarded, in favor of a Urizen who is again set aside because he no longer functions as villain. Finally, the text produces Fuzon, who is little more than a figure for an ending that might proceed beyond the middle. Less a character than a figure for a resolution or at least for change, Fuzon produces Blake's myth as a function of narrative desire.

The process by which the text (de)constructs characters to explain and complete itself renders cosmic history as a series of rifts and permutations profoundly resistant to humanistic reading. For the poem, rather like Byron's *Cain*, interweaves two very different genres. At times it is a cosmogonic narrative, an inquiry into origins that tries to understand the moral structure of the universe by creating a cast of characters who represent different aspects of the cultural mind. Profoundly hermeneutic in its desires, it casts itself in the mode of scripture so as to suggest that exegesis is possible. It inaugurates the romantic concern with myth as anthropology that culminates in Schelling's *Philosophy of Mythology*: a text concerned with myth as part of an ongoing hermeneutics of culture in which we create and interpret myths to understand and recreate ourselves. At other times the poem seems to be describing geological processes that have little to do with scripture. It reminds us of those deteriorationist accounts of the cosmos increasingly popular in romantic natural history, in which the decline of the cosmos has no discernible beginning or end. In contrast to Goethe's studies in biology, which led to the organicist and teleological models of narrative implicit in post-Kantian metaphysics, the model of time and thus of narrative that one might extrapolate from geological research is of a permutational system without a spiritual origin or *telos*, generating superfluous elements that are not integrated into the system. Goethe's model of structure led to a traditional hermeneutic able to grasp the inner form of a text. A model in which narrative is itself an effect of the text, in which writing unsuccessfully generates characters and episodes to explain its surpluses, calls into question the very notion of interpretation.

In other words, it is not just a question of deciding who is responsible for Experience, and whether the poem uses corrective parody to make us reorganize reality or existentially portrays a world from which there is no exit. There is ample evidence that Blake played with these alternatives and found them to be interimplicated. The many copies that omit plate 4, in which Urizen explains his separation, support the first story by removing any inside view of his motivations and thus making his actions arbitrary. The copies that retain the plate create some sympathy for him and leave us wondering whether we would have done otherwise. On the other hand, the omission of plate 4 subverts the very story this omission supports, for it also removes the arrogant declaration of the law that explains the Eternals' rage. Proceeding directly from the disintegration of eternity at the beginning of chapter II to the rage of the Eternals halfway through chapter III, these copies make the Eternals' reaction seem excessive. We wonder who it is that blows the trumpet that ends Eternity. The text only tells us that "The sound of a trumpet the heavens / Awoke" (E71; 3:50–51). Plate 4, which then has Urizen speak, implies that he blows the trumpet as a prelude to the declaration of the ten commandments which rends Eternity apart. But the copies that omit plate 4 make it seem as if the Eternals, having just 'awoken' to the existence of Urizen, whose world precedes the description of Eternity in the order of the text and may thus coexist with it in the order of things, trumpet their rage and thus produce the cataclysms that formally end Eternity. In other words, these copies, by erasing the one segment in which Urizen acts and speaks, efface him as an origin of culpability. As in so many other texts where he changed the order of plates, Blake allows us to create more than one version of the story. But it is not just a question of deciding between these stories or even of combining them. For what they share is a humanistic assumption that events are created by people, and that interpretation tells and retells the story of those people. And it is precisely this anthropomorphism that is challenged by the text's grammatology.

To put it differently, the text borders on what de Man describes as 'unreadability.' This is not to say that the literal activity of reading is blocked, but that the poem seems to defeat any use of it as part of the self-understanding of the reader. The questions about interpretation raised by *Urizen* are thus more radical than anything we have encountered in Blake. For hitherto his emphasis on textuality has produced writings that can be interpreted in more than one way and has recognized how interpretation and culture intergenerate each other. Here, however, it is the very possibility of interpretation, and thus the value of the text as a cultural resource, that is called into question. Reading the whole through the part, we wonder whether this text does not suspend the entire project of Blake's canon. By absorbing mythmaking into a secular scripture, this project makes it part of cultural analysis and therapy. But perhaps there is no Los or Urizen, and perhaps the invention of stories is only a self-complicating deferral of the fact that reality cannot be constructed in anthropomorphic terms. Perhaps, on the other hand, the poem's unreadability is itself a perspective. My discussion of the text's displacements has deliberately ended in a thematics of genre to suggest that even its aporias, unlike those of rhetorical poststructuralism, are about something. They mobilize relationships between this and other texts, reinserting the text's very deconstruction of hermeneutics into cultural dilemmas about the limits of understanding that are still hermeneutic in form.

We can trace this intertextualization of the deconstructive to cultural tensions that may still be relevant today, and that construct deconstruction or its approximations diacritically in a larger field of possibilities. Scientific accounts of the cosmos that made human beings irrelevant were beginning to challenge the androcentric narratives of scripture. But the figures of scripture—figures like anthropomorphism, origin, *telos*—still had a powerful appeal and continued to intersect the very scientific accounts that challenged them. In *Urizen* itself the disfiguration of the characters by the text must be set against the enormous prominence given to the human figure—albeit grotesquely deformed—in the designs. These pictures force us to participate in the anguish of Experience and create a pressure to see beyond it. The radical disfiguration of hermeneutics that results from the language of *Urizen* may be simply one perspective that the poem asks us to consider. It is also clear that *Urizen* itself may be only one perspective in the intertextual dialogue of Blake's canon.

Coda: *Jerusalem* and the Hermeneutics of Becoming

The fact that Blake continued to engrave poems like *Urizen* and *Europe* alongside the final prophecies is evidence of his ongoing struggle with the specter of his earlier texts. Moreover, it allows us to read the final prophecies intertextually instead of according them the canonical privilege of what comes later. But it is also necessary to experiment with reading them autonomously, and as such *Milton* and *Jerusalem* mark Blake's abandonment of the heuristic text in favor of the 'work,' admittedly conceived as ongoing labor, yet tending nevertheless to reify process as a product in itself. *Jerusalem* consolidates the later Blake's commitment to a traditional hermeneutic, and in its discursive passages it provides exegetical principles for normalizing the earlier texts. *Milton* enacts a typological recuperation of the past that provides a paradigm for bringing Blake's Old Testament into the canon. Admittedly, these are not works of the kind Barthes designates as 'readerly.' Despite their assertiveness, they are not repositories of dogmas that we are supposed to consume passively. Instead, what they transmit to us is a semiotics of renovation: an activity that is more important than what Blake produces thereby. But the activity that the later prophecies model is radically different from the perceptual transactions stimulated by the early poems. It is, after all, the creation and not the interrogation of a system.

That *Jerusalem* functions primarily on a hermeneutic level rather than in terms of mimesis or reference, and that it can be read reflexively only if it is treated oppositionally, is what makes it a 'work' in the sense suggested above. Blake indicates the hermeneutic nature of his text in the preface and in the opening plates of chapter I, where he apologizes to the public for the "Enthusiasm of the following Poem" and hopes the "Reader will be with me, wholly One in Jesus our Lord . . . The Spirit of Jesus is continual forgiveness of Sin: he who waits to be righteous before he enters into the Saviours kingdom, the Divine Body; will never enter there" (E145; 3). Excusing the written text as imperfect, Blake asks us to treat it with charity and to recognize its status (in Coleridge's terms) as inspired if not revealed. The uncharitable division of the audience into "sheep" and "goats" that heads the plate is self-mocking only to the extent of conceding that there are imperfect readers as well as authors, and that they, too, deserve to be treated with patience. In the first few plates Blake pictures himself sitting at his desk, writing of the building of Golgonooza, which is not yet Jerusalem but its textual simulacrum, and struggling with the specter of his empiricism, which demands that vision be proved "by demonstration" and "not by faith" (E147; I:4:28). Gradually 'Blake' is replaced by 'Los,' whose struggle with his specter is clearly repressive, but whose tyranny is put to us as necessary for imaginative freedom. It is the specter who works at the forge creating the poem, because it is the dark energies of "doubt & despair" (E153; I:10:33) that must generate vision as a psychological supplement. That Blake represents despair as vital is suggested by the poem's opening image: "There is a Void, outside of Existence, which if entered into / Englobes itself & becomes a Womb" (E144; I:1–2). Unless we enter into the void, nothing will be created. Once entered, the void becomes a contracted embryo with the potential to be a cosmos. Whether anything will be born from it is not clear from this image, which takes us only as far as the anguish of englobing and consolidating vision in the pain of conception.

By situating prophecy in the scene of its own writing, Blake introduces into the poem an awareness of textuality that is counteracted by the invitation to the reader to make the "types" that Blake prints out into truths through applicative reading. Vincent De Luca has persuasively described *Jerusalem* in terms of a textual sublime in which the reader is initially blocked by the visual appearance of the poem as a "wall of words," but then experiences a "countermovement of exaltation" in which he grasps the transcendental (in a Kantian rather than a Platonic sense). Relocating terms like 'gap' and 'abyss' in the vocabulary of the sublime, de Luca absorbs them into a hermeneutics of the sublime as opposed to a deconstruction of sublimation. Signs are passages to mental 'realities' that exist neither in the text nor in a realm of forms that it copies, but in the response elicited by the text.[9] That the poem uses textuality in this way is undoubtedly true. But in addition, *Jerusalem* is part of a specifically romantic genre defined by Friedrich Schlegel when he speaks of a metawork that contains not only the text but also the story of its genesis and a self-commentary. Thus the poem begins with an account of why Blake must write it, which is then repeated more elaborately as an account of why Los must tame his specter; and at various points it produces metadiscursive summaries of what Blake thinks he is saying through his paraphernalia of characters and events. The text described by Schlegel is reflexive in ways that seem to verge on postmodernism but that actually have more to do with a hermeneutics of becoming. Situating itself in the author's life, it conveys the incompleteness of something that has not achieved the impersonality of classical art, and it suggests the urgency of its existential project. By interpreting itself, it conveys not self-mastery but a need for the supplement of reading. These attempts to understand itself are again symptoms of a lack of objectification, gestures toward a reader who will understand the text better than the author, given that the author already understands it better in the act of reflection than in the moment of conception. Schlegel, we must add, did not see the imperfection and involution of the romantic text as a flaw. Rather, he saw such texts as contextualizing themselves in an ongoing process, and asking that that process be continued in the reader.

Crucial to the deferral of meaning to the reader is the use of allegory. Allegory dissociates us from the characters and causes us to see them as 'representations.' That Blake uses an allegorical cast of characters is obviously puzzling, given his condemnation of the mode. One could note with Robert Gleckner that he distinguishes between "sublime alle-

[9]V. A. De Luca, "A Wall of Words: The Sublime as Text," in Hilton and Vogler, eds., *Unnam'd Forms*, pp. 218–41.

gory" and allegory addrresed to the corporeal powers.[10] Kant's theory of the sublime involves an initial dissociation of mind from matter, followed by an experience of (self)-identification in which the mind becomes lord and master. Transvaluing the physical into the metaphysical, sublime allegory would thus avoid the disembodied reification of vision in its physical covering, while using the dissociation of tenor and vehicle characteristic of allegory to make us see beyond the merely literal. In contrast to this metaphysical and visionary view of allegory, Steven Knapp associates sublimity and allegory in order to halt them at the dissociative stage. Foregrounding as it does the personification of figures as realities, allegory is a self-consciously rhetorical mode that risks reversibility: "Once the boundaries between literal and figurative agency were erased, it seemed that nothing would prevent imagination from metaphorizing literal agents as easily as it literalized metaphors." Moreover, allegory was connected in eighteenth-century usage with the sublime, which involved a simultaneous "dissociation from images of ideal power." To experience the sublime "was not quite, as some historians have argued, to identify oneself with a transcendent ideal of pure subjective power, but rather to entertain that ideal as an abstract, fantastic, unattainable possibility."[11] Knapp does not offer this as a description of Blake, who, along with Shelley, is a creator of myth rather than allegory. But even though Blake's allegory is mythopoeic, it seems that he uses the mode as a way of blocking identification with his characters and letting us perceive the 'states' they 'represent' on a screen of possibilities rather than in a world of identities. Los is, as it were, a mask for the reader to assume: an identity that Blake has appropriated but in which he has not yet come to feel at home, and whose otherness is marked by his allegorical status. Our earlier discussion of Coleridge is of relevance here, for *Jerusalem*, too, is a conversion narrative, and conversion offers us models for which we are not quite ready—hence the violence with which we must make ourselves imitate them.

The liminal structure of sublime allegory stops the poem from actually bringing Jerusalem into being, halting it in Golgonooza. As a gigantic construct whose body we cannot inhabit, as a voice without a face, a character like Los represents a series of functions and not an embodiment of Blake's redemptive vision. Through its disembodying use of allegory, then, the text performs a certain kind of activity that is not constatively related to any transcendental or visionary meaning that pre-

[10]*Blake and Spenser* (Baltimore: The Johns Hopkins University Press, 1985), p. 20.

[11]*Personification and the Sublime: Milton to Coleridge* (Cambridge, Mass.: Harvard University Press, 1985), pp. 2–3.

cedes it nor predictively related to anything else that will happen in the 'real' world. *Jerusalem* is not, however, a ghost sonata, for it is hermeneutically grounded in 'Blake,' who models for us the existential necessity of wearing the mask of Los. As part of the process of miming the work of renovation, the text also produces metastatements such as the distinction of contraries from negations (E152–53; 10:7–12. E162; 17:33–36). These credal passages should be seen as generated from within the text rather than as governing its interpretation. In other words, they are not dogmas that cause the poem to come into being in an illustrative capacity, but effects of the poem's need to organize itself as it is written. Not always consistent with each other in what they say, they are consistent at the level of their semiotic function. They tell us that textuality and narrativity must be organized, and that this task is accomplished through the invention of certitudes, bounding outlines, teleologies. The task is ongoing but also progressive, for *Jerusalem* consolidates the labor of *Milton*, whereas *Urizen* may well undo that of *The Marriage*. In this respect the later prophecies suggest a cultural praxis quite different from that of the earlier poems. If accorded a teleological privilege, the final poems represent themselves as advancing if not completing the stubborn structure. The early ones are constructed according to principles that require us to recompose and decompose that structure.

PART II

C. *Deconstruction at the Scene of Its Reading*

CHAPTER TEN

"World within World": The Theoretical Voices of Shelley's *Defence of Poetry*

The relationship between reading and deconstruction has been a recurrent concern of this study. Although the unfixing of meaning is sometimes seen as making texts 'unreadable,' our argument has been that it also confers on them a revisability that *confirms* the importance of reading. The symbiotic if sometimes troubled relationship between reading and deconstruction is a crucial issue in the texts by Shelley that we shall consider, culminating in *The Triumph of Life*, a poem now synonymous with the deconstruction of romanticism. If *Alastor* remains committed to a negative hermeneutic that testifies only to Shelley's uneasiness with its semiotic nihilism, his later texts provide no unproblematic formula for a more constructive relationship between reading and deconstruction. Producing the supplement of reading as a gap between hermeneutics and its dismantling, they force us to scrutinize not only the specific myths that reading enables us to construct, but also at times the very place of language in culture.

Labyrinths, weavings, and related figures abound in Shelley's work, leading us at first to see his theory of language as proto-Derridean. In an essay on imagery, for instance, Shelley describes the mind as a "wilderness of intricate paths . . . a world within a world."[1] A related image is used in *The Revolt of Islam*, where Cythna describes how she traces signs on the sand, to range

[1]"Excursus on the Imagery of Shakespeare and the Greek Tragedians," *Note Books of Percy Bysshe Shelley*, ed. H. B. Forman, 3 vols. (Boston: Bibliophile Society, 1911), II, 102.

> These woofs, as they were woven of my thought:
> Clear elemental shapes, whose smallest change
> A subtler language within language wrought.
> (VII.xxxii)[2]

Ideally, the figure of a structure within a structure, as in the case of the epipsyche that is a "soul within our soul" (*SPP*, p. 474), is associated with an epoché, a grasping of essence. But in this passage the way in which articulation generates a secondary discourse is seen as a process of displacement, by which clear elemental shapes are subtly shifted and complicated. Nor does Shelley allow us a protective dichotomy between conception and expression, for similar figures are used to describe thought, vision, and emotion.[3] Nevertheless, Shelleyan dissemination remains uniquely romantic, for as Geoffrey Hartman comments, Shelley's thinking is both "antireligious" and "radically spiritual."[4] What we find in his work is therefore a phenomenology of disarticulation, a deconstruction of transcendental signifieds that paradoxically remains a defense of poetry. The source of this paradox is precisely that Shelley's deconstruction is not formalist, for he is concerned above all with the power of difference, and with power as something that produces effects. Although Shelley's concern with reception is less explicit than that of Kierkegaard or Schleiermacher, the *Defence* is nevertheless central to this study because it gives us the other side of the equation: the theory of poetry as a self-displacing energy, from which arises both the need for and the reconception of the supplement of reading.

In approaching the *Defence* I focus on two problems: that of writing, or the mediation of conception through expression, and that of reading, whether it means referring the text to a source and recovering the original conception from what survives of it in the text, or whether it means deconstructing and refiguring the text. The question of reading arises as something distinct from writing because it involves for Shelley the application of the text to life and the problem of its authority, rather than the study of its internal relations or of its relation to a transcendental signified. A theory of reading involves the ethics and pragmatics of the text, where a theory of writing is concerned with its metaphysics and ontology. As a sceptic, Shelley was persuaded that metaphysics was a

[2] Percy Bysshe Shelley, *Poetical Works*, ed. Thomas Hutchinson (1905; rpt. Oxford: Clarendon, 1967).

[3] For instance *Alastor*, ll. 48, 154–57, 719–20; *Prometheus Unbound*, I. 805–6, II.i.114–17, IV. 129, 106, 415–17; *The Triumph of Life*, ll. 340–41.

[4] *Criticism in the Wilderness: The Study of Literature Today* (New Haven, Conn.: Yale University Press, 1980), p. 106.

source only of "negative truths" and must be supplemented by ethics.[5] Thus we ignore a crucial part of the dialectic of deconstruction in his texts if we do not consider them in their affective as well as representative dimension. But the problems of writing and reading are also articulated across certain fissures in Shelley's thought. For there are in the *Defence* two radically different theories of writing and reading that reflect two very different views of the stability of the sign. When Shelley sees writing as the inadequate translation of an anterior conception, reading becomes a supplementary act that bypasses language to recover the intention of the work. But Shelley is also unable to posit a 'work' prior to its expression in language. Eventually, if he is to continue seeing reading as that which redirects the negativity of the text, it must be a very different kind of reading: one that makes the text a resource rather than a source.

It is only very occasionally that Shelley views the relationship between signifier and signified as unproblematic. More often, he sees language as interposing between conception and its communication but rationalizes the disseminative effects of representation in terms of a vocabulary of source and emanation. The precise philosophic affiliations of this vocabulary are difficult to pin down. At times it seems neo-platonic, as in the description of poetry as an "echo of the eternal music" (*SPP*, p. 485). Sometimes the neo-Platonism is internalized, as Wasserman points out,[6] and the source is seen as "curtained within the invisible nature of man" (*SPP*, p. 483). But whether conception and expression are opposed as higher and lower or as inner and outer, the point is that Shelley seems to posit an origin outside language, either in some transcendent power or in the consciousness of the author. The famous passage on the text as a fading coal will suffice as an example. Not only does it idealize the differential process of language as alienation from a source, it also explains the autonomous power of language to displace thought in terms of a prophetic spirit that comes and goes, and that thus allows us to marginalize certain parts of the text as mere intervals in the presence of spirit to itself:

> the mind in creation is as a fading coal which some invisible influence, like an inconstant wind, awakens to transitory brightness: this power arises from within, like the colour of a flower which fades and changes as it is developed, and the conscious portions of our natures are unprophetic either of its

[5]Shelley, "A Treatise on Morals," *Shelley's Prose or the Trumpet of a Prophecy*, ed. David Lee Clark (Albuquerque: University of New Mexico Press, corrected ed. 1966), p. 182.

[6]Earl Wasserman, *Shelley: A Critical Reading* (Baltimore: The Johns Hopkins University Press, 1971), pp. 206–7.

> approach or its departure. . . . when composition begins, inspiration is already on the decline. (*SPP*, p. 503–4)

From the sense that expression illegitimately disrupts conception arises a theory of reading as a supplement to the fissured text, a theory paralleled in the German hermeneutic tradition. For at several points in the *Defence* Shelley defers the identity of the work with itself from the written text, which is allowed to be fragmentary and inchoate, to a pre- or translinguistic work that the reader intuits "beyond and above consciousness" (*SPP*, p. 486). Defining 'poetry' as a spirit rather than a specific literary form, he claims that it may be concentrated in separable parts of a composition that allow the reader to reconstruct a conception disarticulated by the text as it exists: "A single sentence may be considered as a whole though it may be found in a series of unassimilated portions; a single word even may be a spark of inextinguishable thought" (*SPP*, pp. 485–86). Such reconstruction, he suggests, occurs because of the ability of single motifs to trigger archetypal patterns shared by author and reader alike: "a word, a trait in the representation of a scene or a passion, will touch the enchanted chord, and reanimate, in those who have ever experienced these emotions, the sleeping, the cold, the buried image of the past" (*SPP*, p. 505). Whether the conception envisioned here is one that precedes the text or one that is produced through a teleological completion of it is not clear. Images of fading, echoing, and reflecting, which imply a substance above or prior to the shadow of expression, alternate with images of growth and process such as the description of thoughts as "germs of the flower and the fruit of latest time" or of words as a "lightning which has yet found no conductor" (*SPP*, pp. 483, 500). Implicit in the former is a hermeneutics of recovery linked to a deferred formalism in which there is indeed an aesthetic whole that precedes writing. Milton, Shelley claims, "conceived the Paradise Lost as a whole before he executed it in portions" (*SPP*, p. 504). But implicit in the second kind of image is a divinatory hermeneutics perilously allied with an aesthetics of process that threatens to deconstruct it. As in Hegel's analysis of art forms that disjoin the idea and its embodiment, the reader divines what is only potentially in the text by relating it to an unfolding whole and seeing it as an episode "to that great poem, which all poets, like the co-operating thoughts of one great mind, have built up since the beginning of the world" (*SPP*, p. 493; cf. also p. 494).

The *Defence* does not at first sight seem to deal with hermeneutics. But we cannot grasp the crucial role that the supplement of reading plays in it, unless we remember how much Shelley is concerned with discrepancies between the Idea of poetry and the historical forms it assumes. Narrative, for instance, being rooted in the circumstantial, is a disfiguration of poetry. Unless 'invested' by poetry, it is a mirror "which obscures and distorts that which should be beautiful," where poetry "is a mirror which makes beautiful that which is distorted" (*SPP*, p. 485). Drama, likewise, is acceptable only "so long as it continues to express poetry," and to dissolve and dissipate only in order to recreate, like a "prismatic and many-sided mirror, which collects the brightest rays of human nature and divides and reproduces them" (*SPP*, p. 491). But virtually all the major canonical texts, not to mention the bulk of Shelley's own writings, *are* either narrative or dramatic. Thus they can become 'poetry' only with the aid of a reader who will save the text from the disfigurations of history or representation. And it is precisely such a reader that Shelley himself becomes in his interpretations of Homer, Dante, and Milton, which provide a theoretical model for the readings often inscribed in what we have called hermeneutic texts. In dealing with Homer, he is confronted with the awkward fact that Homer's heroes do not always display the moral perfection necessary to 'poetry.' As prophetic reader, Shelley must bracket the historically limited text and discern behind the "temporary dress" of historical prejudice in which the writer's "creations must be arrayed" the "internal nature" of the work which "cannot be . . . concealed by its accidental vesture" (*SPP*, p. 487). The case of Dante provides a more elaborate example of the principle of understanding an author better than he understands himself. If Dante's demotion of the Greeks and Romans to purgatory and hell seems sectarian, the 'true' Dante, according to Shelley, comes out in his unusual placement of the non-Christian Riphaeus in paradise. This episode allows Dante to observe "a most heretical caprice in his distribution of rewards and punishments" and to further the goals of a world-historical spirit, without himself being fully "conscious of the distinction which must have subsisted" in his mind between his "own creeds and that of the people" (*SPP*, p. 498). In other words, Shelley's reading of *The Divine Comedy* proceeds on the principle that the work is to be found in unassimilated portions of the text, in revolutionary sparks that a later reader develops, often in opposition to what the major portion of the text seems to say. The reading is essentially similar to one we sketched for Coleridge's *Christabel*, where the conclusion to part II tries to provide such a spark and to invite readers to generate from it the current that will allow them to counterread the text into what it should be.

This traditional hermeneutic is legitimized by the assumption of a conception that exists apart from its representation. But Shelley is profoundly uneasy with this idea, and more positively there is a side of him that sees dissemination as a source of imaginative power. That there is in the *Defence* the embryo of a deconstructive theory of poetry becomes clear toward the end, where Shelley uses two rather unexpected images for poetry. The first passage begins in a characteristically hyperbolic way and defines poetry in terms of a Coleridgean unity of opposites:

> Poetry turns all things to loveliness; . . . it subdues to union under its light yoke all irreconcilable things. It transmutes all that it touches, and every form moving within the radiance of its presence is changed by wondrous sympathy to an incarnation of the spirit which it breathes; its secret alchemy turns to potable gold the poisonous waters which flow from death through life. (*SPP*, p. 505)

On the most obvious level the poisonous waters suggest a Dionysiac source for poetry at odds with the transcendent source implied in earlier images of it as an "echo of the eternal music" (*SPP*, p. 485). Moreover, the curious figure of the poet as alchemist betrays a fear that there may be something illegitimate in the attempt to transmute base matter into gold. At the very least, poetry seems to be a ghostly rather than spiritual force, inhabiting material radically at odds with its intentions. One inevitably asks whether poetry is not just as likely to be inhabited by what it seeks to invest. But the passage is also worth considering on the level of the signifier. For it is an example of how the very copiousness of Shelley's figurative rhetoric unravels the statement to be illustrated through it. Illustration and repetition make expression a differential process, by creating crevices between the parts of an analogy or between the different discursive planes (conceptual and figurative, abstract and concrete) that supplement and repeat each other. What happens in this passage is, on a larger scale, what happens in the logic of the essay as a whole. Shelley repeats the idea of a source prior to language and makes it alternately external and internal to the self. Similarly, he repeats the idea of a work that is more complete than the text and suggests that it has once existed and also that it does not yet exist. He thus unsettles the authority of any single conceptual representation of the 'work' within this field of substitutions.

Even more disruptive is an earlier comparison of poetry to a flower, which exposes a dangerous subtext in the organic analogy:

> Poetry is indeed something divine. . . . It is at the same time the root and blossom of all other systems of thought; . . . It is the perfect and consummate surface and bloom of things; it is as the odour and the colour of the rose to the texture of the elements which compose it, as the form and the splendour of unfaded beauty to the secrets of anatomy and corruption. (*SPP*, p. 503)

'Texture' is, curiously enough, the term that John Crowe Ransom will use to describe a poetry that is part of the world's body, and that thereby becomes more dense and real.[7] For Shelley, however, the implications of the body are less innocent. They extend not only to the nature of poetry, as something involved in the darker side of life, but also to its structure and functioning. As Shelley follows the image, it disarticulates what he is saying; it enacts as well as provides an image of the process of language as difference. The flower is not only a surface, but also an interior, a texture. Moreover, it is not just that the surface conception of the poem is at odds with the narrative articulations that compose it. These hidden articulations and fragmentations, as the word 'texture' suggests, are themselves complexly interwoven and do not compose a monolithic 'inside' or 'reality' that can be opposed to the surface of appearance. Nor can Shelley return thereafter to a 'poetry' that he himself describes as a surface. For poetry is both the root and the blossom, which means that the color of the rose cannot be abstracted from the texture of the elements that compose it.

More significant as a site of theoretical tensions is Shelley's intermittent discussion of language at the beginning of the *Defence*. In praising poetry, he often sounds Platonic, as when he claims that to "be a poet is to apprehend the true and the beautiful, in a word the good" (*SPP*, p. 482). But in dealing with the more philosophically precise subject of language, he is too much of a sceptic to argue for either an immediate or a displaced relationship between words and things. Instead, he takes the Enlightenment view that language "is arbitrarily produced by the Imagination and has relation to thoughts alone," not to things (*SPP*, p. 483). This is not necessarily a problematic formulation, because the relation between thoughts and words, while arbitrary, is also immediate. But then Shelley proceeds to a more complex description of the system of language: "Sounds as well as thoughts have relation both between each other and towards that which they represent, and a perception of the order of those relations has always been found connected with a perception of the order of the relations of thoughts" (*SPP*, p. 484). It is here that his theory of language unravels itself backward to certain seminal and unelaborated suggestions at the beginning of the essay. At first it seems Shelley has introduced a protostructuralist theory of signification by describing a free-standing system in which words (or acoustic images, in Saussure's language) bear a stable relation to thoughts. Acoustic images or "sounds" (to use Shelley's word) "have relation both between each other and towards that which they represent," and it is the former, the syntagmatic and paradigmatic relations among signifiers, that guar-

[7]Ransom, "Criticism as Pure Speculation," in Thomas David Young and John Hindle, eds., *Selected Essays of John Crowe Ransom* (Baton Rouge: Louisiana State University Press, 1984), p. 138.

antee the coherence of the signified and its uptake by the reader. But in at least two respects this formulation is more self-complicating than it seems. For one thing, there is the curious displacement of 'thought' from ground to figure and its consequent implication within a chain of signifiers. At first, words are said to signify 'thoughts,' and thoughts function as referents outside language, though not outside the mind. But in the second passage, "sounds as well as thoughts" have relations to that which they represent, so that ideas are now themselves signifiers representing something else, and thought is itself structured like a language. Even more problematic is the notion of interrelations between the elements of a signifying system. The idea that language is diacritical, that individual words do not contain a meaning but acquire it in relation to other words, *can* be seen as explaining how words clarify each other. But Shelley himself does not so see it. In the first passage quoted, he distinguishes language from other inferior systems of representation by arguing that its relation to meaning is direct rather than diacritical, and thus conceding that the interrelations of elements within a system potentially complicate meaning:

> For language is arbitrarily produced by the Imagination, and has relation to thoughts alone; but all other materials, instruments and conditions of art, have relations among each other, which limit and interpose between conception and expression. The former is as a mirror which reflects, the latter as a cloud which enfeebles, the light of which both are mediums of communication. (*SPP*, p. 483)

Linguistic representation is here described as immediate, and the mediation characteristic of other systems of representation is defined in terms of their tendency to generate local complexities that interfere with the perceiver's ability to link sign and referent. Thus we are surprised to find later on that language actually shares in the complexities of mediation, being a system in which sounds and thoughts have relations among each other. And we are even more surprised to read elsewhere that language is *essentially* mediation: it is *not* conceived in terms of a split between process and product that would keep conception apart from expression, the light apart from the cloud. Language, gesture, and the imitative arts "become at once the representation and the medium, the pencil and the picture, the chisel and the statue" (*SPP*, p. 481). In other words, literature does not say anything abstractable from the process of saying it. But this process, as we have already seen, is a diacritical one in which each signifying element contains the trace of other elements in the system.

How diacritical relationships interfere with the process of reference is best illustrated by Shelley's essay itself. For it is the relations between passages that interfere with what seems to be the conception behind each passage taken individually. In the case of the first passage these interconnections disrupt a binary opposition that privileges language over less satisfactory art forms. In the case of the second passage they undermine its assumption that diacritical systems are stable and self-confirming. And in the third case they expose the problematical subtext of what seems a doctrine of organic unity that fuses medium and message.

Perhaps the best word for the complicating interconnection between elements is Shelley's own term "intertexture" (*SPP*, p. 504), which he introduces disparagingly to suggest that we can go directly to an intuition of the whole without working through the parts of a text. Milton, he tells us, "conceived the Paradise Lost as a whole before he executed it in portions" (*SPP*, p. 504), abstracting the clear elemental shape of the poem from the texture of the elements that composed it. Shelley is thus able to dismiss the "intertexture of conventional expressions" that binds the parts together. But it needs no emphasis that in his own case it is this intertexture that produces some of the essay's most crucial recognitions, because it is the process of intertextualizing the parts of the argument, of seeing how they are interwoven into each other, that prevents us from excerpting one statement and making it stand for the originating conception behind the work. Put differently, what Shelley here dismisses as the intertexture, a mere conjunctive convenience, is what he elsewhere calls the "interstice," the gap between two signifying elements which brings into play their differential interpresence and ultimately their self-difference. And such gaps, he suggests, are productive. Historians like Herodotus and Livy are great because they are poets, and they are poets specifically because they use language to disrupt itself, "filling all the interstices of their subjects with living images" (*SPP*, p. 486), and creating detours in the straight and narrow path that leads instrumental discourse from word to referent.

At other points, too, it seems that one voice in Shelley sees poetry as a heightening of the inherent nature of language as difference. These passages occur toward the beginning of the *Defence*, and often one is uncertain of the intention behind them, as they seem to be the site of a theoretical crossing that is deferred—perhaps deliberately. Curiously, one of them is the opening distinction between reason and imagination, which seems at first to be a predictable romantic distinction between the analytic faculty that "murders to dissect," and the holistic, esemplastic power of imagination which binds disparate elements into a unity. Indeed, Shelley does specifically associate imagination with the capacity to perceive similitudes, following the familiar identification of imagination with love, or in Wordsworth's words, with the capacity to observe "affinities / In objects where no brotherhood exists / To passive minds" (*P* II.384–86). But what is interesting is the precise way in which Shelley describes the creative power of imagination: as "mind acting upon those thoughts so as to colour them with its own light, and composing from them, as from elements, other thoughts, each containing within itself the principle of its own integrity" (*SPP*, p. 480). Though he begins with the familiar image of the mind as lamp rather than mirror, projecting its light onto phenomena so as to synthesize them, he seems to grant the process of thought a certain autonomy from the intentional act that initiates it. He describes not only how the mind acts on a received quantum of thoughts, so as to create new relations between them, but also the process by which thoughts re-act upon the mind itself, so that the light of the mind is no longer a conception prior to expression but the process of expression itself. For what is striking here is that acts of mind are only momentarily synthetic. Inasmuch as they compose from thoughts other thoughts, they are ultimately disseminative, because the new thoughts each contain within themselves the principle of their own integrity and thus cannot be subordinated to each other or to the originating thought. This account of how we think renders very exactly the exploratory and partly deconstructive character of Shelley's own imagistic practice, which William Empson describes in terms of discovering an idea in the act of writing, and which F. R. Leavis criticizes as a "general tendency of the images to forget the status of the metaphor or simile that introduced them and to assume an autonomy and a right to propagate."[8]

Perhaps a good example of how the Shelleyan image functions as a conflictual but productive force, in which an idea is embodied in a figure whose subtext generates a different and autonomous idea, is a disturbing passage in the "Hymn to Intellectual Beauty": "Thou—that to human thought art nourishment, / Like darkness to a dying flame!" (ll. 44–45, *SPP*). Hitherto the ideal, originally referred to only as a power (l. 1, *SPP*), and sometimes operating with capricious inconstancy, has been described in Apollonian analogies such as music, clouds, and moonbeams. The figure of darkness *can* seem to continue the idea of beauty as fostering human development, in the sense that darkness sets off the brightness of the flame. Yet one has to struggle to extract this secondary connotation from the image, given the overwhelming implication that darkness smothers the dying flame. The different associations of the image cause it to function as a switch-point in the poem, composing from

[8]Empson, *Seven Types of Ambiguity* (London: Chatto and Windus, 1930), pp. 155, 160–61; Leavis, *Revaluation: Tradition and Development in English Poetry* (London: Chatto and Windus, 1936), p. 206.

one thought another thought that cannot be synthesised with the first because it contains the principle of its own integrity.

That the imaginative process as described by Shelley is radically different from that conceived by Coleridge is apparent from the fact that Shelley links it in a draft to the power of association.[9] Associationism sees thought as a disseminative process, tracing an idea back to its origin in a train of associations that makes it different from itself, or recognizing it as part of a constellation of ideas that are called into play along with it and disrupt its referential stability. It is no coincidence that what are now described as 'paradigmatic' relations, which expand the particular word into "an indefinite number of co-ordinated terms," were originally described by Saussure as "associative" relations.[10] Far from being rejected or transcended in the idea of an esemplastic imagination,[11] associationism reweaves a certain strand in romantic thinking so as to draw it away from the idea of formal unity. Coleridge himself, as Jerome Christensen points out, is far from unequivocal in dismissing it.[12] He seems at one point to do no more than replace the association of ideas with the association of feelings, conceding the validity of the psychological model but making association a phenomenological rather than a mechanical process.[13] But it is Dilthey who more explicitly clarifies the romantic reconception of associationism, linking his reservations to the fact that it has hitherto been conceived in atomistic and mechanical rather than creative terms. For association as conceived in the eighteenth century mechanically reproduces "given elements in a given combination," unlike imag-

[9]Shelley, *A Defence of Poetry*, in John E. Jordan, ed., *A Defence of Poetry and The Four Ages of Poetry* (Indianapolis: Bobbs-Merrill, 1965), p. 25n.

[10]Ferdinand de Saussure, *Course in General Linguistics*, ed. Charles Bally and Albert Sechehaye, trans. Wade Baskin (New York: McGraw-Hill, 1966), pp. 125–27. Saussure's distinction of associative from syntagmatic relations suggests that they tend to be disseminative and logocentric, respectively: "Whereas a syntagm immediately suggests an order of succession and a fixed number of elements, terms in an associative family occur neither in fixed numbers nor in a definite order. . . . A particular word is like the center of a constellation; it is the point of convergence of an indefinite number of co-ordinated terms" (p. 126).

[11]The conventional view is that Coleridge's theory of imagination stands in opposition to an associationist theory of fancy. James Engell, by contrast, argues that Coleridge's theory is the culmination of the associationist tradition: a reduction of associative multeity to imaginative unity is already implicit in the aesthetics of that tradition: *The Creative Imagination: Enlightenment to Romanticism* (Cambridge, Mass.: Harvard University Press, 1981).

[12]*Coleridge's Blessed Machine of Language* (Ithaca, N.Y.: Cornell University Press, 1981), pp. 76–83.

[13]In an 1803 letter to Southey, Coleridge writes, "I hold, that association depends in a much greater degree on the recurrence of resembling states of Feeling, than on Trains of Ideas. . . . I almost think, that Ideas never recall Ideas, as far as they are Ideas—any more than Leaves in a forest create each other's motion—the Breeze it is that runs thro' them, / it is the Soul, the state of Feeling—": E. L. Griggs, ed., *Collected Letters of Samuel Taylor Coleridge*, 6 vols. (Oxford: Clarendon Press, 1956–71), II, 961.

ination "which produces new combinations from the given elements." As such, it is merely repetitive, where the imagination is fundamentally metamorphic.[14] The fault of eighteenth-century associationism, Dilthey suggests, is that it "starts with representations as fixed quantities. Changes in representations are allowed to occur externally through association, fusion, and apperception." Paradoxically, the romantic imagination is no less associative, but in a more organic way. Association does not simply involve linking elements together but causing them to act and react on each other: "In the real psyche, therefore, every representation is a *process*. Even the sensations which are connected in an emotion, and the relations existing among them, are subject to *inner transformations*."[15]

Drawing on Goethe, Dilthey thus describes a metamorphic imagination in which images transform themselves and "unfold unhampered."[16] Shelley, however, goes much farther in abandoning both imaginative closure and the affiliation of metamorphosis with organic plenitude: "Poetry enlarges the circumference of the imagination by replenishing it with thoughts of ever new delight, which have the power of attracting and assimilating to their own nature all other thoughts, and which form new intervals and interstices whose void for ever craves fresh food" (*SPP*, p. 488). Here the generative power of imagination is traced to its negativity. Imagination keeps itself in being as desire by constantly disarticulating its attempts at closure. In associating and compounding thoughts, it becomes aware of the gaps between them, which it fills by introducing new thoughts, which in turn create further gaps. Perhaps in the light of the above we should reconsider what Shelley means in describing reason as analytic and imagination as synthetic. Analysis fixes the relations between elements so as to use them instrumentally, considering "thoughts, not in their integral unity, but as the algebraical representations which conduct to certain general results" (*SPP* p. 480). Synthesis, which does not have the holistic connotations we might assume, is the dissemination of systematic relations. A "synthetical view of the universe" as described in the "Treatise on Morals" involves being aware that perceptions can be "indefinitely combined," and takes us beyond those "ordinary systems" that use definite combinations and therefore limit the range of our perceptions.[17] Crucial to Shelley's view of imagination as the power of difference and displacement is his description of language as essentially figurative. The language of poets, Shelley argues, "is vitally metaphorical; that is, it marks the before unap-

[14]Wilhelm Dilthey, *Poetry and Experience*, ed. Rudolf A. Makkreel and Frithjof Rodi (Princeton, N.J.: Princeton University Press, 1985), pp. 239–40.

[15]Ibid., p. 68. Cf. also pp. 70, 105.

[16]Ibid., p. 107.

[17]Shelley, "A Treatise on Morals," *Prose*, p. 183.

prehended relations of things" (*SPP*, p. 482). It would be a mistake to treat this passage as another romantic platitude about the organic versus the fixed, the imaginative versus the rational. For like Nietzsche after him, Shelley preserves the form of the binary opposition by which earlier romantics like Coleridge valorize imagination but redefines its content. The view that language either declined or developed from the figurative and concrete to the abstract and conceptual is common enough. What is unusual is the way Nietzsche defines metaphor or the concrete, as the perception of difference rather than affinity. Philosophic language, according to him, identifies and defines, so as to create self-identical concepts. It misleads us into abstracting things from their intertexture, "into grasping things as simpler than they are, separate from one another, indivisible, each existing in and for itself."[18] On the contrary, in Derrida's words there is no simple element that avoids being "constituted on the trace within it of other elements of the chain or system."[19] Thus the function of poetry is to resensitize us to the knowledge that concepts represent not one but several things and are therefore different from themselves. More specifically, because ideas originate through the fundamentally figurative procedure of "equating the unequal," the function of metaphor is to renew, by displacing the ideas it conveys, our awareness of the substitution and displacement at the heart of all representation. Where the formation of ideas, according to Nietzsche, involves a will-to-power that represses difference, the awareness of metaphor "constantly confuses the rubrics and cells of the ideas, by putting up new figures of speech, metaphors, metonymies."[20] Similarly, for Shelley the function of metaphor is to "create afresh the associations" (*SPP*, p. 482) that, as we have seen previously, disseminate meaning. Its function is to put us in touch with that originary difference that is the source of linguistic vitality. Interestingly, Shelley, unlike Nietzsche, does use the word 'similitude' in explaining the words "vitally metaphoric." But he also speaks of the "before unapprehended relations of things," and "relations" have emerged as disruptive elsewhere in the *Defence*. They interpose between conception and expression, which in the present context is desirable, since it impedes the overly rapid conversion of words into readable signs that leads to linguistic atrophy.

We should not be too dogmatic in seeing the *Defence* as the precursor of a Nietzschean and phenomenological deconstruction. But neither is it

[18]Nietzsche, "The Wanderer and His Shadow," *The Complete Works of Friedrich Nietzsche*, ed. Oscar Levy, 18 vols. (1909–11; rpt. New York: Russell and Russell, 1964), VII, 192.

[19]Jacques Derrida, *Positions*, trans. Alan Bass (Chicago: University of Chicago Press, 1981), p. 26.

[20]Nietzsche, "On Truth and Falsity in Their Ultra-Moral Sense," *Complete Works*, II, 179, 188.

anachronistic to place it in transit toward Nietzsche's early work, because writers like Warburton and Blair were already developing theories of figurative language that laid the ground for the romantics to explore the subtexts of their own most cherished postulates. That primitive language was more figurative and that poetry is earlier than prose were of course commonplaces. But Blair goes beyond other writers like Adam Ferguson to consider the structure of tropological thought. All tropes, he argues, "are founded on the relation which one object bears to another; in virtue of which, the name of the one can be substituted instead of the name of the other."[21] As substitutions and condensations, figures are already part of the process of reduction at the heart of representation, which goes even further in abstract thought. Figurative language arose for reasons of economy, because "no language is so copious, as to have a separate word for every separate idea," and hence we made "one word . . . stand also for some other idea or object."[22] But figures, we may argue, are similitudes that reveal how they are constituted on the trace of difference, whereas concepts are dead metaphors that have repressed their origin in difference. Blair does not really develop his suggestions in the direction I am suggesting. But he does lay the ground for others to pursue an archeology of language and to see metaphor as closer than abstraction to that presence-as-difference that underlies all language. For implicit in Blair is a sense that conceptual language is subtended by what Nietzsche calls a "philosophic mythology,"[23] and that the obvious origin of figures in difference makes them an appropriate site for the discovery that all signifying units, whether they function in language or in the language of the world, are implicated in an intertextual network: "every idea or object carries in its train some other ideas, which may be considered as its accessories . . . [it] never presents itself to our view *isolé*."[24]

Equally useful for uncovering the Shelleyan subtext is Warburton's linguistic rather than mystical discussion of hieroglyphics in *The Divine Legation of Moses*. A crucial passage in the *Defence* already cited contrasts language in its original state, where words are "pictures of integral thoughts," with the deteriorated form of language, in which words are "signs for portions or classes of thoughts" (*SPP*, p. 482). Shelley elsewhere expands on the notion of language as picture by praising those poets "who have employed language as the hieroglyphic of their thoughts" (*SPP*, p. 483). At first glance this contrast of hieroglyphic with

[21]Hugh Blair, *Lectures on Rhetoric and Belles Lettres*, 3 vols. (London: Strahan and Cadell, 1785), I, 367.
[22]Ibid., I, 351–52.
[23]Nietzsche, "The Wanderer and His Shadow," *Complete Works*, VII, 192.
[24]Blair, *Lectures*, I, 354–55.

scientific language looks like a valorization of the concrete and pictorial for their logocentric qualities. But once again the hieroglyphic is for Shelley the site of a potential theoretical crossing. Hieroglyphics are roughly equivalent for Warburton to figures for Blair. Indeed, the three kinds of hieroglyphic—curiologic, tropical, and symbolic—seem to correspond approximately to metonymy, synecdoche, and metaphor. More important, hieroglyphics are like figures in that they represent a second stage in the development of semiology, an abridgment or reduction of the cumbersome system in which there is a sign for every thing.[25] At the same time, however, hieroglyphs are less abstract than alphabetic characters, because they are still "signs for things" rather than "signs for words" or sounds.[26] Pictured characters as distinct from simple pictures are figurative condensations still close to their origins in difference. A hieroglyphic puts "one single figure for the mark or representative of several things."[27] It is this sense of the hieroglyph as a similitude containing the trace of difference which is crucial to Shelley. But once again Shelley goes far beyond Warburton in de-sedimenting the concept of the hieroglyph. As pictures of integral thoughts, hieroglyphs must inevitably be symbols for intensive manifolds whose parts have relations among each other that interpose between sign and reference. And this equation of thought with picture in turn casts light on what Shelley means in speaking of the "integral unity" of a thought, or in describing it as "containing within itself the principle of its own integrity" (*SPP*, p. 480). Integral unity is not a synthesis of opposites. Rather the integral thought is an intensive manifold not yet simplified into a sign that will fit into a system. It is a unit that asks to be read aesthetically in terms of its own internal relations and not instrumentally as a palpable design that conducts "to certain general results" (*SPP*, p. 480).

It is not clear that Shelley in the *Defence* explicitly puts forward a deconstructive theory of writing. Rather, the essay is an example of its own doctrine, a lightning that has yet found no theoretical conductor, because at the time of writing the future is still contained within the present (*SPP*, pp. 500, 481). But it is important to remember that this future (our future) is not constrained so much as rearticulated by the resistance it meets in Shelley's present. Hence, in attempting a divinatory reading of the *Defence*, I have avoided a too literal translation of Shelley's essay into contemporary terms, as Derrida and de Man do in interpreting Rousseau and Hegel. A divinatory reading involves a complex symbiosis of past and present. Writing in a later period allows us to 'repeat'

[25]Bishop Warburton, *The Divine Legation of Moses Demonstrated*, *The Works of the Right Reverend William Warburton, D.D.*, 12 vols. (London: Cadell and Davies, 1811), IV, 120.
[26]Ibid., IV, 131.
[27]Ibid., IV, 14.

the past in Kierkegaard's sense: to get everything back double in a way that Shelley's contemporaries perhaps could not. But in the process the past, too, emerges as a dialectical reduplication of the present, a repetition that unfolds the doubleness within the present.

A Defence of Poetry inhabits the fold that divides romantic organicism and idealism from romantic deconstruction but also marks their continuity. As such, it sets in motion a dialogue of the past with(in) the present. It cannot have escaped notice how many of the essay's major statements face, like Janus, in two directions. Shelley insists on the imagination as dynamic and vital but thereby unable to fix meaning. He insists that poetry is infinitely rich, but only because it constantly disseminates meaning in order to recreate afresh the associations disorganized by habit. To say this is to characterize the fold, to point to a 'romantic deconstruction' and to unfold its difference from poststructuralism. For one thing, the former continues to valorize imagination, though hardly in the logocentric way conceived by Coleridge. Moreover, Shelley images the activity of deconstruction in organic terms, through analogies such as the flower whose petals disclose a calyx. These analogies refigure but also bear the traces of Goethe's inquiry into the metamorphic unity of plant structure and claim for the deconstructive activity a processive though not a formal or teleological unity. To argue, as de Man might do, that as metaphors these images are merely sublimatory would be to go against the very assumptions of deconstruction itself, which unsettles any geological arrangement of literal and figural as 'false' and 'true.' Finally, Shelley describes something that sounds very much like deconstruction and describes it not in terms of 'textuality' but through the use of phenomenological and affective terms like 'power,' that make his version of it postorganicist rather than poststructuralist. The term 'power' occurs only twice in the *Defence*,[28] but it seems, with all the connotations that surround its usage elsewhere in Shelley, to inform his concept of poetry. It is at once a site for the deconstruction of a ground behind language and for the characterization of language as an emotional process. Idealizingly linked to the notion of a teleological spirit that produces progressive universal poetry and its divinatory reading, power also emerges as something radically unstable. As in "Mont Blanc" where it can only be known as it appears, the creative 'power' is "like the colour of a flower which fades and changes as it is developed" (*SPP*, p. 504). It is a series of effects or appearances rather than the cause behind them, at best a mode of functioning rather than an essence, described as a

[28]I refer to the passage on the fading coal (*SPP*, p. 504) and to the conclusion (*SPP*, p. 508). There are also references to poetry as a 'power' of the mind having "no necessary connexion with consciousness or will" (*SPP*, p. 506).

cause largely in order to provide a heuristic fiction that will allow the process of interpretation to continue. However, if power is not a source but a self-displacing energy, the very use of the term conveys the involvement of the reader and writer in this displacement. Shelley's 'power' is closer to Nietzsche's use of the term than to Hegel's concept of a world-historical spirit, for there is much in Shelley to suggest that his Hegelian concept of a "spirit of the age" (*SPP*, p. 508) knows itself as a will-to-power. But it is also closer to Nietzsche's use of the term than to Foucault's analysis of power as an institutional and semiotic rather than psychological category.

As the *Defence* contains the seeds of a deconstructive theory of language, so, too, it contains the beginnings of a disseminative theory of reading. Indeed, it encourages the kind of reading attempted here, which paradoxically renews the originality of the text by liberating it from the tyranny of the original intention behind it. A heuristic theory of reading emerges less from formal statements made in the *Defence* than from the interpretive practice it generates if we read it intertextually rather than as the source of certain founding critical doctrines. For as I shall go on to suggest, the fact that Shelley composed his text out of so many voices means that its theoretical position is nowhere embodied in it: what is said is constantly undermined, and what can be said is not necessarily said in any explicit way. The *Defence* works not through logical, sequential argument but through images. It conforms to Shelley's definition of poetry in that the use of image rather than statement gives the sense of a disseminative excess "which consumes the scabbard that would contain it" (*SPP*, p. 491). The essay, in other words, does not contain its meaning. A heuristic theory of reading is thus one that we must construct in those interstices whose void forever craves fresh food. One discerns the presence of such a theory partly because the deconstructive statements on language provide a background against which Shelley's own 'hermeneutic' readings of Homer and Dante emerge as acts of will. His recourse to a traditional hermeneutic is itself an interstitial position that tries to close the gap between what poetry should be and what it is. Disclosing itself as supplementary, this position also manifests to us Shelley's need to see the reader as constructing something positive out of the gaps in Dante's or Milton's text. Thus, the gap created in the *Defence* by the compensatory quality of Shelley's interpretations stimulates us to construct something positive out of what might otherwise be a deconstruction of his hermeneutics. In part, one also discerns a need for a heuristic theory because the emphases of the essay make it clear that an aesthetics for Shelley is incomplete if it considers only the structural properties of language and not also the phenomenology of creation and reception. Again and again, Shelley talks not just of poetry or language but of their effect. To stop at a deconstruction of the essay, to remain inside its aporias and not to consider the outside of the text, is simply too limited a reading.

It is fairly clear that the analyses of Dante and Milton are actually examples of heuristic and not hermeneutic reading. Informed as they are by Godwin's distinction between moral and tendency, they re-vision what these authors were historically precluded from saying by applying the texts to Shelley's own life and finding in them tendencies toward his revolutionary challenge to sectarianism, tyranny, and custom. Shelley's sympathy with Godwin's theory is apparent in his criticism of those who have a "moral aim" and in his insistence that a poet should not "embody his own conceptions of right and wrong, which are usually those of his place and time, in his poetical creations, which participate in neither" (*SPP*, p. 488). It may be for this reason that Shelley speaks vaguely of poetry as creating the "the true and the beautiful, in a word the good" (*SPP*, p. 482), leaving the specific content of these abstractions for different ages to fill in differently. Ostensibly, Godwin's theory parallels the prophetic hermeneutics of the post-Kantians, as does Shelley's insistence on poets as mediums whose words "express what they understand not" (*SPP*, p. 508). But in liberating the reader from the moral authority of the author, Godwin radically historicizes reading, because future readers also cannot be bound by the authority of predecessors like Godwin or Shelley. Poetry becomes a semioclastic energy that we must use to break both the forms it assumes and those we confer on it: "Ethical science arranges the elements which poetry has created, and propounds schemes and proposes examples of civil and domestic life: . . . But Poetry acts in another and diviner manner. It awakens and enlarges the mind itself by rendering it the receptacle of a thousand unapprehended combinations of thought" (*SPP*, p. 487). The radically indeterminate nature of poetic energy is encapsulated in Shelley's description of poets as "mirrors of the gigantic shadows which futurity casts upon the present" (*SPP*, p. 508). In reflecting a shadow the poem is not so much a mimesis as an intimation. Because the shadow is cast by something that does not yet exist, it is we who must partly produce the text's meaning through a negative reading in which we infer the presence of something from its very absence: from the void it creates, which must be the absence of something. On the one hand, the word 'gigantic' attributes a mythic status to what the text portends. On the other hand, we can grasp this meaning only in terms of shadows that contain areas of darkness. Nor can we really see into a mirror that reflects a shadow, for the image suggests not a direct grasping of truth but a displacement of interpretation into the realm of the specular. This indeterminacy is also apparent in Shelley's equation of the imagination with power. Increasingly used in literary criticism by writers like De Quincey, the term 'power' links Shelley to a tradition that begins with Burke's analysis of the sublime and that conceives of literature in affective rather than structural terms. But while the effects of sublimity and beauty can be calculated, power, as we have seen, cannot provide a description of the creative process that supports a traditional hermeneutic.

What, then, is the kind of reading generated by the 'power' of imagination? The clearest indication that his concept of reading is not always traditionally hermeneutic comes in a passage where Shelley returns to those 'relations' that confuse the rubrics and cells of our interpretations:

> All high poetry is infinite; it is as the first acorn, which contained all oaks potentially. Veil after veil may be undrawn, and the inmost naked beauty of the meaning never exposed. A great Poem is a fountain for ever overflowing with the waters of wisdom and delight; and after one person and one age has exhausted all its divine effluence which their peculiar relations enable them to share, another and yet another succeeds, and new relations are ever developed. (*SPP*, p. 500)

It is clear from this passage that Shelley represents the endlessness of reading more positively than does Kierkegaard. Moreover, given the essay's historical treatment of literature and its emphasis on poetry as a social force, we can infer that reading heuristically would involve the inscription of reading within culture—a possibility not raised by the German tradition. This kind of reading is best described by Kristeva's concept of intertextuality, although she does not develop the term in the direction of a theory of reading. In an intertextual framework, history and society are "seen as texts read by the writer, and into which he inserts himself by rewriting them."[29] For Shelley, the relationship between text and reader is similarly transformational. Rewriting the *Divine Comedy* by organizing its relations according to cultural perspectives that would not have been possible in an earlier period, Shelley discloses Dante's own society as a text by treating certain aspects of the poem as written by the cultural metaphors in which it is temporarily arrayed and not as a reflection of truth. The textuality of the poem, a 'feigning' in the word Shelley takes over from Sidney, discloses the textuality of the social codes it reflects and facilitates the poem's transformation by its reader into something that can in turn transform not only the past but the future. This process continues beyond Shelley, for different people and ages keep interpreting the text in new ways that make it valuable not for

[29]Julia Kristeva, *Desire in Language*, trans. Leon Roudiez (New York: Columbia University Press, 1980), p. 65.

what it 'says' but for the heuristic role it plays in the self-understanding of each reading community.

This description of the text as a productivity whose identity is not fixed but historically variable is very different from the notion of it as a conception that precedes expression and that requires us as readers to resist dissemination in order to return to a source. To search for that first acorn is now absurd, as Droysen similarly suggests.[30] The poem survives not as what it originally was but as a series of self-transformations that generate and are further generated by social transformations. But just as importantly, Shelley's account of textuality and reception differs from current ideas of unreadability. It links the life of the text to its deconstructibility, making its interstices and gaps the shadows that futurity casts upon the present. For dissemination is precisely the site of a paradox: dissemination as the scattering and unfixing of unitary meaning, dissemination as communication.

But we must also avoid giving too firm an identity to Shelley's theory of reading. Precisely because the *Defence* contains so many voices its theoretical position is nowhere embodied in it, and this mobility on the part of the text unsettles our attempts to incorporate our own theories in it through a kind of transference. The concept of dissemination just described experimentally posits an aesthetics on the basis of the difference between the idealistic and deconstructive voices in the essay. But this so-called position must be seen as the difference between and not as the synthesis of the two voices. In other words, it suffers the anxiety of being supplementary. Shelley's essay contains no positive terms. Its identity—if one can use that word—emerges through relations between its voices: the idealistic and the deconstructive, the ontological and the pragmatic, the essentialist and the historicist. Preferring image to statement, the essay defers the theorizing of a position on either writing or reading. Contemporary critics who turn to earlier theory as to a mirror-stage, hoping it will confirm our own identity as unitary intellectual subjects, find that Shelley's text reduplicates not one but several positions, and that the movement of substitution and exchange between these positions resituates our own positions and discloses differences within them. In turning to his later poems as mirrors that stage his theory, we similarly find that they defer the provision of a firm answer to the death of the transcendent *logos*. The two poems we shall consider are very different and are themselves engaged in an internal dialogue. Written before the *Defence*, *Prometheus Unbound* plays with a traditional hermeneutic that survives in the essay and probes its limits in ways that explain why the latter must contain more than one voice. Written after

[30]See Chapter 3, n. 5.

the *Defence*, *The Triumph of Life* renounces the traditional hermeneutic of the allegorical mode that it negatively evokes and generates from the defacement of its own representations something akin to a heuristic practice of reading, but one that must live with the gigantic shadows that the past casts upon the present.

CHAPTER ELEVEN

Deconstruction or Reconstruction: Reading Shelley's *Prometheus Unbound*

More conspicuously than those of Wordsworth or Keats, Shelley's poems are accompanied by prefaces that place a hermeneutic frame around them, pleading with the reader for their sympathetic reception yet thereby recognizing that what they try to 'say' is subject to dissent. The writing of prefaces, however, is only a symptom of a more pervasive awareness that the imagination is not autonomous. The ways in which reading becomes the dialogical supplement of writing are a central concern of the two later poems we shall consider. But the problem of reading, though deferred, is present on the margins of more hermetically visionary poems as well. In this respect *Alastor* can provide us with a pre-text for raising problems that Shelley explicitly confronts in his later work. For its defense of 'poetry' is attempted through a hermeneutics of negativity that stops just short of consuming what it struggles to protect and that requires us to reconceive both the role of deconstruction in semiosis and the nature of reading.

Alastor is a highly reflexive poem that enacts simultaneously the processes of making and reading. In conflating these two activities, it nevertheless elides the deconstructive dialogue between them that Shelley must confront in *Prometheus Unbound*. The poem is in the first place about the writing of itself. As a poet himself, resuming his "long-forgotten lyre" (l. 42, *SPP*), the Narrator has the task of animating what reverts at the end to "An image, silent, cold, and motionless" (l. 661, *SPP*). He must give substance to the Poet, who is otherwise an empty sign, threatening to deconstruct a romantic ideology of vision that becomes no more than an intent of consciousness. But this struggle against the counterspirit of language proves to be a troubled one, because the

Narrator's attempt to make the Poet speak to us takes form not as the inspired song he originally plans (l. 19, *SPP*), but as poetic narrative: in a form that keeps complicating the drive toward idealization by entangling it in a story of particular facts. Converting lyric into narrative, the text defers the identity of the Narrator with his own mood. For subjective narrative of the kind produced in *Alastor* is caught in a series of differences: in the difference of the Narrator from an alter ego with whom he cannot quite identify, and in this case in the internal differences of a story that must be told twice over and that is eventually abandoned rather than concluded.[1] Moreover, as a text addressed *to* someone rather than simply "overheard," as Frye says of the lyric,[2] such narrative is 'poetry' produced at the site of interpretive dissent. It is already aware that its readers might think otherwise, incipiently dialogized by this awareness.

But at the same time the Narrator's attempt to write the figure of the Poet is already a hermeneutic, not a mimetic or creative act; the Narrator does not commemorate someone he has known intimately, like Wordsworth remembering Lucy. Like the speaker of the conversation poems he tries to understand from the outside an experience he has not had but struggles to believe in. That he tells it twice testifies to his persistence in trying to get to the heart of the Poet's story. His attitude to a visionary ideology whose authority is felt only as an absence thus models for us the role of the reader who must overcome doubts that are created by the fact that we live in the twilight of the idols. It is therefore difficult to imagine the Poet except as a "twilight" phantasm (l. 40, *SPP*), and indeed to construct him except as a character without interiority, a mere sign of what he wants to be. Indeed, the hermeneutic modeled here is considerably more negative than that of Coleridge. Where Coleridge is able to invest the experience he would have us recover in another person, the Narrator does not clearly represent the Poet as having had a visionary experience. 'Vision' is disturbingly accompanied by fainting (ll. 188–91, *SPP*). and if "meaning" once flashes on the Poet's "vacant mind" (l. 126, *SPP*), it is never represented in language. That the Poet is essentially a representation is marked in the preface, where his life is described as "allegorical" (*SPP*, p. 69). As sign, he posits nothing except the desire to posit. For the preface negates the Poet as "self-centred" but then negates

[1]I discuss the doubling of the narration and the relationship between lyric and narrative in "The Web of Human Things: Narrative and Identity in *Alastor*," in Kim Blank, ed., *The New Shelley: Later Twentieth-Century Views* (New York: Macmillan, forthcoming). For a general discussion of lyric versus narrative modes see my essay "Romanticism and the Death of Lyric Consciousness," in Chaviva Hosek and Patricia Parker, eds., *Lyric Poetry: Beyond New Criticism* (Ithaca, N.Y.: Cornell University Press, 1985), pp. 194–207.

[2]Northrop Frye, *Anatomy of Criticism: Four Essays* (Princeton, N.J.: Princeton University Press, 1957), p. 249.

the "meaner spirits" who do not follow his example, so as to signify through this double negation a desire for the visionary that is not embodied in the Poet himself (*SPP*, pp. 69–70).

What the Narrator attempts is, however, a hermeneutics of negativity that makes us aware both of a powerful resistance to deconstruction and of the crisis faced by such resistance. Crucial to his strategy is the estrangement of the Poet, whose journey through regions that are culturally and temporally distant draws our attention to a hermeneutic problem, while also putting the Poet in the space of the auratic. Scattered through the poem are references to the Orient that try to make the vacancy repeatedly alluded to in the poem into an occultation of meaning. Nature finally builds a "pyramid" over the Poet's moldering bones (l. 53, *SPP*), and while alive he is represented among obelisks and sphinxes (ll. 111–16, *SPP*), lingering among "memorials / Of the world's youth" in places where "dead men / Hang their mute thoughts on the mute walls around" (ll. 119–22, *SPP*). These images function as signals to the reader which reverse what Geoffrey Hartman has presented as a 'westering' movement in romantic poetry[3] and ask us to construct the sublime from within the hermeneutic. But it is not a question of deciphering that cipher which is the figure of the Poet, for the Oriental exists only as the negation of our own world, and thus as a dead world. More helpful than theories that associate hieroglyphs with a lost origin is Hegel's account of Egyptian art as the crystalization of the symbolic phase:

> Egypt is the country of symbols, the country which sets itself the spiritual task of the self-deciphering of the spirit, without actually attaining to the decipherment. . . . But their works remain mysterious and dumb, mute and motionless, because here spirit itself has still not really found its own inner life and still cannot speak the clear and distinct language of spirit. (*A*, I,354)

Hegel's description helps to explain why the visionary mode in *Alastor* is conceived only negatively, in terms of silence, absence, vacancy. For the visionary is still only a figure of itself. Crucial to the negativity of Egyptian art are the pyramids that take form as "a double architecture, one above ground" and obviously constructed only for the sake of the "inner meaning" it envelops, the other "subterranean" but consisting of an intricate network of labyrinths and hieroglyphs, one might say of further signs. These signs, moreover, construct a world that is dead. According to Hegel, Egypt turned from the phenomenal world to the inward, but conceived "as the negative of life, as death," such that "the

[3] *The Fate of Reading and Other Essays* (Chicago: University of Chicago Press, 1975), pp. 126–27.

immortality of the soul" is still only conceptualized as the "preservation of corpses" (*A*, I, 355). The 'reorientation' of *Alastor* therefore involves grasping the text as the sign of some inner meaning that is absent. It also involves seeing an otherwise nihilistic emphasis on death—on the Poet's moldering corpse—as an embalming of that which remains still (to be) born. Augmenting our sense of the visionary mode as lifeless is the fact that the Poet almost never speaks, spending his days among "speechless shapes" (l. 123, *SPP*). But muteness for Hegel is not the death of the sign, but rather the site of the text's delivery to and by the future. Egyptian art is summed up by the statues of Memnon, which "numb, stiff and lifeless, are set up facing the sun in order to await its ray to touch them and give them soul and sound." Unable to "draw animation from within" like the human voice, these statues require "light from without which alone liberates the note of the soul from them" (*A*, I, 358).

For the reader outside the text, however, it is difficult not to see the hermeneutics of negativity described here as a mystification. Denying itself the constructive force of prophecy, the poem's elegiac orientation toward the past constantly thwarts our attempts to posit something on the ground of the Poet's absence, by reinscribing them in the Narrator's failure to represent him. The phenomenological recuperation of death as a state of consciousness thus comes up against the materiality of death, against the sense that it is the obliteration of what survives only as a trace. Or to put it differently, the Poet's death still has the force not of transcendence but of a double negation: a negation both of the ordinary and of the visionary. Any attempt to make it into a transcendence is suspended by the way in which this text exchanges author and reader functions so that neither can be self-grounding. For the Narrator's attempt to give the Poet an identity emerges as a hermeneutic act, such that writing is already interpretation and not a reflection or expression of truth. But, on the other hand, the reading of identity emerges as figurative because the muteness of the Poet prevents it from being a reconstruction of something already said or thought. We have seen how such instability can become an occasion for reformulating the relationship between text and reader. Indeed, the double negation of the preface asks that we read beyond the poem and open it to historical reformulations of the dialectic between the visionary and the social. But the poem itself seems committed by its form as a quest (for truth) and by the hermeneutics of elegy to an essentialism that preempts heuristic reading. As elegy, *Alastor* stands at the opposite pole from *The Triumph of Life*, where it is not the living who must turn toward the dead but the past that must encounter the present. Michael Fried has described how painters in the age of Diderot found it necessary to include the beholder as witness to their truth, only to turn away from him as the site of their insertion into a world outside the hermetically sealed enclosure of the canvas.[4] This tension between 'absorption' and 'theatricality' parallels the ambivalent attitude of traditional hermeneutics toward the reader: an ambivalence particularly evident in the fact that the elegy frames the role of the reader within the death of its subject. Like those paintings that invite us to watch them turning away from us, romantic elegy asks us to join in re-membering its subject, while sealing it against further reading by leaving us with the reproach of the Poet's death. For the dead elicit sympathy but also guilt, such that any understanding that is also critical becomes like a violation of the sacred.

To compare *Prometheus Unbound* and *Alastor* may seem unusual, but the later text is again concerned with the mediation of a visionary ideology. The problem of mediation is raised by the very mode of lyrical drama, which Shelley defines in the preface to *Hellas* as a difference between vision and history that signals the intentionality of the former:

> The subject in its present state, is insusceptible of being treated otherwise than lyrically. . . . I have, therefore, contented myself with exhibiting a series of lyric pictures, and with having wrought upon the curtain of futurity which falls upon the unfinished scene such figures of indistinct and visionary delineation as suggest the final triumph of the Greek cause. (*SPP*, p. 408)

We can reformulate this by saying that the materiality of narrative and drama, of writing vision into the language of events, inevitably defers the re-visioning of history as the phenomenology of mind. Appealing to futurity, Shelley experiments with the idea of a prophetic hermeneutics that will read beyond the indistinctness of his play. But in transposing lyric into drama, he also submits vision to the theatricalization of which the romantics were so deeply suspicious.[5] We can therefore expect that he will deal much more explicitly with the problematic relation of 'poetry' to its audience.

For much of its history, critics have emphasized how *Prometheus Unbound* fails as an act of representation. Such assessments, though insensitive to the ways the play encodes its own textuality, seem more accurate in describing its construction than the organicist readings that replaced them. From the nineteenth century onward, critics have accused the play of being "intangible," "vague and hollow," populated by characters who

[4]*Absorption and Theatricality: Painting and Beholder in the Age of Diderot* (Los Angeles: University of California Press, 1980), pp. 103–4.

[5]Ibid., p. 104.

are "spectral, often formless, sometimes only voices."[6] Some of the gaps in its logic are thematic. The movement of history toward the far goal of time is seen in linear and eschatological terms, but the historical process is also imaged as a cyclic one in which the infirm hand of Eternity may allow Jove to return again. Other gaps are dramatic. Demogorgon, a volcanic and amoral power who sees the deep truth as imageless in the early part of the play, suddenly becomes Olympian and beneficent in a fourth act that lifts the veil and does image ultimate reality. Yet other gaps have to do with the semiotics of the play's characterization, which hovers uncertainly between the external and the internal. For instance, while Prometheus himself remains chained to the rock, two secondary figures carry out the task of ending the Jovian age. Asia, whose ethic of love is consistent with Prometheus' forgiveness of Jupiter, must be seen psychologically as a force within Prometheus, if the latter's change of heart is to be viewed as something active and not merely contemplative. But Demogorgon, whose violent overthrow of Jove represses rather than forgives him, is conceived allegorically as a power beyond Prometheus himself. Yet if Asia is internal to Prometheus, can we really dissociate Demogorgon from a Prometheus who is then caught in the paradox of using violence to achieve peace? It is hardly surprising, in view of such contradictions, that the triumphant fourth act seems an aria tacked on to a three-act drama, rather than an organic resolution.

Perhaps the most troubling lacuna in the play has to do with the unilateral nature of Prometheus' forgiveness of Jove, on which the entire action depends. If Promethean love is indeed to inaugurate a new age, then surely this love cannot remain a paradise for a sect. Yet it is only the Jove within Prometheus who is overcome by love. The actual Jove, in a scene reminiscent of *Paradise Lost* where Satan is hurled headlong only to rise again, is cast into the abyss: repressed rather than reintegrated. These local aporias are, moreover, reflected in the text's ambiguous genre. *Prometheus Unbound* is often described as a political allegory. As a political work it assumes the legislative, even the executive, authority of words. But as an allegory it concedes that the world it represents exists at a certain distance from actuality and must be rendered abstractly rather than realistically. Moreover, Shelley himself described *Prometheus Unbound* through another paradox when he subtitled it a lyrical drama. As drama, it claims an objectivity at odds with its often diaphanous language. A dramatic action is concretely, materially present before us. Drama is, moreover, a communal mode: because it communi-

[6]See L. J. Zillman, *Shelley's Prometheus Unbound: A Variorum Edition* (Seattle: University of Washington Press, 1959), pp. 41–42, 44.

cates to an audience, it assumes a shared ideology and an affective link between words and the world outside them. Yet Shelley's play is a lyrical drama, by definition impossible to stage in the theater of the world, and acknowledging for itself a merely private and subjective status. Interestingly, Shelley himself expected it to be read by no more than twenty people, perhaps as few as five.[7]

Faced with such disjunctures in the play, the response of modern critics has been to use an aesthetic version of the argument from design. K. N. Cameron, for instance, raises the question of why Demogorgon is described as having existed from time immemorial and then is introduced in act III as the child of Jupiter and Thetis born to overthrow his father. Making Demogorgon the fatal child is necessary to show how tyranny breeds its own destruction. But an awkward by-product of this new parentage is that Demogorgon, previously an abstract force outside time, now becomes historically specified as a revolutionary power within the world of time, liable to be consumed by the future as he has consumed the past. Cameron's response is to argue that this ungrammaticality makes sense on a deeper level. Jove is mistaken when he identifies his fatal child with Demogorgon, and evidently Demogorgon himself, when he identifies himself as Jove's child (III.i.54, *SPP*), is speaking only metaphorically, although he is speaking literally when two lines earlier he identifies himself with Eternity.[8] This argument, however, seems ingenious. If Shelley simply wanted to have Jove overthrown by his child, we must ask why he had to create confusion by identifying the child as Demogorgon when Hesiod and Aeschylus make no such identification. He wished, of course, to show the revolution as engendered within history. But he could have given the fatal child some other name, except that identifying it with Eternity is also necessary if the Promethean revolution is to have a transcendental guarantee and not to be a purely local event. Moreover, it is not simply Demogorgon's identity as the child of Jupiter but also his identity as "Eternity" which is in question. In act III he announces that he is Eternity (III.i.52, *SPP*); in act IV he refers to "Eternity, / Mother of many acts" (IV.565–66, *SPP*), as though Eternity is something other than himself, and as though he is not supreme but subject to some other force. Between Demogorgon the first cause who resides in the realm of *res cogitans*, and Demogorgon the effective cause operating in the sphere of *res extensa* or historical events,

[7]See W. E. Peck, *Shelley: His Life and Work* (1927; rpt. New York: Burt Franklin, 1969), II, 125; Shelley, *The Complete Works*, ed. Roger Ingpen and W. E. Peck (London: Ernest Benn, 1926–1930), X, 354.

[8]K. N. Cameron, "The Political Symbolism of Prometheus Unbound," *PMLA* 58 (1943); rpt. in R. B. Woodings, ed., *Shelley: Modern Judgments* (London: Macmillan, 1968), pp. 121–24.

the link is as unclear as the one Descartes constructs between his two spheres via the pineal gland. Or to put it differently, Shelley cannot make the transition from the sphere of thought to that of actuality, a problem not untypical of revolutionary thinkers, and also fundamental to the status of the play's revolutionary discourse. One could go on, but the point is a simple one. It is that one can construct exits from the interpretive labyrinth of the play if one tries. But any attempt to clarify the play's dramatic syntax simultaneously generates further ungrammaticalities.[9]

Described this way, the play invites scepticism. But *Prometheus* is a consciously metafictional text whose deconstruction is part of the dialogue on aesthetics set in motion by the *Defence*. It includes at least two scenes of understanding which reflect on the process by which a unified truth is constituted, communicated, and confirmed: the dialogue between Asia and Panthea at the beginning of act II and Asia's visit to the Cave of Demogorgon later in the act. The first of these comes immediately after act I, which reluctantly recognizes the discourse of hope as hypothetical. The two crucial episodes of act I—the encounter between the reformed Prometheus and the Phantasm of Jove, and the psychomachia that balances the Furies against the Spirits of hope—do not simply convey the play's optimistic propositions. They also reflect back on themselves and must be viewed semiotically as well as thematically. In Prometheus' revocation of his curse, voice is deliberately decentered. His words are split away from their original speaker and attributed to Jove, himself not a person but a phantasm, an empty schema like the subject in Lacanian psychoanalysis. The words do not seem to come from anywhere or from anyone: they do not belong and are therefore inappropriate. This curious device, which has an effect similar to that which Brecht describes as *Verfremdung* or alienation, suggests that the Jovian element in Prometheus is no longer a part of his thinking. But it is also used to remove from those words the ability to affect the real world that comes from their being centered in a speaking self. Deprived of the validating authority of the emotions that generated them, Prometheus' words become simply words, grounded in nothing outside themselves. But the decentering of the text of hate inevitably makes us aware that its successor, the text of love and forgiveness, is also an intent of consciousness. To put it differently, Prometheus uses the fact that he exists within

[9]I borrow the term 'ungrammaticality' from Michael Riffaterre, who uses it to indicate an element that disrupts the manifest grammar of a text and that thus threatens "the literary representation of reality or mimesis": *Semiotics of Poetry* (Bloomington: Indiana University Press, 1978), p. 2. Unlike Riffaterre, I do not believe that the ungrammaticality is part of "a deviant grammar or lexicon" that is eventually integrated into a unified system of signification.

the prisonhouse of language precisely to argue that the semiotic manacles he has created by perceiving his relationship to Jove in a certain way are mind-forged. But in making the past into a text that he can rewrite, he semiotizes the future, making it, too, into a text that may lose its grounding in reality if it does not find readers with a similar emotional tropology. The result is a displacement of the play's subsequent action from the status of signified to signifier. This displacement will be accentuated throughout the play in the use of aesthetic rather than natural analogies to evoke the process of Promethean renewal.[10]

The summoning up of the phantasm can in fact be seen as mise-en-abime of the larger play. Occurring entirely inside Prometheus' consciousness, it reduces the play's action to a play with images, disclosing the immateriality of what Shelley describes as writing "drawn from the operations of the human mind" (*SPP*, p. 133). Equally problematical is the remainder of the first act. The Furies are depicted as insubstantial phantasms from "the all-miscreative brain of Jove" (I.448, *SPP*). But the matching of the spirits against the furies suggests that they may be no different. Not only do the spirits have difficulty envisioning a world in which ruin is no longer love's shadow, the fact that their tenuous vision of a redeemed world takes the form of a dream acknowledges that imagination cannot give a foundation to what it posits except as an intent of consciousness.

It is against this background that we must see the dialogue between Asia and Panthea in which Shelley reflects on the rhetorical problem at the heart of the play: that of whether he can make his vision of a Promethean Age convincing, given the lacunae in it. Again, the vision takes the form of dreams, subliminally felt as Panthea sleeps in Ione's arms in the depths of the sea. The scene focuses on the difficulty she has in articulating her two dreams about the psychological resurrection of Prometheus and the future heralded for the rest of mankind by his transformation. Thus it raises the two problems central to the poetic process: that of expression, the finding of signs to signify the ineffable, and that of persuasion, the creation of an interpretive community that will give assent and solidity to an otherwise esoteric vision. It is the latter alone that can fulfil the imperatives of Shelley's form by translating lyric into dialogue and finally drama, visionary intention into communication and action. Panthea in this scene functions as the implied author, the hierophant of "an unapprehended inspiration, (*SPP*, p. 508), while Asia is the reader desired by the author and one who "produces" the meaning of the text by intuitively grasping his intention. Shelley's essential work, as distinct from his published text, is figured here in the form of the

[10]Cf. *Prometheus Unbound*, ll. 661–63; III.iii.160–66; IV.153–58, 212–13, 236–40, *SPP*.

dreams. The word 'text,' meaning something that is woven together, designates a collection of signs with grammatological but not pneumatological status. Its relationship to the term 'work' is, to borrow his own distinction, like that of a mosaic to a painting, a mosaic being a conglomerate of parts and a painting being a unified whole (*SPP*, p. 504). Although Panthea's words (like Shelley's text) serve as conductors of the play's vision, this vision remains scattered as long as Asia attempts to ground it in the words themselves, which are transitory and fragmentary, imaged in terms of winds and air (II.i.37, 109, *SPP*). In short, at the beginning of the scene we are able to scan the textual mosaic but unable to grasp the work.

The roles of Panthea and Asia correspond almost exactly to those Schelling assigns to the two sides of the self at the beginning of *The Ages of the World*. Schelling conceives of understanding as a dialogical process, but one that culminates in identity rather than difference, the difference being due to the process of articulation and the ultimate identity of questioner and respondent being also a finding of identity. Understanding is first of all a process of recollection and recognition by which we reawaken the "archetype of things [that] slumbers in the soul like an obscured and forgotten, even if not completely obliterated, image" (*AW*, p. 85). But this we accomplish through dialogue, which enables us to make conscious what we sense only obscurely, by learning it from another who turns out to be an objectification of ourselves. In the phenomenology of understanding, which can serve as a model for the reading process, there are two participants: "an asking one and an answering one, an ignorant one which, however, seeks knowledge, and a knowing one which, however, does not know its knowledge." The higher, intuitive self, in Schelling's words, "is mute and needs a mediating organ in order to attain expression" (*AW*, p. 89). Similarly, in *Prometheus Unbound* Panthea, though in possession of what Shelley calls "the uncommunicated lightning" of the play's vision, (*SPP*, p. 134), is ignorant of what she knows and needs Asia to produce her vision. That the vision is inarticulate until it is read is a significant point, and one whose deconstructive consequences will emerge in the visit to Demogorgon. But for the present it is enough to say that the reader here is given the responsibility of recovering and in some sense co-creating a vision that otherwise would "not speak to us, but remain dead" (*AW*, p. 88).

Communication proceeds only when the internalizing of knowledge described by the German word for recollection, *Erinnerung*, occurs through an identification of author and reader. Suddenly, Asia discovers the right method of reading by gazing into Panthea's eyes and there reading Prometheus' "written soul" through a paradoxically "wordless converse" (II.i.110, 52, *SPP*). The logocentric concept of the "written soul" resolves the paradox of traditional hermeneutics: the paradox that in order to preserve vision one must fix it in writing, but that writing is always external and supplementary to what it transmits.[11] The process of moving beyond the linguistic sign to the language of the eyes suggests how the reader, too, can break the hermeneutic circle by moving beyond a semiological reading that decenters vision to a psychological reading that allows us unmediated access to the inner core of the work. The breaking of this circle serves as a catalyst for the communication of Panthea's second dream, which turns out to have been Asia's also. Thus we can see in this scene the outlines of a Shelleyan hermeneutic designed to reverse the deconstructive potential within a text that fails to confirm itself by meeting the classical criteria for unity. The published text, composed of disjunctive elements that can be brought together only by imaginative leaps, is seen as a product of the semiotic fracture described in the *Defence*, which occurs when inspiration is signified through composition (*SPP*, p. 504). But the scene dramatizes the imaginative project as interpersonal communication rather than simple linguistic intention involving a dyadic relationship between the sign and the thing or concept signified. In other words, it presents reading as a psychological and not just a semiological process. Asia responds to Panthea's dream, not on the level of its fractured signifiers, but through a process of what Dilthey calls "reconstruction" (*Nachbildung*). By translating a language initially "given us only from the outside" in terms of "our own sense of life," Dilthey argues, we center the isolated signs "given to our senses" in a "coherence experienced from within."[12] This coherence, though subjective, is also shared between author and reader. Panthea's attempt to voice her dream is an invitation to Asia as implied reader to re-cognize the dream she herself has had. As such, the dialogue between the two sisters serves as a model for the dialogue intended to occur between author and reader. Critics have often complained that the fourth act is like a castle in the air. But the insubstantiality of the play's action is not the point, because the action cannot become real until we as readers recognize it as the dream we have had. The fourth act, in which Shelley stages an objectively unverifiable outcome in the theater of his own mind, invites us to stage Shelley's vision in the theater of *our* minds and thus bridge the gulf between intention and actuality conceded in the notion of lyrical drama.

As an intratextual allegory of the transmission of text to reader, this scene is of course stage managed. By imaging the author and implied

[11]Wilhelm Dilthey, "The Rise of Hermeneutics," trans. Fredric Jameson, *New Literary History* 3 (1971–72): 232–33.
[12]Ibid., p. 231.

reader as sisters, Shelley assumes a reading based on sympathy, a dialogue that is no dialogue because the Other is the emotional twin of the self. It is this same assumption of psychic affinity which allows him in *The Defence* to construct a hermeneutics of understanding in which reading is the redemption of a fragmentary text through the animation of archetypes that point to the intention in which the text has its genesis (*SPP*, p. 505). But it is necessary to distinguish between the implied and the explicit readers: using the term "explicit reader" as H. R. Jauss uses it to distinguish the actual historically differentiated reader from Iser's idealized "implied reader" whose role is prescribed within the text.[13] Though this reader by definition is not figured in the play, the reader's presence as a potentially negating force is something of which Shelley seems aware even in the dialogue between Asia and Panthea, but more strongly in the visit to the Cave of Demogorgon.

One of the changes that Shelley made in the draft manuscript of the play casts considerable light on the way he problematizes the hermeneutic journey undertaken in the second act. When Asia asks her sister to raise her eyes so that she can read Prometheus' soul in them, the draft shows Asia experiencing an ecstatic communion with the burning image of Prometheus in Panthea's eyes: "It is his spirit in their orbs."[14] This passage is deleted in the published version, which goes straight on to Panthea's troubling question: "what canst thou see / But thine own fairest shadow imaged there?" (II.i.112–13, *SPP*). Panthea here points out that her eyes may not be a window into some ultimate reality but a mirror in which Asia sees the projected text of her own desire. Read in the light of the deleted passage, the sceptical potential of this question is neutralized, and Panthea's question can be taken positively as meaning that the soul of the work, the vision of Prometheus, is also a reflection of Asia's epipsychic essence, her fairest shadow. It thus guarantees the culmination of the interpretive dialogue between author and reader in a fusion of horizons, accomplished literally through an act of vision. Read without the deleted passage, the question becomes more sceptical and suggests that the supposed essence of the work is a projection by the interpreter of her own self, which is itself a construction, an 'image' momentarily constituted in the kaleidoscopic process of communication rather than preceding it. We will return later on to this point about the semiotics of identity: that of author, reader, and character. Suffice it to say that Asia's response to Panthea's question about the nature of the text read in the eyes is contradictory: she at first confirms the hermeneu-

[13]"Theses on the Transition from the Aesthetics of Literary Works to a Theory of Aesthetic Experience," in Mario J. Valdes and Owen J. Miller, eds., *Interpretation of Narrative* (Toronto: University of Toronto Press, 1978), p. 142.

[14]See Zillman, *Shelley's Prometheus Unbound*, p. 187.

tic myth of transparent communication by paralleling Panthea's eyes to "the deep blue, boundless Heaven" (II.i.114, *SPP*). But then she suggests that what she reads there is a labyrinth of tropes: "dark, far, measureless,— / Orb within orb, and line through line inwoven.—" (II.i.116–17, *SPP*), an image for visionary communication that is repeated in the "life of life" lyric, where Asia's eyes are paralleled to mazes (II.v.53, *SPP*). It is true that Asia here goes on to announce that the hermeneutic circle has been broken when she declares: "The dream is told" (II.i.126, *SPP*). But the seeds of the later scene have already been sown. We are aware that the notion of a language that is grounded in something beyond language may be itself a linguistic construct and therefore subject to doubt and dismantling.

Even more unsettling for a hermeneutic reading is the second interpretive interlude, Asia's dialogue with Demogorgon. Immediately after their conversation the sisters follow the echoes of voices into a forest that presumably leads into the depths of consciousness and toward the origin of things. This journey is the narrative equivalent of the process that Husserl describes as reduction or epoché, by which one seeks to reach the transcendental subjectivity, in this case, of the author. The shift from dialogue to lyric at the end of the first scene and in the dialogue of the Fauns signals a bracketing of the external world. The voices of the speakers are no longer dramatically differentiated, and their lyrical oneness is an attempt at what Schelling describes as the annulling of "all duality in one's self, so that we would be, as it were, only inwardly, and live altogether in the supramundane, discerning everything immediately" (*AW*, p. 88). But the sisters' journey ends in the Cave of Demogorgon, where the philosophical foundations of traditional hermeneutics are eroded, as Shelley once again brings into the foreground the problems of communication, interpretation, and reading. Asia's conversant is no longer her sister but Demogorgon, a being who is sexually and ontologically other than her. The scene reflects on the opacities of communication, and though the explicit reader is not figured in the text, the reader's potentially negating presence emerges from the gaps and silences where the dialogue within the text fails to become a meeting of minds and thus reflects back on reading as dialogue. But the scene is only obliquely about the relationship of the implied to the explicit reader, and in fact is about something more radical which subtends this relationship: the relationship of the reader to the work itself. Ostensibly, the scene repeats the earlier one and ends with Asia as implied reader "producing" the meaning of Shelley's work when she acts on her perceptions and perceives in a positive light what is actually a very ambiguous event: the appearance of the two chariots that herald some momentous historical change. Ostensibly, then, it is the active mirror image of its contemplative counterpart: in the first scene Asia understands the work and articulates its vision; in the second scene she translates it from the sphere of expression to the sphere of events. But in fact the scene renders highly problematical the reading for which Asia serves as missionary, by dismantling our earlier security as to what the work says, and what the animating intention behind it is.

Crucial to this second scene is the figure of Demogorgon, a character who again seems an empty schema rather than a tangible personality. If Panthea was the means by which the reader made contact with the essence of the work and the spirit of its author, then Demogorgon is her antithesis: the means by which we recognize that the inner core of the work is absent, its voice "lacking," its cryptic and contradictory text all that there is. 'His' eyes cannot be read. 'His' curious lack of personality denies the possibility of communication except on a grammatological level, and indeed the inconclusive dialogue between Asia and Demogorgon often revolves around the signifier. It is halted by grammatical problems such as the specification of an antecedent to a pronoun, as in Asia's attempt to find out what is meant by "He reigns" (II.iv.28, 31, 32, *SPP*), and it is held up by the need to identify an abstraction that stands in place of someone whose identity we are never told, such as the destiny in the chariot (II.iv.146, *SPP*) or "God" (II.iv.112, *SPP*). Asia is once again the implied reader who believes in the sacred necessity of hope: the reader we might suppose to be desired by Shelley or by a part of him. As a dramatic character, she seeks a meeting with her creator or his intermediary that will allow her to understand the destiny of the created world. As implied reader, she seeks a fusion of horizons with the author that will enable her to grasp the essence of the work and then act on her intuition. But she succeeds in neither aim, for Demogorgon, apparently the originating or intending force behind the play's events, proves ungraspable. Consequently, what in the earlier scene was the "soul" of the work, the vision of hope discovered behind its flawed form and language, now becomes itself a linguistic construct. Meanwhile, the inner core of the work, which Asia was once able to read in Panthea's eyes, has disappeared, to be replaced by a vacancy. The scene therefore complicates severely a traditionally hermeneutic reading that allows the unity of the work to be potential rather than actual. The reconstruction of the original work encouraged in the dialogue with Panthea is presented as the reconstruction of a unity that may not be there, a passionately optimistic attempt to center something that is decentered and unfocused, having, like Demogorgon itself, neither "form—nor outline" (II.iv.6, *SPP*).

Crucial to the philosophic dismantling of hermeneutic reading is the rigorously antiphenomenological character of this episode. For the scene probes not only the authority possessed by individual acts and speech acts, but also the semiotics of the self in which action and language have their origin. Traditional hermeneutics assumes the existence of a transcendental ego, an essential core within us which gives value to our words and which is guaranteed by its link to a similar spirit on the level of the macrocosm. It is this ego that we had seemed to grasp in the dialogue between Panthea and Asia, whose shared discovery of identity enabled them also to grasp the Promethean spirit of the age. The figure of Demogorgon, however, deconstructs any notion of history as an organic manifestation of a spirit, a developing SUM or I AM. It casts in doubt the phenomenological notion of a *Geist* or world-historical spirit elaborated by Hegel and also assumed in such catch phrases as 'the spirit of the age.' Moreover, what this scene does on the level of the world-historical spirit a much earlier passage, which is explicitly linked to this scene by its introduction of Demogorgon, does on the level of the individual self. Close to the beginning of the play, in Earth's enigmatic description of how the Magus Zoroaster met his own image in the garden, Shelley already raises the question of what there is behind the possibly kaleidoscopic formation we call the individual. Ostensibly, the question is raised to dismantle the credibility of Jupiter by phantomizing him. But the implications of Earth's speech resonate through the rest of the play and unsettle our reaction to other characters and hence the authority of what they say and do. We are told by Earth that behind the flesh-and-blood forms of those who "think and live" is an appearance, not a reality: that the essential self is variously an image, a phantom, a "vacant" shade (I.198, 216, *SPP*).

> For know, there are two worlds of life and death:
> One that which thou beholdest, but the other
> Is underneath the grave, where do inhabit
> The shadows of all forms that think and live
>
> . . . .
>
> There thou art, and dost hang, a writhing shade
> . . . all the Gods
> Are there, and all the Powers of nameless worlds,
> Vast, sceptred phantoms;
>
> (I.195–206, *SPP*)

Moreover, as Shelley suggests in a canceled line, the encounter between the self and its other dooms us henceforth to interweave the two worlds of life and death, the ego and its deconstructed image.[15] Thus, it is not

[15]See ibid., p. 143. The canceled line following "For know there are two worlds of life and death" is "Which thou henceforth art doomed to interweave."

only Jove who becomes an echo within this ghost sonata, but Prometheus also, Demogorgon, and indeed everyone who thinks and lives. In Asia's visit to the cave, for instance, the thinking and living Demogorgon who will later overthrow Jove is dismantled before we meet him by our encounter with his vacant image, an encounter that exposes the later, active Demogorgon as a linguistic constitution. Although Prometheus in this play is not similarly dismantled by his shade, he is perplexingly absent from the drama he initiates. With the exception of one scene, act III, scene iii, he speaks only one line after act I (III.iv.97, *SPP*). Critics have sometimes rationalized the disappearance of the play's characterological center by seeing various secondary figures as projected parts of Prometheus, such that he is reassembled, like Albion, from his parts.[16] But this only makes us question whether what we call Prometheus is a holistic entity, or a conglomeration of selves. When he and Asia retreat to the cave at the end of act III, we must ask, is this the cave that like the hermeneutic circle conceals a potential totality to be brought to light by a sympathetic reader? Or is it, like the Cave of Demogorgon, the site of a return behind what Lacan calls the mirror-stage, to a space where we uncover the original self, a vacant sign as yet untenanted by author or reader?

Asia, indeed, does tenant the space vacated in this episode. The scene ends with Asia acting out her reading by ascending in the chariot of hope, following her own statement that in the absence of any ultimate meaning, one may make one's heart the oracle of its own truth. But this time we must consider more closely the status of the discourse of hope that she offers us as the hermeneutic matrix of the play. The long dialogue between Asia and Demogorgon begins with a theogony in which she places Prometheus' transformation as a moment in the phenomenology of the world-historical mind, thus also accounting for the Jovian age as a fortunate fall. It ends with her decision to see the arrival of the two chariots positively, which prepares the way for her reunion with Prometheus, and metaphorically for the union of the revolutionary mind with the material world. Thus, the scene might seem to encapsulate and reveal the entire action, the *arche* and *telos*, of the otherwise obscure Promethean drama. But if Asia starts from the assumption we have already encountered in Schelling, that the spirit of the work is a "voice unspoken" (II.i.191, *SPP*) that emerges in dialogue, the scene disturbingly challenges the hermeneutic conception of understanding. For what it offers us is a dialogue that is Lacanian in structure, a dia-

[16]See for instance Frederick A. Pottle, "The Role of Asia in the Dramatic Action of Shelley's Prometheus Unbound," in G. M. Ridenour, ed., *Shelley: A Collection of Critical Essays* (Englewood Cliffs, N.J.: Prentice-Hall, 1965), pp. 133–43.

logue that does not so much reveal the identity of the text as bring to light its difference from itself. Asia's redemptive theogony, as Stuart Curran has pointed out, is radically different from the cosmic history provided earlier by Earth, who suggests that there "never was a golden age, but only the continuous tyranny of Jupiter."[17] Though it is told in the past tense, Asia's account is no more than an interpretation. Crucial to its tenuous status is its dialogical setting, which in the relative silence of Demogorgon registers the possibility of another side to what is being said. That dialogue can function to accentuate our sense of language as difference was pointed out a long time ago by Harold Pinter, who suggests that "the speech we hear is an indication of that we don't hear. It is a necessary avoidance . . . which keeps the other in its place."[18] Indeed, Asia cannot quite avoid the other side of what she says, for the very length of her speech gives her space in which to complicate the idea of the Jovian age as a mere interregnum between the Saturnian and Promethean ages. It seems that Prometheus created Jupiter by giving him "wisdom, which is strength" (II.iv.44, *SPP*), even though Asia also claims that "Jove now reigned;" as though he is an autonomous entity (II.iv.49, *SPP*). The uncertainty about whether Jove is an external oppressor or a figure for some self-destructive potential within the human race leaves us unclear whether the "speech" and "Science" that Prometheus gives humankind in a second attempt at organized innocence (II.iv.71–75, *SPP*) will not recreate 'Jove.' And indeed that doubt is registered in Asia's description of the "legioned hopes" that Prometheus awakens as narcotics that "hide with thin and rainbow wings / The shape of Death" (II.iv.59–63, *SPP*).

As significant as the insecurity of Asia's theogony is the tenuous way in which the sisters construct a link between signifier and signified in the interpretation of the two chariots. For this scene, after all, initiates the resolution of the plot. Carlos Baker speaks for Asia and for a long critical tradition when he sees the chariots, one dark and one light, as intended for Demogorgon and Asia, respectively.[19] By associating Asia with the light chariot, and by making the force within the dark chariot serve the purposes of good, he sidesteps the possibility that the dark chariot may herald a second coming in which the center no longer holds. He makes destruction a prelude, rather than a Manichaean alternative to, construction. Yet the text is by no means so clear. Asia at first assumes that the dark chariot has come for her (II.iv.145, *SPP*), a possibility that the

[17] *Shelley's Annus Mirabilis* (San Marino, Calif.: Huntington Library, 1975), p. 40.

[18] "Between the Lines," *The Sunday Times*, 4 March 1962, p. 25.

[19] *Shelley's Major Poetry: The Fabric of a Vision* (Princeton, N.J.: Princeton University Press, 1948), p. 107; cf. also K. N. Cameron, "Political Symbolism of Prometheus Unbound," pp. 119–20.

spirit never actually denies, as he announces ominously that the reality of what he is, is worse than it appears: "I am the shadow of a destiny / More dread than is mine aspect—" (II.iv.146–47, *SPP*). Moreover, it is not certain whether "Heaven's kingless throne" (II.iv.149, *SPP*), which the dark charioteer threatens to demolish, refers to Jove's throne or to the authority of some power higher than Jove, whose overthrow might lead to total chaos. Although the spirit in the light chariot does announce that it has come to bear Asia to Prometheus (II.iv.168, *SPP*), the spirits, as we know from a canceled passage at the end of the act, may well be voices from a heart that is its own oracle. Again, the positive construction put on the scene's ending is no more than an interpretation, supplied, significantly, by Panthea and eagerly taken up by Asia. And again the silence of Demogorgon makes us aware of another side to this interpretation. Panthea, we recall, was earlier the author who functioned as a medium for "the gigantic shadows which futurity casts upon the present." But the author, to quote Roland Barthes, is now a "guest" in his own text, "inscribed . . . like one of his characters, figured in the carpet."[20]

The deconstructive reading encouraged by Asia's visit to the Cave of Demogorgon would see the play's hiatuses as dismantling its attempt at a transvaluation of values through a logocentric act of mythmaking. For the authority of mythmaking is eroded by the contrivances of which it makes use: by the disjunctive structure and characterization. But the reading urged earlier might see the very disjunctiveness of the text as something that antithetically stimulates the reader to break the hermeneutic circle and grasp the synthetic totality of the work across its negativity. It may seem that the play consumes the hermeneutic reading it offers. Or to put it differently, it may seem that the scene in Demogorgon's cave resists any attempt to reduce it to a concessive clause in the play's dramatic syntax. Indeed, my argument has been that hermeneutics contains the seed of its own deconstruction, because making the reader a mediating element allows for an explicit as well as for an implied reader, and so renders problematical any sentimental reconstitution of text as work. But the presence of the reader similarly complicates a deconstructive interpretation, because the explicit reader may, after all, follow a range of reconstructive options from sympathetic understanding to demythologization.

The plethora of choices available to us is nowhere more evident than in the play's method of characterization as it guides us, again equivocally, to seek or resist a phenomenological understanding. It is helpful here to distinguish between allegorical and psychological or symbolic character-

[20]*Image, Music, Text*, trans. Stephen Heath (New York: Hill and Wang, 1977), p. 161.

ization, using the distinction between symbol and allegory as de Man uses it with reference to rhetorical figures.[21] Shelley's method of characterization, for the most part, is allegorical. Jove, the Furies, the various spirits, and Earth, are conventionally allegorical characters. Prometheus and Demogorgon are more complex. They have the abstractness, the hollowing out of "individuality," that Hegel sees as natural to allegorical characters (*A*, II, 1177), and the concomitant emphasis on character as actant rather than personality, signifier rather than signified. But if their characterization manifests the split between tenor and vehicle proper to allegory as a figure, the tenor is less clearly specified than in the case of the other characters. Still, they, too, are products of an allegorical characterization that decenters personality, by splitting the discourse in which the subject manifests itself from the originating subjectivity behind the words, and giving us only the former. Allegorical characterization seems the logical extension of the semiotics of selfhood that emerges from the play's two encounters between the magian ego and its empty origin. But Asia and Panthea, on the other hand, are somewhat different: personalities rather than signifiers. Shelley's characterization is nowhere realistic, but these two figures, who are not dramatically fissured in the manner of Prometheus and Demogorgon, are drawn symbolically rather than allegorically. There is no split between discourse and self, and the words of the sisters therefore provide us with immediate access to the inner core of their psyches. The allegorical subject is a schema that we know through a relatively conventionalized discourse and not in its interiority. This method of characterization, which makes the various characters into constructs rather than persons, cuts against the psychological identification between the reader and the central voice(s) in the text crucial to hermeneutic understanding. Allegorical characters can only be read grammatologically, though in a framework that may be either structuralist or poststructuralist. But psychological characters, whether realistic or symbolic, demand a phenomenological reading. Since it is partly through its characters that one grasps the identity of a dramatic text, the play's ambiguous method of characterization leaves its identity in doubt.

This is not to say that a hermeneutic reading offers us the key to the play. The text itself clearly undermines the epistemological authority of such a reading, though it supports its ethical authority. But the reinscription of the hermeneutic as desire displaces us from any schematic use of deconstruction. Indeed, one might argue that a third approach is

[21]Paul de Man, "The Rhetoric of Temporality," *Blindness and Insight: Essays in the Rhetoric of Contemporary Criticism*, rev. ed. (Minneapolis: University of Minnesota Press, 1983), pp. 187–208.

suggested in Shelley's representation of the text as drama, as performance: a designation with profoundly antimetaphysical consequences. With Asia's decision to interpret the arrival of the chariot positively, the play seems to move to an optimistic conclusion. Indeed, Harold Bloom complains that in "Act IV the imagination of Shelley breaks away from the poet's apparent intention, and visualizes a world in which the veil of phenomenal reality has been rent."[22] More precisely, it is after act II, scene iv, rather than after act III that the play makes its great imaginative leap, electing quite consciously to produce the meaning of the play according to one particular version. Yet if we are to understand the status of the play's discourse beginning with Asia's ascent in the chariot, we must understand its relationship to the earlier part of the play. The second or active half of the play stands in relation to the first reflective or reflexive part rather as a dramatic performance stands in relation to the script that elicits it.[23] The relationship between script and performance is not strictly symmetrical, because a performance is a production of the script, not a reproduction related to the script as a photograph to its negative (as Asia might like us to believe on her emergence from the Cave of Demogorgon). Script and performance exist in different spaces, the former being intentional and complex, the latter being a concrete actualization, which succeeds in being such only by a deliberate act of simplification: by repressing the traces of alternative performances that exist in the intentional space of script. What this means, given that the individual production of a play is personally and historically variable, is that Shelley's *Prometheus* as script is open to the deconstructive production that as performance it chooses to exclude. Or to put it differently, his staging of the Promethean myth in the theater of his mind has, as performance, the status of a concrete possibility: it is more than a merely abstract potentiality, but less than a reality. Shelley himself suggests in the preface that he is aware of his play as a performance. It is in the nature of drama, he argues, to use a certain "arbitrary discretion" in its reworking of inherited subject matter, to produce rather than reproduce an action (*SPP*, p. 132). Moreover, he concedes that his production of the myth is historically limited, being an effect of culturally conditioned tropes of understanding that operate through the individual: "Poets, not otherwise than philosophers, painters, sculptors and musicians, are in one sense the creators and in another the creations of their

[22]*The Ringers in the Tower: Studies in Romantic Tradition* (Chicago: University of Chicago Press, 1971), p. 96.

[23]For a discussion of the relationship between script and performance see Keir Elam, *The Semiotics of Theatre and Drama* (London: Methuen, 1980), pp. 208–9; see also Terry Eagleton, *Criticism and Ideology: A Study in Marxist Literary Theory* (London: Verso Editions, 1978), pp. 64–66.

age" (*SPP*, p. 135). That the Shelleyan version is formed by the spirit of the age (a more romantic term for what we now refer to as "discursive formations") is the source of its momentary authority and also of its vulnerability. But the fact that the gospel according to Asia is performance and not metalanguage has another side to it. For it means that any interpretation of the play is also not metalanguage but performance: or as Josué Harari puts it: "any theory of the text *is itself text*."[24]

That the plot as a performance of the myth cannot be reified into an imitation of an action is a point that can be further clarified if we borrow the distinction between story and discourse made, among others, by Seymour Chatman.[25] The story comprises the actual events of the narrative, while the term 'discourse' refers to a telling and thus an interpretation of the events. But the discourse of *this* play is ungrounded in a story. For the story of who invested Jupiter with power and of what the limits and extent of that power are is never clarified, because the various cosmogonic fictions provided only serve to complicate the matter further. Indeed, the story of Prometheus' forgiveness of Jove, the most pivotal event in the play, is also unclear, for all we really know is how Prometheus tells the story of his attitude to Jove from l. 59 onward, but not what actually happens within his psyche. For instance, only a few minutes before he announces that the quality of mercy is not strained, Prometheus vengefully pictures Jove being forced to kiss his bloody feet (I.49–52, *SPP*). One may argue that this is before the crucial recantation, though the transformation is too instantaneous to be wholly persuasive. But several lines after Prometheus' spiritual transformation, in his confrontation with the Furies, he appears still to feel the darker emotions of which we thought him purged and describes his mastery over these emotions by disturbingly paralleling it to the repressiveness of Jove: "Yet am I king over myself, and rule / The torturing and conflicting throngs within / As Jove rules you when Hell grows mutinous" (I.492–94, *SPP*). Thus we do not know whether line 59 states an intention or an actuality, and whether the optative mode ("the Curse / Once breathed on thee I would recall") is used because Prometheus has not yet met the phantasm of Jupiter or because he has not yet become fully capable of forgiveness. In other words, we do not know what happens at line 59, and know only how Shelley later stages the meaning of the play. The displacement of the action from story to discourse, from signified to

[24]Josué V. Harari, "Critical Factions/Critical Fictions," in *Textual Strategies* (Ithaca, N.Y.: Cornell University Press, 1979), p. 40.

[25]*Story and Discourse: Narrative Structure in Fiction and Film* (Ithaca, N.Y.: Cornell University Press, 1978), pp. 1, 19–22. For a critique of the Platonic dualism implicit in Chatman's distinction see Barbara Herrnstein Smith, "Afterthoughts on Narrative," in W. J. T. Mitchell, ed., *On Narrative* (Chicago: University of Chicago Press, 1980), pp. 209–32.

signifier, is crucial to Shelley's emergent recognition that if the text of desire is to be saved, it can be saved only as performance and not as mimesis.

One indication of Shelley's willingness to untie the text he actually published is the curious organization of the manuscript in the Bodleian library, possibly one on which he worked both before and after publication.[26] It begins with act IV and proceeds to alternate act I on the left-hand side of the page with the remainder of act IV on the right-hand side. The manuscript continues up to the middle of II.ii, then alternates part of the third scene on the left side with the remainder of the second scene on the right, and finally places the remainder of the third scene (the song of the Spirits) on the left-hand side alongside the crucial dialogue in the Cave of Demogorgon (II.iv).[27] Textual scholars have explained away the state of the manuscript by suggesting that it is an intermediate draft in which Shelley transcribed the first three acts and then inserted the fourth act, known to be an afterthought, "wherever there happened to be a vacancy."[28] Yet the mechanical explanation does not entirely clarify why he left several pages at the beginning of the notebook blank, if he was not toying with the idea of putting something there. Still less does it explain why the unweaving of the play's linear

[26]Zillman, *Shelley's Prometheus Unbound*, p. 12.

[27]The Bodleian manuscript consists of three notebooks. MS E1 begins with act IV and proceeds for 427 lines, slightly beyond Earth's ode on humanity as "one harmonious soul of many a soul" to some lines spoken by the Moon. At this point Shelley commences act I on the left-hand pages and continues to insert the remainder of act IV on the right-hand side. This notebook ends in the middle of the scene involving the Furies. MS E2, at least equally confusing, begins with the remainder of act I on the left-hand side. Several pages on the right side are left blank, and it is not until he reaches the middle of act II, scene ii, that Shelley again returns to his dizzying practice of dividing the play between the two sides of the notebook. Having placed all of the dialogue between Asia and Panthea and part of the next scene (II.ii.1–63: the semichorus of Spirits) on the left side, Shelley suddenly shifts the remainder of II.ii to the right-hand side. Thus the first part of II.iii, Asia's conversation with Panthea as they approach the volcano, is placed on the left side, beside the remainder of II.ii (the dialogue between the Fauns: ll. 64ff.). The second half of scene ii does not occupy as much space as the first half of scene iii, and Shelley therefore leaves one of the right-hand pages blank as he continues scene iii up to the end of Panthea's and Asia's conversation (II.iii.53). The remainder of scene iii is now shifted from the left to the right-hand side. Thus the crucial interview between Asia and Demogorgon (II.iv) now occupies the left side, while the remainder of scene iii (the song of the Spirits: ll. 54ff.) is juxtaposed opposite it. MS E2 ends in the middle of II.iv. MS E3, far simpler in its disposition of the play, begins at II.iv.124 and continues straightforwardly to the end of act III, sometimes but not always leaving the right-hand pages blank for corrections.

[28]C. D. Locock, *An Examination of the Shelley Manuscripts in the Bodleian Library* (Oxford: Clarendon, 1903), pp. 28–29. Zillman also points out that the transcription of act IV begins before that of act I. But his account of the remaining acts makes them sound simpler than they are: "This act (I) was completed on page 20^v, with Act II following on 21^v and continuing to the end of the book (page 43^v, line II.iv.74). Again Shelley continued directly into the next notebook (E.3), with the next line of Act II starting on page 1^v and ending on 10^v" (p. 22).

succession is continued through the disarrangement of the second act. The redeployment of the parts of act I, moreover, is not just eccentric. The second and third scenes are split at logical points, and from the middle of the second scene onward the effect is antiphonal. Lyrical scenes are divided from and juxtaposed with dramatic ones. The lyrical segments are separated and transposed to the right-hand side, as if to stage a confrontation between the imaginary world projected by desire and the greater complexities of the linguistic order.

The manuscript is therefore quite different from the published text. For the linear action of the latter may seem to distinguish it from the 'open' texts described by Umberto Eco, which "the author seems to hand . . . on to the performer more or less like the components of a construction kit."[29] Indeed, it would be wrong to say that Shelley's text is ever completely open, that he is unconcerned about its "eventual deployment,"[30] and it would be more accurate to say that he places a model for the text's deployment within a structure that exposes it as problematic. Nevertheless, the mobile text that emerges from the manuscript dissolves space and time, juxtaposing different temporal planes and placing the cancellation of the Hours alongside the period of Prometheus' enchainment. One is reminded of Shelley's statement that pronouns and tenses are grammatical intrusions (*SPP*, p. 483), and of the many romantic projects for dissolving boundaries, whether they be between different spatiotemporal orders or between different perceptual modes. Indeed, as in Blake's later prophecies, the impulse behind this aesthetic and temporal syncretism is partly to redeem time by making all time eternally present. But one may also be reminded of Nietzsche's statement that to abolish grammar might finally be to get rid of God.[31] For the cubist disassembling of the text radically upsets our sense of a fixed perspective on events. The interpretive results of placing the last act at the beginning, for instance, are by no means easy to discern. It may occupy a prefatory position and inform us how to read the play. Or it may project a lyrical vision, only to parody the dangers of moving too quickly to the end of the play by exposing the perilous underpinning of this vision in the preceding three acts. That parts of the play can be placed in different spatial positions emphasizes that every event must be viewed in more than one way. For instance, Demogorgon's exuberant addresses to the Earth, the moon, and the "happy dead" (IV.524ff.) must seem curiously hollow when placed, in a kind of collage, opposite

[29]*The Role of the Reader: Explorations in the Semiotics of Texts* (Bloomington: Indiana University Press, 1984), p. 49.

[30]Ibid.

[31]*Twilight of the Idols*, in *Twilight of the Idols and The Anti-Christ*, trans. R. J. Hollingdale (Harmondsworth: Penguin, 1968), p. 38.

the Magus Zoroaster's encounter with his own shadow and the subsequent disclosure that Demogorgon, too, is no more than a shadow. Similarly, the song of the Spirits, with its movement beyond the veil of life and death, is set against the equivocal conversation between Asia and Demogorgon, and displaced into the vacant pages used for corrections and afterthoughts. It thus loses its lyrical immediacy and becomes an echo of itself, the object of a Brechtian alienation effect. Again and again, it is as though the play is quoting itself and reducing mimesis and voice to text. But the odd juxtapositions do not necessarily work toward dismantling the Promethean drama. The conjunction of the last and first act, like one of those windows into eternity of which Blake speaks, can also be seen as opening up a vista that act I by itself denies us, thus reducing act I to quotation. It is as if copying out the text without preparing it for print freed Shelley to compose and decompose it, so as to dissolve in his mind any illusion that the form he finally gave it was inevitable.

It is appropriate to conclude with some theoretical reflections. The idea of the text as performance, while it accommodates a hermeneutic reading, is philosophically very different from the reading dramatized in the dialogue between Asia and Panthea, which assumes that we can grasp the identity of the text. But as I have already suggested, traditional hermeneutics contains the traces that lead to its own deconstruction, as to some extent does poststructuralism. Both contain tendencies to reify interpretation that are at odds with their insistence that we intertextualize fiction and reality. Hermeneutics, as we have seen, requires that literature enter the world of communication in order to be brought to life, yet clings to a dualism of work and text that makes the work an essence unchanged by its existence in the communicative process. Poststructuralism, on the other hand, de-idealizes the notion of literature as a special form of language, protected by a dualism that privileges it above other forms of discourse. But it often ends by underprivileging literary discourse, thus reverting to a dualism that denies language the power to affect reality. I have suggested here that what *Prometheus Unbound* responds to is an approach that intertextualizes fiction and 'reality,' and recognizes that they mutually make and remake each other. But the attempt to construct this approach from interpretive interludes in the play and from the theory of the romantic period itself marks a reluctance to engage in the ahistorical and paradigmatic reading that Frank Lentricchia criticized in Yale deconstruction:[32] reading that assumes that the interpretation of a particular text is a paradigm for the interpretation of all other texts. *Prometheus Unbound* is a particular kind

[32]*After the New Criticism* (Chicago: University of Chicago Press, 1980), pp. 310–17.

of text, and a strictly poststructuralist approach may well be appropriate for a different kind of text such as the French *nouveau roman.* As a play that has elements of political allegory, it belongs with works like Blake's *Songs* and prophecies, the reformist novels of Godwin and Wollstonecraft, even Wordsworth's *Prelude*: in other words, with works that assume the interaction of fiction and sociopolitical reality, fiction and personal life. But as a text that claims some relationship between literature and history, it also recognizes its own vulnerability to having its significance constituted differently by different readers. For the semiotics of theater is not identical with the semiotics of the book, the former being a performance that is subject to change. In choosing the mode of drama, Shelley departs from *Alastor* to set his work in the space of historical difference and forfeits for it the closure of a classic that can codify its message. To adapt a phrase from "Mont Blanc," the text "governs thought" but does not originate it: it remains a presence in the world, but no longer one that can institutionalize meaning.

CHAPTER TWELVE

The Broken Mirror: The Identity of the Text in Shelley's *Triumph of Life*

In *Prometheus Unbound* Shelley goes as far as he can in separating the pragmatic from the metaphysical, the positive activity of reading or more properly acting out, from what he sees as the deconstructive activity of writing. But there is something evasive about this solution. Denying that reading can return us to a point of origin, the play nevertheless affirms that it can enact a work identical with itself. For in making his text into a play, Shelley allegorizes reading as performance rather than interpretation, a discourse that legitimizes itself by doing what it says rather than by conveying an anterior and provable truth. At the end of her encounter with Demogorgon, Asia gives up the attempt to interpret anything and simply acts as if certain suppositions were true. We are not bound by these suppositions, since the fourth act is a masque that knows itself to be sustained only by Demogorgon's rough magic.[1] Yet if we stand back from the play, we begin to sense that *Prometheus Unbound* only represents a solution. For the notion of reading as performance ignores the fact that there is no such thing as an act of pure will unmediated by language. Or to put it differently, it avoids recognizing that performance also occurs in a linguistic world. Indeed, in one of the manuscript versions of the *Defence* Shelley sees perception or poetry, expression or art, and "invention" or "the application of art" to knowledge and use, as gradations of the same power, thus implying that they

[1] For a discussion of how the lyrical elements in Shelley's lyrical drama, particularly in the fourth act, provide a Dionysiac undertow that threatens to dissolve the Apollonian fiction, see Ross Woodman, "Nietzsche, Blake and Shelley: The Making of a Metaphorical Body," *Studies in Romanticism* 29 (Spring 1990).

must be structurally similar.[2] By this token, the attempt of romantic hermeneutics to reverse the negativity of the text at the level of expression by a reading that returns to the original 'perception' behind expression or by one that applies art to knowledge and use seems highly problematic. For although psychological and applicative reading are different from grammatical reading and from the rhetorical reading that has replaced exegesis in an era that no longer regards expression as stable, their very real qualitative difference is, so to speak, constituted on the trace of their structural similarity. To read on the psychological and applicative as well as the rhetorical level is to restore the affective (or emotive) and the referential power of literature. But that is not to suggest that emotion and action are less complex than verbal language, more easily decipherable, more self-identical.

Shelley concedes as much when he describes the performance of the fourth act as a "perpetual Orphic song, / Which rules with Daedal harmony a throng / Of thoughts and forms, which else senseless and shapeless were" (IV. 415–17). Action, whether it be acting out something in the theater of the mind or acting in the stage of the world, is here seen as a will to power, a surface orientation given to a state of mind more complex and conflicting than we represent it as being. It involves a process of substitution and abstraction by which we make one act represent a differential complex of motives. That all performative readings are thus deconstructible is something that Shelley in *Prometheus Unbound* considers as a philosophical problem but brackets as an experiential problem. How to preserve the psychological and applicative dimension of literature without engaging in an abstract compartmentalization of the practical and the metaphysical is thus the problem that he must work through in *The Triumph of Life*. For the use of drama in *Prometheus* has two rather different implications, both of which a phenomenology of disarticulation must comprehend as symbiotically related. In moving from the first scene of reading, which lyricizes dialogue by creating a unity between two different voices, to the second scene, which focuses on dialogue as difference, Shelley recognizes dialogue and drama as the dissemination of unitary vision. On the other hand, drama is not quite the same thing as dialogue, nor is the play reducible to what happens in the Cave of Demogorgon. For theater also disseminates vision in a quite different sense: it produces ideas, materializes them on the stage of the world.

In *Prometheus* Shelley elides the difference within drama, subsuming one form of dissemination into the other. In *The Triumph of Life* he

[2]Shelley, *A Defence of Poetry*, in John E. Jordan, ed., *A Defence of Poetry and The Four Ages of Poetry* (Indianapolis: Bobbs-Merrill, 1965), p. 31n.

returns to this aporia to ask whether language can produce meaning if its very process effaces it. The Car of Life with its procession of historical figures seems to represent the language of events as a chain of substitutions: one figure merely taking the place of another in a way that will make us, too, into figures if we follow Rousseau's injunction to try and enact meaning within the text (ll. 305–8, *SPP*). These figures are repeatedly described as shadows or phantoms, as if the vision being rolled on our brains is of the twilight of the idols, the fading of the subject (ll. 251, 253, 289, 487–88, 534, *SPP*). But they are also the "mighty phantoms of an elder day" (l. 253, *SPP*), traces of a cultural grammatology in which the erasure of figures remains entangled in their survival. Turning toward the past instead of the future, the poem asks us to read these traces: to become mirrors of the gigantic shadows that the past still casts on the present even as it is being effaced.

Reinscribing Difference: Speech, Dialogue, and Dia-logos

At first sight, *The Triumph of Life* seems simply to dismantle the assumptions of *Prometheus Unbound*. Not only does it recapitulate negatively such motifs as the chariot of the hour; as a fragment it aborts meaning, where as theater *Prometheus* produced it. No analysis of the poem can now ignore the seminal essay by Paul de Man that sees the diegetic level of the text as preempting all attempts to approach it thematically. All interpretations of the poem hitherto have assumed that it 'says' something, that it has a content other than the processes of its own language. Such interpretations would include those of Bloom and Woodman, who make the poem didactic or apocalyptic, viewing it as a critique of Rousseau for having been seduced by nature and perhaps as a rejection of life in the manner of *Adonais*. But they would also include more recent ones like my own in *Dark Interpreter*, which deconstructs the binary oppositions crucial to earlier readings only to make the poem's indeterminacy the regenerative prelude to what it does not quite succeed in saying. My reading elides the fragmentary status of the poem and provides a hermeneutic completion for it by arguing that it is in the process of rehabilitating Rousseau. His shifting view of himself is thus explained by the fact that he is in transit from the Platonic repudiation of the phenomenal world associated with the sacred few to an existential embrace of life in which activity is its own Sisyphean reward.[3] Describing

[3]Harold Bloom, *Shelley's Mythmaking* (1959; rpt. Ithaca, N.Y.: Cornell University Press, 1969), pp. 220–75; Ross Woodman, *The Apocalyptic Vision in the Poetry of Shelley* (Toronto: University of Toronto Press, 1964), pp. 180–98. Woodman's argument is characteristic of

a range of interpretations that either view the movement of the poem as negative (a rejection of life) or positive (a discarding of old positions in order to work through to new ones), de Man dismisses them as captive to an idealizing genetic metaphor, which insists that there is psychological growth in the poem, that it moves toward some insight. Instead, he shifts his attention to its rhetoric, which he characterizes in terms of erasure, disfiguration, the syntax tying itself into a knot. In figuring the poem as a scene of reading in the larger setting of Western culture, de Man sees it as challenging the hermeneutic foundations of that culture, which represents reading as the recovery of something meaningful and its application to the life of the reader, and which thus places texts as spots of time to which we can repair for increased self-understanding.[4]

The power of de Man's essay lies in his exposure of the ways in which previous readings have made something out of the poem without attending to its most pervasive feature: the status of a language unable either to state or to perform anything that is not already different from itself. Yet it remains to be seen whether the poem's lack of 'identity' renders it 'unreadable' or brings into being a reconception of the supplement of reading. For one thing, de Man (as he would be the first to admit) *has* provided a 'reading,' by making form take the place of a vanishing content through a hypostasis of the poem's method. Or to put it differently, even this text, which asks to be approached diegetically rather than mimetically, has a referent, that referent being the process of the poem itself. If we grant that de Man has provided a reading, the issue raised by his concept of unreadability is not whether the poem has any meaning, but whether the way it foregrounds its own discourse invalidates its power to create something meaning*ful*. Put differently, the issue is whether the poem still permits reading as it is understood by the developing tradition of hermeneutics discussed in this book. The greatest challenge to answering this question affirmatively is not the language of the posthumously printed text but the tangle of the manuscript in which Shelley himself left the poem. De Man does not refer to the manuscript except in passing, but it plays an important symbolic role in his reading, the mutilated text becoming a disfiguration of any attempt to read Shelley or to read Shelley as a paradigm of romanticism. As a synecdoche for Shelley's drowned body, which is inscribed in its last page, the manuscript thwarts our attempts to incorporate the scandal of disfiguration into literary history.[5] We could speculate that if de Man

a certain phase of romantic criticism but is unlikely to represent his view now. Tilottama Rajan, *Dark Interpreter: The Discourse of Romanticism* (Ithaca, N.Y.: Cornell University Press, 1980), pp. 58–71.

[4]Paul de Man, "Shelley Disfigured," in Harold Bloom, Paul de Man, et al., *Deconstruction and Criticism* (New York: Continuum, 1979), pp. 39–74. See esp. pp. 39–42, 44–46.

[5]Ibid., p. 67.

had discussed its details, it would have become the trace left by an irreducible aporia at the heart of language and the site of our submission to that aporia. Thus, any attempt to re-vision the poem's discourse must deal not only with its language but also with the intervention made by the manuscript in the institutional structures of literary criticism.

Our discussion of the poem will focus on how it functions: on its repetitions, its syntax, and on its foregrounding of speech over writing, as elements that create differences within the rhetoric of erasure, so that disfiguration is not just the effacement of figures but also the production of new figures. In many ways this discussion subsumes my own previous analysis, which saw Shelley's poem as generated by a process of self-revision. Crucial to that analysis was the unsettling of a pattern of binary oppositions by which earlier readings had schematized the poem so as to criticize Rousseau for participating in life. Such oppositions included those between the sacred few and the multitude that was not wise enough to avoid life (ll. 128–37, *SPP*); between the bards of elder time and Rousseau himself, whose lack of distance from the world he wanted to change resulted in his infecting his audience with his own misery (ll. 274–81, *SPP*); and most importantly between the two shapes, the shape all light generated by the spark with which heaven initially lit Rousseau's spirit, and the shape in the car that replaced it when he put on the "disguise" of life. There is no question that the text is profoundly ambivalent about "Life," and that that ambivalence disrupts not only the earlier view that the poem was written by a 'Platonic' rather than 'radical' Shelley,[6] but also the recent emphasis on its semiotic nihilism. But instead of embedding that ambivalence in a genetic narrative that absorbs aporia into the dialectic of Rousseau's (and the poet's) maturation, I will assume that my earlier reading is a heuristic construction. It must therefore be reinscribed in the text that generates it, and is present in the text only as a trace and not as what Godwin called the poem's 'tendency.' The details of this reading are less important than the linguistic processes that make it possible, while also generating the kind of reading provided by de Man. And these processes, too complex to be summed up in the term 'effacement,'[7] are in some form intrinsic to all poetic narrative, even though they may be foregrounded in this poem. But the details of the reading are also not unimportant. For the eschewing of the thematic in favor of the figural elides both the possibility that the nature of the figural may be altered by what we pick out as being (dis)figured, and the recognition that much Yale poststructuralism takes form as a thematics

[6] I borrow this distinction from Milton Wilson, *Shelley's Later Poetry: A Study of his Prophetic Imagination* (New York: Columbia University Press, 1959), pp. 176–77.

[7] For a discussion of the concepts of face and effacement, see de Man, "Shelley Disfigured," p. 46.

of figures: in other words, as a reading that can be challenged thematically as well as linguistically.

For the sake of convenience, we can divide the poem into three sections: an opening segment in which 'Shelley' falls asleep in a transfigured natural landscape only to witness its transformation into the dismal scene of the procession; a dialogue between him and Rousseau in which the latter describes in detail the significance of the same procession; and a dream narrative that describes an experience parallel to 'Shelley's' initial experience, namely, the transformation of the shape all light that Rousseau conceived at the moment of his creative birth into the shape in the chariot with its attendant procession. On the most obvious level the poem tells a characteristic romantic story about the collapse of illusion. Its return (three times) to the procession emphasizes in an emblematic way the chariot that erases hope and the chain of historical figures without origin or end. But the fact that the poem's title does not specify whose triumph it details (that of Life over humankind, or the triumph that is life, the triumph of surviving) suggests that it cannot simply be reduced to its most traumatic images: the car that wipes out what preceded it as the shape obliterates Rousseau, and the procession of disfigured dancers who follow it. These are in turn the figures that de Man uses to represent figuration and must be set against other images whose presence suggests that language is a form of the unconscious, and that so far we have only succeeded in representing, not in understanding it. Among these other images are the car's "creative ray" (l. 533, *SPP*); the association of life with dance, music, and embroidery (ll. 98, 110, 142, 448, *SPP*); and the image of life as a cleaving apart that sculpts the "marble brow of youth," allowing form to emerge only through disfiguration (l. 523, *SPP*).

We can locate the poem's indeterminacy partly in its repetitions: the repetition of the procession; the repetition of 'Shelley' as Rousseau; the temporal repetition of Rousseau's life in the form of a retrospective narration; and finally the repetition of Rousseau's attempt to understand the core experience of the transformation of something beautiful into something hideous in the discursive form of a conversation with 'Shelley,' and in the symbolic form of a dream sequence unimpeded by conceptual filters. Because the poem is a dream, its repetitive organization suggests an incomplete attempt at mastery: an attempt that we repeat each time we interpret the poem. Blocking progress, the figure of reading as repetition halts any attempt at the teleological completion of the poem. But though repetition may be intended to confirm trauma, it also allows reading-again to become the production of differences. We do not repeat something in different words if we mean to say exactly the same thing. Repetition implies the insufficiency of what was said: we repeat because there is still something more to be said, something more to be read in the political unconscious whose shadows are mirrored in this poem. Moreover, the attempt to understand the poem's core experience is repeated by Rousseau at different stages of his life: as the young man who experiences the transformation of the shape, as the older man who remembers it, and as the subject in dialogue with Shelley, in conversation with a future that discloses new perspectives to him even as it seems to close itself against him. It is repeated by 'Shelley,' both as the autonomously later subject who sees the procession, and then as the subject in dialogue with the past who re-views the procession in his conversation with Rousseau. By repeating itself at different points on a personal and on a historical axis, by allowing these axes to intersect in different ways, the poem generates more than one perspective from which we can view it and gives to the repetition that is reading a complex and still unfinished historical dimension.

The Triumph is organized so as to foreground repetition on a narrative level and so as to make it a figure for understanding. But the poem's structure simply raises to a level of self-consciousness what is a feature of all extensive utterance: namely, a tendency to repeat along different axes, to illustrate concepts through figures or fables, or conversely to reduce symbols or narratives to conceptual paraphrases. We become aware of how the poem is complicated by such micrological repetitions in the very first segment. For the most part 'Shelley' describes the followers of the car with condescension and takes the view that their error is involvement in life. But his argument is constantly disarticulated by the figures he uses to convey it, this despite his attachment to similes, which maintain a formal commitment to the exact equivalence of image and referent. For instance, in dismissing the procession he tells us that it includes:

> All but the sacred few who could not tame
> Their spirits to the Conqueror, but as soon
> As they had touched the world with living flame
>
> Fled back like eagles to their native noon.
> (ll. 128–31, *SPP*)

This binary opposition between the multitude who are captivated by life and those who see through it is more explicitly unsettled in Rousseau's account of the procession. But even here it is undermined by the description of the sacred few as "fleeing," Thel-like, from the generative world, and by the fact that the noon of transphenomenal vision that they embrace only seems to be outside the temporal cycle. And on the other hand, the dancers in the procession are described with an energy and vitality that belies their portrayal as part of a sad pageantry. One example is the account of how they are destroyed by their own desire for life. To begin with, they are described as moths attracted by the light (ll. 153–54, *SPP*), but then they are paralleled to

> . . . two clouds into one vale impelled
> That shake the mountains when their lightnings mingle
> And die in rain.
>
> (ll. 155–57, *SPP*)

The second simile displaces the first by continuing its emphasis on self-destruction but making this a generative rather than a futile activity: productive of rain that will fertilize the land. This is only one example of how a statement is unraveled by its multiplied figurative repetition and how the process of articulation generates new perceptions about the car's followers which refigure the pageant of error as a vital and Dionysiac dance.

The dialogue of text and subtext in 'Shelley's' monologue generates quite naturally his repetition of himself in the person of Rousseau and his placing of himself in a dialogical setting. Rousseau seems at first to confirm 'Shelley's' rejection of life. But a measure of how unsettled his position is is the discrepancy between his initial advice to 'Shelley,' "Forbear / To join the dance" (ll. 188–89, *SPP*), and his later suggestion that involvement is the only means to understand it:

> "But follow thou, and from spectator turn
> Actor or victim in this wretchedness
>
> "And what thou wouldst be taught I then may learn
> From thee.—
>
> (ll. 305–8, *SPP*)

Nor does Rousseau's account of the procession simply duplicate 'Shelley's,' for the participants are now named and individualized, which makes it difficult to dismiss them as an anonymous multitude. The roll call of names, moreover, includes all the great figures of Western culture and leaves us wondering who the "few" who have avoided life might be. Bacon, compared in the manuscript to an eagle and thus imagistically linked to the sacred few,[8] is in the procession, as is Napoleon with his

[8]References to the manuscript are to Donald Reiman, ed., "*The Triumph of Life*: A Facsimile of Shelley's Holograph Draft," *The Bodleian Shelley Manuscripts: A Facsimile Edition, with Full Transcriptions and Scholarly Apparatus*, vol. I (New York: Garland, 1986).

"eagle's pinion" (l. 222, *SPP*). But it now seems to be Bacon's error that like the sacred few he wanted more than the phenomenal world and tried to force "The Proteus shape of Nature" to yield him a truth (ll. 269–71, *SPP*). Socrates, once exempt from the procession, seems to enter it vicariously through Plato, who "Expiates the joy and woe his master knew not" (l. 255, *SPP*), as if Plato's very inferiority is a greater knowledge and Socrates' superiority a sin. Plato, moreover, has been conquered by "love" (l. 258, *SPP*), not something for which we can criticize him, especially since Socrates in avoiding woe was also ignorant of joy. Though repeating 'Shelley's' account of the procession, Rousseau's is actually quite different. One could do an extensive thematic analysis of the section, showing how as he speaks, Rousseau creates a space in which he can think and in which he can unravel not only his earlier radicalism but also his present condemnation of himself for having entered life. It is specifically the diacritical nature of dialogue which causes it to unsettle and generate penumbral positions, for the presence of the other person makes us recognize that we are other than what we are, and yet that we are not the other or the other's perception of us. But my concern is also with a characteristic linguistic feature of the poem, which complicates the movement of syntactic erasure. I have in mind the way in which negative statements are constituted on the trace of positive ones, or to be more precise, the way in which negative statements are in their turn negated, so as to produce the trace of something positive, though only as a shadow that futurity casts upon the present.

We notice how often the trace of self-assertion is masked within Rousseau's statement that he is *not* something, or to put it differently, how often erasure generates a construction, both in terms of syntax and in terms of the syntax of identity and action. A significant example is the passage on the bards of elder time, which has been edited differently by Mary Shelley and by Donald Reiman, thus raising the ancillary question of how the state of the manuscript affects our attempts to (de)construct the poem's significance. Mary Shelley's version, as Reiman's transcription indicates, was deleted, though less definitively than he implies. However, I begin with it partly because it was the text that most people read until Reiman published his reading text of the poem in the 1977 Norton critical edition. Moreover, given the unfinished state of this poem, in which convenient deletions are not always made and final intentions are hard to extract, no deletion can be sufficiently absolute to counteract the material force of the manuscript as a palimpsest in which the trace of an earlier version survives in emendations that repeat and displace it. For instance:

"See the great bards of elder time, who quelled

"The passions which they sung, as by their strain
May well be known: their living melody
Tempers its own contagion to the vein

"Of those who are infected with it—I
Have suffered what I wrote, or viler pain!
And so my words have seeds of misery—

"Even as the deeds of others, not as theirs."
And then he pointed to a company.
(ll. 274–82)[9]

Grammatically, these lines are destabilized by a curious tension between Rousseau's statement that he is *not* the equal of the bards and the self-assertive position of the personal pronoun in l. 278, which prevents them from neatly settling into a representation of Rousseau as inferior. Entangled in the next line (279) is a sense that Rousseau has suffered more than the bards and thus is *not* as great as them, but also has lived at a greater intensity. Even more interesting are lines 280–81. They castigate Rousseau for writing words that have destructive consequences in the world of action and therefore are "not as theirs," not like the tranquilizing words of the bards. Yet this does not exhaust the meaning of "not as theirs," which dangles oddly at the end of the line, attempting to erase the forceful impression of what Rousseau *has* done by reintroducing the bards in a rather unprepossessing and pronominal way as something that Rousseau is not, through a word ("theirs") that has no clear antecedent in something actually achieved by the bards. To elaborate, it is not clear whether "theirs" refers to the words of the bards or to their deeds, which are not "as the deeds of others." And at this point we begin to recognize that perhaps the bards have no deeds, but only words, and that in this they are not like Rousseau, whose words reach out beyond the monastery of language. My point is that at no place in Rousseau's discourse are grammar and statement fully adequate to each other, so that the grammar paradoxically deconstructs the poem's logic of erasure, leaving a residue, a trace, that makes it different from itself.

What emerges from this analysis is that although the text is constantly erasing itself, that process is by no means unidirectional. In attempting to deny the value of his own work, Rousseau is unable to construct the bards as a positive counterpoint and instead reconstructs their position

[9]Mary Shelley's version is reprinted in *The Complete Poetical Works of Percy Bysshe Shelley*, ed. Thomas Hutchinson (London: Oxford University Press, 1905).

by telling us what it is not. The result of this double negation is to efface his self-rejection, but without immediately representing himself in a positive light. The double negation dilutes the force of the binary opposition by which Rousseau tries to measure his failure against the norm furnished by the bards. But on the other hand, the fact that his rehabilitation is initially no more than a syntactic trace, and the fact that his assertion of his own achievement is deferred to a passage some stanzas later (ll. 292–95, *SPP*) gives this self-assertion a tentative and supplementary quality. The vindication of Rousseau also leaves out something—which is perhaps why the manuscript could not be finished. We will return at the end of this chapter to the hermeneutic problems posed by the manuscript. But for the present it is worth noting that the line about which there is disagreement exists in three manuscript states: an 'original' state (already a reading that jumps from f. 33r. to f. 33v., omitting 'irrelevant' material) the version chosen by Mary Shelley, and the version (by no means final) chosen by Reiman. Set in between the two other versions of the line, the anxious negativity of the one we have just analyzed becomes all the more interesting:

1. Thus have my words been seeds of misery—
   Even as the deeds of others—*even as* theirs
   And then he pointed to a company

[original; italics mine]

2. "And so my words have seeds of misery—

   "Even as the deeds of others, not as theirs."
   And then he pointed to a company,

[Mary Shelley's version]

3. "And so my words were seeds of misery—
   Even as the deeds of others."—"Not as theirs,"
   I said—he pointed to a company

[Reiman's version]

Reiman's version, to which we will return, breaks up line 281 and assigns the second half to 'Shelley' instead of to Rousseau (a questionable attribution, since the manuscript at no point uses quotation marks). In the 'original' version, (reconstructed by undoing Shelley's cancellations), it seems that Rousseau speaks the entire line and that its meaning is relatively straightforward: his words sow misery, like the deeds of others, "even as" the deeds of those to whom he then points. In the intermediate version Rousseau reassigns the antecedent of "theirs" from the company of despots to the bards: his words are like the deeds of others, and not as theirs (the words [?] of the bards [?]). In Reiman's version, which does not definitively replace the second one,[10] the poem once again avoids the double negative. The words "not as theirs" are reassigned so that they neither support nor confuse the opposition between Rousseau and the bards. Rather, they prepare the way for Rousseau's later distinction between creative and destructive forms of power by having 'Shelley' differentiate Rousseau's verbal deeds from the actions of the despots: his deeds are "Not as theirs," not like the atrocities they commit. Somewhere in between an opposition that devalues Rousseau and an uncharacteristic response by 'Shelley' that rehabilitates him is Mary Shelley's version, a version that makes the positive a trace within the negative. In this interstice in Rousseau's speech, he emerges as the difference between a self-rejection in which he cannot find identity and a self-assertion whose lack of finality is evident in the fact that the poem continues, as if this is just one more figure cast on the "fragile glass" (l. 247, *SPP*) in which identity (dis)appears:

> —"Their power was given
> But to destroy," replied the leader—"I
> Am one of those who have created, even
>
> "If it be but a world of agony."—
> (ll. 292–95, *SPP*)

The self-displacing energies of speech are equally evident in Reiman's version of the passage, which seems at first to invalidate our reading. Removing the awkward phrase "not as theirs" from Rousseau's speech, Reiman tidies up what Rousseau says and allows it the neatness of a straightforward opposition. But the new version is no simpler, because the referent of what is now 'Shelley's' half-line intervention is less clear than we have made it seem, depending as it does on whether we connect the phrase to what precedes or to what follows it. We can take the antecedent of "theirs" to be the bards, in which case 'Shelley' seems to be confirming Rousseau's self-repudiation by adding to the latter's claim that his words are like vicious deeds a clarification that tells us that Rousseau's words are indeed unlike the words of the bards: "Not as theirs." Alternatively, we can take the statement as referring to the despots 'Shelley' proceeds to list, in which case he is dissenting from Rousseau's self-condemnation to observe that Rousseau's verbal deeds have not produced the misery created by tyrants and demagogues. It seems logical to connect 'Shelley's' intervention to what precedes it and to see him as condemning Rousseau, because that is what 'he' usually does.

[10]See my discussion later in this chapter.

Moreover, it is Rousseau (not 'Shelley') who points to Caesar and Constantine, so that the list of despots does not seem to come as an illustration of 'Shelley's' statement. On the other hand, it is just as logical to connect 'Shelley's' intervention to what follows it, because it is after all he who recognizes tyranny for what it is, thus enabling Rousseau to make his subsequent distinction between creative and destructive power.[11] At issue is whether 'Shelley' repudiates or rehabilitates Rousseau, and the problem cannot be resolved because he seems to do both. Diverging from Mary Shelley's version in the assignment of words to characters, Reiman's version differs only in extending the entanglement of positive and negative from Rousseau to 'Shelley.' In the course of the dialogue Rousseau moves from self-rejection to a self-justification that, being an equal and opposite reaction, has no final authority. In his brief intervention, and in the silent meditation on tyranny that follows it, 'Shelley' exhibits a similar ambivalence produced, it would seem, by the tendency of extended discourse (whether silent or verbal) to revive the traces of what it does not say.

If the sense of poetry as difference emerges linguistically at the level of the poem's grammar and generically from its dialogue form, it is also presented mythopoeically in the scene of Rousseau's creative birth, where he imagines the shape all light that later becomes the destructive shape in the car. The background in which the shape appears is a complex intertexture of light and shadow, shadow and substance:

> "but all the place
>
> "Was filled with many sounds woven into one
> Oblivious melody."
>
> (ll. 339–41, *SPP*)

Though this is apparently a scene of paradisal origins, oblivion alone makes us ignore that it is woven of many elements. Of particular interest throughout the poem are the figures of music and dance, but specifically in this passage of melody, for herein lies the deconstruction of Rousseau's oblivious perception of unity. We may think of Nietzsche's use of music in *The Birth of Tragedy* to symbolize the originary difference that is the ground of all systems of representation. But Shelley himself discusses music in the *Defence*, in terms of a vertical/referential axis and a horizontal/associative axis, which at another point he attributes separately to poetry and all the other arts, respectively. Harmony is the internal adjustment of sounds to their referents, but melody is the un-

[11]This is how Reiman reads the passage in his notes to the Norton critical edition (*SPP*, p. 463n.).

schematized play of external and internal impressions over the mind (*SPP*, p. 480), a perpetual motion of impressions that develop relations among each other that interpose between conception and expression. Hume, similarly, had linked music to the interpresence of apparently separate elements within a syntagmatic chain. In discussing the passions, he compares the mind to a stringed instrument "where, after each stroke, the vibrations still retain some sound. . . . Each stroke will not produce a clear and distinct note of passion, but the one passion will always be mixed . . . with the other."[12] Rousseau's error, if we can speak of one, is to create a unitary form (a shape *all* light) out of this differential ground through an act of Orphic will. Or rather, since the shape seems autonomously generated by a combination of light and optics—by a process at once perceptual and natural—, his error is to isolate the shape from its spatial and temporal context. For the apparently single shape emerges from a background of difference, as a moment in a process that consolidates and fixes an impression only to complicate it, threading "all the forest maze / With winding paths of emerald fire" (ll. 347–48, *SPP*):

. . . "there stood

"Amid the sun, as he amid the blaze
Of his own glory, on the vibrating
Floor of the fountain, paved with flashing rays,

"A shape all light, which with one hand did fling
Dew on the earth, as if she were the Dawn."
(ll. 348–53, *SPP*)

It seems clear that what is described here is the making of a figure through a process of substitution and displacement. To begin with, it is not the sun that we see, but the sun's image in a body of water that is confusingly a well or a fountain, in other words, the sun as constituted by reflection (ll. 345–46, 351, *SPP*). The shape is then generated by a series of synecdoches in which a diffuse and formless radiance imaged in the water is represented by an anthropomorphized sun described as "he," which in turn is represented by an inner, more focused female shape, metaphorically identified as the dawn, and as the dawn of a new era. There is indeed nothing unusual about a romantic poem's drawing attention to its construction of a myth. But here the process by which a myth is traced from its genesis in a moving army of metaphors and

[12]David Hume, "Dissertation on the Passions," quoted by Engell, *The Creative Imagination: Enlightenment to Romanticism* (Cambridge, Mass.: Harvard University Press, 1981), p. 54.

metonymies to its misprision as truth is presented as a hypnotism. Long before Rousseau explicitly perceives that the shape is not as simple as he takes it to be, the destructive effects of its formation are described:

> "And still her feet, no less than the sweet tune
> To which they moved, seemed as they moved, to blot
> The thoughts of him who gazed on them, and soon
>
> "All that was seemed as if it had been not,
> As if the gazer's mind was strewn beneath
> Her feet like embers, and she, thought by thought,
>
> "Trampled its fires into the dust of death."
> (ll. 382–88, *SPP*)

As Rousseau allows himself to be captivated by the unitary shape that momentarily forms itself out of the play of differences, the ground of his creativity is erased. The sparks of his mind (l. 201, *SPP*), Shelley's image in the *Defence* for thought as a productivity, are trampled out as one idea is made to represent a differential complex of ideas and "All that was seemed as if it had been not." For as long as the mind is inhabited by a variety of different thoughts, as long as we remain aware that the dominant thought is constituted on the trace of what it does not say, the mind remains in Shelley's image both here and in the *Defence* a 'fountain' (l. 351, *SPP*), or more precisely a source of elements between which we can form new relations. Thus the creative oblivion Rousseau suffers in these lines is not something done by the shape to him, but rather something that he does to himself as he yields to the impossible desire to create a unity out of multeity. For the shape, as light, is not a fixed form but a moving army of particles. She is, moreover, a dancer, dancing "i' the wind where eagle never flew" (l. 381, *SPP*), beyond the grasp of those who reject the differential flux of life for the native noon of single rather than manifold vision. Those who will survive the dance of language dance with her, as Rousseau comes to do and enjoins Shelley to do. Those who abstract a single form from the dance, as Rousseau once did, find the spark of their creativity killed.

Even after his first encounter with the shape of his own mind ends with its disintegration, Rousseau's sense of what constitutes truth remains simple. Thus the unitary construction of the shape as 'all light' is now replaced with an equally partial perception of it as entirely destructive. Dimly, however, he is beginning to grow aware that the figures the mind constructs, whether negative or positive, contain the trace of their own difference from themselves:

> "So knew I in that light's severe excess
> The presence of that shape which on the stream
> Moved, . . ."
>
> "So did that shape its obscure tenour keep
>
> "Beside my path, as silent as a ghost."
> (ll. 424–33, *SPP*)

On a diegetic level, then, the poem, while essentially deconstructive, does not present a process of pure erasure. Rather, it shows us how the power of deconstruction at the heart of language actually produces meaning. The image of erasure crucial to de Man's analysis,[13] of the waves perpetually erasing the tracks of wolves and deer on the sand, is Rousseau's image, used with reference to what is chronologically the earliest segment of his life, to describe his initial sense of vertigo at the destruction of old positions (ll. 405–410, *SPP*). A variant of it turns up in Rousseau's dialogue with Shelley in the present, namely, the image of figures painted on a bubble (ll. 248–51, *SPP*). But if indeed the words are his,[14] he uses this image in response to a comment by Shelley, which he qualifies by pointing out that if cultural heroes are merely historical *figures,* this does not make them identical, erasible, reducible one to the other. Plato, he tells us, "Expiates the joy and woe his master knew not" and is uniquely different from Socrates. The poem does, to be sure, operate in terms of grammatical and conceptual displacements. But if this were purely a matter of erasure, we would feel a sense of loss at Rousseau's inability to rest with his rejection of the phenomenal world, instead of feeling that the presence of other responses creates openings in the poem.

Paradoxically, then, *The Triumph of Life* is profoundly committed to the power of LOGOS, or rather DIA-LOGOS. If it deconstructs writing as an enduring monument by refusing to let Rousseau rest in peace, it valorizes speech as closer to a presence-as-difference. As writer, Rousseau had used the power of the published book as a means to fix meaning and achieve canonical status. But by the same token he was dead, catalogued like Adonais in the abode where the eternal are. Paradoxically, it is because 'Shelley' does not let him rest but deconstructs him that he comes to life, for to be deconstructed is to be read, and Rousseau is at least read, where 'Adonais' in some sense is killed with reverence. But more importantly it is through the power of speech that Rousseau returns to life, because until he speaks, he is simply a root in the hillside.

[13]De Man, "Shelley Disfigured," pp. 45–46.

[14]Since there are no quotation marks in the manuscript, it does not follow that Rousseau speaks these words. It is just as possible that his part of the dialogue begins at l. 252.

The dialectic of author and reader, as Shelley dramatizes it here, is a complex one, which transforms writing into speech through a process in which the reader deconstructs the writer, but in which the writer also speaks back and in some sense deconstructs the reader. Two things occur in the extended interchange between 'Shelley' and Rousseau. Rousseau loses his authority over his own words in entering the circuit of reading: they can be appropriated in different ways by different readers, such dissemination being the price of the communication for which Shelley uses the image of the spark and of the acorn that contains all future oaks (*SPP*, p. 500). But 'Shelley,' too, loses his authority over his reading, which becomes part of the differential process of speech between writer and reader. He becomes what we might describe as a *lector* rather than a reader, following Barthes' distinction between the author who controls the circulation of meaning and the *scriptor* who is a function of his own language.[15] Though 'Shelley' does not recognize his changed status and does not speak again after Rousseau's account of his dream, such a shift seems implicit in the fact that Percy Shelley takes *both* author and reader out of contexts that may be thought to exist outside language (death in Rousseau's case, ordinary life in 'Shelley's'), and places them in a world of language.

The Triumph of Life is thus committed to speech and reading, to the human participation in the dance of words. Shelley's poem is characteristically romantic in actually valorizing speech, but speech (whether fictional, psychological, or political) is something very different from what Derrida criticizes in his distinction between speech (equated with a language that is self-identical) and writing (equated with difference and the loss of presence). For these terms Shelley substitutes an opposition between writing (equated with codification) and speech (equated with presence, but also difference). The written book offers a certain security, as something that confers on words the finality, recognition, and also the complacency of publication. But speech, which Rousseau engages in when he leaves the archives to encounter 'Shelley,' exposes and also revitalizes his words by placing them in a dialogical relationship with an other or with a world that dismantles and reconstitutes them. Nor is this view of speech confined to Shelley, for the renewed interest in Platonic dialogue evident in eighteenth-century British philosophy, in the hermeneutics of Schleiermacher and others, and in forms like the conversation poem, is at least potentially an interest in speech-as-difference: in speech as superior to writing because it is more fluid and indeterminate.

Similarly, the poem actually valorizes reading. In some sense it is, as de

[15]Roland Barthes, *Image, Music, Text*, trans. Stephen Heath (New York: Hill and Wang, 1977), pp. 145–46.

Man suggests, a deconstruction of reading, because it presents language as a process of repetitive expansion that unreads itself and therefore unreads any attempt at unitary interpretation. But this is only to say that it deconstructs the kind of allegorical reading practiced by the character 'Shelley,' who tries to establish a one-to-one correspondence between figure and referent, to read the scene he witnesses into a book and out of his life. It is no accident that 'Shelley' uses simile rather than metaphor, that he describes the dance as a "just similitude" (l. 117, *SPP*), and that he tries to construe it in terms of literary conventions such as the medieval dream-vision and the Petrarchan triumph that will help him to label its characters and themes (ll. 40, 118, 176, *SPP*). But in a deeper sense the poem can be seen as developing a complex symbiosis between reading and deconstruction. As 'Shelley' reads Rousseau and more importantly as Rousseau reads himself, narrating the growth of his mind not to arrange and monumentalize his past like Wordsworth in *The Prelude* but to reread it, he unweaves his past self in such a way that his rereading unreads itself and creates a further language within language. It is, moreover, the fact that we can discover ever new relations within the poem that keeps us and future generations reading it. It is, of course, a far cry from this defense of reading to the one constructed by a traditional hermeneutics that sought to recover the original meaning of the text. We may discover how the poem functions as process but we do not discover its original meaning, any more than Rousseau, in recounting his past, is able to discover the original meaning of his life. Rather, we appropriate the poem to our own experience and create something meaningful out of it by participating in it, by becoming actors rather than spectators, and teaching the text what we would learn from it.

The Fading of Philology: The Manuscript and the Subject of Reading

But what does it mean to read heuristically and to realize that what we perceive in the text is partly what we create through reading? In the *Defence* Shelley speaks as though dissemination is a plenitude. But in this poem, which reduplicates the earlier theory in a glass darkly, the process is more recursive. Any reading we construct of Rousseau or of the text must be inscribed in its own differences: in the difference of our interpretation from a manuscript that will always in some way contradict what we attribute to it. No interpretation can now proceed without taking account of the original, which is unusually tangled, and in such a way that we wonder whether it is as it is because of the accident of Shelley's death or because of something in it that resists completion in the form of a conventional poem. The state of the manuscript raises fundamental questions about the status of the reading subject, about the nature of textual origins, and about the relationship between a printed text accessible to technical reading and a manuscript that encourages psychological reading, but in a radically intertextual way.

To read this manuscript, in contrast to surviving manuscripts of *Hellas* or *Prometheus Unbound*, is to experience an enormous gulf between its chaos and the iconic clarity of the printed text. It is also to reassess our very conception of what Schleiermacher called the indefinite thought process that precedes the finished thought complex. That *The Triumph* survives only in manuscript may be an accident. But the accident is part of the text's history and produces that history as a kind of mirror-stage on which the identity of editing, of philology, and of reading is projected and broken. We could do an extensive study of the points at which editors have (necessarily) cut, bridged, or otherwise amended the manuscript to make a readable text out of it. We will, however, confine ourselves to two recurrent aporias in the manuscript: the problem of (un)canceled passages and that of punctuation.

Not surprisingly, there is much more in the manuscript than appears in the printed text. Indeed, the discrepancy is so severe that Reiman has recently found it necessary to call into question his entire editorial activity by going beyond the re-edited text with notes on the manuscript that he published in 1965,[16] and providing a facsimile of the manuscript itself with a full transcription. From the manuscript it is evident that editors have played a role in producing the poem not entirely dissimilar from that of Ezra Pound in relation to *The Waste Land.* From Mary Shelley's to Reiman's, reading texts choose one version of a phrase or a line, where the alternatives are not clearly canceled out in the manuscript, and more often they shape a stanza out of a passage that contains uncanceled bits of lines that are surplus to the terza rima form. If the reading text facilitates coherent reading(s) of the poem, the publication of the manuscript compels us to go beyond a technical to a psychological reading, in which we recover the subtextual and collateral thoughts that keep deferring Shelley's attempt to give the play of language a direction. The manuscript, in other words, encourages us to read the poem as a palimpsest of traces, as the site of its own constant displacement. One of its more interesting features is the way it introduces alternatives that are sometimes quite radically opposed to each other. In general, Shelley chooses between these alternatives, but when he does so, the unfinished and self-canceling nature of the manuscript tends to make us erase the cancellations and see his choices as constructed on the trace of what they

[16]Donald H. Reiman, *Shelley's 'The Triumph of Life,' A Critical Study* (Urbana: University of Illinois Press, 1965).

do not say. Close to the beginning of the poem as it is printed, 'Shelley' describes the multitude who follow the chariot and comments that "none seemed to know / Whither he went, or whence he came" (ll. 47–48, *SPP*). But in the manuscript Shelley writes and then crosses out the line "And by their motions they appeared to know." On the question of whether the multitude are unthinking victims of life or enter its dance knowing full well what they are doing depends the further problem of whether Rousseau's participation in life is an error or an existential commitment. And at least at one point Shelley sees the question as yielding completely different answers.

Likewise, in the passage on the sacred few it seems that Shelley was uncertain whether the few "were there" in the procession or were "neither mid the mighty captives seen." In completing an incomplete revision, Reiman erases what is in effect an aporia.[17] This pattern of opposed alternatives recurs throughout the manuscript, reaching a point (in the middle of the passage on the great bards) where Shelley in frustration erases all alternatives:

These ~~the creators, the destroyers they~~
~~And then~~ *By words & deeds*,~~—& such as these~~
~~And both both or neither~~
~~Are both or neither~~

[17]Mary Shelley's reading text seems more faithful to ll. 127–28 of the manuscript than Reiman's, though by the same token it is less coherent. Mary Shelley's:

All but the sacred few who could not tame
Their spirits to the conquerors—but as soon
As they had touched the world with living flame,

Fled back like eagles to their native noon,
Or those who put aside the diadem
Of earthly thrones or gems . . .

Were there, of Athens or Jerusalem,
Were neither mid the might captives seen.
(ll. 128–35)

Reiman's:

All but the sacred few who could not tame
Their spirits to the Conqueror, . . .

Were there;—for they of Athens & Jerusalem
Were neither mid the mighty captives seen.
(ll. 128–35)

The first version preserves a syntactic aporia that the second version corrects on the basis that Shelley must have meant to write what Reiman prints. In Mary Shelley's version the text begins by exempting the sacred few from involvement in life but then proceeds to an elaborate description of them in the course of which we almost forget the original "All

Confusing words and deeds, and unable to distinguish creators from destroyers, this passage intervenes in the manuscript in such a way as to undo any meaningful contrast between the bards and Rousseau, between words that absorb life into art and verbal deeds that extend the infection of art into life. Nor does the disruptiveness of the passage end here. The fact that Shelley introduces, confuses, and then erases a distinction between creative and destructive power casts a shadow over his attempt, several lines later, to have Rousseau reintroduce the distinction. For the (op)position between Rousseau and the despots may simply be a displacement of the opposition between the bards and Rousseau: an attempt to wrest a position out of this tangle in which there are neither positive nor negative terms.

These passages of extreme aporia are (un)canceled, in the sense that a manuscript cannot sanitize their removal in the way that a reading text can. A related problem occurs in those cases where the cancellations are less definitive than they seem in edited versions. The passage on the great bards again provides an example. Because the manuscript contains no quotation marks, the attribution of certain words to certain characters is entirely speculative. Reiman, we recall, divides line 281 between Rousseau and 'Shelley' so as to strengthen Rousseau's opposition between himself and the bards, and so as to make it clear that 'Shelley' disagrees with Rousseau's equation of himself with Caesar and Constan-

---

but." The result is that it sounds as if Shelley is saying that the sacred few "Were there," and as if he then remembers what he set out to say and corrects himself by explaining that Jesus and Socrates "Were neither mid the mighty captives seen." Although it is possible to read the text logically by bracketing everything between "the sacred few" and "Were there," the logical reading is inhabited by a syntactic reading that keeps deferring it. Precisely because Mary Shelley's reading makes no grammatical sense, we are inclined to read the passage not just in terms of what Shelley was trying to say but also in terms of what he was having difficulty saying. Reiman takes the problematic juxtaposition of the lines "Were there" and "Were neither" and cleans it up by adding the clarifying phrase "For they." In fact, this phrase is only partly in the manuscript:

~~The twi~~ Were there;—
~~For they~~ of Athens & Jerusalem,
For

In his notes to his 1965 edition (cf. n.16) Reiman explains that he has restored the phrase "For they" that Shelley crossed out, because Shelley wrote in "For," thereby indicating that he meant to restore "For they." But it is just as likely that Shelley thought of restoring "For they" and then changed his mind. The aporia left in place by Mary Shelley's version is significant for two reasons: first, it is picked up later in the poem, when Rousseau's account of the procession begins to indicate that virtually no one *is* exempt from life; second, several canceled lines intervene between "of Athens and Jerusalem" and the line "Were neither mid the mighty captives seen," and in these lines Shelley again defers the exemption of the sacred few, becoming increasingly fascinated by those who are in the procession.

tine. Reiman's emendation of Mary Shelley's edition is based on the claim that Shelley inserted the words "I said" into the text and deleted the words "And then" in order to make place for them:

> not as
> ~~but~~
> Even as the deeds of others—~~even as~~ theirs
> ~~And then~~ he pointed to a company
> I said
>
> [Reiman's transcription]

But a closer look at the facsimile provided by Reiman shows that Shelley did not simply cancel "and then"; he canceled "And then he." The text, in other words, ought really to read "I said pointed to a company," which makes no sense unless we read its non-sense symptomatically. We can argue that Shelley meant to emend the text to write what Reiman prints. But it is just as possible that he made a change to which he was not clearly committed. Why, after all, did he not revise the text to read "I said and pointed to a company"? We will return yet again to this textual crux and to the way it unravels our attempts to read it and through it the poem. Suffice it to say that the manuscript shows Shelley making an incomplete change, and that that is why its editors render it differently. Moving between a version in which Rousseau repudiates himself and one in which 'Shelley' rehabilitates him, the poem seems doubtful about whether Rousseau really dismisses himself. But it is equally hesitant about having 'Shelley' leap to his defense. Uncertain whether to assign the revaluation of Rousseau to Rousseau or to 'Shelley,' the text projects and dislocates that revaluation, unsettling it when it reappears as a distinction between creative and destructive power but also blurring Rousseau's repudiation of himself.

By deferring the choice between alternatives, the manuscript's unfinished status allows it to inhabit the space of its own differences. The manuscript, in other words, forces any reading we might construct to confront those places where the poem refuses to become identical with itself. Those readings are based on reading texts that are themselves hermeneutic constructions, and it is to make this point that I focus on certain 'inaccuracies' in Reiman's transcription. But this is not to criticize the work of Shelley's editors, without which the text would be literally unreadable and without which this chapter could not be written. The manuscript, the reading texts, and the publication of the facsimile are all part of the poem's history, and it is not a question of choosing between them but rather of exploring their intertextual impact on each other. That impact is both constructive and recursive. Generations of scholars have not accepted the unreadability of the text, and their readings are now part of the text's history: supplements to which we can add but which we cannot subtract from the text. The fact that the manuscript was *not* left in a state in which it had neither form nor outline, the existence of the reading texts and of the hermeneutic constructions they have generated, these phenomena testify to what the poem itself images in the procession of dancers at its center. They are intertextual effects that reveal the way the human mind continues to construct meaning on the trace of its absence, as generations of readers participate in the life of the text and learn from themselves what they wanted to be taught by the poem. Until recently we could have made the dialectic of manuscript and text into the Sisyphean story of our triumph over life. But with the republication of the manuscript we have entered a further stage in the process of intertextual reading. If there was a phase in the poem's reception history when an editor could simply shape a work out of the manuscript and put the original behind her, that history is now a palimpsest that we must reenter each time we read the poem. The appearance of the Garland facsimile leads us to reflect on the ways in which different reading communities establish the identity of a text so as to legitimize their own philosophical or ideological positions, and on the strategies of transference that underlie our use of literature to reinvent ourselves.

The coexistence of reading texts and facsimile results, as we have already suggested, in a dialogue between technical and psychological reading. Our dialogue retraces the dialogue in Shelley's own mind, as he sought to represent that imageless anxiety (or perhaps excitement) that moved him to write the poem, recognizing all the while that nothing he wrote down had any finality. As we read the manuscript we feel in it a pressure toward what Schleiermacher calls 'composition' and 'meditation,' a pressure that has led Shelley's editors to complete his work by shaping the indefinite thought process into a finished thought complex. But we also feel the text's resistance to the selection and exclusion required by composition, and we feel it with a materiality that we cannot recover without returning to the manuscript. It seems that this particular poem was the site of Shelley's encounter with a radical textuality. To enter the contradictory palimpsest of the manuscript is to see that its utterances have no constative status. As Shelley sits down to write, he does not know 'that' the multitude are ignorant of what they are doing or 'that' they are self-aware. The significance of their actions comes into being in the moment of writing and is textualized rather than performed by its writing. Aware that events and characters have no mimetic status, Shelley writes with a sense that whatever he says can be said, and will then exist, quite differently. And given that knowledge, he can no longer write anything in the firm persuasion that it is so. The psychological reading encouraged by the manuscript, which does after all invite us to reconstruct the author's 'intention,' gives us back what Schleiermacher calls the 'discourse of the text,' and that discourse makes us aware that writing is subtended by a radical indeterminacy. What the discourse of the text is for the reader, speech is for Rousseau. Both are the medium in which we recover the sense of a perpetual difference within representation.

What are the consequences of this indeterminacy for the reader of the poem? Crucial to the hermeneutic process is our ability to locate characters with whom we can engage in some combination of identification and distance. Even the reading provided here assumes a Rousseau distinct from 'Shelley' and identifies with the former, or assumes that we can at least identify certain words as his. But one of the more extraordinary aspects of the manuscript is that Shelley did not use quotation marks, and that the editorial attribution of certain words to certain characters is entirely speculative. Though it is often clear (especially in longer passages) who is speaking, there are points at which the boundaries between Rousseau's and 'Shelley's' words are blurred, or where the speech of a character is not clearly demarcated from his unspoken thoughts. In the passage we have considered, for instance, there is no reason for Reiman to assign half rather than all of line 281 to 'Shelley.' If we look at the transcription, it seems that Shelley wrote "not as theirs" and not (as Reiman prints it in his reading text)" 'Not as theirs.' " The absence of the capital letter from "not" suggests that line 281 may be one sentence (fragment) spoken by one voice, albeit a referentially vague sentence. Attempting to limit this vagueness, Reiman substitutes a capital letter that is simply not in the manuscript and adds in his Norton critical edition a footnote that provides the referent of 'Shelley's' words. Rousseau condemns himself, according to Reiman, and 'Shelley' disagrees. But what if 'Shelley' speaks all of line 281 and Rousseau's part of the dialogue ends "And so my words have seeds of misery"? Because the addition of 'Shelley's' "I said" was clearly an afterthought, there is no means of knowing how much Shelley meant his persona to say and how he might have repunctuated the previous lines to accord with the reassignment of line 281 to 'Shelley.' To give all of line 281 to 'Shelley' is to make him agree with Rousseau's self-criticism. "Your words," 'Shelley' now says to Rousseau, "are like the vicious deeds of others, and are thus completely unlike the words of the bards."

My purpose is not to quibble with Reiman but to raise a larger question. The problem of who speaks which words is, at certain points, undecidable, and in adding a fourth version of line 281 I have resolved nothing. Even to try and decide the problem is to assume that Shelley meant to divide the dialogue clearly between the two characters and intended to add quotation marks later. But why, unless he meant to do so, should he have omitted only the quotation marks in a text that includes other forms of punctuation? Because he uses personal pronouns and character names, it is clear enough that Shelley expected the reader to try and assign words to characters. But it is also possible that he meant us to see such assignments as dubious, that he himself did not know who spoke what in a text that is, after all, a dream. At issue in the punctuation of the dialogue is the (dis)location of our readings. The assignment of specific words to specific characters has been a feature of all editions of this poem from Mary Shelley's to Reiman's, and has been responsible for our assumption that there are characters in this poem who have identities. Having constructed these characters, we can then assign certain positions to them, which enable us to interpret the poem in definite ways. Thus we can say with Bloom that Rousseau should have known better than to trust life, and we can see 'Shelley,' either from the beginning or at least by the end, as a locus for this insight. This identification of the insight a reader gains from the poem with a character in the text is a feature not only of traditional readings of *The Triumph* but also of so-called revisionary interpretations. My own analysis of the poem in *Dark Interpreter*, which argues that the poem reevaluates its rejection of Rousseau and thus of life, embodies this changed understanding in Rousseau, who stands in a relation of predictive parallelism to a 'Shelley' whose education remains incomplete because the poem is unfinished. But it is precisely the hermeneutic use of a character to confirm an interpretation that the manuscript questions. We are unable once and for all to identify 'Shelley' or Rousseau, and thus unable to locate whatever reading we have chosen in the text, as something that the text finally says.

This is not to say that Shelley dispenses with notions of character or identity. After all, he uses proper names and personal pronouns, and the burden of my argument has been that Rousseau in some sense survives, though it is far from clear for what he is a locus. What we experience in reading the manuscript is rather what Lacan calls the "fading" of the subject, a phenomenon that has been powerfully analyzed by Jane Gallop. Fading is not disappearance, but something more haunting: a presence that cannot be located and yet cannot be definitively renamed as absence so that we will cease searching for it. In Gallop's analysis it becomes an epistemological structure that makes us reflect on the status of a knowledge that seems to be in the text but that we cannot attribute to any specific person: author or character. Commenting on Lacan's idea in terms of her own experience of writing a chapter on Lacan's "Subversion of the Subject," Gallop speculates on why she feels compelled to set down as part of her interpretation a dream narrated by Freud, which is not the dream Lacan mentions in his essay, but which she *thinks* someone may have linked with the dream from Freud that Lacan does discuss.

The association of the two dreams enables Gallop to 'understand' what Lacan has written. But as a scholarly source for her reading of his essay, 'Lacan' is in the process of fading and so, too, is the hypothetical critic who may have linked the two dreams but whom Gallop may also have imagined. And yet she feels compelled to see her reading of Lacan as coming from somewhere other than herself.[18] Our position as readers of Shelley's text is very similar. We knew, when Bloom wrote his seminal chapter on *The Triumph*, that the text was critical of Rousseau for having been seduced by life. Yet with the re-editing of the poem that knowledge can no longer be clearly located in the text because it cannot be identified once and for all with the character 'Shelley.' As far as I am concerned, Bloom's reading has been replaced by my own knowledge that Rousseau achieves a certain measure of self-respect in the course of his conversation with 'Shelley.' Although the rehabilitation of Rousseau is tentative, I know that I gain a certain insight from reading the poem: an insight not into what he is but into his identity as the difference between positions that do not quite represent him. That Rousseau keeps speaking, that he does not simply fall silent when his interlocutors (life, 'Shelley,' or even Rousseau himself) negate his self-representations, suggests that he is that difference which consists not in anything he says but in the fact of speech. Yet this insight cannot be identified with a subject who is the source of my knowledge. Though it is intermittently given voice by Rousseau, I am troubled by the fact that he finally drops out of the poem, causing my insight to fade with him. Moreover, after reading the manuscript I can no longer quite locate Rousseau's words, which means that I must now ask myself whether it is not I who want 'Rousseau' to achieve self-respect because I still believe in the value of human life. But on the other hand, that knowledge is not my invention because I can point to specific passages in the text that account for my reading of it. The knowledge is somewhere in the text, produced and dislocated. Or rather, it is produced by my reading, but not purely in my reading. For I could not have told the text what I would have preferred to learn from it unless I had turned actor in this particular text.

The fading subject has significant consequences for a theory of reading, for the notion of fading applies not only to the author but also to the reader. Linking it with Barthes's notion of the death of the author, Gallop points out how much more complicated Lacan's subversion of the subject proves to be for a theory of reading. For Barthes the death of the author becomes, fairly unproblematically, the birth of the reader: "Proclaiming the death of the author asserts that one does not care, is not at all troubled by the still unknown source."[19] But the Lacanian subject is

[18]Jane Gallop, *Reading Lacan* (Ithaca, N.Y.: Cornell University Press, 1985), pp. 172–80.
[19]Ibid., p. 183.

not a dead but a disappearing subject. The site of this (dis)appearance is the poem's first-person speaker: the 'Shelley' who, unlike Wordsworth in *The Prelude*, is not named, must be in quotation marks, but has not yet left his poem. Unable to locate Shelley or to locate him through his characters, we feel that our readings lack authority. But because Shelley is not dead, we also cannot invest them with our own authority, since they may not quite correspond to what he meant. As the question of authorial intentions recurs, the reader becomes subject to that very fading that brought her into being.

What Shelley meant remains important, because the fact that the poem survives as a manuscript frames the reader's response within the generic conventions of philology. It seems appropriate to conclude by considering Shelley's poem not simply as a thematization of reading, but intertextually as a scene of reading within the larger process of culture: one that generates new relationships between various critical positions. Perhaps by virtue of a historical accident, the poem survives as manuscript rather than text and thus induces an archeological attitude that preserves the hermeneutic impulse, but only as that which unsettles the identity of a performative reading. It is surely significant that hermeneutics survives only as that which introduces difference into reading. Among the cultural effects of this manuscript is the fading, not the death or the rebirth, of hermeneutics. But the fading of hermeneutics is also the difference between its consolidation and its dismemberment. In other words, the fact that the hermeneutic reappears at the site of the poem's deconstruction, that our reading of the text is undone by our attempt to re-member what Shelley actually wrote, is the reason why it is insufficient to see the manuscript as the disfiguration of the printed text(s). The manuscript, it is true, obliterates the printed text: as we struggle with it, our brains become as sand, and the traces of what we have previously constructed from our reading are effaced, "half erased" (ll. 405–407, *SPP*). But this dis-figuration takes the form of a psychological reading in which the forgetting of one reading allows us to remember another: to recover something else that Shelley might have meant. Or to put it differently, among the cultural effects produced by the manuscript is also the fading of deconstruction.

Afterword

The choice of a text with which to conclude is always in some sense subjective, functioning as a musical rather than a decisively philosophical statement. One could justify a decision to end with *The Triumph of Life* on chronological grounds, but the real reasons are personal and critical. This book was written over seven years, in the course of which a debate between hermeneutics and deconstruction expanded into a dialogue between hermeneutics and cultural criticism. The chapters on Shelley, in an earlier form, were almost the first ones to see the light of day, and to place them at the beginning would have been to leave unquestioned the idea of a 'progress' beyond deconstruction claimed by current critical trends. In other words, to conclude with the sections on Wordsworth, Wollstonecraft, and others would have been to grant a teleological privilege to a certain positivism implicit in cultural criticism, however recursive. But Shelley, more than other writers considered here, forces us to reflect not just on the limits of particular readings but on the supplementarity of reading itself. I have tried to recognize this in discussing how the multiplicity of voices in *The Defence* eludes any attempt to extract from it a 'positive deconstruction.'[1] More particularly, I have tried to recognize it by making *The Triumph of Life*, which has been constantly associated in my own work with attempts at recuperation, a scene of reading for the project of this book. On the other hand, if

[1]This would be my one disagreement with Jerrold E. Hogle's excellent study *Shelley's Process: Radical Transference and the Development of His Major Works* (New York: Oxford University Press, 1988), which appeared too late for me to take account of it in the chapters on Shelley.

concluding with Shelley's last poem sounds a cautionary note, there are also more positive reasons for placing it at the end. Since the publication of *Deconstruction and Criticism*, the poem has become a synecdoche for the self-effacement of language and of romanticism as a cultural project that continues to mobilize the economy of criticism. If it can be shown that the essence of the poem resides not simply in those places where it ties itself into a knot, but in the transactions between a manuscript that displaces our interpretations and what readers have made of it, then it can be argued that demystification is not the ultimate horizon of our reading but must itself be inscribed in the intertextual processes generated by the poem. Moreover, as the narrative salvages from Rousseau's disfigured writings a figure who can still speak to us, by revisioning speech as *differance* rather than *logos*, so by refiguring difference as speech it gives it an originary quality, thus crossing and suspending the hermeneutic and the deconstructive within each other.

As such comments suggest, this study, although it focuses on problems played out in romantic theory and literature, also has as a subplot the network of linkages and differences that make up the contemporary theoretical scene. Thus it tries to be not simply a theory of romanticism, but also a book about the position of hermeneutics and reader-response theory in the current critical field. That position, like the position of any other critical approach, is necessarily diacritical. I began with a sense that a deconstructive approach needed to be supplemented by one that saw texts as related to readers. But as the very word 'supplemented' indicates, to introduce the reader into the critical equation as a way of filling a gap left by a more purely text-oriented deconstruction is also to reflect on the needs that lead one to fill that gap. If a recuperative emphasis on the reader converts into a positive term, what is more properly understood as a difference from deconstruction, the gaps in a traditional hermeneutic also emerge in relation to various forms of cultural critique now current. For hermeneutics has hitherto constructed in the author an idealized subject immune from analysis in terms of his or her cultural self-interest. Yet it is precisely hermeneutics, or the difference within it disclosed by reconsidering it from the perspective of cultural criticism, that makes possible such analysis by emphasizing the importance of reading. A traditional hermeneutic committed to truth in interpretation necessarily unravels itself into a cultural reading sensitive to literature as a site of ideological difference, precisely because hermeneutics emphasizes reading as much as it yearns for authority. At the same time a cultural criticism generated by the emphasis on reading is logically subject to reading itself and cannot simply replace the self-identical author with a self-identical reader. Thus in analyzing Blake's *Songs*, the very fact that we assert our difference by occupying subject-positions distinct from the bardic one (such as those of Thel or Earth) means that we must also experimentally identify with 'Blake' as a way of recognizing the subjectivity of these positions. Reinstating as a tool if not a goal what Gadamer terms a "fusion" of horizons between author and reader, such an approach does not simply dismantle hermeneutics as a relic of transcendentalism. It also resituates cultural criticism as part of a hermeneutic, as part of the reader's attempt to understand herself through her difference from others.

To put it differently, this study does not come to rest in any single critical position but works the spaces between them. Crucial to the dialogue it tries to mobilize between different approaches are two concepts touched on elsewhere in this book: narrative and intertextuality. The relationship between narrative and hermeneutics is material for another book. Suffice it to say that as a critical style whose use is legitimized by its wide provenance in romantic literature, narrative enables us to move from a deconstruction centered on tropes to a hermeneutics that is speculative rather than exegetical. Allowing us to experience the text as story rather than rhetoric, it constructs characters to whom we relate in varying degrees of identity and difference. It thus encourages what Ricoeur calls "appropriation" and what Dilthey calls "re-experiencing." At the same time, where exegesis allows us to occupy only one subject position (that of the author), narrative makes the process of reexperiencing dialectical, by offering us several positions that allow us to emplot the ideological cruxes of the text in several ways. To narrate the text (as we did in the case of Coleridge's poem to Wordsworth) by contextualizing it in the author's life and recontextualizing it in our own is thus a critical and self-critical process. Insofar as narratives are fictions, they remain experimental. Insofar as they contain several characters, including ourselves, they require to be told from more than one perspective. Perhaps another way to describe the functioning of narrative is to say that narrative is intertextual, a term that Julia Kristeva defines as the "transposition" of one signifying system into another.[2] Denying to the text an autonomous and self-enclosed existence, intertextuality makes meaning a passage between one text and another, which is to say between the text and its readings. Many of the texts we have considered are constructed intertextually: Coleridge's conversation poems, Blake's mobile texts, and texts like *Frankenstein* and *Prometheus Unbound* or other writings of the Godwin-Shelley circle which are addressed to each other. By constructing one text as a reading of another, these texts implicate both their own writing and our response to them in further reading. The story of her-

[2]*Revolution in Poetic Language*, trans. Margaret Waller (New York: Columbia University Press, 1984), pp. 59–60.

meneutics as it culminates in Kierkegaard and as it is played out in romantic texts is the story of a development from exegesis to intertextuality or sometimes of a sub-version of the former by the latter. The subplot of this story may well tell us that criticism, too, is intertextual: a transposition of one method into another.[3]

[3]For further discussion of how intertextuality transposes deconstruction and reader-response theory into each other, see my article "Intertextuality and the Subject of Reading/Writing," in Jay Clayton and Eric Rothstein, eds., *Influence and Intertextuality* (Madison: University of Wisconsin Press, forthcoming).

Index

Library of Congress Cataloging-in-Publication Data

Rajan, Tilottama.
The supplement of reading : figures of understanding in romantic theory and practice / Tilottama Rajan.
p. cm.
Includes bibliographical references and index.
ISBN 0–8014–2045–8 (alk. paper). —ISBN 0–8014–9749–3 (pbk.:alk. paper)
1. English literature—19th century—History and criticism—Theory, etc. 2. English literature—18th century—History and criticism—Theory, etc. 3. English literature—19th century—History and criticism. 4. English literature—18th century—History and criticism. 5. Romanticism—Great Britain. 6. Reader-response criticism. I. Title.
PR457.R34 1990
820.9'007—dc20 90–55122